Readings in African History
Edited by P. J. M. McEwan

AFRICA FROM EARLY TIMES TO 1800
NINETEENTH-CENTURY AFRICA
TWENTIETH-CENTURY AFRICA

NINETEENTH-CENTURY AFRICA

EDITED BY

P. J. M. McEWAN

LONDON
OXFORD UNIVERSITY PRESS 1968
IBADAN NAIROBI

Oxford University Press, Ely House, London W.1

GLASGOW NEW YORK TORONTO MELBOURNE WELLINGTON
CAPE TOWN SALISBURY IBADAN NAIROBI LUSAKA ADDIS ABABA
BOMBAY CALCUTTA MADRAS KARACHI LAHORE DACCA
KUALA LUMPUR HONG KONG TOKYO

Maps drawn by Regmarad

PRINTED IN GREAT BRITAIN BY
THE CAMELOT PRESS LTD, LONDON AND SOUTHAMPTON

Preface to
Readings in African History

FOR the past eighty years the continent of Africa has been steadily increasing its proportion of the limelight in world affairs. There have also occurred, during the same period, a general educational awakening and a dramatic refinement of the techniques available for the advancement of knowledge. The coincidence of these developments has led to African studies, social, political and economic, past as well as present, becoming a recognized part of a balanced university curriculum.

The history of Africa holds a special position as a subject worthy of study. In the first place, it is that part of man's heritage which most strongly captures the interest of modern African men and women. The long-run contours of African history are rich in content and often revealing in their illumination of the present.

African history has, indeed, the same claims to be studied as British history or American history, and just as its role in Africa is much the same as the role of British history in British schools and universities, or American history in American schools and colleges, so is its role in these countries similar to that which the study of British and American history has to play in Africa.

But in addition to the intrinsic importance of the subject, it has a further significance within Africa itself. It provides a context of man's development into which many of the problems and aspirations of the present can be meaningfully placed, thus stimulating a broader sense of tradition and a deeper pride of achievement which lend natural and legitimate support to the growth of nationhood.

In the second place, the rapid growth of African influence and importance in the world, together with previous neglect of its history, gives the study unusual significance. For too long, and with increasing incongruity, nations have studied and taught, often exclusively, the history of their own people. As the world shrinks and the extent of national interdependence expands, our knowledge of other civilizations and other continents becomes commensurately more necessary.

There is a third, more technical, reason for the importance

of African history. This is the direct relevance to it of other disciplines, principally archaeology, ethnography and comparative linguistics, and the further problems raised by oral tradition. The nature of their respective associations and the issues that each separately raises brings the student of history in continuous contact with these other studies, making him more responsive to their application and value.

African historians have tended to fall into two groups. There are those who seek to identify common factors in disparate regions of space and differing periods of time and who, perhaps mindful also of the practical need for comprehensive texts, write in unifying and comparative terms of tropical Africa as a whole. There are others who prefer to narrow the focus so that it embraces one selected area or a single nation. The former provide the condensation necessary for comparative study and for a more complete understanding of those developments, such as partition, which have been transcontinental in character and origin. The latter, on the other hand, provide the detail and depth necessary for detailed understanding. As time goes by and our knowledge extends so may the more intensive studies increasingly outnumber the continental histories. For the present, however, there is room for both.

In addition, there are a number of historians who concentrate still more intensively, writing only in learned journals.

Where, in this scheme of things, does the present work stand? The aims of the three volumes are several. First, their essential aim is to provide the student of African history with a comprehensive but detailed understanding, written by recognized authorities, of the major events and developments in their subject. Whether the readings are studied on their own or in conjunction with one of the several general histories now available, the reader will have at his disposal the most significant events and movements as recorded and interpreted by leading historians.

A second aim, and a corollary of the first, is to provide a necessary adjunct to general history texts. It is impossible to deal adequately with even the most influential sequences of events in Africa's past within the confines of a single volume. It is difficult to do so even in a regional history. The present volumes will allow the student to undertake a closer examination of the more important of these developments. It also offers a useful corrective against the bias of a single author when dealing with such discursive material as, for example, partition, or the rise of nationalism, making direct comparison possible between different points of view.

A third important objective has been to bring together definitive writings which are not generally available, either because of inadequate library facilities or because of their original appearance in a comparatively obscure publication, perhaps in a language other than English.

A book of readings is inevitably susceptible to the sins of omission and commission. Selections always invite criticism not only for the subjects chosen but for the writings chosen to cover them. The present work can be no exception. In determining what to include, the following criteria have been employed. With regard to design, three volumes were decided as being the least possible number to allow adequate treatment of the major themes. In order to follow the flow of history and to draw appropriate comparisons, with due reference to regional and temporal inter-relations, each volume deals with a different period of time. Volume I takes the reader to the end of the eighteenth century, Volume II is concerned with the nineteenth century, and Volume III with the twentieth century. Thus, while early times are by no means neglected, there is an emphasis on the history of the last two hundred years.

Within each volume the material is presented in sections. These follow the same geographical pattern throughout, in the order: West Africa, North Africa, Egypt, Ethiopia, East Africa, southern Africa. In the sections themselves, the readings are presented in the order approximating most closely to the connection, logical and temporal, between the material they discuss. Thus, within a framework based on chronology, the readings are organized in accordance with geography as well as with time. In this way, it is hoped that convenient reference will be facilitated without sacrificing the occasional need for ignoring spatial boundaries in the interest of historical accuracy.

There are, however, a number of issues which do not fit neatly into any conventional category of either time or space. These include the spread and influence of the two great religious movements Islam and Christianity, partition, and the rise of nationalism and pan-Africanism. In accordance with their closest logical affinity, treatment of the religious questions is included in Volume I, partition in Volume II, and nationalism and pan-Africanism in Volume III. In each case, the subject is treated as a whole in its own specific section with the same geographical order of presentation, wherever this is appropriate.

There is a further subject amenable to study only in a single, continent-wide context. This is the study of pre-history, which comprises the opening section in Volume I.

As will have been observed from the geographical order of presentation, two countries have been singled out for specific reference, Egypt and Ethiopia. The long history of Egypt cannot, of course, be encompassed in a work of this nature and, in any case until the nineteenth century, Egypt was closer in her development to Asia Minor than to Africa. Since, however, our concern is with the whole continent of Africa and because the influence of Egypt had been felt to the south and west for many centuries, its inclusion was demanded. In order to account for Egypt's peculiar role in African affairs, as a nation at the cross-roads of three continents, its individual role has been accordingly recognized in the text.

Ethiopia has been singled out in the same manner on account of her long history of independence and for the long periods of her isolation from outside influences. Where her development has been associated with other forces, as has occurred increasingly since the early part of the nineteenth century, these factors are discussed in the sections dealing with Ethiopia.

An examination of the section headings will indicate a slight bias towards political history and, in Volume III, towards political science. Although every effort has been made to give full attention to economic, religious and social developments, it is perhaps inevitable that the main emphasis has been on political change, on the fluctuating powers of government and on conflict. Detailed comparative studies of African economic and social history are still awaited.

There is another bias which should be mentioned. Movements and events that are discussed in the following pages have been chosen not only on account of their intrinsic importance but also because, in the majority of cases, they figure in one or more of the commoner examinations in the subject.

In spite of this consideration, it must not be thought that the readings have been streamlined to fit probable examination questions. This would be a task not only impossible but contrary to our intention of providing a comprehensive selection. Thus, for example, considerable space has been given in the third volume to the question of *apartheid*. This subject, which seldom appears in any examination, has been analysed in detail because of its importance for the whole continent, not only as national policy but as a rallying point for international opposition.

Turning from design to detailed content, it was only when the choice seemed to lie equally between two or more readings that other criteria than pure merit were introduced. Length and accessibility were then considered, the less readily accessible and the more concise being preferred. Articles were generally more suitable than extracts from books, especially if the book had just been published and was in most libraries. Articles, apart from being less widely known and more difficult to find, have the advantages of being self-contained, of paying greater attention to the general historical context of their subject matter, and of bringing a sharper focus to bear on a narrower front—all important factors for our purpose. At the same time, where there has seemed no adequate alternative, rather than have no reference to an important question, an extract has occasionally been chosen from a book, however recent, and, if unavoidable, however derivative.

There are a number of works which, although strongly criticized in their main thesis, nevertheless contain, often as an introductory chapter, a summary of an important sequence of events which in accurate conciseness is not to be found elsewhere. Such books present a problem: should the extract be included, at the risk of inviting ready criticism, or should general suspicion be allowed to drown incidental quality? In a limited number of cases, which it would be invidious to identify, where the alternative has been less than satisfactory the editor has included what has seemed to him a sound extract from an otherwise doubtful source.

One final category of choice should be mentioned. In three cases, readings have been included because of their own historic quality as classical statements on important issues, in spite of more modern treatments of the same topic. These are Professor Schapera's paper on 'Economic changes in African urban life', first published in Volume I of *Africa* (1928), Dr Gann's paper on 'The significance and suppression of the slave trade in British Central Africa', which first appeared in the *Journal of the Rhodes-Livingstone Institute* (1954), and an extract from Sir Winston Churchill's *The River War*, first published in 1899. In their contrasting ways, each is a model of its kind.

Finally, a word about interpretation. History, once it passes beyond being a mere chronicle of events, becomes inevitably interpretative. Interpretation implies selection. The historian of an epoch or a movement or a personality selects his data and reaches a general conclusion. In many cases, more numerous than is sometimes appreciated, the conclusion is reached prior to the selection. The result may be accepted at once, in which event it will pass into the realm of historic fashion, or it may evoke alternative, perhaps contradictory, interpretations, firing a general dispute. Occasionally, when it is openly polemical or intentionally provoking, the bias is transparent and may therefore be easily countered. But it more often happens that the selectivity is hidden and the assumptions and personal prejudices of the historian are occluded by an aura of objectivity, and an apparently scrupulous concern with accuracy. Whether this obscuring is conscious or otherwise makes no difference to its effect, which is that the unprepared observer accepts as proven what is only hypothesis, and is left in ignorance of the existence of any solid grounds for an alternative explanation. It is true, of course, that certain subjects in history, as in other things, are more emotive than others. Subjects also vary in their degree of certitude. It is these two factors, emotion and doubt, which most often give rise to the hidden premiss and an unhinted selectivity. Thus, to mention just two examples from the study of African history, one has to be particularly cautious when considering colonialism (particularly in southern Africa), and the factors leading to partition.

In the first (emotive) case, fashions have changed, and to be implicitly anti-colonial is to be as modish as was the almost unconditional praise of the colonist by white historians in the 1900s. Thus we find writers suppressing data that reflects badly

on the colonized while concentrating on evidence that reflects
adversely on the colonizer.

This is not intended as a general indictment of historians
but as a warning against the common academic hypocrisy
of believing that in one's own work the hidden value-judgement
is not only hidden but non-existent.

Faced with this situation, the aim of the present volumes
has been to give expression, as far as space permits, to alternative interpretations, exposing the critical reader to more than
one point of view, leaving him, with the guidance of his
teachers, to make up his own mind.

Similarly, in an area of doubt, such as the principal causes
of partition, where opinions are no less biased for being openly
divided, there have been included alternative explanations,
Stengers as well as Robinson, Hyam as well as Gallagher. The
same applies to other discussions—the comparative influence of
Islam and Christianity for example—wherever space has
allowed, and contentious selectivity demanded.

For myself, as editor, the selection of readings has been
as objectively chosen as it is possible for one man to make it.
My main regret is that there have not been many more African
written texts from which to choose. One may be confident,
however, that in twenty years time, if these volumes should be
revised or others written, the ratio of texts written by Africans
to others would be about reversed. Such is the rate of change
in all things African.

Contents

Maps

Maps 3, 4, 5, 6 and 7 are based on maps which appear in *A Political History of Tropical Africa* by Robert I. Rotberg (Harcourt Brace & World, Inc. and Oxford University Press, 1965). Map 8 is by courtesy of D. Van Nostrand Company, Inc.

Acknowledgements

THESE volumes, prepared in three continents over a period of two years, would not have been possible without the co-operation of a very large number of people.

Although, of course, I am alone responsible for all the deficiencies involved in the selection and exclusion of material, I wish to express my deep appreciation for the manner in which so many scholars allowed me to consult their wisdom and consume their time. Often this was done more intensively than anyone has the right to request, but always more willingly responded to than anyone has the right to expect.

Mention cannot be made of all the help I have received, but a special word is due to Professor J. D. Hargreaves, Professor J. F. Ade Ajayi, Professor George Shepperson and Mr Anthony E. Atmore. Their constant advocacy of alternatives proved invaluable. My greatest debt in this regard, however, is to Dr Robert I. Rotberg, whose patient criticisms and comments extended as fully in time as they did in detail. I am extremely grateful and I hope that the final result will not be too disappointing to him.

I would like to record my thanks to the many librarians who gave so freely of their time and who allowed me the use of their facilities, often from a distance, and to all the authors and publishers who kindly gave permission for me to include their material. The fact that only two readings have had to be excluded from a final list of 140 choices reflects the extent of their co-operation.

Dr Ian Lockerbie, of the Department of French at Aberdeen University, did a magnificent job in rapidly organizing the translation of difficult material when he and his colleagues could ill afford the time. To him and his team I am deeply grateful.

My sincere thanks to Carol Stein and Ruth Spivack, who hunted countless books through countless shelves, and to Madeleine Allen, Dorothy Roberts and Florence Zamchek, who spent many daunting hours establishing order out of chaos.

An immeasurable debt of appreciation is due to my wife. Without her long-term patience and encouragement through many vicissitudes these volumes could never have been completed.

P. J. M. McEwan

Boston, Massachusetts
January 1967

Introduction

THIS volume is concerned with the history of Africa in the nineteenth century. The dominant theme of the period is the unfolding story of change. In Europe the expanding nature of industrialization was reaching its height, and from this began to flow its major corollaries—political ambition, economic growth and social upheaval. At the same time as these external influences were increasing in their intensity, throughout Africa itself there was developing a growing self-consciousness. New states were being formed and tribal realignments were being assembled.

In the north, where European and Asian influences were most immediate, dramatic and often violent change became the order of the day. Not only was Egypt undergoing transition from medievalism to the structure, function and outlook of a modern nation, but new concepts of political self-awareness were establishing themselves throughout the Maghreb.

In the west, Holy War and tribal rebellion were giving way to the equally rigorous but more subtle force of European control. The slave trade was to be gradually replaced by more respectable commerce; from being a major source of exported labour, the peoples of the Western littoral were to become producers and consumers in their own land. By the end of the century Britain and France had forged their zones of influence, areas which were to reflect increasingly the language, the political and educational systems, and the philosophies of their mentors.

Particularly when considering West Africa during these times but also when thinking about other parts of the continent, it is useful to distinguish between three separate but closely inter-related threads. These are (*a*) the rivalries, motivations and activities of the competing European powers, (*b*) the socio-economic condition and the political response of the many African peoples during this time, and (*c*) the socio-political relationships and reactions between these sets of situations and events. In this way it is possible to gain a fuller appreciation of how and why developments occurred as they did, and of the forces which emerged and came to dominate the continent during the century that was to follow.

Parallel events to those in the west were taking place in the central and eastern parts of the continent, although the influence of France was here largely replaced by that of Belgium and Germany.

The so-called partition of Africa has been given a section on its own in this volume, both because of its intrinsic importance and because alternative interpretations have to be considered impartially. The effects of this era are, of course, still being felt, so that its assessment is vital if later history is to be properly understood.

The reader will find it rewarding to compare the rise of national leaders and national parties in diverse areas of Africa; the Mahdist idea in the Sudan, the development of political consciousness in Algeria and Morocco, and the establishment of new political forces in British and French West Africa—these are exciting and informative precursors to similar developments elsewhere during the following century.

During this time also the struggle between Islam and Christianity intensified and was to have important repercussions later.

In the south, European domination was slower in coming and was perhaps harsher. This was primarily because the motivation behind it was different. Europeans came to settle rather than merely to trade, so that military conquests and personal security needed to be more complete. The reactions of the African population were, for the moment, correspondingly more limited. But the fact that the time-scale in the south was different has had tremendous significance for the future. Furthermore, it is necessary to remember that the Republic of South Africa, if perhaps the most backward politically, is certainly the most advanced nation in the continent industrially. This is also the one part of Africa where Europeans have engaged in civil war.

During the nineteenth century, then, we find the political history of Africa dominated by the story of its relationship with Europe. The resurgence of the African Spirit, the adjustment of characteristic African value-systems to the facts of modern life, and political freedom, were soon to follow.

For the convenience of readers, a short bibliography and a list of major events with dates are provided at the end of the text.

I. POLITICAL AND SOCIAL DEVELOPMENT IN WEST AFRICA

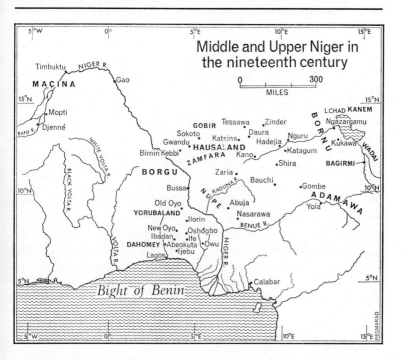

Middle and Upper Niger in the nineteenth century

1. The Fulani *jihād*: a reassessment

MARILYN ROBINSON WALDMAN *Journal of African History*
Vol. 6, No. 3, 1965 Cambridge University Press; pages 333–55

MANY authors have written about the Fulani *jihād* of 1804, but despite their efforts no comprehensive account exists which does justice to the complexity of its nature. Most writers emphasize one aspect at the expense of others. Many view the *jihād* as a movement towards purer religion. Others stress the ethnic homogeneity of the leaders and of much of the following in calling the *jihād* a racial uprising. A growing number of writers sees the movement as a rebellion of economically and socially oppressed groups against their harsh masters. Recent investigation of the writings of the leaders of the *jihād* has encouraged the view that, 'in origin it was also an important intellectual movement involving in the minds of the leaders a conception of the ideal society and a philosophy of revolution.'

Taken separately, these factors are inadequate to explain the seemingly self-contradictory nature of the *jihād*. All of them were certainly present, but only because of their interaction was the *jihād* possible and successful. A few writers have recently begun to recognize the complexity of the movement, but they have not yet explained how the various factors converged to produce the *jihād*. An adequate explanation depends on a proper understanding of the way in which the various elements were inter-related. A balanced account, however tentative, should be useful as a guide to future research, especially at this time, when the editing and translation of a rapidly increasing number of manuscripts written by the leaders of the *jihād* promises to shed new light on the persistent problems which have confronted students of Usuman dan Fodio's movement.

This article traces the transformation of Usuman from an itinerant preacher to a militant reformer, and pays special attention to the development of the relationship between Usuman as a leader and his following. For the key to the *jihād*'s complexity lies in the gradual development of this relationship. To do justice to the development of Usuman's movement, it is necessary to view it as the result, not of a conception complete in his mind from the start of his preaching, but as one which unfolded itself in three gradual stages. Initially, Usuman travelled from area to area teaching religion to the people. In the second phase, during his involvement with the Gobir court, he probably began to express publicly his growing discontent with the failure of the Sarkin Gobir to put his demands for reform into practice. Usuman's continuing reformist preaching in this phase, though artic-ulated in a religious and intellectual manner, could have been perceived to express many people's feelings, motives and aims, some of which could easily have been unrelated to, or even fundamentally opposed to, his. In the third phase, when, because of a crisis in his relations with the Sarkin Gobir, Usuman changed his goals and called for political overthrow of the Hausa system rather than for reform within it, the appeal of his movement became even broader, so that it encompassed all of those who might have had *any* interest in a change of rulers for Hausaland. Usuman had created, over a long period of time, the bases upon which his subsequent call to arms could take hold, but not necessarily with the conscious aim of some future *jihād* in mind. The followers were able to associate themselves with the leaders without initially sharing all, or even a large number of, the leaders' religious ideals. The *jihād* itself resulted from a tentative though essential convergence of the motives of the leaders and the motives of the followers. To the degree that an identity of motives other than the overthrow of the rulers existed between the leaders and their followers, that identity was not essential to the success of the movement.

During his early adult years in the Sudan, Usuman dan Fodio played a role similar to that which other *mallams* (Arabic: '*ulamā*'—Muslim scholars) had played there for four centuries. He was a link in a chain of reforming Muslims who had repeatedly sought to bring about the acceptance and practice of orthodox Islam by the Sudanese rulers and their subjects, and thereby to destroy pagan and syncretistic practices. About 1781, Bawa Jangworzo, the fifty-fifth *sarki* (ruler) of the Hausa city-state of Gobir, engaged Usuman to act as tutor to the royal family. In so doing, he was continuing a centuries-old pattern of interaction with the tradition which Usuman represented. Bawa, like many of his predecessors, was hospitable to Islam but did not himself enforce a Muslim form of government. Usuman's appointment to the court of Gobir was similar to many such appointments throughout the preceding three or four centuries. For the Hausa *sarkuna* had never developed an explicit theory of the place of Islam in their States. Nor were they consistent in the policies towards Islam which they did adopt. Rather they accommodated themselves to the needs of the moment without making a definite commitment to establish Islamic States. In order to understand Usuman's early relations with the court of Gobir, it is necessary to explore the history of the tradition of the Hausa *sarkuna*'s *ad hoc* policies towards Islam.

The introduction of Islam neither profoundly affected the social and religious life of Hausaland, as Burns says, nor left it totally undisturbed, as Delafosse suggests. Missionaries brought Islam to Katsina and Kano in the early and middle fourteenth century; and it was, in some ill-defined manner, accepted by their rulers. Yet if, in Kano, Sarki Yaji had his first mosque built *under* the sacred tree of his cult, the introduction of Islam need not have involved a forced and radical change in Hausa life or rule. The effects of these early conversions to Islam were not long-lasting. The military successes which had resulted 'miraculously' from the adoption of the new religion were short-lived; reversions to the former religion soon resulted. For example, Sarkin Kano Kanajeji (r. 1390–1410), facing an unbeatable enemy, received the following advice from the head of an animist cult begun a century before: 'Re-establish the god that your father and grandfather destroyed.' The *sarki* heeded the warning, revitalized the cult, and, as it happened, was successful in his war effort. The issues illustrated in this incident recurred periodically until the *jihād* itself. The adoption of Islam by the rulers did not lead, in these early cases or even in later ones, to the complete extirpation of non-Muslim cults or of non-Muslim politico-religious advisers, whom the *sarkuna* could easily recall in times of stress.

Although, in the late fifteenth century, the rulers of Kano and Katsina again took up Islam and began an illustrious century-long period of patronage of Muslim personages, they did so only because of the influence of Songhay. The latter never achieved more than tributary political control over some of the Hausa States; nevertheless, it was culturally influential, especially through the innovations of Askia Muhammad I. Reversing the policy of Sunni Ali, who had alienated Islamic scholars, Askia Muhammad conscientiously attached the party of *mallams* to himself, thereby bringing religion successfully into the service of the State. He then proceeded to offer his example to the Hausa rulers for their imitation, mainly through the activities of his chief adviser in religious matters, al-Maghili, the famous North African and Sudanese theorist of reform. During Muhammad's reign, there occurred in Hausaland, because of Songhay's missionary activity, two striking conversions of reigning *sarkuna*—Ibrahim Maji of Katsina and Muhammad Rimfa of Kano—whose predecessors had long shown no interest in Islam.

The motives of one of these converts seem to have been as opportunistic as those of the earlier converts. Sarkin Kano Rimfa was known as a progressive and innovating *sarki* in matters other than religion. He no doubt foresaw benefits to be gained by his adoption of Islam. It is clear from the 'Kano Chronicle' that Rimfa's conversion indicates that he was giving his hospitality and encouragement to those willing to tutor him in religious and secular culture and learning, and who would attract to his town numerous other holy men. As Rimfa's case illustrates, whenever the chronicles say that Islam flourished anywhere in Hausaland, it is more likely that the reigning *sarki* showed himself willing to encourage, and possibly to protect, the presence of Isalm and of learned men in his State and in his entourage, than that any extensive conversion took place among his subjects.

Despite the above qualifications, the period of the late fifteenth and early sixteenth centuries was a stimulating one for Islamic learning in Hausaland. Because of the receptiveness of a few of the *sarkuna*, and the increasing prestige of the Hausa States as commercial centres in the Sudan (especially during Muhammad's reign in Songhay and for some time afterwards), 'many marabouts of Djenne and Timbuktu stopped there [Kano and Katsina] on their return from the pilgrimage to Mecca and taught theology and Mālikī law there to the native students.' Some even settled in Hausaland. There were probably more scholars in Hausaland than the present incomplete information suggests.

The experience of one of these visitors helps to illustrate the nature of their relationship with the Hausa *sarkuna*. In 1509, the author al-Tāzakhtī returned from the *hajj* and settled in Katsina, where he was given the title of Alkali (Arabic: *Qādi*—judge, or perhaps in this case, chief judge) by the Sarkin Katsina. The fact that he was appointed tempted Lady Lugard to argue misleadingly: 'It may, I think, be taken for granted that the appointment of Cadi was not made by a pagan Sultan, nor would a pagan court have offered attractions as a residence to one of the most cultivated traditionists of Timbuctoo.' On the contrary, the history of Islam in Hausaland shows that learned men often came and even resided there for many reasons other than the ones suggested by Lady Lugard.

The desire to proselytize or to reform, political disaffection from their own countries, the hospitality and protection of a ruler—all had their appeal. There is no evidence to indicate that the attractiveness of Hausa courts for Muslim scholars in the sixteenth century was due to the Muslim, let alone orthodox, nature of these courts. The encouragement of Islamic learning and the protection of Muslim learned men depended ultimately upon the goodwill of the rulers; scholars accepted support from a wealthy and comfortable court, even though the court itself might not be thoroughly Muslim. On the other hand, even a partially pagan court would not necessarily deny itself the prestige that ensued from the presence of the most learned men, even though they might be Muslim. Much of Usuman's own criticism of the Hausa rulers of his day stemmed from just this fact, which had been evident from the early sixteenth century on, that rulers' patronage and encouragement of Muslim scholars and of learning did not necessarily indicate an acceptance of the restrictions and demands which an orthodox Muslim ruler would have to place upon the polity and society.

Although both in Katsina and in Kano Islamic learning 'flourished', in the limited sense described, Ibrahim Maji's conversion did not have long-lasting effects on his successors. After his conversion, the Katsina king list makes no further mention of Islam until the *jihād*. The place of Islam in Kano was somewhat different from that in Katsina. After its acceptance by Muhammad Rimfa, Islam seems to have remained at least a recurrent if not a fundamental issue. But strained relations between Islamic and traditional principles of government began again to be evident towards the end of the sixteenth century. New stimuli were needed throughout the century to encourage the fostering of Islam by Hausa rulers. This tension, which should not be put simply under the general heading of a tension between animism and Islam—between, on the one hand, the religious and secular demands of the 'patronized' learned class and on the other, a succession of rulers and a political order fundamentally unchanged by the doctrines of Islam—persisted without resolution in Hausaland after the demise of Songhay influence. Each tradition remained separate and intact, even when rulers chose to bring the two together tentatively in the familiar practice of patronage. The tension and co-existence continued without a violent clash, as far as is known, until the end of the eighteenth century.

The picture which has been drawn—of an Islam which scholars maintained despite the fickleness of the rulers, although sometimes with their approval—is essential to an understanding of the relations which Usuman was to have with the *sarkuna* of Gobir. In Hausaland, in the eighteenth century, the will of the individual ruler determined the extent to which Muslims would be tolerated or the principles of Islam applied. Most of his subjects were non-Muslim or at best partly Muslim. As an orthodox Muslim, Usuman entered a setting which was bound to arouse his criticism, but unlikely to provide any adequate outlet for his grievances. Yet the early years of his preaching showed no signs of the forthcoming violent opposition to the Hausa rulers which had failed to arise for so many centuries.

According to Abdullah dan Fodio, the year 1774–5 marked the beginning of Usuman's preaching tours. By that time Usuman had studied with many learned men in Hausaland and Agades, and the basic tenets of his thought had already begun to form. Of all his teachers, Jibrīl b. 'Umar had the greatest influence on him. Although Usuman owed much of his inspiration to Jibrīl and his movement, and saw himself as following in his footsteps, a serious quarrel over doctrine early divided them. Nevertheless, about 1781, Usuman travelled with Jibrīl to Agades. Abdullah dan Fodio claims that his brother returned to Hausaland shortly afterwards because their father had not given Usuman permission to continue with Jibrīl on the *hajj*. Jibrīl, because of his fanatical activities, had angered the Hausa *sarkuna*, and may in fact have been ousted from Gobir by Bawa. His decision to make the pilgrimage may thus have been forced on him. Indeed, two reasons other than lack of parental consent to undertake a *hajj* may have drawn Usuman back to Gobir from Jibrīl in Agades. Since he had already diverged from the more radical ideas of Jibrīl, it is possible that he decided to return to Hausaland to carry on the work of Jibrīl in a more moderate and therefore less dangerous manner. Alternatively, Bawa may have called Usuman from Agades to enter the court as tutor to the royal family. It is equally possible, though, that Bawa engaged him only after his voluntary return from Agades.

The nature of Bawa's relationship with Usuman after Usuman's entry into the court of Gobir is illustrated by one incident which occurred about 1787 or 1788. According to Abdullah

> the Sultān of Ghubīr, who was Bāwa, sent word to all the 'ulamā' that they should gather together at his court. . . . We gathered together before him, and he said what he had to say, and gave much wealth in alms to the 'ulamā'. Then Shaikh 'Uthmān stood up before him and said to him: 'Indeed I and my community have no need of your wealth, but I ask you this and this,' and he enumerated to him all matters concerning the establishing of religion. The Sultān replied to him: 'I give you what you ask, and I consent to all that you wish to do in this country'.

On the surface this incident seems to support Arnett's judgement that, 'In the early days of his preaching it is said that Shehu was on the most cordial terms with the Sarkin Gobir; that Sarkin Gobir Bawa Jangworzo gave him every encouragement . . .' . Yet Abdullah's last sentence reveals a deeper significance. Despite the willingness of Bawa to accede to Usuman's requests, his words indicate that he was dealing with Usuman according to the age-old pattern already described. Although Bawa himself did not enforce the sharī'a, he was interested in attaching to himself the most famous scholars, and consented to their activities as long as they did not become too troublesome. Usuman had already been associated with Bawa for some time, and had already explained the true Islam to him when he first came to the court in 1781; if Bawa had intended to institute the sharī'a as the result of Usuman's prior requests, this repetition of demands would not have been necessary. Judging from Jibrīl's fate, Bawa was quite ready to dispense with any individual whose criticisms became too harsh and dangerous. Had he not—within a short period of time— expelled one mallam who had become too troublesome, and taken into his court another younger one, equally renowned, but not extremist in his views? In this latter light, Bawa's giving of alms and his consent to Usuman's requests may be seen also as rewards for the continuing good will of the mallams, which he desired but did not view as indispensable.

At the time Usuman became involved with the court, he may have been encouraged by his cordial reception to hope that Bawa would both accept and implement the desired reforms. He must soon have realized that although Bawa tolerated Islam, he would not practise it—that the way to spread Islam was to preach among the people and yet to remain on cordial terms with Bawa while resisting his pressures. If the rulers were not completely won over to the true faith, then it was still possible that the people could be; for instance, in the preaching tour of Zamfara and other areas which Usuman began about 1786.

From 1786 to the end of his reign, Bawa remained cordial to Usuman. The latter continued to devote much time to circulating and preaching among the people. Although his preaching was steadily attracting a following, there is nothing to show that at this time he intended to use this support for a movement against the government rather than for his avowed purpose of bringing the people into the fold of Islam. However, with his growing dissastisfaction with the *sarkuna*'s continuing indifference to Islam, his criticisms of the government may have found their way into his preaching, possibly only as illustrations of the way in which Muslim law was being violated. From Muhammad Bello's description of Usuman's discourses to the people, it is clear that Usuman taught them the rules of the *shari'a* and insisted on the perfect observance of them. His attraction for the clerical class and the Fulani in general was enhanced by his membership in those groups. But his appeal to all people was strengthened by the diverse nature of his grievances against the practices of the non-orthodox rulers. Sincere conversions to Islam did take place, and many who were already good Muslims were associated with him; but many more people may have become attached to him or interested in him more because he expressed a religious justification for their general dissatisfaction, or for one of their own grievances, than because of any initial religious sympathy with him or any desire to become converts.

Initially, the core of Usuman's support consisted mainly of personal disciples, fellow-clerics, and other orthodox Muslims who shared his criticisms of Islam in Hausaland. He was in contact with many of them, who may in turn have been preaching his message in their own areas and reporting to him about their own difficulties and objections. If Usuman's desire to raise the status of the learned class symbolized a larger wish to make Islam compatible with the political order, it also expressed his special sympathies with a group whose plight was very familiar to him. Primarily, the orthodox *mallams* suffered from being 'a small but cultured group in a society where standards were generally low . . .'. In addition, they were not, for many reasons, financially independent. They were not allowed to hold land, at least as long as they remained *mallams*. Farming, trades, or trading, were not desirable pursuits for those who felt that manual labour would take them away from the religious life. Those *mallams* who did not wish to perform services for the many non-Muslims who desired them would further restrict their incomes. The income of the cleric was furthermore dependent on the whims or generosity of the influential and wealthy among the Hausa. Bawa's largesse to the Fulani chiefs was, aside from the other motives already discussed, an example of such generosity.

Despite their apparent plight, not all of the *mallams* were sympathetic to Usuman's preaching. Although he should have seemed to them their appropriate representative, he was never to be accepted as such by all of them. By Abdullah's own admission, during the period under discussion, many *mallams* of his own clan were not entering the community. Some of them claimed that they doubted Usuman's mission of reform. Many, both Hausa and Fulani alike, were either satisfied with their positions at the Hausa courts or in Hausa society, or comfortable enough to dislike the prospect of change. The latter seems very likely in the light of Abdullah's revealing statement that, after Bawa had accepted Usuman's demands in 1788, 'we returned to establish religion, and the rest of the '*ulamā*' returned with their wealth'. Usuman fundamentally opposed *mallams* who, in accommodating themselves to the system, sanctioned and supported the *sarkis'* non-Muslim practices; they in turn were loath to exchange comfort for his form of orthodoxy.

The wealthiest among the Fulani were Fulanin Gidda (settled Fulani) rather than *mallams*; some of the wealthiest were unmoved by religious criticisms of the existing Hausa order in which they had been successful. Nevertheless, there were probably some wealthy Fulanin Gidda among Usuman's associates or followers. An undefined sense of racial affinity, and the presence of holy men in their clans were factors which may have kept the Fulanin Gidda in contact with Usuman. By the last decade of the eighteenth century some of them had begun to manifest and succeed in political ambitions, if only in a limited sense. The office of *Sarkin Fulanin* (ruler of Fulani) indicates that they achieved political power or status, but only as the heads of fellow-Fulani. The seventeenth and eighteenth centuries had seen a great increase in the number of Fulani in Hausaland. Unlike the Bararoji, the Fulanin Gidda dwelt in town and participated in town life, and in many cases began to speak Hausa and to adopt Hausa customs. Nevertheless, their assimilation was not complete—even by the end of the eighteenth century they were regarded as distinct from the Hausa. The extent to which this separation was due to Hausa social discrimination is not known. It seems reasonable that Fulanin Gidda, desirous of more power and dissatisfied with the Hausa governmental system, might have joined in Usuman's criticisms of the system which had excluded them.

The Bararoji (pastoral Fulani) could have come into touch with Usuman in two ways, though they probably did not contribute significantly to his following during the period under discussion. First, although in the early part of his career Usuman may not have had frequent contact with them, the Bararoji were closely related to the Fulanin Gidda and often economically dependent on their services. Second, Usuman condemned abuses by the Hausa which directly affected the Bararoji, as well as the Fulanin Gidda, though on the grounds that they were violations of Muslim law rather than because fellow-Fulani were abused. Ethnic sympathy, either with the Gidda or the Bararoji, played a minor part in Usuman's articulation of his grievances. In his condemnations of injustices done to cattle-owners and cattle-keepers by the Hausa, he does not speak of the plight of the Fulani in particular. This omission, though, is not incontrovertible proof against the charge of racial sympathy: 'herdsmen' or 'cattle-owners', after all,

meant 'Fulani'. Even if Usuman were secretly championing the
cause of the cattle-owners and cattle-keepers because they were
Fulani, a purely religious articulation of that defence would
have been most natural to him. If his religious writing has
obscured any particular ethnic sympathies, only further
research into his thought will reveal them. At the present time,
all that can truthfully be said is that his specific condemnation of
the *jangali* (cattle tax)—among other things—on religious
grounds, merely coincided with the hatred that the Bararoji
themselves felt against the impost. Usuman opposed it because
the Hausa *sarkuna* were exploiting the Muslim tax structure by
equating the *jangali* with *jizya*, the traditional Muslim head-tax
applied to non-Muslims. The Bararoji, most of whom had
remained non-Muslim, resented the tax on non-religious
grounds—that it was deleterious to their economic well-being
and subject to arbitrary increases.

Although some of their number tended the royal herds, most
of the Bararoji tried to remain aloof from town life while
maintaining what Stenning describes as a symbiotic relationship with the settled agrarian cultivators and landowners. Out
of this relationship arose further dissatisfaction among the
Bararoji over their rights to grazing land. Furthermore, they
were subject to raids on their cattle by the Hausa; they were
often forced to sacrifice, in the interests of security, the best
pasture lands for semi-permanent settlements, occasionally
within the town walls, and to pay for these rights with military
service to the *sarkuna*. Usuman himself condemned the unwritten rule among the Hausa rulers that when cattle strayed
into the royal herds, they were to be appropriated with no
compensation to the owner. Thus the Bararoji, and to an extent
the Gidda, had been enduring for several centuries the very
abuses—*jangali*, raids, appropriations—which Usuman attacked
on religious grounds.

The Hausa peasantry and non-Hausa pagan groups living
outside the towns shared the oppression of the Bararoji; they
too were the objects of 'indiscriminate, oppressive, and frequently excessive imposition of taxes'. In the event that pagan
headmen collected these local taxes, it would have been quite
likely that the peasantry, virtually untouched by Islam, and
the non-Hausa pagans, had little or no idea of the religious

import of these burdens before Usuman preached among them. Here too, as in the case of the Gidda and Bararoji, Usuman's religious attacks coincided with the prevalent economic grievances. The peasantry may have made up a large part of Usuman's following; at least he seems to have spent much of his time preaching among them. As Abdullah said, in Zamfara, the majority of the people to whom Usuman preached '. . . had not smelt the scent of Islam'. Furthermore, even if these two discontented elements had not heard or sympathized with all of the specific issues of Usuman's message, their own discontent would probably have led them to subscribe to any general movement which offered them further justification for, and expression of, their grievances.

Part of Usuman's attraction for the people must be attributed to his own personality and preaching skill. But it was the broadness of his appeal, in which many grievances found their expression, that attracted many of his followers. At the end of the eighteenth century, Hausaland was filled with people dissatisfied with the Hausa order, and who were thus potential supporters for a movement of protest. As a result of oppressive and arbitrary actions, Hausa rulers alienated many more elements than they benefited or satisfied. All the groups which have been discussed shared one important characteristic; to a great extent they depended for their livelihood and security on the goodwill of others more powerful than they: the *mallams* on the Hausa rulers and Hausa patrons; the Gidda on the Hausa rulers; the Bararoji on the rulers, landholders, and cultivators; the peasants on the government. Discontent prevailed where goodwill was lacking. Usuman criticized both the harshness and arbitrary nature of the exercise of control by those in power, and also the specific practices to which much of the population objected; he then taught the people about a religion in which these practices would be outlawed and in which government would be administered with social justice. His sympathies were particularly with the clerics and other Muslims who shared his ideas, but the fact that not all of his followers shared his religious motivations or grievances did not make him any less attractive as an articulator of their discontent with the existing régime. The fact that many of his followers were also Fulani or Muslims or clerics was not essential to his attraction for them, but merely served to enhance and strengthen it.

During his early adult years in Hausaland, Usuman's avowed aim was to bring Hausa rulers and subjects to the acceptance and practice of orthodox Islam by preaching the reform of the faith. Under Sarki Bawa, he achieved at least limited success because of the approval and friendship of the *sarki* that he enjoyed. Although by its nature his preaching attracted those discontented with the government, he himself tried to avoid this result. Abdullah reports, and this does not seem mere self-justification, that Usuman tried to avert a quarrel between the people and their rulers, saying, 'I will not interfere between anyone and his chief; I will not be a cause of parting.' Usuman might have been content to work within the system rather than to call for its overthrow if Bawa's successors had continued their predecessor's policies towards him and his work. Bawa's successors maintained the appearances of cordiality. According to Arnett, 'Yakubu, Nafata and Yunfa, as each in turn became Sarkin Gobir, visited Shehu at Degel and received his blessing'. This statement is not difficult to believe. Usuman withdrew from the court because of Nafata's reversions to animism; but even by the time of Yunfa's accession, he had not completely broken with the royal house. Yet despite the superficial respect of the later *sarkuna* for Usuman, Bawa's death marked the end of official approval of Usuman's activities.

The *sarkuna*'s hostility was related to the increasing size of Usuman's community and its alienation from the Hausa ruler's as well as to the rulers' own attitudes to Islam. The community at this time was large and separate enough to constitute a threat to the rulers, yet not so large as to provoke forceful or total suppression. According to Abdullah, 'Men kept leaving their countries and coming to him [Usuman] with all they possessed, leaving their Sultans. Then the Sultans became angry. . . .' Towards the end of his reign, Sarki Nafata became angry enough about the existence and continued growth in the number of Usuman's followers to take action against them. After verbal threats and constant harassment of his supporters had failed to cause Usuman's community to disband, Nafata took steps to check its growth by issuing the following orders:

He announced that he would not allow a single man to be Muslim except he had inherited the Faith from his father. He who had not inherited Islam was to turn to that which he had inherited. Secondly, that no man in future should wear a turban. Thirdly, that no woman should cover her head with a cloth.

Nafata had good reason to be disturbed by Usuman's preaching and by his following. By demanding the application of the *sharī'a*, Usuman was calling on the *sarki* to abandon his traditional system of government and to substitute a Muslim form based on religious law as taught by the *mallams*. As Usuman himself wrote, 'He upon whom is laid the Command, and who has undertaken to follow the Sharia, asks a learned man, relies on his learning, and obeys him.' Although Bawa had never completely put Usuman's demands into practice, he had accepted his advice and had consented to his activities in Hausaland. Nafata, on the other hand, had never undertaken to follow the *sharī'a*, had not required Usuman's or any other cleric's advice, and certainly would not have made even a pretence of obeying his words, although he may still have felt and expressed the personal respect of a student for his teacher.

In addition to posing a challenge to a centuries-old pattern of rule, Usuman, by withdrawing from the court to avoid conflict and by speaking out against the government perhaps more than he had done during Bawa's reign, appeared even more menacing and antagonistic. Usuman's community had been growing for at least four years, and possibly more, between Bawa's death and Nafata's proclamation. Whatever its exact size, the following which Usuman was attracting with his preaching was alarming, not because it represented a disgruntled minority of religious men led by one reforming *mallam*, but because it was drawing adherents from all segments of the population through the efforts both of Usuman and of many other *mallams*. A rival centre of authority and power was developing which could have resulted in a diarchy. The stability of the Hausa State depended on the loyal participation of all elements at their various levels. Usuman's separation from the court and the nature of his preaching obviously threatened to undermine the allegiance of all discontented persons to the secular authority.

Yet the seriousness of Nafata's measures need not be over-stated. That he merely issued a proclamation indicates that at this stage he thought he could stop the growth of the movement with measures short of force: by taking away its formerly pagan adherents, by preventing it from attracting more of them, and by denying to the remaining core their symbols of unity and their privileges as a special community which had been granted during Bawa's reign. Nafata thought that Usuman's followers would not be dangerous if they were not allowed access to the rest of the population or to dress distinctively. Orthodox Muslims who were not distinguishable as a separate community were not a threat to him; on the other hand, a growing community involving all elements in the population, and obeying laws other than those of the *sarki*, obviously would be.

Sarki Yunfa's continuation of his father's policy did not preclude an initial show of respect for Usuman. But Yunfa soon realized that the situation resulting from Nafata's proclamation was far more serious than the one which had provoked it. The effect of Yunfa's continuation of his father's policy was not the one intended: so far from re-establishing the *sarki*'s authority, it had actually encouraged the growth of a separate community. Realizing the failure of the proclamation to achieve the desired result, Yunfa began to make repeated threats to Usuman's followers. The threats served only to drive a group of them, under a disciple named Abdu Salame, to the town of Gimbana, which they fortified against the *sarki*. After they had refused to obey his order to return to the capital, in mid-1803, Yunfa summoned Usuman to his court. Usuman obeyed, and arrived accompanied only by Abdullah and one other. According to Abdullah, an attempt on Usuman's life followed, but failed, as the gun which Yunfa directed at Usuman backfired, burning his own clothing.

The motives behind Yunfa's actions are not clear. Perhaps he had hoped to secure Abdu Salame's return by putting pressure upon Usuman, and then fired on him in sudden anger or because Usuman refused to accede to his demands. Perhaps, as Lacroix says, he was at last becoming exasperated with the unrest which the Fulani had caused ever since the time of Jibrīl. Moreover, he was probably beginning to feel that violent action was the only way to avoid the compromise with Usuman which he was unwilling to make. After his attempt on Usuman's life had failed, Yunfa told Usuman of the hatred he felt for him, but allowed him to leave, perhaps reasoning that in the event of Usuman's murder or arrest, he would still have to deal with his followers. Usuman's reluctance, even at this stage, to commit himself to calling for the overthrow of Yunfa which he must have desired, is revealed in Abdullah's report of their departure from the Gobir court: 'And the *shaikh* said to us, "Both of you conceal this, and pray God most high that we may never again meet with this unbeliever".'

Yunfa proceeded to prepare an expedition against Abdu Salame in Gimbana, which took place in December 1803, and was successful. Yunfa took Gimbana, and killed, put to flight and captured many Muslims. When the captives passed Usuman's town of Degel on their way back to the capital, Usuman, incensed, somehow caused the Muslims to be released. His order to return the captives having been ignored for two months, Yunfa threatened to destroy Degel as Gimbana had been destroyed if Usuman's intransigence continued any longer. Usuman refused to leave his community as Yunfa wished, and instead fled with it to Gundu on 21 February 1804, the flight being called by the participants the '*Hijra*'. The declaration of *jihād* was imminent.

Usuman had not been trying to provoke such a serious threat from Yunfa as a pretext to declare war, although he must have been aware that both his preaching and his defiance of the *sarki* might have this effect. Rather, he was acting consistently with his policy of persistent pressure against the Gobir *sarkuna*. He was clearly not in the tradition of the intentionally antagonistic reformers of, for example, North Africa. Yet his provocative behaviour on this occasion marked a departure from the type of pressure he had applied in the past, and proves his complicity in bringing on the war to a greater extent than the major apologists for the *jihād* would care to acknowledge. He must have seen that a firm stand was necessary to protect his followers from further aggression. Perhaps he also believed that, with stronger pressure, Yunfa would accede to his wishes. His willingness to try to force the issue at this particular moment was encouraged by the existence of his large following, was facilitated by the chance to use the captives to put pressure on Yunfa, and was made necessary by the fact that the captives included some of his own supporters. Unfortunately, he over-estimated the strength of his bargaining position.

His pressures having failed, and his community being endan-gered rather than protected by his actions, he was forced to the decision that a change of rulers rather than a change in Yunfa's attitudes was necessary if his goals for Hausaland were to be achieved. He was forced to invoke the religious penalty which Hausa violations, or neglect, of Muslim law theoretically required. If Usuman had merely been waiting for a pretext to declare a *jihād*, as Delafosse and Meek contend, one can only say that he had waited a very long time to seize an opportunity which must have presented itself earlier in other less obvious forms. His final break with the court occurred after more than twenty years of a compromising involvement with it, and then only because he was faced with an anti-Muslim ruler, who not only proved unamenable to pressure, but also threatened the growth and even the very existence of a Muslim community in Hausaland. The propriety of *jihād* against the unbelievers must have long been in Usuman's mind, as it would naturally occur to any Muslim reformer; the possibility of a successful *jihād* may have been suggested by the late eighteenth-century revolutions in the Futa regions; but the decision that *jihād* actually had to be waged in Hausaland came when Usuman was faced with the choice of war or destruction. In a sense, Usuman decided that *jihād* was obligatory only when it had become inevitable. The catalytic incident was a pretext only in the sense that the defence of Muslims was a more urgent issue than the reform of the faith in general. No longer merely a preacher of gradual reform, Usuman strengthened his appeal to the populace and devoted himself entirely to gathering support for a movement to overthrow the existing government. It was in a movement explicitly for this purpose that the grievances which had attracted people to Usuman could achieve their overt expression.

Although it is clear that, once the *jihād* had been declared, Usuman began to see his whole life as a preparation for it, the student of the *jihād* should not be led to this view. The very nature of the documents which Usuman began to produce in

1804 indicates that the war was one for which he had not prepared himself intellectually. *Tanbīh alikhwan* was only one of his
attempts to rationalize a war against people who considered
themselves Muslims. For once the war had been declared,
Usuman was forced to return from his more moderate ideas on
unbelief to the more extreme doctrines of his master Jibrīl:
to conclude, as in the *Tanbīh*, that the Hausa who followed
non-Muslim practices could be considered heathens for
purposes of a *jihād*, even though they considered themselves
Muslims.

Late in 1804 Yunfa was to inform his neighbouring Hausa
rulers that 'he had left a small fire in his country but it had
surpassed his power and had overcome him'. His statement
was both true and untrue. It was untrue for him to say that he
had ignored Usuman's movement; he had on the contrary
made several misguided attempts to counteract it. However,
it was true that Usuman's movement had grown from a
nuisance to a threat before any of the parties were aware of
what had happened. The war which was to come had not been
planned or actively sought by Usuman. However, over many
years, and for a long time with the support of the *sarki*, he had
unwittingly laid the basis for it, in the context of a society
where discontent was already widespread. Perhaps he was able
to be more successful than his predecessor Jibrīl only because
he had done so unintentionally, and thus without arousing
distrust until it was too late.

The history of the *jihād* itself served as a stage for the further
interplay of the forces which led to its declaration. It affords
further evidence that Usuman was initially seeking to force
Yunfa to submission by pressure rather than by force; that
Usuman had not planned or organized the war; that participation in Usuman's movement, and in the war, was not based
purely on ethnic or religious affinities; and that many of
Usuman's supporters did not share his high ideals or goals for
religious reform, but rather appropriated because of their own
grievances, in a generalized and simplified form, his justification for the overthrow of the existing order. Yet despite all these
facts, the events of the *jihād* confirm that Usuman's articulation
and justification of war on behalf of his supporters and on

behalf of Islam was essential; for he without doubt remained the sole moral, spiritual and, in fact, political authority for the conquest.

After the *Hijra*, the Sarkin Gobir ordered attacks on Usuman's followers who were trying to reach him in Gudu. When they continued to go to him nevertheless, Sarkin Gobir Yunfa called on him to return to Degel. Usuman agreed to do so, but only on the condition that Yunfa would adopt the reformed religion and restore the property which had been seized from Usuman's followers. Yunfa refused Usuman's demands, and was aided, according to Bello, by many of his 'own' *mallams* in making his decision. The urgency of the situation prompted Usuman's formal transformation from the spiritual leader of a movement of reform to the commander of a holy war through his election as *Sarkin Musulmi* (Arabic: *Amīr al-mu'minīn*, Commander of the Believers) by his closest followers.

According to Bivar, *Wathīqat ahl al-sūdān* may be the apologia issued 'at the moment when, after his election as *Amīr al-mu'minīn*, the Shehu launched his sacred war against the rulers of the Hausa States'. It at once outlined the rules by which the *jihād* was to be waged, and stated Usuman's case against the Hausa rulers. The document failed to make a strong impression in either respect. In setting out the standards by which the war was to be waged, Usuman denounced wilful and indiscriminate appropriations, killings and plunderings, which the law could not possibly sanction. Yet from the early months of the fighting, 'onlookers saw with dismay that the Fulani raids spared neither Muslim nor pagan and that any town or village in their way was looted quite impartially'. Niven attributed this phenomenon to the fact that religious fervour had already worn thin. It is more likely that, although Usuman had instilled in his followers his enthusiasm and his feeling of divine mission, his 'fanaticism' for the *jihād*, he could never have imposed upon them systematic rules for the conduct of the actual fighting. Such rules might have influenced an inner core of close disciples, but many of Usuman's followers lacked his sophistication and his religious motivation. Most of them were suddenly being called upon, after a long period of growing discontent, to fight with the prospect of easily obtainable booty. The restraint noticeable in some of Usuman's treatises disappears completely in the fervour of other writings, and especially in his popular appeals. In meeting the demands of the new political developments, Usuman unintentionally encouraged the indiscriminate extremes of his followers by the extremism of his own thoughts on the duties and mission of the fighters in a holy war.

Although in the *Wathīqa* Usuman demanded the general allegiance of all Hausaland to the Sarkin Musulmi, he was not to need to call the force of his words into play with respect to his lieutenants in the other Hausa States until more than a year after the *jihād* had begun. The activities of the first year of the *jihād* were mainly in Usuman's own area of Gobir, Kebbi and Zamfara, and showed both the comparative weakness of his position and his continuing desire to force the Sarkin Gobir to a speedy capitulation, possibly with the help of the other *sarkuna*. The victory of the Fulani over the Gobirawa at Tabkin Kwotto, 21 June 1804, was probably a surprise to both sides, since the Fulani archers were far less numerous than the armed and chain-mail-clad cavalry on the Hausa side. According to Abdullah's account of the battle, many Fulani were among the armies of the Sarkin Gobir. Although this shows that something other than ethnic affinity was involved in the Fulani's choice of sides, Abdullah's victory poem extols the triumph of a people of predominantly pastoralist origin (that is, the Fulani) over the powerful heathen. The participation of so many Bararoji on the side of Usuman may have been due to their perception of a general threat to all Fulani. While Arnett adduced the evidence of Fulani fighting on the side of the Sarkin Gobir in order to reject the view that Yunfa actually issued an order to exterminate the Fulani as a race, he did argue reasonably that, 'it seems probable that in a general movement to attack adherents of Shehu and the reformed faith, anyone of the Fillani race was specially liable to suspicion and attack'.

The next attempt to negotiate with Yunfa and the other *sarkuna* followed in July 1804. The *Wathīqa* may also be the document which Usuman used at this time to announce and explain his declaration of war against the Sarkin Gobir to the other *sarkuna*. Usuman's message probably failed for two reasons: first, the other *sarkuna* were not yet fully apprised of the danger to themselves, although they were sufficiently alarmed by Yunfa's defeat to attack Fulani in their own areas; second, Usuman's following may not have appeared in its most fully menacing light, since many of his own kinsmen and a large number of Fulani and Hausa still had not rallied to his side. In October 1804, when the Wazirin Gobir visited him in the interest of achieving a peaceful settlement, Usuman promised to offer an armistice to all of Gobir except Dangeda (a small town which his forces were attacking at the time) until the Sarkin Gobir should sue for peace in person to him. But Yunfa's final refusal, after he had almost decided to accept, finally closed the attempt at negotiation. Usuman was not yet in a position strong enough to force Yunfa to concede without further fighting.

By July 1805, one year after the war had begun, Usuman's cause was still not secured. Apart from Birnin Kebbi, no major towns had fallen to his forces; the first attempt on Alkalawa, the capital of Gobir, in November 1804, had failed. He had suffered a serious defeat after a surprise attack by the Gobirawa and their Tuareg mercenaries in December 1804; and many of his men had perished. The only Hausa state in any way allied to the Fulani—Zamfara—had defected to Gobir, and supplies were difficult to obtain in hostile territory. In the absence of a large and organized army, there could be no planned strategy for the future. Not even all Muslims had agreed to fight with Usuman; Usuman and Bello were constantly forced to appeal for help from them and others. In fact the Shehu's cause was at this time by no means assured of success. This does not mean that there were not many factions desiring the overthrow of the Hausa rulers; on the contrary, it emphasizes that their ultimate participation in the *jihād* was so opportunistic, and so lacking in commitment to Usuman's religious cause, that many of them preferred to join him only later, when there seemed to be a better chance of his being victorious. He probably entered the war with the more devoted contingent from each of the groups which have been discussed; as the war progressed, more joined him.

Meanwhile, a diverse group of other leaders—or flagbearers as they came to be known—were taking up Usuman's cause in the other Hausa States, most often on their own initiative. Although the news of Usuman's war with Gobir and of his early military successes was the most important catalyst to uprisings elsewhere in Hausaland, in no sense does his relationship with the flagbearers suggest a conspiracy. He was not a strong military leader in his own area. He had not, as the actions of the flagbearers show, formulated any general plan for the conquest of Hausaland, although he and Bello later, as an improvised measure, sent help to the fighters in other areas. He did not lead or even control, in a military sense, the *jihād* elsewhere in Hausaland. The way in which the *jihād* spread shows that the underlying discontent which led to Usuman's own movement in Gobir was present in the other Hausa States, but required his example and justification, and possibly the need for self-defence, to activate it.

Although there had been reformist preaching in the other Hausa States, and although Usuman considered all Hausaland to be subject to the *jihād* and had his appeals circulated throughout it, the first men to seek his sanction were not sent for by him, and may not have come to him until at least one year after the *jihād* had been declared in Gobir, and then only after hostilities had broken out in their respective areas. Although Usuman had wide connexions in cleric circles, many of the men who approached him at the time of the *jihād* were not clerics, and were not even the type of leader he would have chosen. They were not always men of outstanding intellectual achievements, but were primarily the delegates of the influential Fulanin Gidda interests. Usuman did not always make the selection of the flagbearers, but often accepted the man whom the muslim-Fulani community sent as its representative. The only two men whom Usuman did select as flagbearers and sent out, apparently with no prior request on their parts and not as rewards for service, were students who were with him when the *jihād* was declared. Furthermore, they were sent to 'pagan' areas where, because of the lack of a sizeable Fulani-Muslim community, Usuman could have no hope that leadership would arise spontaneously. In two emirates, men were made flagbearers as recognition for former service on behalf of the *jihād*. It was a mark of Usuman's prestige as the legitimizing authority of the *jihād*—the philosopher of the revolution and the indispensable unifying force—that his flagbearers considered him the sole source of approval for leadership and the sole sanction for conquest, and that he was able to impose his will upon those who tried to defy his authority. However, once he had entrusted power to a flagbearer, he interfered only when he felt that interference was absolutely necessary.

Meanwhile, in the Gobir area, Usuman suffered one more severe defeat—at Alwassa, November 1805, at the hands of a Kebbawa-Gobirawa-Tuareg alliance—before his cause took its final upswing. Despite the severity of the defeat, after the battle the Kebbawa were not able to mass enough strength to attack Usuman's camp at Gando. Having survived Alwassa, 'Shehu's cause continued to gain ground and was never again in any great danger'. In 1808 Alkalawa finally fell to Usuman's forces, after a second fruitless attempt had been made in 1806; then the Tuareg deserted the Gobirawa for Usuman's camp, having themselves been soundly defeated by the Fulani in March 1806. With the fall of Alkalawa, where Yunfa and most of his followers were killed, the *jihād* in Usuman's area, and in fact in all Hausaland, was virtually accomplished.

The oppressive situation in Hausaland at the time of Usuman's recruitment to the Gobir court was one which was likely to provoke discontent. But in 1804, although Hausaland possessed the components necessary for a revolution, revolution was not inevitable. Hausaland had failed to produce a leader of its own. In the main, the available leadership lay in the settled Fulani. Usuman himself served as the essential spark. His movement was not only a group of Muslims overthrowing a pagan government. It was not merely one race expressing its natural hostility to another. It was not simply the overthrow of the hated oppressors by the oppressed. Nor was it limited to those learned men who shared Usuman's intellectual motivation. It is true that individuals fought for one or a number of these reasons. But they fought in a body only because of their connexion to Usuman and his representatives, and that connexion was the result of many different attractions. In causing his various followers to transcend their individual motivations for the purpose of fighting for a single cause, Usuman maintained control over the general purpose of the movement.

2. Political conditions in the western Sudan

A. ADU BOAHEN *Britain, the Sahara and the Western Sudan*
Clarendon Press, Oxford 1964; pages 239–47

BARTH's accounts throw a good deal of light on the political conditions in the kingdoms and empires of the western Sudan by the middle of the nineteenth century and on the changes that had taken place since the visit of the earlier explorers. In the basin of the Chad, it was clear from the reports of Lucas, Park, and Hornemann, based mainly on information supplied by Arab and Tuareg traders, that Bornu and Bagirmi were the dominant states. By the time of the visit of Denham and Clapperton, Waday had joined these states and the three of them were engaged in a bitter struggle for the mastery of the basin. Bagirmi was then courageously challenging Bornu, and in December 1823 even invaded her. When Barth visited the basin, the three states were still predominant though a significant shift had occurred in the balance of power. Bagirmi's offensive of December 1823 would appear to have been her last determined effort in the protracted struggle for the control of the Chad basin. For in a later engagement, of which Denham and Hillman were eye-witnesses, the Bagirmi army was decisively defeated and nearly annihilated. Bagirmi never recovered from this defeat, for Barth discovered that she was paying tribute to both Bornu and Waday. 'Ruined by a most disastrous civil war and trodden down by its neighbours,' Barth reported, 'the country of Bagirmi seems to linger till it is destined either to rise again or to fall a prey to the first invader.' Bagirmi did not in fact rise again but lingered on till, like Waday and Bornu, she fell a prey to Rabeh, the adventurous Arab warrior, formerly of the Khalifa's army, in 1892–3. Until the conquests of Rabeh altered conditions in the Chad basin in the 1890s, Waday and Bornu remained the main powers.

It was, however, in the area west of Bornu that political conditions underwent a fundamental and revolutionary change in the nineteenth century. By the beginning of the century, as is evident from the reports of Lucas, Park, and Hornemann as well as the research of Barth, Hausaland was divided into about fourteen separate and independent states. Hornemann sent

DNA

home a rough map sketched for him by a *marabout* on which Kebbi, Nupe, Noro(?), Daura, Kano, Katsina, Gobir, Zamfara, and Solan(?) were shown. Of these states Katsina was certainly the most powerful, the most prosperous, and the best known in the Sahara and the Barbary states. But when Clapperton visited Hausaland, he found that in place of the Hausa states was a single Fulani Empire stretching from the Niger in the west to the borders of Bornu in the east and to Adamawa on the Benue in the south-east. The Empire was at that time divided into two: the area from the Niger to Katsina, including Nupe and Ilorin in the south, was under the Emir of Gwandu, and the area from Katsina to the western border of Bornu was under the Sultan of Sokoto. Clapperton also found that Kano and not Katsina was the main commercial emporium of Hausaland. As he and Denham gathered from people who had actually taken part in the wars, the phenomenal change was the outcome of a predominantly Fulani rebellion led by Usman dan Fodio, the great Fulani scholar and ascetic, against the Hausa rulers.

The Fulani had been infiltrating into Hausaland and Bornu from the Senegal and the Futa Jallon regions since the thirteenth century. Some of them, the *Bororoje* (Cattle Fulani), were wandering about in the rural areas; while others, the *Fulani Gida* (Town Fulani), had settled in the towns, where their higher education soon won for them positions of influence as *mallams*, secretaries, and political advisers at the courts of princes. Usman dan Fodio, the leader of the rebellion, was one of the Fulani Gida and had lived for some years at the Court of Gobir, where he acted as a tutor to the princes Yakuba and Yunfa. The increasing pagan practices at that Court forced dan Fodio to leave his job and to settle in the village of Degel, a few miles west of the modern town of Wurno. There he began to preach against the prevalent unorthodox practices with ascetic zeal and devotion and gradually won a large following. Alarmed by the growing strength of this zealot, his former pupil Sarkin Yunfa was alleged to have given secret orders for his murder. This leaked out and led to the flight of Fodio and his followers from Degel on 23 February 1804, an event whose anniversary is still celebrated in Northern Nigeria. From now on, assisted by his son Bello, afterwards Clapperton's host, and his brother Abdullahi, Usman planned the revolt, and letters were written by Bello to the Fulani *mallams* in the other Hausa states. Having gathered a large following, Usman raised the standard of revolt about May 1804 by attacking the neighbouring Goberawa towns. Proclaimed *amir al-mu'minin* (Commander of the Faithful), he gave his blessing in the form of flags to various Fulani *mallams* who initiated similar rebellions in the states and kingdoms in which they lived. For instance, *Mallams* Bauchi and Adama began the Jihad in the pagan states of Jacoba and Fumbina respectively, and their conquests were named after them. Whatever the true nature of this rebellion—and from modern research it is clear that it was a complex one—its successful outcome cannot be doubted. By 1831 the various independent Hausa and other states had superimposed on them the Fulani Empire of fourteen emirates owing allegiance to the Commander of the Faithful, who resided in Sokoto, the new town founded by Usman dan Fodio. Before his death Usman divided the Empire into two Sultanates, Gwandu for his brother and Sokoto for his son, who was recognized as the religious head of the whole Empire.

When Barth visited Hausaland in the 1850s, the twin Fulani Empire of Sokoto and Gwandu still held sway. But from his observations of the state of the Empire he concluded: 'it cannot be denied that the Empire of Sokoto, if going on in the present way, will soon be dissolved and thrown into pieces.' Barth's fears were unfounded, for in fact the results of the rebellion have lasted to this day. The present Northern Nigeria is more or less coterminous with the Fulani Empire, the Sultan of Sokoto is still a direct descendant of Usman dan Fodio, he bears to this day the title of *amir al-mu'minin*, and is recognized as the religious head of Muslim Nigeria. Most of the present emirs of the region are also the direct descendants of the founders of the emirates.

That Barth's forecast did not come true is not at all surprising, since the picture he painted of the whole Empire as a Hobbesian state of nature, a picture which many historians, especially those of the 'Lugard' or 'Pax Britannica' school of thought, have only too readily accepted, is grossly misleading. There is no doubt that in the provinces of Yarui, Gwari, and Nupe to the south-west, as well as in the former Hausa states of Gobir, Kebbi, and Zamfara, wars and revolts continued throughout the century. Clapperton and Lander found that the people of Yauri and Gwari had revolted against the Fulani and were maintaining their independence. Though nearly all these regions were conquered and formed into the Fulani emirate of Kontagora by Umoru Nagwamache, one of the sons of the fifth Sultan of Sokoto, they still remained exceedingly restless and insecure in the fifties. In Nupe, too, the struggle between the Fulani and the former rulers continued intermittently, as the Landers, Laird, and Baikie saw, until the fifties, when the issue was finally decided in favour of the Fulani. Farther north in Sokoto, Barth arrived in 1853 to find that the Sultan was campaigning against the same people, the Goberawa and Kebbawa, who had revolted during Clapperton's visits of 1823 and 1826. During his travels in this neighbourhood Barth often met troops on the move and heard echoes of war drums. He once had to wait in Katsina for seven weeks because of a threatened invasion of the district by the Goberawa. Undoubtedly these wars and revolts must have caused some devastation and insecurity.

This situation should not, however, be exaggerated. In the first place, these wars and revolts were usually sporadic and of short duration. Secondly, they were mainly limited in the north to the area immediately north of Katsina and west of Sokoto and in the south to Nupe and Gwari. In other words, they were chiefly confined to the Emirate of Gwandu and should not therefore be taken as a reflection of the state of the Fulani Empire as a whole. Thirdly, Barth was certainly wrong—and so of course are Lugard, Meek, Bovill, Trimingham and other scholars who follow him—in describing these wars either as raids for slaves or as the 'struggle carried on between paganism and islamism'. What he observed was no less than a struggle for independence by the Hausa, the Gwari, and the Nupe. Far from reconciling themselves to their fate, the Courts of Gobir and Kebbi moved to Argungu and Matadi and from there spasmodically continued the struggle, with the assistance of some of the other dethroned Hausa dynasties and some of the Tuareg tribes, until the British occupation.

Whatever may have been the situation in the areas under Gwandu, it was different in those under Sokoto. During his travels through the emirates of Kano and Zaria in 1826, Clapperton did not notice any rebellions or civil wars. On his return journey after the death of his master, Richard Lander proceeded, to use his own words, 'on my way unmolested' and with a perfect sense of security through the southern districts of Kano and the northern and eastern parts of the emirate of Zaria, and through the emirate of Bauchi to within a day's march of its capital; nowhere in these districts did he come across any rebel armies. Nor had Vogel, who travelled through the emirates of Gombe, Bauchi, Zaria, and the southern part of Kano, any story of wars, revolts, and insurbordination to tell. If anything, especially in Bauchi and Adamawa, it was the Fulani who were on the offensive. Instead of attempting to regain their independence, most of the people of the south-eastern emirates merely emigrated across the Benue or sought refuge in the almost inaccessible reaches of the hills and plateaux. From Barth's own observations, as well as from the information he collected about the Sokoto Sultanate, it was only in the emirate of Hadeija, in the northernmost districts of Katsina, and in Zamfara that he found disturbances. In Hadeija the deposed governor, Bukhari, was still carrying on the campaigns for the reconquest of his post which he began in 1851. By 1853 he had killed his successor, had retaken his emirate, and was still attacking the districts of Gumel and Katagum. The disturbances in Katsina and Zamfara were due, as we have seen already, to the people of Gobir and Kebbi. These districts were all on the fringe of the Sokoto Sultanate. Indeed, when, in order to avoid the Goberawa, Barth had to proceed southward instead of westward from Katsina to Sokoto in March 1853, he himself was astonished to find that the country within a single day's journey south of Katsina was 'populous and well cultivated', with extensive cotton and tobacco fields and large plantations of indigo. Of the other provinces of the Sokoto Sultanate, Barth informed the Foreign Office in January 1853 that 'there was nothing particularly to be said'.

In the regions of Timbuctu and the upper reaches of the Niger, conditions were also entirely different from those that Houghton and Park had portrayed. The area did not consist of a series of independent Tuareg and Songhay principalities.

As may be recalled, in the days of Barth as in those of Laing and Caillié the whole stretch from Timbuctu to Jenne formed part of the Fulani Empire of Masina. This empire was founded at the same time as that of Sokoto and would seem to have been a product of the same movement—the Jihad of Usman dan Fodio. Though Shehu Ahmadu, the Fulani *mallam* and founder of Masina, may not have actually taken part in the Hausa wars as Westermann thought, he was influenced by the puritan ideals and fanatical zeal of Usman dan Fodio. About 1813, while the wars in Hausaland were still raging, Ahmadu raised the standard of revolt against what he considered the idolatrous and semi-pagan rulers of Masina. He soon overthrew these rulers, attacked and conquered Jenne, the important trading centre, and from there invaded Bambara at the time when Dochard was waiting a few miles from Segu for a reply to his request for freedom of passage. From Bambara Ahmadu again turned his attention eastward, overran the petty Tuareg and Songhay principalities, and in 1826, only a few weeks before Laing's arrival, conquered Timbuctu. Like Usman dan Fodio, Shehu Ahmadu founded a capital for his new empire which he characteristically named Hamdallahi (God be praised). Ahmadu ruled with fanatical zeal till his death in 1844, and his empire lasted until it was overthrown by the Tuculor Tijani, Al-Hajj Umar, between 1855 and 1862. Undoubtedly it was the religious fanaticism of Ahmadu and his successor, a feeling which had not burned itself out even by the time of Barth's visit, which made the regions of the Niger bend so dangerous for European explorers after 1826.

The relations between these various empires and kingdoms of the western Sudan as revealed by the accounts of the explorers are also noteworthy when compared with the ideas of the 'Pax Britannica' School. As we have seen, Bagirmi, Waday, and Bornu were in the days of Denham and Clapperton bitterly struggling among themselves. The warlike spirit of Bagirmi declined after 1823, but Waday and Bornu continued the struggle in the thirties and forties. During the stay of Barth and Vogel, however, while relations were not at all friendly, the two states were not in armed conflict. Farther west, Bornu and Sokoto were also far from being permanently at war with each other. Relations between the two would even appear to have been quite friendly at the time of the Denham–Clapperton mission, mainly because Al-Kānami had his hands full with the Waday–Bagirmi wars. When at one of their palavers in 1823 Clapperton told Bello that Al-Kānami would seize any guns and presents sent to him through Bornu, the Sultan replied confidently, 'Oh no, he will never do that, he will never do that, he is my friend.' But, as may be recalled, Clapperton arrived in Kano the second time only to meet an invasion of Sokoto by the army of Al-Kānami. This invasion was successfully beaten back, and from then on till Al-Kānami's death in 1837 peace prevailed between the two states. His son and successor, Umar, revived his father's aggressive policy towards Sokoto and during the first five years of his reign launched a number of attacks on that state. These were mostly unsuccessful, and in 1942 he concluded peace with the Fulani. During Barth's long stay he found that the two states were still officially not at war, that the rulers were 'professing to be on the best terms with one another' and that messengers were going to and fro. But he did discover that covertly Bornu was aiding Bukhari as well as Gobir, that clashes between the governors of the border provinces were not infrequent, and that both states were giving asylum to each other's political refugees. Indeed, when he was leaving Bornu for Timbuctu, Barth was specifically asked by the Government of Bornu not to go to Kano, because that would 'interfere with their policy'.

This hostile attitude particularly on the part of Bornu towards Sokoto dates from the *jihad* of Usman dan Fodio, which was not confined to Hausaland, for two Fulani *mallams*, Ibrahim Zaki and Gwani Mukhtar, led the Fulani of Bornu in 'sympathetic risings' against the Sultan in about 1808 and were in fact later given flags by Usman dan Fodio. By 1812 the Fulani had conquered most of the western provinces of Bornu and completely burnt down Birni Ngazargamo, its capital since its foundation in 1470. However, under the inspired leadership of Muhammad Al-Kānami, another celebrated scholar and ascetic who was called in from Kanem by the helpless Sultan, the Bornu army reconquered most of the lost provinces except Katagum.

Al-Kānami became so indispensable to the Sultan that he was invited to stay permanently in Bornu. He accepted the invitation, built a new capital, which he named Kukawa, in 1814, and became from then till his death in 1837 not only the king-maker, but, as Denham and Clapperton observed, the effective ruler of Bornu.

On Barth's arrival he discovered that the office of Sultan had been entirely abolished and that sovereign power in theory as well as in practice was exercised by Umar, the son and successor of Al-Kānami. This change took place, Barth informed Palmerston, in 1851, 'in consequence of an attack from Waday'. The invasion of Bornu in 1846 by the Sultan of Waday had been undertaken at the request of the people of Bornu, who wanted to rid the country of the Kānami family and restore Sultan Ibrahim 'to the authority of his forefathers'. The Sultan of Waday defeated Umar at the first encounter and went on to raze Kukawa to the ground. He then appointed Ali, the last surviving member of the Sefuwa dynasty, as Sultan in place of Ibrahim, who had been executed by Umar. During the second battle, however, Umar defeated and killed Ali, whose death ended the Sefuwa dynasty which had been reigning in Bornu since the tenth century. From that time till today the descendants of Al-Kānami have continued to rule Bornu under the title of Sheikh or Shehu.

The *jihad* then had very far-reaching consequences in Bornu, including a legacy of hostility and jealousy towards Sokoto owing to the loss of Katagum, Kano, Katsina, and Daura, all of which owed Bornu nominal allegiance before the *jihad*. But from the visit of Barth and Vogel to the death of Umar in 1880 this feeling of jealousy and hostility did not lead to any invasions or wars.

Equally strained in the fifties were the relations between the Gwandu–Sokoto and Masina Empires. When Barth was leaving for Timbuctu, the Sultan of Sokoto repeatedly asked him not to visit the ruler of Masina. According to Barth, this was due to the insulting message which Shehu Ahmadu had sent to the rulers of Sokoto to the effect that unless they reduced the number of their wives to two and renounced their effeminate dress, he would 'pay them a visit'. The two sister empires, however, never took the field against each other.

From this brief survey of the observations of the explorers, it seems that during at least the first half of the nineteenth century, the states of the western Sudan were not permanently at each other's throats. As between the states of contemporary Europe, jealousies, animosities, and rivalries existed and these led occasionally to wars and invasions. Indeed the Fulani wars were contemporaneous with the Napoleonic wars in Europe. But as in Europe, there were long periods of peace between states in the western Sudan. During the fifties, while Europe was in the throes of the Crimean War, the states and kingdoms of the area from Timbuctu to Chad were at peace with each other: the area was in a state of 'cold war' not dissimilar to what we are experiencing today.

Another interesting aspect of political life on which the accounts of the explorers shed some light was the structure of government of the states and kingdoms of the western Sudan. As Denham and Clapperton discovered, at the head of each was a sultan who, either by himself, as in Bagirmi, or assisted by a council of ministers, as in Sokoto and Bornu, governed the kingdom or empire. Provincial administration was in the hands of governors or emirs who were appointed and could be deposed by the sultan. Except in Bornu the structure remained unchanged at the time of Barth, and indeed as a result of the system of indirect rule adopted by the British, the traditional arrangement has continued as the framework of local administration in Northern Nigeria to this day.

3. The Ashanti war of 1900: a study in culture conflict

B. WASSERMAN *Africa* Vol. 31, 1961 Oxford University Press for International African Institute; pages 167–78

An Historical Perspective

THE Ashanti Nation was a federation of Akan tribes united in 1697 under the Golden Stool. This federation, while functioning effectively in war, was loose with regard to internal administration. The chiefs of the constituent tribes had very wide autonomy, and a tendency to assert their independence from the Asantehene at Kumasi.

The British occupied neighbouring territory on the Gold Coast and were primarily interested in trade. For trade to prosper it was necessary to have order in the area. There were two policies which would have made this possible: the British could have supported the power of the Asantehene, who would then have been sufficiently strong to keep his constituent tribes in order, or it could have taken the entire region under its protection and enforced peace among the tribes.

The history of British policy in the nineteenth century is one in which neither alternative was taken, until the last decade of the century when the Government's hand was forced by the colonial rivalry of Germany and France and by pressure from British commercial interests.[1] On the one hand, the British Government consistently refused to undertake additional responsibilities regarding the administration of Ashanti, because it was concerned with keeping its expenses at a minimum.[2] On the other, it granted protection to dissident Ashanti tribes because it regarded the Ashanti Federation as a savage régime maintained by tyranny.

The result of this policy was that when Ashanti tribes had disputes with the Asantehene, they would cross into British territory and ask for the protection of the British Government. The Asantehene, therefore, found it almost impossible to maintain his authority, as his constituent tribes could disobey him and escape punishment by crossing into British territory.[3] In order to keep his nation together the Asantehene was frequently forced to undertake expeditions against his disaffected tribes who had gained British protection. As a result he found himself in a series of wars with the British which he wished to avoid.

The history of Anglo-Ashanti relations in the nineteenth

[1] Ashanti was formally annexed in 1902.

[2] The British several times refused to extend their commitments in Ashanti even at the request of the Asantehene, because of the expense involved. For instance, in 1888 they refused his request to establish a Resident in Kumasi.

[3] Some dissident tribes—notably the Adansi—continued raiding into Ashanti from British territory.

century, therefore, is one of constant warfare[1] between two nations both of whom desired to avoid war with the other.[2] The wars were an indirect and unintended consequence of their policies and thwarted the interests of both parties—of the British because they damaged trade, and of the Ashanti because they weakened the Union. They were primarily the result of mutual and protracted misunderstanding.

As each misunderstanding in Anglo-Ashanti relations arose out of a previous one, it is necessary to go back at least until 1863, in order to present an intelligible account of the causes of the war of 1900. The war of 1863 occurred because the British Governor, Richard Pine, refused to give up to Ashanti justice one Kwasi Gyani (or Janin) who had fled to the British for protection.[3] The Ashanti thereupon invaded British territory. The war which ensued was not concluded because the Ashanti were struck down by sickness and dysentery after their initial victories, while the British Government was not prepared to finance the expedition necessary to subdue the Ashanti. The issues which had led to the conflict remained unsettled and continued to poison Anglo-Ashanti relations.

The strained relations between the British and Ashanti again led to conflict in 1873 as an unintended consequence of the Anglo-Dutch exchange of forts on Cape Coast, which took place between 1869 and 1872. One of the forts transferred to the British was Elmina Castle, which was under the suzerainty

---

[1] There were seven wars—1806, 1811, 1814–15, 1823–6, 1863, 1873–4, 1900—three large-scale military operations hardly distinguishable from wars—the 1853 Ashanti invasion, the 1881 alarm, and the 1896 British expedition—and frequent skirmishes between the British and the Ashanti in the nineteenth century.

[2] Both parties desired to avoid war even to the extent of enduring humiliation. Thus, for instance, the British did not counter the 1863 Ashanti expedition, while the Ashanti passively submitted to the British in 1881 and 1896.

[3] Gyani failed to surrender a gold nugget to the state, as he was supposed to do under Ashanti law, and fled to the Cape Coast Colony. The British Governor, Pine, did not feel justified in giving up a man to the embassy sent by the Ashanti (for the offence was an important one in Ashanti law) for something he did not regard as a crime. The Ashanti regarded this refusal as an insult, especially in view of the reparation treaty between the two parties, and the war which ensued followed primarily from their two different conceptions of Law. See W. W. Claridge, *A History of the Gold Coast and Ashanti*, vol. i, pp. 509–10.

of the Asantehene, to whom the Dutch paid £80 per year rent. The British took over Elmina only in 1873 after receiving a letter allegedly from the Asantehene renouncing his claim to it. This letter was, however, unknown to either the British or the Asantehene,[1] a forgery by an African clerk, Henry Plange, and when the British took over Elmina they again found themselves invaded by the Ashanti. This time the British sent out an expedition under Sir Garnet Wolseley, which defeated the Ashanti and concluded the treaty of Fomena in 1874.[2]

The defeat of 1874 seriously weakened the central power of the Ashanti Federation. Most of the important tribes (including Mampon, Nsuta, Bekwai, Kokufu, and Tuaben) refused to obey the central authority: the outlying provinces declared their independence and the Asantehene, Kofi Kakari, was destooled. His successors devoted all their efforts to reasserting the authority of the Golden Stool over the rebellious provinces and disaffected tribes and on restoring the former position of the Ashanti Federation. This led to a series of protracted tribal wars, which dislocated trade and embroiled the British as protectors of the dissident tribes.

The British Government at first pursued a policy of non-intervention. When this failed to restore trade or even to keep them out of war[3] with the Ashanti, they gradually changed to a policy of taking the whole of Ashanti under their protection.[4]

[1] See Claridge, op. cit., pp. 609–12. Being unaware that the letter was a forgery, both the British and the Ashanti later suspected each other of the worst intentions.

[2] Under this treaty the Ashanti had to pay an indemnity of 50,000 ounces of gold, renounce their claims to the Denkera, Assin, Akim Adansi, and Elmina tribes, keep the Kumasi road open to trade, and abolish human sacrifices.

[3] In 1881 war nearly broke out over a misunderstanding (in which the Golden Axe was involved) centred on a possible heir to the stool of Gyaman, one of the disaffected tribes. The British, thinking the Ashanti were about to attack them, undertook military preparations. The Asantehene, having no such intentions, thought these indicated a British attack. War was averted only by the Asantehene surrendering the Golden Axe and paying an indemnity for a war he did not intend.

[4] In the 1890s Germany and France became potential rivals with the British for West African colonies. Moreover in the late 1880s and 1890s pressure was brought by the British Chamber of Commerce to take over Ashanti because of disturbances to trade. See 'Further Correspondence on Affairs in Ashanti': 1896 (Parliamentary Papers), hereafter F.C.A.A.

When, therefore, further disturbances broke out in 1892, the British demanded that a Resident be established in Kumasi. While the Asantehene temporized over this demand by sending an embassy to England, an expedition under Sir Francis Scott was dispatched and entered Kumasi unopposed in 1896. The expedition established a British fort in Kumasi, signed separate treaties with Bekwai, Ogona, Ofinsu, Ejisu, Nsuta, Mampond Kumawu, Bampata, Obodom, and Kokufu, and deported Prempeh, the Asantehene, and his chief counsellor to the Seychelles.

The 1896 expedition left the Ashanti without a king and with a deep feeling of resentment, at what they regarded as the treachery of the British.[1] This resentment was particularly felt by the people of Kumasi, for the Asantehene had been chief of Kumasi as well as king of Ashanti and his deportation disorganized the administration of the Kumasi division. Kumasi was deserted and disturbances occurred in Wam in 1898 and in Agona in 1899.

It was therefore against a background of unrest that the Governor visited Kumasi in 1900. His speech to the assembled chiefs of Ashanti on 28 March included a demand for the Golden Stool. This demand 'was received with "silence". A few days later we were at war.'[2]

The British Perspective

The Ashanti war of 1900 was not desired by the British, yet its immediate cause was the British Governor's speech to the Ashanti chiefs on 28 March 1900. From this speech[3]—and

[1] The Ashanti had accepted the British demand for a Residency at Kumasi but, unfortunately, the latter had deported Prempeh without warning, giving as their pretext the unpaid indemnity of Fomena.

[2] Rattray, *Ashanti*, p. 292. The quotation continues 'The Ashanti were "silent" but every man left that meeting to go and prepare for war. I am sure that if the Government of that day had ever known what is here described it would never have asked for the stool "to sit on".' The first engagement of the war was that of Captain Armitage's expedition to look for the Golden Stool. (Armitage had previously been sent on a similar expedition in February.)

[3] Parliamentary Papers 1901: 'Correspondence relating to the Ashanti War 1900', pp. 10–26. (Eye-witnesses at the Palaver of 28 March who published accounts were Lady Hodgson, *The Siege of Kumasi*, and Captain Armitage, *The Ashanti Campaign of 1900*.)

from other eyewitness accounts—it is possible to infer Sir
Frederick Hodgson's estimate of the Ashanti situation on his
arrival in Kumasi. From his final report,[1] after the conclusion
of the war, Hodgson's post-mortem estimate of that same situation can be discovered. Both these estimates diverge widely
(and contain inaccuracies); nevertheless both fall within a very
stable framework of assumptions about the Ashanti. An examination of these underlying assumptions reveals the source of the
Governor's miscalculations—and in particular of his decision
to search for the Golden Stool, which led to the outbreak of
1900.

On his arrival in Kumasi, Sir Frederick Hodgson was quite
unconscious of any unrest in Ashanti.[2] His speech was, from his
perspective, firm but fairly friendly,[3] and his demands seemed
reasonable enough in the circumstances. His demand of an
annual payment of 4,000 ounces of gold a year was small
considering that the indemnity of 50,000 ounces—which the
Ashanti undertook to pay in 1874—was still unpaid; that the
1896 Expedition had cost a further 50,000 ounces; and that
the British had for four years and without charge maintained a
Residency in Kumasi at considerable annual expense, the

[1] Parliamentary Papers 1901: 'Correspondence relating to the Ashanti
War 1900', pp. 110–16.

[2] This is quite clear from the tenor of his speech, Lady Hodgson, op. cit.,
p. 59, and the Governor's final report, where he writes 'Up to the date of
my departure from Accra there had been no reports received from Kumasi
which could lead to the inference that the Ashantis were in a disturbed state
bordering on rebellion; or that they were in a state of preparation for revolt.
. . . There was, therefore, really no reason for me to consider the opportune-
ness of my visit. . . . As it was, I left Accra quite unconscious of any danger.
This is clear from the fact that I had only the usual escort of some 30 Hausas.'
Moreover he only became aware that Kumasi was deserted after his arrival
there and points out that this unawareness of unrest in Ashanti was shared
by the other British officials in the Gold Coast, who had not regarded the
various incidents as serious (in all the annual reports of the Gold Coast from
1896 to 1900 there is only one line with regard to the state of Ashanti, in the
report of 1899).

[3] P.P. 1901, p. 17. 'Kings and chiefs, I want you to look to me as your
friend. I have been in this country for a long time . . . and I know a good deal
of your native customs . . . and although at times I might have to do certain
things that may not be altogether palatable to you . . . yet I shall try to do all
I can to be your friend, and to let you see that you have someone to turn to
if you have difficulties.'

benefit of which he did not doubt the Ashanti appreciated.[1]
He reiterated the British Government's decision that Prempeh
would not be returned and finally stated that, as the representative of the paramount power in the area, he was entitled
to sit on the Golden Stool.[2] Nevertheless he resolved that
the Ashanti disobedience in not producing it for him would
affect neither the impartiality nor the firmness of British
rule.

In his final report, after the conclusion of the conflict,
Hodgson maintained that the war had been premeditated by
the Ashanti over a long period. The Ashanti, he states, are a
warlike race accustomed only to domination and resentful of
being subordinate to the British.[3] They were smarting under
the unopposed loss of their king—a stigma which 'only the white

[1] Ibid. 'You know perfectly well that with the entry of the British Government into Ashanti the power of making human sacrifices ceased; that your
lives are now safe. You have only to advise the white officer who is resident
in Kumasi when you are in danger and you have the strong arm of the British
Government to defend you. There is one other matter that has come to an
end at the same time, that was the buying and selling of human beings as if
they were cattle or bales of goods. In all countries of the Queen everyone is
free. . . . You know by this time what the state of things is under the British
Government. You have had four years of it and I venture to say that if you
were to speak out what is in your hearts, you would say that you do not want
to return to the old dissensions among yourselves, and that in fact, you do
not want to return to the old state of things.'

[2] Ibid. 'Now Kings and Chiefs . . . . What must I do to the man, whoever
he is, who has failed to give the Queen, who is the paramount power in this
country, the stool to which she is entitled? Where is the Golden Stool? Why
am I not sitting on the Golden Stool at this moment? I am the representative
of the paramount power; why have you relegated me to this chair? Why did
you not take the opportunity of my coming to Kumasi, and give it to me to
sit upon?'

[3] Ibid, pp. 112–13. 'The collection of the enormous quantity of warlike
stores, which the siege of Kumasi, and the determined opposition to the
gallant force under Colonel Sir James Willcocks showed them to be possessed
of, must have been spread over a long period. It is in itself evidence of a
pre-determined outbreak. The whole history of the Ashanti is a record of
wars, wars against their neighbours, who until the power of the British began
to be manifested, were either directly subservient to them or in a state of
vassalage. . . . It is perhaps not to be wondered at that the warriors of a warlike race, unaccustomed to any other life than that of pre-dominance,
should have decided to make an attempt to throw off the British yoke at the
first opportunity which might appear to them fitting.'

man's blood could remove'.[1] Moreover they resented the abolition of 'all their savage modes of Government'—slavery, human sacrifice, etc.—the imposition of fines, the demand for compulsory labour for public works, and trade freedom. They therefore took the opportunity of the Governor's visit to revolt.[2]

There are considerable divergencies between Hodgson's contemporary and retrospective estimates of the pre-28 March situation in Ashanti, and these may be taken as an indication of what he learned from the revolt. In the former estimate, he is unaware of any unrest and believes that the Ashanti were pleased to be under British rule. In the latter he points to premeditated and protracted hostility among the Ashanti and to their resentment against British rule. Nevertheless both accounts reveal a consistent attitude towards the Ashanti. Hodgson clearly regarded them as 'lesser breeds without the law'—as inferior people with savage ways, moved by lower forces such as bribery and coercion. Thus, in his speech on 28 March, Hodgson assumed that the savage Ashanti were grateful for the innovation of 'civilized' rule,[3] while in his final report he attributed the war in large measure to their warlike and bloodthirsty qualities.[4] He regarded Ashanti history as a record of conflict among savage tribes, their Federation as a union subject to a common tyrant, and the Golden Stool as his seat and symbol of power.

In terms of these assumptions Hodgson's actions were perfectly rational, from the point of view of British interests. Given that the Ashanti respect little other than force and authority, it was quite rational for him to seek to establish the

---

[1] P.P. 1901, p. 17. 'The Kumassis, the dominant Ashanti tribe, were, I was to discover, smarting under the loss of their king—Prempeh—without having struck a blow in his defence. . . . The whole incident was a stigma upon the valour of the Kumasi warriors—a stigma which, by native custom and native tradition, blood alone—the blood of the offending white man—could wipe out.'

[2] The Ashanti, in Hodgson's opinion, conceived of his visit as a favourable opportunity to revolt because they wanted to capture him and exchange him for Prempeh (see Parliamentary Papers 1901, p. 90, and also Lady Hodgson, op. cit.), and also because the British Government was at the time pre-occupied with the Boer War.

[3] See note 1, p. 39.

[4] See note 3, p. 39 and note 1 on this page.

representative of the British Queen as 'paramount chief' in their eyes. Assuming that the Golden Stool was the paramount chief's source and symbol of power, his quest to obtain it in order, thereby, to gain the allegiance of the Ashanti for the British is perfectly understandable.[1] Assuming unquestioningly that the British mode of government is superior it follows that the Ashanti must be grateful for it and can have no legitimate objection to paying for it.

Hodgson's policy failed—and led against his wishes to consequences detrimental to British interests—because the assumptions on which it was based were unsound. His interpretation of the Ashanti was one which saw them as acting against their own interests—as pursuing war for its own sake, rejecting the benefits of civilized Government, and indulging in bloodthirsty and senseless practices. It was contradictory because, although he regarded the Ashanti as irrational savages, he also attributed considerable cunning and reason to them regarding their premeditated war preparations, and their choice of opportunity. It was untestable because his assumptions about the inherent characteristics of the Ashanti could not be established by any conceivable evidence. It was unempirical because the Ashanti did not respect power and authority for their own sakes, but only when they were constituted in accordance with established customs and traditions; their Federation was not a union subject to a common tyrant but an association united for common purposes; the Golden Stool was not the seat and symbol of the paramount chief's power, guaranteeing allegiance to anyone who possessed it, but the keystone of the Ashanti political and religious system which could not be allowed to fall into alien hands.

Why did Hodgson base his policy on such patently unsound assumptions about the Ashanti? The answer is that he did not know his assumptions were unsound—indeed he did not know that he was acting in terms of any presuppositions at all. He

[1] In his final report *after the war* Hodgson wrote (pp. 113–14) 'So long as it [the Golden Stool] remains in the hands of the Ashanti, so long does the power of the king—whether the king exists or not—remain with them . . . "the whole history of Ashanti is attached to it and only the possessor of it is acknowledged as Head or Master of the Ashantis". . . . The Golden Stool is, therefore, a valuable assest to the Colonial Government, and it is a matter of regret that its delivery was not insisted upon in 1896.'

ENA

believed rather that his descriptions of the Ashanti and their practices, intentions, and actions were 'factual' descriptions of neutral events, occurrences, and objects.[1] Actually they were interpretations based upon an unconscious set of preconceptions—e.g. about life, the individual, property, government, procreation, material substance, disease, etc.—derived from an upbringing in an industrial, Christian, constitutional monarchy. When viewed unconsciously in terms of these presuppositions, the Ashanti did become savages with senseless and barbarous practices. Such an interpretation involves uncritically assessing others' actions in terms of one's own preconceptions and finding them wanting and inferior thereby. The Ashanti, however, acted as they did not because they were 'lesser breeds without the law' but because their actions were based on different assumptions. In terms of these their conduct was perfectly rational and intelligible, and an unconscious interpretation of it derived from unquestioned British[2] preconceptions, therefore, could not fail to lead to miscalculation.

---

[1] Being unconscious of his own preconceptions Hodgson did not realize that he did not understand the Ashanti. See p. 38, note 2, for Hodgson's estimate of his own understanding of the Ashanti.

[2] As all British officials concerned with the Ashanti—including even the Parliamentary Opposition—shared a more or less common set of unquestioned presuppositions, virtually all agreed with Hodgson's misinterpretation of the Ashanti, his views of the history of Anglo-Ashanti relations, and the character of the Ashanti régime, the 1896 Expedition and the Golden Stool, etc. This is illustrated by the following quotations from Opposition Speeches in the House of Commons Debate on 18–19 March as published in Hansard:

Rt. Hon. Joseph Chamberlain. 'What are the customs of the natives with which we are interfering? Human sacrifice is one, fetishism of all kinds is another and slavery is another . . . and when you come to ask what is the cause of the subsequent disturbance I have no hesitation in saying that it was the bloodlessness of the previous expedition. The people of Ashanti in common with every savage tribe hold it to be a point of honour to fight for their chief . . . they are ready to accept defeat but they are not ready to accept the consequences of defeat without actual conflict. . . . Let me first deal with the incident of the Golden Stool. . . . I entirely approve of his [Hodgson's] attempt to secure it. The Golden Stool is of very great "moral and intellectual value" . . . in the opinion of the tribe and according to the custom of the tribe the possession of the Stool gives supremacy. And if, therefore, we could secure this Stool we should be doing more for the peace of Ashanti than, probably, by any armed expedition.'

W. Redmond (Labour). 'They might be called savage people, and no doubt

The Ashanti Perspective

The Ashanti felt that they had no quarrel with the British yet they found themselves in a war with them, which they ascribed to the latter's rapacity. Their conception of the British progressively deteriorated during the last decade of the nineteenth century. Prempeh's letters, following his accession in 1888, reveal a strong desire for friendship with the British Government. This attitude, however, turns ever more to hostility and suspicion with the latter's failure to co-operate in restoring the dissident Ashanti tribes. Following the 'treachery' of 1896 the Ashanti became convinced that the white man was intent only on their ruin and expropriation. The British Governor's demands and expeditions for the Golden Stool were the last straw.[1]

The letters of the Asantehene (1888–96) to the British Governor revolve around the central theme of regaining the dissident Ashanti tribes. Prempeh addresses Sir Branford Griffith in most friendly terms, at first.[2] His attitude towards the tribes is one of an indulgent parent towards children who have misbehaved. He believes that they have run away to the British Protectorate because they have offended him and wish to return, but seek British intercession to escape punishment.

it was a great mistake that the Almighty, when He created the world, did not make all populations as highly civilized as the English people.'

Broadbent. 'The Liberal Party . . . would not attempt to teach savages the wickedness of human sacrifices by indulging in a great slaughter, with modern weapons, of the poor savage people we sought to rule.'

See also the speech of the Rt. Hon. Sydney Buxton (the Liberal Under-Secretary of State for the Colonies in 1895–5) and his letter of 14 December 1894 on p. 237, F.C.A.A. 1896 ('. . . the Queen cannot receive these persons [the "Ashanti Ambassadors"]. The King of Ashantee is now only head of a tribe and does not hold a position which would entitle him to send "ambassadors" to the Queen of England, neither are they the class of person whom the Queen could be asked to receive. Further there are ample and solid grounds for believing that the Ashantee Kings, Chiefs and people still continue the practice of human sacrifice; on which ground alone his messengers could not be received here').

[1] W. E. F. Ward, *A History of the Gold Coast*, p. 303, maintains that the Ashanti believed that Hodgson was coming to Kumasi to search for the Golden Stool in person.

[2] Around 1890 Prempeh addresses the Governor as 'My Good Friend'. See letters of 7 April 1890, 22 August 1890, 20 January 1891, F.C.A.A. 1896.

Desiring them back, he is prepared to forgo punishment and wishes the British to reassure them on this so that they will pluck up courage and return.[1]

The failure of the tribes to return and of the Governor to intercede on his behalf[2] led Prempeh to suspect the Governor's friendship and intentions. He became convinced that the tribes would return but for the action of the British Government, which was preventing them from doing so.[3] When the British— exasperated by the disturbed state of tribal affairs and, therefore, of trade—proposed to establish a Protectorate over Ashanti in 1895, Prempeh no longer trusted them and sought to temporize by sending an embassy to England. When his embassy was not received he had no alternative but to accept

[1] See letter, p. 16 (27 December 1889). Prempeh writes to the Governor: 'Your true and firm friendship you stated in your letter with me, I am sorry to say it wants wanting, for I believe that when two persons are keeping friendship each of them seeks the interest and welfare of the other, but it is not the case here. I thought that my subjects had come to you to solicit your intercession for their safe return, for I believe that when a friend's boy or servant offends his lord he runs to his lord's friend to ask pardon for him, so when there is any punishment whatever, through the intercession of the other friend, the offended servant is pardoned, and then he returns to resume his former duties. This is real friendship, but I am extremely sorry it is not so with us; I am deprived almost of all my subjects; on whom then shall I rule'. See also letters on pp. 35 and 40–41. Prempeh's assessment is not without foundation, because when his message of pardon and welcome back was delivered to the Kokufus and Dadiasies, they elected to return. Ibid., pp. 37–9.

[2] The British Governor's assessment of the situation, in contrast, was that the dissident tribes were refugees from oppression. See his letter of 16 July 1890 to Prempeh, ibid., p. 27: 'You must fully understand the views, policy and firm determination of this Government with regard to refugees seeking its protection. . . . If any of the Adansis, Kokufus, Bekwais, Dadiassies . . . wish to return there is nothing stopping them, but this government, not-withstanding its sincerely friendly wishes toward you, does not consider that it would be in any way justified in advising any of the people referred to upon the question of returning to Ashanti.'

[3] This is already evident in Prempeh's letter of 27 December 1899 to the Governor: 'You stated . . . that the king of Kwahu have signed treaty with the British Government; may I ask for what cause, have I had palaver with him, or is it only the wish to the British Government that he should do so. The Sefwis I learn from them that during the late disturbances they have run to the British Government, and that if I seek for them they will gladly give in their allegiance to me, all these and many others I find that if it is the British Government's wish they all will return.' See also letter, pp. 70–1.

the British terms. The British, refusing to deal with the embassy[1]
and receiving no timely reply to their ultimatum from Kumasi,
dispatched their expedition despite the fact that their terms
had been accepted.[2] The expedition met no opposition. It
deported Prempeh and his councillors, imposed an indemnity,
and established a fort in Kumasi.

The Ashanti regarded this action by the British Government
as constituting the greatest treachery. The British terms had
been accepted and no opposition had therefore been offered,
yet they had persisted with their expedition and forcibly
removed the Asantehene on the most flimsy excuse.[3] Every
move of the British Government was now suspect, and the
Ashanti believed that the British had no desire other than to
ruin and to subjugate them.[4] It was with forebodings that they

[1] See quotation from Sydney Buxton's letter in note 2, p. 42.

[2] The British were so suspicious of the Ashanti that they did not believe
the latter's acceptance of their demand for a Residency in Kumasi which
made the 1896 Expedition superfluous. See correspondence between the
'Ashanti Embassy' and the Colonial Office., ibid., pp. 107–37 (e.g. p. 126):
'I . . . acknowledge . . . your letter . . . protesting against the continued
expenditure upon military preparations, which you say . . . is quite unneces-
sary seeing that the Kings, Chiefs and people have already accepted to the
fullest extent the demands of the British Government. In reply I am to say
that . . . the fact that the messengers made no offer to accept British terms
until the expedition was ordered and that the King has not, even to this date,
shown the slightest disposition to comply with them, strengthens Mr.
Chamberlain's distrust as to the real object of the communications of which
you have been the channel, since he cannot conceal from himself the fact
that, if it were the intention of the King and the desire of his messengers to
procrastinate, and delay the expedition until the wet season was at hand,
the course taken was one well calculated to effect that object.'

[3] The Asantehene submitted to the British and their demands on the
arrival of the Expedition in Kumasi. He was arrested on being unable to pay
an immediate indemnity of 50,000 ounces of gold (he did not possess this
sum and offered an immediate first payment of 680 ounces). Ward, op. cit.,
p. 303, maintains that the Ashanti gained the impression from this that
Prempeh was deported as security for money.

[4] Casely Hayford's book, *Gold Coast Native Institutions*, written in 1902, can
be taken as more or less representing the Ashanti conception of the British
(Hayford was a British-educated Fanti barrister). He writes on p. 4:
'Whether you call them spheres of influence, territories, possessions, protectorates, or colonies, there is hardly a European power which will not fight
for their acquisition, even though there is derived from them not one
farthing's worth of profit, taking the outlay it costs into consideration. . . .

went to the Palaver on 28 March 1900.[1] The Governor's speech confirmed their worst fears and his expedition to seek the Golden Stool led to the first clash of the war.[2]

The Ashanti acted quite rationally in terms of their conception of the British. Their friendly overtures had been rebuffed, their submission to British terms had been of no avail. They conceived of the British as intent on the 'insane' despoliation and expropriation of their nation, land, and trade. The demand for the Golden Stool came to them, therefore, as the culmination of a rapacious policy of aggrandizement and had to be resisted if the Ashanti people were to survive.

The Ashanti conception of British intentions was unsound. Their interpretation was one which saw the British as acting against their own interests—as intent on war and domination for its own sake, on 'insane' and unprofitable aggrandizement,[3] and on the despoliation of trade. It was contradictory because whereas on the one hand they believed that the British sought (to ruin the black man for) their own capitalistic profit, on the other they believed that they were inherently acquisitive and predatory irrespective of the loss. It could not be tested because their assumptions about the British 'primitive instinct of acquisitiveness' could not be refuted by any conceivable evidence. And it was unempirical because the British did not seek war or domination for its own sake, but earnestly desired peace in the area; they did not wish to exterminate the Ashanti people by robbing them of their constituent tribes and their Golden Stool, but wished to foster trade with them; they did not desire costly aggrandizement, but were most niggardly

There is in some cases an insane thirst for territoral acquisition cost what it may. . . . To state the proposition broadly, it is simply the primitive instinct of acquisitiveness in man which operates in the case of nations no matter the extent of their boasted civilization.'

[1] Cf. Kufi Kafia's remark before the Palaver that the Ashanti would fight if the Governor had not brought a good message. Claridge, op. cit., vol. ii, p. 437, and Lady Hodgson, op. cit., p. 59.

[2] Armitage, op. cit., p. 10, quotes the Ashanti war cries as follows: 'The Governor came to Kumasi on a peace palaver. He demanded money from us and sent white men to bring him the Golden Stool. Instead of money the Governor shall have the white men's heads sent to him in Kumasi. The Golden Stool shall be well washed in the white man's blood.'

[3] See note 4, p. 45.

and reluctant to extend their commitments and expenses.

The Ashanti approached the situation in the light of certain presuppositions about the Golden Stool, the dissident tribes, the Ashanti Union, human personality, the hereafter, etc. Evaluating the British in terms of these, they came to regard them as 'insanely' rapacious because they failed to co-operate with them in matters—such as intercession with regard to the dissident tribes—which were reasonable enough on their own assumptions. The British, however, were acting not in terms of the Ashanti assumptions (and, therefore, insanely and against their own interests) but of their own different ones. The unconscious applications by the Ashanti of their own assumptions to actions of the British led, therefore, to their misconceptions.

Both the British and the Ashanti formed hostile and misconceived pictures of each other. Once formed these were difficult to dispel by contrary evidence—for this became interpreted as confirming rather than refuting the unsound picture.[1] Undoubtedly, the unconscious application of inappropriate assumptions was instrumental in generating misconceptions. However, another factor—perhaps more immediately obvious in the case of the Ashanti than of the British—was that the fundamental assumptions in which their respective policies were rooted were themselves inadequate.

[1] The Ashanti distrust of the Lands Act of 1897—'the sole object of which is to Protect the Chiefs against speculators' (Chamberlain)—and the British of the 1896 Ashanti Embassy's acceptance of their terms illustrate how each party interpreted to its own disadvantage the other's intended acts of co-operation as evidence for rather than against their hostile image of the other. Similarly each, in line with their hostile image of the other, interpreted the other's friendly professions as hypocritical despite the apparent implausibility of this interpretation. (Cf. Hayford, op. cit., p. 269, '. . . the talk about human sacrifices, barbarous customs and slave raiding is all cant. What lies behind it all is the desire for the good things of Ashanti that would come into the pockets of the British Capitalist'; Sir Branford Griffith, the British Governor, reprimanding the District Commissioner on being 'duped' by the friendly professions of the Ashanti—Parliamentary Papers 1896, volume 48, p. 29: 'With all natives you cannot be too cautious in what you say but especially so with regard to Ashantis. It requires considerable experience of this people with their plausible ways and apparently friendly disposition before the belief can be entertained that they are artful, unscrupulous, treacherous. . . .')

The Realms of Conflict

The policies of the British and the Ashanti were rooted in their fundamentally different conceptual frameworks. The issues of the war of 1900 had no common significance to the disputants. Each interpreted common events, objects, and situations differently in terms of his own particular assumptions and each generated an image of the other based on his own frame of reference. As a result both found themselves in a war which neither wanted, but which appeared rational enough to each in terms of his particular conceptualization of the situation. Part of this conceptualization consisted of their mutual interpretations of each other's intentions as being hostile, and has already been analysed. Its significance for the disputants derived from the way of life which was considered to be threatened.

The Ashanti believe in a pantheistic world of spirits, which pervade all matter—animate and inanimate—and control all actions and events. Human beings are conceived of as the embodiment of an enduring racial spirit, which never dies but is perpetual through the matrilineal lineage or clan (*abusua*). The individual, therefore, is not regarded as an autonomous acting agent, but as a member of the undying racial (corporate) personality of common blood descent, whose spirit he bears. His actions are watched over and protected by the spirits of his departed ancestors, who reside in the nether or ghost world (*samandaw*) and who can be recalled to their shrines (their blackened stools). His course of conduct, fate, or teleological potentiality is predetermined by his immortal soul or spirit (*kra*) which enters his body shortly after birth and leaves before death. Birth and death do not mark the beginning and end of life for the Ashanti, but transitions between different realms of life.[1] Life in this world represents for him only one of the forms of existence—i.e., the conjunction of the immortal spirit (*kra*) with the mortal physical basis of life or vitality (*sunsum*).

---

[1] The concept of death (*owu*) as the termination of life (*nwka*) is foreign to the Ashanti. It is rather the reverse of birth (*awu*). Danquah writes (p. 157): '. . . death (*owu*) is only an aspect of birth (*awu*), an instrument of the total destiny, the continuity of the kind, the permanence and persistence of the organic whole, which is the greatest good of endeavour.' See J. B. Danquah, *The Akan Doctrine of God*, especially section 5, chapter 3.

The Golden Stool is the keystone of the Ashanti political and religious system, because through it the nation is united with its ancestors and its God. It is revered above all else including the king, for it contains the *sunsum*, vitality or life-force of the race, upon which the health (physical) life and well-being of the people depend. They would never have surrendered it voluntarily because they believed their nation would perish if it fell into foreign hands.[1] In fighting for the Golden Stool the Ashanti believed that they were fighting not for a king's throne but for the physical survival of their race.

The British approached the Ashanti in terms of their unquestioned preconceptions of an inanimate physical universe, composed of material substance and obeying mechanical laws: of individuals as autonomous acting agents with a limited spatio-temporal existence and of Government as constituted by such individuals. In terms of this conceptual framework, the Asantehene was the paramount chief or most powerful individual in Ashanti;[2] the Golden Stool was his throne and source

[1] The Golden Stool was allegedly produced out of the sky by Okomfo Anokye at a great gathering of clans in Kumasi. Anokye had convinced Osai Tutu, King of Kumasi, that he had a divine mission to unite the Ashanti tribes. Tutu united the Ashanti tribes and the Golden Stool became revered as containing the *sunsum* or life-force of the nation which would perish if it fell into foreign hands.

In 1921 war nearly occurred again as a result of a false rumour that the British were again after the Golden Stool. It was averted as a result of the British Governor's renunciation of any desire for the Golden Stool on the advice of Rattray, the Government Anthropologist. See *Annual Report for Ashanti* (Colonial Office), 1921; Rattray, *Ashanti*, chapters 23 and 24, and *Ashanti Law and Constitution*, chapter 24; also Busia, *The Position of the Chief in the Modern Political System of Ashanti*, p. 91.

Rattray also maintains that the Ashanti fear of taking the Golden Stool to a war they were certain to lose was the reason for their submission in 1896 'deeming the loss of their king a trifle in comparison with the loss of their Golden Stool' (*Ashanti*, p. 291).

[2] For the Ashanti, the Asantehene held his authority as the embodiment of his ancestors, not as an individual, as supposed by the British. The confusion resulting from the British and Ashanti acting in terms of two different conceptions of the individual can be illustrated from the episode of the British refusal to receive the Ashanti embassy of 1895. One of the reasons given for the British distrust of the embassy was that its head Prince Ansah claimed to be the grandson of King Prempeh who was only 25 years old, whereas Ansah had already been in the employment of the Colony for over 23 years (see p. 120, Parliamentary Papers 1896). Ansah was the grandson

of power. Having become paramount (individual) in the area
the British Governor felt entitled to sit upon the Golden Stool,
believing it to be a throne.[1] Still acting in terms of his unconscious assumption, he interpreted the Ashanti refusal to
produce it as a sign of their disloyalty and disobedience. His
purpose in seeking it, therefore, was to facilitate the peaceful
government of the area.[2]

The other issues in the dispute between the British and the
Ashanti similarly derived their significance from their respectively different conceptual frameworks. The Ashanti, believing
in life after death, killed people (particularly a chief's attendants) at the funerals of their chiefs and high tribal dignitaries
so that these important personages should not go unattended
into the nether world. Those killed were not regarded as dead
but as moving into another world, where they were supposed
to resume their activities under their royal master.[3] In terms
of the British conception of an individual's life as confined to
the here and now, the Ashanti practice of killing at funerals
was human sacrifice and murder, whereas in terms of the
Ashanti theory it was the continuation of life in another realm.
On the other hand the British, in terms of their notion of
private property or individual ownership, regarded it as quite
natural to hang their soldiers for looting[4] Ashanti property,
whereas for the Ashanti, with their notion of communal or clan
ownership, such action was incomprehensible and indeed tanta-
mount to human sacrifice. Similarly, the Ashanti, in terms of

of the Asantehene Kwaku Dua (1838–67) and therefore of the Royal Stool.
As the present Asantehene is the embodiment of his ancestors, Ansah was
regarded as a grandson of Prempeh, occupant of the Royal Stool.

[1] Hodgson's assumption that the Golden Stool was a seat or throne is
implicit in his demand of it to sit on (see note 2, p. 39). It was never sat on.

[2] The effect of seeking the Golden Stool was likely to be the exact opposite
of what the Governor intended thereby (see note 1, p. 41). Rattray writing
in 1921 states: 'I believe it will be found that all the obedience, respect and
great loyalty we have been given by the Ashanti is given through and by
reason of the Golden Stool. I believe that far from benefiting had we ever
taken this stool . . . its power would have worked against us' (*Ashanti*, p. 293).

[3] See Rattray, *Religion and Art in Ashanti*, chapter 4.

[4] On the 1874 Expedition a British soldier was hanged for looting in the
centre of Kumasi. This made a big impression on the Ashanti, in whose eyes
it was completely unjustified (particularly as hanging was abhorrent to
them).

their notion of a world of spirits, propitiated the spirits of their departed ancestors with offerings of food and drink, and also the spirits of the Earth, the rivers, the lakes, the trees, and taboo animals. The British, in terms of their notion of an inanimate universe obeying mechanical laws, looked upon these Ashanti practices as 'fetishes' while never questioning their own observances—such as holding a parade to commemorate the Queen's birthday in the besieged fort at Kumasi, playing the national anthem, etc.—which to the Ashanti without the Western notion of national sovereignty must have seemed very similar.[1]

The Ashanti war of 1900 was in the interests of neither Britain nor Ashanti, yet it was the result of their policies. This study has sought to explain it as the unintended consequence of national actions based on false assumptions. There are two senses in which the disputants may be said to have based their policies on false assumptions. Firstly they misinterpreted each other's intentions. Secondly they pursued mythical objectives or 'interests'.

In the first case one can take the conceptual framework of the disputants as given and show how each, unconsciously evaluating the actions of the other in terms of his own assumptions (and not realizing that the other was operating on different ones), generated a hostile but unsound and rigid image of the other party. Consequently, each party acting rationally in terms of this hostile image of the other[2] found himself forced by the other to take measures which eventually resulted in a war desired by neither.

---

[1] I have attempted to illustrate how the issues between the British and the Ashanti had a different significance for each in terms of his respective assumptions, rather than to attempt a comprehensive exposé of all their differences in terms of their underlying assumptions. Numerous other differences rooted in their different conceptions of God, procreation (which affected their attitudes to slavery), disease, agriculture, hygiene, friendship, etc. have not been dealt with.

[2] In this way, through the mutual generation of fear, suspicion, or distrust, a hostile situation developed in Anglo-Ashanti relations, so that the same measure—i.e. the establishment of a Residency in Kumasi in 1888—which was welcome to the Ashanti at the earlier period of less distrust, became repugnant to them and an object of conflict at the later date of increased suspicion (1896).

In the second case one can question the conceptual frameworks in which the interests or objectives of the disputants were rooted and ask in what sense it was in the Ashanti interest to fight for the Golden Stool. Sudh questions are usually banished to the now unfashionable realm of moral philosophy but it is my belief that they can be treated scientifically. Objectives or interests such as the Golden Stool derive their significance to the parties concerned from the assumption by which they are interpreted—i.e. from their location within a conceptual framework. Thus the significance of the Golden Stool to the Ashanti was rooted in their animistic conception of the universe, while its significance to the British lay in their mechanical, atomistic conception.[1] Neither of these conceptual frameworks is uninformative,[2] but the British is more informative and gives better prediction than the Ashanti one.[3] In this sense it can be

[1] I refer now to the way in which the British conceived of the Golden Stool—i.e. as a throne, a material inanimate object—not to the importance they attached to it, which was dependent on their interpretation of its importance to the Ashanti.

[2] While the concepts of primitive societies are of lower explanatory power than those of western (or scientific) societies it must not be supposed that considerable knowledge about the world is not available to them, including much that is unknown to the West (e.g. many modern wonder drugs, such as quinine, were first discovered in the potions of medicine men). However, this knowledge is formulated in terms of less scientific or efficient concepts than Western knowledge is. Thus, for instance, the Ashanti attribute the periodic eruptions in Lake Bosomtive (when the water turns black, fish are thrown to the surface, and a stench is given off) to the Lake spirit who 'explodes his gunpowder', whereas the western geologist explains it in terms of decaying organic matter, on the bottom of an enclosed lake, which becomes buoyant with gases and rises to the surface and, forming a black scum, gives off a stench.

[3] The following two examples from Anglo-Ashanti relations illustrate what I mean by saying that the British acted in terms of more scientific assumptions. The 1874 Expedition blew up the sacred trees and groves of Kumasi. The Ashanti, believing in a world of spirits for which these trees were the shrines, were terror-stricken, expecting fearful vengeance from their spirit gods. The British, acting in terms of the framework of inanimate mechanics, expected nothing of the sort and it never came. Similarly Hodgson's notion of the Golden Stool as a material object (a throne) was more mature than the Ashanti one, who regarded it as the repository of their physical well-being which it was not (i.e. they would not have died had it been taken away). The concepts of high universality or explanatory power give better protection—i.e. the consequences of acting in terms of them are less likely to be unsuccessful than on lower explanatory assumptions.

said that the British policy was based on more enlightened, explanatory, or universal assumptions than the Ashanti was. Thus the failure of the British, and even more of the Ashanti, to pursue policies more conducive to their interests was due not only to their misconception of each other's intentions but also to the immaturity or illusory nature of the assumptions in which their objectives were rooted.

4. Juaben and Kumasi relations in the nineteenth century

A. ADU BOAHEN *Ashanti Research Conference* Legon 1964; pages 25–33

The Ashanti Empire at the height of its power consisted of two parts: metropolitan Ashanti, made up of the principal Ashanti states of Nsuta, Kokofu, Bekwai, Juaben, Mampong and Kumawu, and provincial Ashanti, made up of the conquered states and kingdoms such as Gyaman Krachi, Banda, Gonja, Kwahu, Akin Denkyira Wassaw and Assin. The royal families of Nsuta, Kokofu, Juaben and Bekwai belonged to the Oyoko clan. Of the metropolitan states the greatest, according to the evidence of Bowdich, Dupuis and Freeman, was Juaben, second only to Kumasi in area, wealth and population. In 1817, Bowdich estimated its military strength at 35,000, more than twice that of each of the other states. Indeed, he regarded the power of the Juabenhene as 'equal to that of the king of Ashantees'.

The foundation of Juaben appears to have been contemporaneous with that of the other metropolitan states though it had the most rapid growth due to its strategic position and the courage of its first two kings, Osei Hwedee and his brother Adaakwaa Yiadom. Founded in a rich kola nut and gold-bearing region, the town itself was situated at the junction of two important commercial highways, one running north-westwards to the coast and the other northwards to Salaga, the centre of the Ashanti kola trade. Expansion began with Osei Hwedee and by the end of his reign, probably about 1700, all the provinces now constituting the Juaben state had been absorbed.

Thus for Juaben the eighteenth century was one of consolidation and internal organization while for most of the metropolitan states, as well as Kumasi, it was the period of further conquest and expansion. And the most characteristic feature of eighteenth- and early nineteenth-century history of Ashanti and the main reason for the greatness of that Empire was the exceedingly smooth and fruitful co-operation between Juaben and Kumasi.

Okomfo Anokye, the traditional priest of the Ashanti nation, realizing the importance of this co-operation, had it embodied in the Ashanti unwritten constitution that under no circumstances whatever should Kumasi ever take up arms against Juaben. Indeed, he is said to have planted a large species of *bromeliacae* between Kumasi and Juaben to be a constant reminder of this compact. This compact appears to have been meticulously observed throughout the eighteenth and early nineteenth centuries. Bowdich was particularly impressed by this co-operation on which he observed:

This common interest (of Juaben and Kumasi), preserved uninterrupted more than a century, by two rising powers close to each other, with a view of a more rapid aggrandizement, and their firm discretion in making many serious disagreements subservient to the policy, is one of the few circumstances worth considering in a history composed of wars and successions. . . .

Unfortunately for both Juaben and the Ashanti Empire, this phase of fruitful co-operation did not continue far into the nineteenth century. In 1832 and again in 1875 Kumasi declared war on Juaben. These wars appear to be mainly the outcome of the increase in the power of Juaben by the 1830s, a clash of personalities and the interference of the British in Kumasi–Juaben affairs.

The first obvious reason for the rift between Kumasi and Juaben was the tremendous increase in the power and wealth of the latter by the 1820s. As it has been pointed out already, as a result of the industry of its people and the bravery of its kings,

Juaben appears to have become, by the nineteenth century, the most famous of all the metropolitan Ashanti states, and the Juabenhene had become as powerful and as revered as the Asantehene. There could obviously not be two people at the top and it was clear that sooner or later a decision would have to be taken as to who, to all appearance, was the real power in Ashanti. Even before 1830, there is evidence that the Asantehene Osei Bonsu was getting concerned about the increasing power of Juabenhene and contemplating his reduction. Bowdich is positive on this: 'It is clear that the king of Ashanti contemplates the reduction of the king of Juaben from an independent ally to a tributary.' Osei Bonsu, however, did not attack Juaben. His successor, Osei Yaw Akoto, was on the other hand not only aware of the great power of Juaben but was also personally hostile to Akuamoa, partly because, according to Reindorf, he was 'envious of the favours shown to Boaten by Bonsu during his life'. To worsen the situation, a section of the Juaben royal family began to intrigue against Akuamoa in Kumasi. Not long after Akoto's accession to office, a series of incidents occurred which made war between Juaben and Kumasi virtually unavoidable.

The first of these occurred during the Akantamasu war. During this war, the Ashantis were defeated and the Golden Stool was captured from the Asantehene. It was the Juabenhene who succeeded in retrieving the Golden Stool. While this on the one hand increased the already great prestige enjoyed by the Juabenhene, on the other hand it intensified Osei Yaw Akoto's envy and animosity. Thus on their return to Kumasi, contrary to all expectations, Osei Yaw Akoto accused Akuamoa of having stolen the treasure-box containing gold dust worth about £1,000 that was kept with the Golden Stool. Clearly this was a false accusation calculated to tarnish the reputation of the Juabenhene or even excite the entire Ashanti nation against that potentate. Akuamoa was naturally stupefied by this accusation.

Reconciliation of the two was further ruled out by the Nsuta enstoolment episode. Nana Yaw Sekyere the Nsutahene was accidentally killed in the Akantamasu war, and two people, Owiredu Kwatia and Maafo, contested for the vacant stool. Kwatia appealed to the Juabenhene while Maafo appealed to the Asantehene. Now, according to custom, before any person is placed on any of the Ashanti Oyoko stools, the Juabenhene, being the constitutional head of the ten Ashanti Oyoko families, has to be consulted. Kwatia was therefore right in appealing. But Osei Yaw Akoto took this as an opportunity to clip the wings of the Juabene. Without consulting the Juabenhene, he not only put Maafo on the Nsuta Stool but also caused Owiredu Kwatia and some of his supporters to be murdered. Boaten was enraged by this act and for over a year he refused to go to Kumasi. After an ambassador of the Asantehene had been pelted with stones in Juaben and that of Juabenhene had been killed in Kumasi a year later, Akoto declared war against Juaben. It must be noted that the Asantehene was reminded by his elders of Okomfo Anokye's advice, but he contemptuously shouted them down.

In 1832 therefore, probably for the first time in Ashanti history, Kumasi fired on Juaben. After a strong initial resistance, Juaben was finally defeated. Consequently, the king, his brother and his mother, the celebrated Juaben Sewaa, and the entire population emigrated *en masse* to Kibi where they were hospitably received by the King and Queen mother of Akim Abuakwa. Among the captives sent to Kumasi were Asafo Agyei, the son of Akuamoa Boaten, and Afrakuma I, the only daughter of Juaben Serwaa.

The Juaben people remained in Akim from 1832 and returned to Juaben between 1839 and 1841. Two factors led to their return. The first was the pressure exerted on them by the European powers on the coast, led by Maclean, the President of the Council of Merchants in Cape Coast. The second was the death of Osei Yaw Akoto and the accession of Kwaku Dua I in 1834. Soon after his accession Kwaku Dua despatched numerous ambassadors to persuade Juaben Boaten and Serwaa to return.

Before the actual return march started, there occurred the 'drinking of the gods' by the kings and people of Juaben and Akim. Rattray says that this was done 'to the effect that they would never disclose any private matters that might have come to their knowledge concerning the affairs of Kibi'. My informer, Okyeame Agyepong, states that this event did take place and besides undertaking not to divulge any Akim secrets, the Juabens also swore never under any conditions to take up arms against the Akims.

After this pact, the significance of which will become apparent below, the return journey to Juaben began in 1839. Shortly after their departure from Kibi, Akuamoa died at Saaman, and his successor, Akuamoa Kofi, also died at Oboo only eighty days after his enstoolment. In the absence of any male heir and, more important still, since she had passed the menopause, Nana Ama Serwaa was proclaimed the Juabenhene. Thus it was under her leadership that the Juabens re-entered their capital in 1841 and she died on the stool three or four years later.

The reign of Kwaku Dua I and that of his successor, Kofi Karikari (1867–74), ushered in another period of smooth relationship between Kumasi and Juaben. Unfortunately, this ended in 1875 when Kumasi once again invaded Juaben. It appears from my studies so far—and there are still many important documents I have not as yet been able to consult—that if the first civil war was essentially the result of the hostile attitude of Osei Yaw Akoto, the second seems to be the outcome of the Juaben non-aggression pact with Kibi and, above all, the policy of the British on the coast towards Ashanti after the 1873–4 war.

It must be emphasized that even as late as the end of 1873 Kumasi-Juaben relations were, as Ramseyer and Khune testify, exceedingly smooth. The Juabenhene attended all the meetings of the Council as well as all the durbars and festivals in Kumasi. More important still, he belonged to the party that was vehemently opposing the release of Ramseyer, Khune and Bonnat and vociferously clamouring for war against the British and the coastal states. When a huge Ashanti army under Amankwa Tia invaded the coast in December 1872, the Juabenhene contributed a strong contingent of about 13,000 men under Yaw Okyere. When the British began the counter-invasion of Ashanti in January 1874, Asafo Agyei was to march eastwards against the British army under Captain Glover. According to Crowther, Claridge and Fuller, Asafo Agyei agreed to do so but decided to wait for Glover in Juaben and, on hearing of the fall of Kumasi, submitted without consulting the Asantehene. This view is wholly unacceptable. If Asafo

FNA

Agyei really wanted to fight against Glover, he would certainl
have marched out to meet him on the Pra or in Ashanti Akim
What was the sense in allowing himself to be besieged in hi
capital? Ward, on the other hand, states that 'the Juaben hel
the line of the River Anum' and blocked Glover's advance from
Konongo. This is also wrong, for the written accounts show tha
Glover met with no resistance from Juaso through Konongo t
Juaben.

On the other hand, we learn from oral tradition that Asaf
Agyei disobeyed the Asantehene's order to contain Glover'
army behind the Pra and remained neutral during the entir
fighting. Not only does this version make more sense but it i
also confirmed from primary written sources. Since Asaf
Agyei was one of the kings who clamoured for war, hi
behaviour was regarded by all as an act of treachery and i
caused a rift between Juaben and Kumasi. Why then did Asaf
Agyei behave in that way?

Secondary sources are silent on this but oral tradition give
a plausible explanation for his behaviour. Asafo Agyei wa
clearly anti-British and was indeed anxious to fight, a
evidenced by the strong contingent he sent to the coast i
December 1872. But unfortunately for him nearly half o
Glover's army consisted of Akims, and the Queen of Juabe
resolutely refused to allow Asafu Agyei to fight against th
Akims because of the non-aggression pact. The entire cit
rallied behind the Queen and Asafo Agyei thus found himself
general without an army.

After the war, Asafu Agyei was summoned to Kumasi t
explain his conduct, but he refused to go. Though this widene
the rift, he nevertheless had a good but an unfortunate reaso
for this. Though he was the son of a former Juabenhene, Asaf
Agyei was an Asona and a Kwabu by birth and not an Oyok
and an Ashanti. He was allowed to occupy the Juaben Oyok
stool because there was no male heir at the time, and even the
only after a special appeal to the Juaben people by the the
Asantehene, Kwaku Dua I. The other Ashanti Oyoko familie
therefore felt that he behaved so treacherously because he was
foreigner. Thus there was every likelihood that Asafo Agyei
being an Asona and therefore not enjoying the immunity of a
Oyoko, would have fallen victim to the wrath of both the livin

and the dead kings of Ashanti if he had gone to Kumasi.

The situation was further complicated by the intervention of the British. They were indeed initially invited to intervene by the Asantehene, Kofi Karikari, himself. In his anxiety to win the friendship of the British he had determined to adhere strictly to the terms of the Fomena treaty, which enjoined the maintenance of 'perpetual peace' and freedom of trade between Ashanti and Her Majesty's forts on the coast. Reluctant therefore to employ force to bring back any of the Ashanti states that had seceded, he began to despatch ambassadors to the Governor to demand his assistance in a peaceful solution of the Juaben as well as the Adansi disputes. His successor, Mensa Bonsu, at first continued the policy of appealing to the Governor for help.

The view which has hitherto been canvassed by British historians such as Claridge, Ward and, more recently, Gallagher and Robinson that the British adopted 'a policy of non-interference' towards Ashanti after 1874 is not borne out by the evidence. In July 1874, Governor Strachan agreed to send an official to mediate between Juaben and Kumasi on condition that 'the king of Juaben be allowed to remain unmolested as a friendly but independent neighbour of Ashanti'. The Asantehene reluctantly accepted this condition and Captain Lees was consequently sent to Kumasi to draw up a treaty which was signed by both the Asantehene and the Juabenhene in August 1874. By this treaty, the Asantehene agreed to 'the complete independence of Juaben and that both kings swore to keep open the roads, to give up prisoners then in their hands, and to allow old disputes to die out'. Both Juaben and Kumasi established embassies in Cape Coast which enjoyed the same diplomatic recognition.

The Lees treaty finally ruled out all possibilities of reconciliation between Juaben and Kumasi by peaceful means. Indeed, fully aware that the British were biased in his favour, Asafo Agyei now adopted a more defiant attitude towards the Asantehene. For instance, he successfully persuaded Asokore, Afidwaase, Oyoko and Asaaman to join his Empire. Moreover, he killed two leading wing chiefs of the Juaben State, the Mmorontoohene, Barima Okyere and the Annohene, Nana Twumasi, for, among other allegations, an alleged attempted murder of two Juaben heiresses. Since both of them were members of the Oyoko Clan and should not under any circumstances whatsoever have been touched by the knife, this was not only a barbaric act but, according to Ashanti law and custom, also an absolutely heinous crime. It therefore further enraged the Oyokos throughout Ashanti.

All these acts of the Juabenhene were reported—and of course the Juabenhene also lodged his own complaints—but the Governor merely asked both parties to observe the Lees treaty. The murder again by Asafo Agyei of an important ambassador sent to Juaben by Mensa Bonsu, the newly installed Asantehene, and the arrival of the news that the Governor had despatched an officer, Dr Gouldsbury, to warn both parties to keep peace precipitated an invasion and defeat of Juaben by Kumasi in October 1875. On the invitation of the British, the Juabens emigrated into the Protectorate where, with the help of the Governor, they acquired land and founded new settlements between 1876 and 1880 which they nostalgically named after those they had abandoned—New Juaben (Koforidua) Asokore, Oyoko, Afidwaase. Asafo Agyei did want to return but, fearing that he might provoke further wars, the British refused to allow him to do so. When he was caught preparing for war against Kumasi he was first imprisoned in Elmina and later exiled to Lagos in 1880, where he died in 1885.

Why did the British adopt the pro-Juaben attitude? Governor Strachan himself has answered this question in two despatches to the Colonial Secretary in October and November 1875. In these he advocated that the Ashanti Empire should be divided 'into two or more tribes who would be independent of each other', on the grounds that if Kumasi were allowed 'to establish itself in its former power, this would act as a barrier to the opening up of trade with the interior, re-imposing perhaps four- to ten-fold the extent the tribute which was exacted from the inferior tribes'.

It is clear then that the Juaben-Kumasi co-operation was absolutely indispensable for the peace, glory and stability of the Ashanti Empire. This was guaranteed in the seventeenth and eighteenth centuries. But it collapsed in the nineteenth century and its results were disastrous not only for the Juaben state but also for the Ashanti Empire as a whole.

5. The establishment of Sierra Leone

J. D. HARGREAVES *Cambridge Historical Journal* Vol. 12, No. 1, 1956 Kraus Reprint Company and Cambridge University Press; pages 56, 57–66

The Colony of Sierra Leone originated in settlements of freed slaves on the West African coast carried out on the initiative of British philanthropists in the later eighteenth century. For over a century, British responsibility was as far as possible restricted to the small mountainous peninsula on which Freetown stands, and to certain nearby islands; but influence was inevitably obtained over nearby coast and hinterland, and during the nineteenth century some additional territories were incorporated in the Colony, though not always brought under effective administration. In 1896 the remaining regions not conceded to be under French or Liberian influence were proclaimed a British Protectorate; which also included, for administrative purposes, certain chiefdoms formerly part of the Colony. In this period, therefore, the term 'Colony' is applied to the peninsula and islands originally settled, with a few predominantly tribal areas around the river Sherbro; the term 'Protectorate' to territories the size of Ireland, which form the great bulk of the area marked 'Sierra Leone' on a modern map and whose social organization was at this time exclusively tribal. At the beginning of 1898 British officials began to collect a House Tax which had been imposed on three of the five districts of the Protectorate. In February, resistance to the tax by certain Temne chiefs developed into open warfare in the north, and at the end of April a series of savage attacks took place on British and American subjects, mostly of African birth and descent, among the Mende and Sherbro people further south. These two outbreaks constitute the insurrection to be studied in this paper. . . .

The impact of the West upon the traditional society of the

Protectorate did not come solely, or even principally, through governmental channels. The philanthropic sponsors of the eighteenth-century settlement had hoped that, from Freetown, Christianity and civilization might be disseminated through Africa. The influences actually carried into the interior by the inhabitants of the Colony had rarely corresponded closely with this ideal. From the early decades of the nineteenth century, Creole[1] traders, missionaries, and occasionally settlers had begun to move up the rivers to conduct their affairs among the native tribes; as the range of the Pax Britannica expanded, the Creoles went in larger numbers and further afield. In the Colony, they had by this time evolved a distinctive 'cultural pattern', which owed more to Western than to tribal influences; the type of man it produced, while liable to move European observers to scornful contempt, was often regarded with equal distaste as an intruder in the tribal community. Many Creoles were, of course, able to achieve happy and balanced relations with the people among whom they moved; many chiefdoms welcomed the trade they brought on account of its less satisfactory features—the cheap trade gin, the fire-arms which could be used for slaving. But in general, Creole influence upon tribal society was disruptive. Unprejudiced observers had for many years been noting in Creoles tendencies to bully or to interfere in chiefdom affairs, arrogant airs of superiority, defective standards of commercial morality; the Native Affairs Department had often needed to invoke the authority of the Governor to settle their quarrels with native chiefs. So in the Mende rising of 1898 it was the Creoles who suffered more than any others, even though many of them had in the early stages taken leading roles in opposing the House Tax. They were treated, not as fellow-Africans, but as 'White man's children'; the grievances of the Mende against them seem to have been no less deep, and of longer standing, than those against government officials and their tax.

[1] This word has an interesting but complicated semantic record. It is used here interchangeably with the contemporary meaning of 'Sierra Leonean', to mean an inhabitant of the Colony, almost certainly descended on one side at least from one of the various groups of liberated slaves but in any case regarding himself and behaving as a 'civilized' inhabitant of British territory rather than as a member of any local tribe.

Christian missions in the Protectorate were predominantly Protestant, and most of their staffs were Creole; in Mende and Sherbro country, their leadership was largely American. Their work tended to be concentrated in a few centres, notably Rotifunk, Shenge, and Taima; smaller outposts were often short-lived. Even in the centres, mission influence might hardly extend beyond a group of devout Creole immigrants. Few of the missionaries had studied the social organization and traditional beliefs of those to whom they were preaching; often the converts, even the African clergy, were apt to lapse from grace at the approach of temptation. In Shenge, missionaries seem to have interfered in chiefdom elections on behalf of converted candidates.

In Temne country, their philanthropic work, if not their preaching, seems to have been much appreciated; but the Mendes more often regarded them as partners with the government in 'cultural aggression'. Such impressions must have been deepened by the sermons on the subject of payment of taxes to Caesar which were preached in at least two churches in 1898. There were exceptions; but in general, Mende responses to missions showed more indifference and mistrust than zeal or gratitude. Not one of the 'Western' influences at work in the territory over which British administration was extended in 1890 had established truly sympathetic contact with African society; tensions already existed on which the administrative policy adopted was to put a breaking strain.

Official contacts with the interior were not, of course, unknown before 1896; indeed, government servants had for several years loosely applied the term 'Protectorate' to the British sphere of influence there. This influence rested, in the last analysis, on the assumed possession of paramount military force, which might on occasion actually be used to settle such inter-tribal disorders as were impeding the passage of trade to the coast. But the keys to effective control—the presence in the interior of British political agents, supported in their attempts at pacification by standing forces of armed police—had been conceded only gradually by the Imperial government. The Frontier Police force, founded in 1890, comprised by 1894 twelve British officers and about 500 African rank and file; it was mostly dispersed in very small detachments. Near the coast

—and more particularly to the south of a track which joined the navigable heads of the principal rivers—British authority had sometimes been partly formalized by treaties with chiefs. But no chiefdom in the British sphere was large enough to offer a territorial basis for strong and centralized political institutions. In a region the size of Ireland there were well over a hundred independent chiefdoms, inhabited by peoples of some fourteen tribal groups. No single African ruler approached the status of a Sultan of Sokoto or a Kabaka of Buganda, or even of the Mandinka warrior chief Samori on the northern border. The establishment of the Protectorate implied an arbitrary work of political unification.

The decision to seek Colonial Office approval for the formal proclamation of a Protectorate was taken early in 1893, on the initiative of J. C. E. Parkes, the African head of the Native Affairs Department. But first it was necessary to define the area to be protected; and on this subject the Foreign Office had for years been leisurely conducting difficult negotiations with the French. Throughout 1894 these were held up by an attempt to settle the more contentious Nile and Niger questions in the same reckoning; since these fell within the private African empire of the Foreign Office, many in the Colonial Office feared long delays and over-generous concessions in Sierra Leone. However, separate agreement on the Sierra Leone frontier was reached on 21 January 1895; and though it was not an advantageous frontier, it could hardly have been radically improved by the most ardent of negotiators. British governments had long been indifferent as to who should rule in the southern Sudan; the French had shaken off their indifference first; and British claims which might have been founded upon expeditions or treaties of the earlier nineteenth century had by 1890 gone by default. The Protectorate was not only composed of small chiefdoms; it was itself restricted in size.

The difficult task of establishing a Protectorate administration fell to Colonel Frederick Cardew, who came to Freetown in March 1894. Cardew, who was born in 1839, was a Regular officer who had served in South Africa, China, and on the North-West frontier; between 1890 and 1894 he had been Resident Commissioner in Zululand, a territory with recent traditions of powerful African political institutions. Immedi-

ately on arrival he decided to journey into the interior to investigate the latest reports of Sofa raids; within two years this
energetic soldier had travelled well over 2,000 miles, mostly on
foot or by hammock, and spent seven months in the hinterland.
From the start he was profoundly moved by the petty internal
slave-trade which was still continuing, and by the destruction,
depopulation, and economic stagnation caused, especially in
Kono country, by the Sofa raids. His conviction deepened that
the extension of the Pax Britannica in the interior was his
urgent humanitarian duty. Though well aware that British
rule could be extended only gradually, he was to be led by this
sense of mission to move at a speed hardly justified by the
material resources at his disposal, or the extent of European
knowledge about the peoples to be ruled.

In a despatch of 9 June 1894, written after his first journey,
Cardew attempted a general appreciation of the problem. The
peace and order of the interior depended on suppression of the
internal slave-trade and the petty wars it engendered. Once
the Anglo-French boundary had been settled, there should be a
substantial increase in the Frontier Police, at an annual cost
of £7,000. There should be restrictions on the import of trade
guns and powder—later, perhaps, of trade spirits also. The
civilizing agency of 'legitimate' trade should be promoted by
railway construction, which had been under leisurely discussion
for years, and by governmental development of roads, bridges,
and ferries.

When the Protectorate was declared, Cardew thought it
should be administered 'as far as possible by native law and
through the chiefs'. But Cardew knew, what some of his
predecessors had forgotten, that 'native law and custom' might
sometimes sanction or encourage practices, like ritual murder
and slavery, which were repugnant to 'natural law and justice';
or at least to the conscience of Liberal England; and he proposed to reserve extensive judicial powers to the District Commissioners. While admitting that domestic slavery was deeply
entrenched in tribal society, Cardew hoped to abolish it, at a
year's notice, in the fairly near future. In some of these
proposals, he seemed to the Colonial Office to be under-
rating the difficulties. But his chief difficulty was financial.
Although the Protectorate could reasonably claim a share of

customs duties collected in the ports of the Colony on imports destined for the interior, and although it would contribute directly a small amount in licence fees, a large and rapid increase in the colonial revenue was necessary if Cardew's plans for administration and development were to go rapidly ahead. Direct Imperial assistance being excluded, some sort of direct taxation seemed to Cardew unavoidable. Between 1851 and 1872, house, land, and road taxes had been levied in the Colony; but these, and the provision for exacting forced labour on the roads from defaulters, had been bitterly resented by many Creoles. In the latter year Governor Hennessy achieved a popularity which long outlived him by abolishing them all in favour of heavy import duties on tobacco, liquor, fire-arms, and gunpowder, which in 1895 still provided nearly two-thirds of the total colonial revenue. As Cardew complained, three of these staple imports would have been better suppressed than encouraged; but Hennessy was content to have 'shifted the incidence of taxation from the settlements to the consumers in the interior'. To re-introduce direct taxation in the Colony would be politically very difficult, as had been shown by the reluctance of the new Freetown municipality to levy a rate. But in the Protectorate—where the money was immediately needed —Cardew believed that a House Tax could be collected without much opposition. Even on this first journey he had begun a count of the houses in the towns visited, as a preliminary to assessment.

Implementation of these proposals had to await a final boundary settlement with France; meanwhile Cardew's subsequent tours amplified his ideas without modifying their fundamental principles. His second long journey, early in 1895, convinced him that the worst evils of the slave trade had already been suppressed by the Frontier Police; that economic development would naturally follow the restoration of tranquillity; and that domestic slavery was sufficiently innocuous to be left to disappear in the normal course of social evolution. When Cardew went on leave in June the boundary had at last been settled, and he was able to enter into detailed discussion of the new administration during visits to the Colonial Office. Simultaneously he obtained approval for work to begin on the first section of railway—Chamberlain in an incisive minute overriding the financial caution of his officials. Cardew and Chamberlain alike saw that communications were the key to economic progress in the Protectorate, and so to all future planning. But railway construction in Sierra Leonean conditions could not be rapid; it would inevitably be many years before its benefits could be felt in the Protectorate.

Detailed provisions for the administration of the Protectorate were completed after Cardew's return to Freetown, and given final legislative form in an Ordinance of 10 September 1897. Cardew's underlying principle was that 'the jurisdiction of the Protectorate should be continued as far as possible through the Chiefs, and its administration kept as far as possible distinct from that of the Colony'. Superficially, it seems tempting to apply to it the label of 'Indirect Rule'; yet to do so, in view of the connotation which the phrase has acquired, might be seriously misleading. To a post-Lugard generation, it implies the conscious adoption of certain principles and methods of administration which have come to have a fairly wide application; but in Sierra Leone, and many other places, the structure was designed locally, as an almost inevitable product of local conditions. Miss Perham has defined Indirect Rule as 'a system by which the tutelary power recognizes existing African societies, and assists them to adapt themselves to the functions of local government'. Cardew's proposal had no such conscious purpose; his approach to African societies was that of a Victorian missionary rather than of a modern administrator. There was nothing sacrosanct to him about native institutions, certainly not those of the rather sordid petty chiefdoms with which he had principally to deal. The chiefs had of necessity to constitute the usual channel of communication; but in the last analysis they were only savages, to be classed with their people as 'ignorant, superstitious and uncivilized'. He assumed too readily that chiefly power was, by its nature, uniformly despotic. If chiefs seemed hesitant in executing the policy of the Imperial government, they must be either refractory or weak rulers; the possibility that they might be constitutional rulers was hardly considered. There is little sign in the correspondence of these years that administrators made serious attempts to understand the basis of tribal constitutional custom, or even the political functions of such obviously powerful societies as the Poro.

Under Cardew's predecessors, many rulers had felt the respect of their people weakened by the disregard for native hierarchy shown by the Frontier Police. Their prestige would not be restored by this attempt to discipline them into the role of government agents.

Nor was the system rendered more consistent by criticism in the Colonial Office, which appears to have been inspired firstly by financial caution; secondly by regard for certain humanitarian principles (these derived partly from international treaty obligations, partly from concern about the reaction of the House of Commons, partly from moral conviction); and only thirdly by empirical comparisons, generally destructive, with the experience of other dependencies. There was no attempt to collate and reflect upon such experience in anything resembling the modern 'African Studies Branch'. Little more could be claimed for the administrative system introduced than that it recognized the limitations imposed by the slender resources available.

The primary purpose of the Protectorate was to establish public order; and the chief responsibility for this fell on the District Commissioners. Their judicial powers were extensive, partly because many practices permissible in native law were morally intolerable to British eyes, partly because of the need to provide acceptable justice for the Creole immigrants, who in some parts of the Protectorate were settling in such numbers that chiefs feared even to attempt to control them. Sitting alone as a court of first instance, the District Commissioner had jurisdiction in all civil cases involving a non-native; for a time, in all land cases; in all criminal cases of offences against a person not native; and in all cases of pretended witchcraft, faction or tribal fights, slave-raiding or slave-dealing. In native cases of murder, rape, cannibalism, or offences connected with Human Leopard or Alligator societies, he was to sit with, and record the opinions of, two or more assessor chiefs, but the finding was to be his own. To the Courts of the Native Chiefs were reserved only civil cases between natives, not involving title to land, and the lesser criminal cases.

In addition to these wide judicial powers, District Commissioners had authority to make arbitrary settlement of any matter liable to cause breach of the peace, even if it concerned native law and custom. Their responsibilities as representatives of the Imperial power in the five Districts (each larger than Yorkshire) were enormous; and at every point were liable to infringe the traditional authority of the chiefs. Much therefore depended on their personal qualities. With one exception—a young barrister who after less than a year was transferred to Freetown as Solicitor-General—the duties of District Commissioner were, until after 1898, performed exclusively by officers of the Frontier Police, sometimes temporarily relieved by a doctor. The problem of recruiting European civilians willing to serve (for salaries rising from £400 to £500) in the isolation and the still-notorious climate of the interior of West Africa had not yet been squarely faced. Creoles were serving as District Commissioners in the Colony, which included the tribal district of the Imperri; but official opinion was reluctant to utlize them in the Protectorate. There was no alternative to employing these young captains and lieutenants from the British army and militia; and Cardew regarded them as not unsuitable choices.

Their appointments were accepted by the Colonial Office with resignation rather than enthusiasm. 'We used to employ constabulary officers in that capacity on the Gold Coast, and on the whole they did very well', wrote Antrobus; and Bramston added 'and matters are not yet advanced enough to employ barristers as D.C.s. We must be content with men of common-sense and integrity without legal education.' But although some of these officers eventually did well, and have left a good report in Sierra Leone, others seem to have lacked even 'common-sense and integrity'. One acting District Commissioner was asked to resign in October 1897 after admitting that he had been continuously drunk for three months; another was censured for accepting presents from chiefs and for other improprieties. Even the best were bewildered men, dealing, in addition to heavy office duties, with a host of problems unknown in their experience.

Their previous association with the Frontier Police did not make them more acceptable. Though this force had had considerable success in suppressing inter-tribal slave wars in the interior, its members had often abused their authority. Most of its rank and file were Protectorate men recruited in Freetown;

all these, presumably, had in some way become dissatisfied with tribal society, and some were malefactors or runaway slaves. The dispersal of the force in small detachments, sometimes of a corporal and two men, made abuses easy to practise and hard to detect. Charges of extortion, looting, rape, and brutality were common, and continued even after Cardew, in his early days, had made provision for better supervision by officers. Undoubtedly, many complaints were exaggerated or fabricated, but even the best friends of the Force could not discount them all. The Frontier Police, or some such force, was clearly necessary to assist the administration as much as to put down tribal wars, for the few Court Messengers were not yet effectively discharging their varied police and intelligence duties; but its actual operations did much harm to the prestige of the government.

That the new administrative and judicial structure was imperfect was well appreciated in the Colonial Office; but though Cardew's original proposals were amended in important details, his general structure was preserved. The most drastic intervention from London was on the Lands question. Approval was withheld from those provisions of the Ordinance of 1896 which vested in the Crown all mineral rights in the Protectorate, placed under the Governor's control all transfers of land to non-natives, and granted him extensive powers arbitrarily to dispose of 'waste or uninhabited lands'. The motives of Cardew were of the highest—to protect the natives against deception and exploitation by concession-hunters, European and Creole, such as had already begun to enter the Protectorate; and the Colonial Office were objecting to incidental provisions, rather than to his main principles. But much alarm was caused by the Governor's temporary assumption of power to dispose of waste lands. Under a system of shifting cultivation, much land actually in tribal or individual 'ownership' can easily be assumed to be waste, as can land from which individuals have been accustomed to gather wild crops like palm kernels. Rumours that the government was planning to take the land from the people became powerful and wide-spread.

Even more controversial was Cardew's proposed House Tax. In 1895 he had suggested that houses of three or more rooms should pay £1 annually, those with two rooms 15s., and single-roomed houses 10s. The Colonial Office insisted on reductions; and the 1896 Ordinance imposed a tax, from 1898, of 10s. for houses of more than three rooms and 5s. for smaller ones. Even now some, inspired by a timidity which later events made to look like prudence, thought this too ambitious. Antrobus and Mercer questioned the validity of Cardew's comparison of these rates with the higher ones paid in many other African territories, and notably with the 14s. in Zululand. 'The areas are much smaller, the people more civilized and intelligent, and there are numerous magistrates to help in the carrying out of the law [wrote Mercer]'; he feared that the system would break down, and that the revenue would fall much below expectation. There is also a serious moral danger in trying to collect a tax which might not be understood, and which the natives might be tempted to evade or resist. But Cardew insisted that immediate direct taxation was essential to all plans for developing or merely administering the Protectorate; though he agreed that in 1898 the tax should be collected only in those three districts—Karene, Ronietta, and Bandajuma—which were in closest contact with the trade of the Colony, and had suffered least from the Sofa wars.

There were soon signs of resistance. In 1896 Cardew attempted briefly to explain the Ordinance and the tax to such chiefs as he happened to visit, but took little trouble to ensure consent. 'They appeared to acquiesce in the scheme as it was unfolded to them,' he wrote, optimistically, 'and many expressed approval of it'. But the idea of paying taxes to a remote and alien potentate was not so easily acceptable. Sierra Leone had no memory of a centralized African state drawing tribute or services from its vassals, such as existed in northern Nigeria, and had until 1879 existed in Zululand. Nor was the idea familiar that taxes are payment for services rendered by a government; and in any case nearly three-quarters of the £30,000 spent annually on the Protectorate was paying for the unpopular Frontier Police. The principle of tribute was familiar, but only as payment to a conqueror. Not only had the British government not conquered the peoples of the Protectorate—in several cases it had not even sought treaties of protection. The most common interpretation of the tax seems to have been that it was payment for the houses—an idea with alarming implications when considered in conjunction with the rumours about the land legislation. But Cardew's deep conviction that direct taxation was both just and necessary led him to underrate the opposition.

6. The formation of the Government General in French West Africa

C. W. NEWBURY *Journal of African History* Vol. 1, No. 1, 1960 Cambridge University Press; pages 112–23

... From a general viewpoint, the French experiment in West Africa was an attempt on the part of a new ministry, faced with enormous responsibilities for developing its colonies, to heed a guiding principle—summed up by a French colonial official and historian: 'On gouverne de loin, mais on ne peut, de loin, que se borner à gouverner.' The details of administration were for the colonial federal authority to work out. French administrators in West Africa during the early 1890s would probably have seconded this advice not to interfere from afar with the primary task of establishing law and order along the rivers and trade routes from the coastal ports to the interior. Their approach to the task was, for a period, isolated and pragmatic. This administrative separatism was assisted by the relatively independent economic life of the coastal territories where the bulk of imports into Senegal, Guinea, the Ivory Coast and Dahomey came from Britain and Germany rather than from France. Separatism was also influenced by the uncertain position of the Colonial Department in Paris, prior to 1894. And it was recognized formally in the legislation which ended the joint administration of the Senegal and South Rivers' Dependencies by constituting Guinea, the Ivory Coast and Dahomey as unitary colonies between 1891 and 1893.

Yet much was achieved while separatism was at its height. French control of the oldest colony, Senegal, was incomplete as late as 1890. During the next five years, under the energetic governorship of Lamothe, the areas of Cayor and the Rip were pacified, the Traza Moors were kept on the right bank of the

Senegal river, and the administrative policy of *désannexion* placed most of the interior, other than the river posts, under indirect rule. Most important, communications between Saint-Louis and the Soudan were assured; and General Faidherbe's old plan for a chain of military and commercial posts was realized as far as Bamako on the Niger. By then, too, French administration in the Soudan had officially begun with the creation of the *Haut-Fleuve* territory under the political and military control of an army officer responsible to the Governor of Senegal.

Opposition to further French expansion north-west of Bamako centred around Segou, the capital of the remnant states of the empire of El Hadj Omar and his son Admadou.[1] South of Bamako, the brigand cavalry of the Mande opportunist, Samory, prohibited regular communication by land with the Ivory Coast.[2] In the Fouta Djallon area of Guinea, the Peul chiefdoms constituted a solid Muslim hierarchy which paid little regard to a French protectorate treaty signed in 1881.

Operations against Ahmadou and Samory and negotiations with the Fouta Djallon Almamys were lengthy and expensive. Moreover, they severely tested the weak links between the military administration of the *Haut-Fleuve* (or the French Soudan as it was officially known after 1891) and the civil administration of the coastal colonies. In the view of colonial under-secretaries of the early 1890s, army officers were merely on loan to the Governor of Senegal. But the army was a difficult servant. Decrees aimed at constraning the Commandant of the Soudan to his civil duties at Kayes or Bamako were ignored. Colonel Archinard who had run the Soudan since 1888 corresponded directly with Paris, took the field against Ahmadou and Samory on his own initiative, and sought advice from Saint-Louis rarely. Unimpeded by distant officials on the coast

[1] Paramountcy over El Hadj Omar's Fulani and Toucouleur states of the Upper Senegal and Niger was disputed, but finally went, in the 1860s, to his son Ahmadou. The best unpublished history of the area is in Haut Commissariat, G/1/63, 'Notices sur El Hadj Omar' MS, 1878. See too, Alphonse Gouilly, *L'Islam dans l'Afrique Occidentale Française* (Paris, 1952), 72–6.

[2] The Almamy, Samory, was an intelligent brigand who carved out his fief in Upper French Guinea. It was never an empire—in the sense of the earlier Sudanic states—but rather a nomadic court which lived off and recruited from the local populations, leaving some external forms of Islam behind it. See, Gouilly, op. cit., 80–1; A. Mévil, *Samory* (Paris, 1899).

or in France, he conquered the Upper Niger between Segou and Siguiri and drove Ahmadou northwards towards Nioro. At the height of his African career he was recalled; and in November 1893, to weaken the hand of his subordinates, the Soudan was placed under a civil governor, Grodet, whose permission was required for military campaigns. During this uneasy partnership between the governor and the lieutenant-colonels, the empire of El Hadj Omar was dismembered, and Ahmadou was replaced by his brother as Emir of Macina, under a French resident. As a result of the superb indifference of the army to the caution of colonial administrators the way to the Chad from the west was now open.

In the southern Soudan, however, Samory's forces fell back into the rich forest areas of Guinea and the Ivory Coast. A campaign against him in 1893 failed; and the abortive and piecemeal sorties that followed only served to emphasize the need for a clearer definition of civil and military authority. The attempt to end the financial irresponsibility of the Commandant by recalling Archinard left Grodet and the Governors of Senegal, Guinea and the Ivory Coast in some confusion about the area under their control and about the ultimate responsibility for the joint use of French troops. Precise directives about inter-colonial boundaries were hardly enough to counter the nomadic forays of Samory; and the policy of leaving a civil governor to make military decisions resulted in a disastrous inactivity on the part of the Soudan militia at a critical point in the campaign.

At the same time, opposition to military expenditure in Paris itself provoked a sharp reaction against administrative separatism in West Africa, once the Ministry for the Colonies was in a position to assert itself in March 1894. It was recognized in the new ministry that French expansion had provided a link between the coastal territories, and had cut off other rivals from much of the interior—notably the Gold Coast and Togo.[1] But no French governor in 1894 knew exactly where

[1] By 1893, diplomacy had assured the Guinea frontier with Portuguese territory and with Sierra Leone. The frontiers of the Ivory Coast were also demarcated, as far as the ninth parallel, with Liberia and the Gold Coast. Farther east, the French enclave in southern Dahomey was recognized by Germany in 1885 and England in 1888. See E. Hertslet, *Map of Africa by Treaty*, 3 vols. (London, 1894).

Senegal, Guinea or the Ivory Coast met the Soudan, so long as Samory remained undefeated and the Fouta Djallon area was in doubt. A co-ordinating authority was needed—and in West Africa, rather than in Paris.

This became clear from two episodes in 1894: once, when Governor Lamothe of Senegal exceeded his authority by making reprisals against villages in the Fouta Djallon— nominally under Governor Ballay of Guinea; and again, when a small column, led by Lieut.-Col. Monteil, was sent into the Kong region of the Ivory Coast against Samory and was forced to withdraw after failing to come to grips with the Almamy. In the first instance, Governor Grodet of the Soudan argued that he should have been consulted; in the second, he neglected to send any help from the French troops stationed in his colony.

With these lessons in mind, the Minister for the Colonies, Chautemps, drew up the Decree of 16 June 1895 which established the first federal authority in French West Africa. The day after this legislation was ratified, Chautemps explained some of his reasons to the French Senate. The separatism that had grown up since the late 1880s and the conflicts of authority between the governors were his main targets.

On y voit une administration du Sénégal diriger une expédition contre des villages du Fouta-Djallon, alors que le protectorat du Fouta-Djallon est placé dans les attributions du gouverneur de la Guinée française; et c'est le gouverneur même du Sénégal qui, dans ses rapports, s'attache à démontrer que les villages dont il a autorisé le pillage appartiennent à son collègue de Konakri, le but de cette démonstration étant d'anéantir les prétentions d'un troisième gouverneur, celui du Soudan, lequel soutient que c'est chez lui que le gouverneur du Sénégal a porté indûment les armes.

Les violations de frontières qui se produisent parfois en Europe ne donnent jamais lieu à des correspondances diplomatiques aussi compliquées, aussi passionnées que celles qui se sont produites en ces circonstances entre trois gouverneurs de colonies voisines. . . .

C'est à cette situation anarchique, messieurs . . . que nous avons mis fin en instituant un gouvernement général de l'Afrique occidentale française.

But colonial federation, as laid down in the 1895 Decree, was very limited. Only the military powers of the lieutenant-governors of the coastal colonies were surrendered to the new governor-general, Chaudié, who, at the same time, was appointed head of the Senegal administration.[1] Their political correspondence was supposed to be sent to Paris through him; but, financially, they remained independent, and their budgets continued to be approved by the Ministry for the Colonies, not by the governor-general at Saint-Louis. Indeed, Dahomey was left out of this new arrangement altogether. The lieutenant-governor of the Soudan, however, was made directly responsible in all matters to Chaudié; and all military operations conducted by the new military commandant, Colonel de Trentinian, were to be first approved by Chaudié's commander-in-chief, Colonel Bolève. In addition, large areas between Senegal and the Sierra Leone frontier were joined to the Senegal protectorates and to French Guinea which made it possible for Chaudié to direct affairs in the Fouta Djallon without reference to the Soudan.[2] In short, all military decisions and the general administration of the Soudan were centralized at Saint-Louis. Whether this rudimentary federalism would work or not depended to a great extent on co-operation between Chaudié, who approved the Soudan budget, and de Trentinian who determined, in fact, how much was spent.

The principal difficulty with the new organization, moreover, was not the Decree itself, but what was laid down in Chautemps's confidential instructions to Chaudié which envisaged a much wider political and diplomatic role for the governor-general. His main functions were to act as the 'arbitre nécessaire des diverses colonies de l'Afrique Occidentale Française', to co-ordinate their native policies, and to share out the expenses of the Government General between them, while keeping a special eye on the finances of the Soudan. Native policy was limited to the questions of the Fouta Djallon and Samory. Relations between the former area and French Guinea had improved slightly, after the Almamy, Bokar Biro,

---

[1] Jean-Baptiste Chaudié, born in 1853, had served under the Ministère de la Marine as naval commissioner and inspector. He had reached the rank of inspector-general in the Ministère des Colonies by 1894, and it was largely in this capacity, though with a change of title, that he was expected to serve in West Africa.

[2] The *cercle* of Bakel, an important river post, and a portion of the *cercle* of Kayes were transferred to Senegal. The Farana *cercle* on the northern Sierra Leone frontier passed to French Guinea.

came to power; but Chautemps thought it essential to set up a French resident at Timbo by force, if necessary.

Là seulement est le moyen de rendre désormais régulières, au point de vue commercial non moins qu'au point de vue politique, nos relations avec le Fouta Djallon. Il n'est pas admissable qu'un pays définitivement placé sous la domination française reste plus long-temps fermé à toute manifestation de notre autorité.

As for Samory, the governor-general was to follow the same policy as Archinard: the Almamy had so disrupted French communications 'que l'on peut dire que la disparition de Samory est absolument indispensable au développement et à la prospérité de nos possessions'. Despite this intention to destroy the militant leaders of Islam, Chautemps attached great importance to the tolerant supervision of Muslim religious and judicial institutions and to the preservation of the Koranic schools at Bakel and Bamako. For, he advised Chaudié, Islam was not simply another West African religion, but a confraternity with authority and strength—'une sort de maçonnerie théocratique en même temps qu'une congrégation militaire'—which might be used to preserve order throughout the wide area under French rule. And with this end in view, he suggested that a Muslim section should be added to the Department of Native Affairs at Saint-Louis.

At an international level, Chaudié was expected to improve France's zone of influence between Lake Chad and the Niger, as demarcated roughly by the Anglo-French Convention of 1890.[1] This might be achieved, thought Chautemps, by extending Dahomey as far north as possible, when the results of various French, German and British expeditions into the Borgu region were known. On other frontiers, especially those

---

[1] Chautemps (like most French officials) was dissatisfied with the provisions of the Convention of 5 August 1890, based on the Joint Declarations of August 1889, which limited French rights along the Niger on a line from Say to Lake Chad, drawn so as to leave the Sokoto area to the Niger Company. Ministère des Affaires Étrangères, Possessions Anglaises de la Côte Occidentale/128, 'Résumé de la situation respective de la France et de l'Angleterre â la Côte Occidentale d'Afrique, avant et après l'arrangement définitif signé le 10 août 1889 au Ministère des Affaires Étrangères.' Minute, n.d. See too, Hertslet, op. cit., 11, 763–5.

between Senegal and Sierra Leone, infringements were to be scrupulously avoided.

The governor-general, then, was instructed to do more than his powers over his lieutenant-governors strictly entitled him. It was difficult to share out the expenses of the Government General, so long as Chaudié had no control over the budgets of the coastal colonies, except that of Senegal. Even in the Soudan, where he was expected to ensure a fair share of customs revenues collected on goods entering from Senegal and Guinea, it was not easy to determine the value and volume of imports, still less to persuade the Guinea administration or the Senegal General Council to yield up a portion of such revenues.[1] Finally, the only body which could advise the governor-general on his policy of arbitration was the Government General Council, set up by Decree in September 1895. But, on this council, composed of Senegal officials and military officers, the other territories of French West Africa were not represented.

These discrepancies between intention and practicability became clear during the first few years of Chaudié's tenure of office. His role as 'arbiter' between the colonies was success-ful only in the matter of the Fouta Djallon protectorate, where he worked closely with the administration of French Guinea. Similar co-operation with the Soudan in dealing with Samory was wrecked by the chaotic finances of the northern colony.

The advisory Government General Council met only once, in February 1896, when it was agreed that a residency at Timbo in the Fouta Djallon was essential in order to keep open new trade routes between the coast and the Soudan. In April, Chaudié went to the area himself to renew the protectorate treaty with the Almamy. But, in November, a show of force was

---

[1] The General Council was a body of officials and traders elected from the coastal towns of Senegal since 1879. It had certain restrictive powers over the Senegal budget—including the expense of subsidies to the Soudan. The revenues of the Senegal local budget were set at some 4,000,000 fr. for 1895 about 3,000,000 of which were from customs. Chautemps thought the Soudan should have at least 150,000 fr. of this. The Soudan's own budget for 1895 was set at 890,500 fr. in revenues and 885,927 fr. in expenses, excluding credits from France for the Kayes-Bamako railway, Rolland, op. cit., 79–80; Ministère de la France d'Outre-Mer; Afrique/Correspondence Générale/I, Chautemps to Chaudié, 11 October 1895.

necessary at Timbo to install the new resident, and Bokar Biro was deposed and killed by his rivals.[1]

In the Soudan, political and military control remained in the hands of Colonel de Trentinian. Both he and Chaudié were opposed to the provision in the 1895 Decree for a senior commander-in-chief at Saint-Louis—but for different reasons. De Trentinian disliked referring his military decisions to Boilève; Chaudié objected to the expense of extra military personnel, paid for from his slender budget for the Government General. To this budget each of the colonies, except Dahomey, was expected to contribute—no more than a hundred thousand francs from Senegal, in 1895, and some ten to fifteen thousand each from the other territories. The Ministry for the Colonies was anxious to increase Senegal's contribution. But Chaudié feared a clash with the Senegal General Council where traders' representatives were reluctant to help finance a federal authority part of whose purpose was to allocate a share of Senegal customs to the Soudan. Worse, Guinea and the Ivory Coast reduced their contributions to only five thousand francs each. And with that Chaudié had to be content, 'étant donné que ces colonies ont conservé une autonomie administrative et financière complète', he wrote, 'et je ne connais d'elles que leur correspondance politique; à cet égard seul, je leur donne des directions'. The Soudan, however, was legally subject to more direct control; and Chaudié, while on tour there, gave de Trentinian full instructions for every department of local administration. Soudan revenues from taxation were therefore expected to rise from one and a half million francs to just over two millions in 1896; and the Soudan's contribution to the expenses of the Government General was increased accordingly to twenty-two thousand francs. The northern colony was to pay for the parsimony of the others.

It was a charge that the local budget could not support. The price of military conquest in the Soudan, as borne by the State

[1] J. Quinquand, 'De Beeckmann au Fouta-Djallon' in *L'Expansion Française en Afrique Occidentale* (Société de l'Histoire des Colonies Françaises, Paris, n.d.), 1–77. The area, however, was not completely pacified till after the revolt of the Almamy, Alfa Yaya, in 1903. See A. Demougeot, 'Notes sur l'organisation politique et administrative du Labé avant et depuis l'occupation française', *Mémoires de l'Institut Français d'Afrique Noire*, no. 6 (Paris, 1944), 23–9, 47–56.

Budget for the Colonies, had reached a maximum of eleven million francs in 1894. For the next three years the expanding colony cost France an average of seven and a half million francs a year and earned a reputation for insolvency as the high prices for transporting provisions from the coast to the scattered military posts exceeded both state credits and local revenues.[1] In May 1896, Chaudié and de Trentinian warned the Ministry for the Colonies that the Soudan could not pay for the proposed Niger railway or a section of the road from Conakry without further metropolitan subsidies. They both suggested the reduction of local forces as a remedy; but, even so, Chaudié concluded that the Soudan budget for 1897 could not be less than seven million francs without risk of bankruptcy.

This delicate financial situation coincided with de Trentinian's return to France which left the position of lieutenant-governor and military commandant vacant. Despite Chaudié's request for a civil administrator, Colonel Audéoud was appointed. For the moment, his deficiencies as a functionary were off-set by his brilliant military campaigns which extended the Soudan eastwards to Mossi and Gourounsi and ended in the capture of Samory in September 1898.[2] But the high prestige of Audéoud and his lieutenants was founded on the ruins of financial administration in the Soudan and the breakdown of all controls exercised from Saint-Louis. Audéoud clashed with Chaudié's delegate at Kayes; and when Chaudié himself went on leave in 1898, the colonel ignored orders from the acting governor-general, Ballay, to stop levying customs on goods coming into the Soudan from Senegal and Guinea. After a year of military success and three months of acrimonious paper warfare with Saint-Louis, Audéoud resigned, shortly before Chaudié and de Trentinian returned to their former appointments in November 1898. Both the governor-general and the lieutenant-governor immediately called for two

---

[1] Soudan receipts in 1896 for the local budget—as distinct from credits from the State Budget—were 2,034,500 fr. The bulk of these consisted in head taxes, paid in specie, or more usually in gold, ivory, gum and hides—minus 10 per cent of revenue for village chiefs and tax collectors. Other sources were market fees and the *oussourou*—a caravan tax of one-tenth of produce and one-fortieth part of livestock passing through French territory. Frantz, op. cit., 78–9.

[2] Samory was exiled to the French Congo where he died in 1900.

million francs in credits to pay for the recent campaigns. Work on the Soudan railway came to a stop; and, in April 1899, Chaudié estimated that the total excess of expenses for the year over state credits and local revenue would not be less than 2,200,000 francs.[1]

Two other developments increased the pressure for a revision of the 1895 Decree—a crisis over the appointment of de Trentinian's successor, and a conference on the future of French West Africa. In March 1899, Chaudié heard that de Trentinian had been nominated as inspector-general of troops in Senegal without his knowledge. In a private letter to Binger, director of African affairs in the Ministry for the Colonies, he complained of the oversight and the delegation of the Soudan administration to inexperienced hands. This was not the moment, he pointed out, to allow the affairs of the colony 'aller au petit bonheur', when there was a serious deficit in the budget. More important, he explained, the announcement had frightened the trading community on the coast which was convinced 'que de Trentinian descend pour prendre la direction du Gouvernement Général'. A wild rumour perhaps; but it was also a reflection of Chaudié's personal suspicion that he was to be enclosed in a network of authorities between the coast and the interior 'dont la marine et les militaires tiendraient tous les fils'. So strongly did he feel about his diminishing control that he urged Binger to persuade the Minister for the Colonies, Decrais, to accept one of three solutions to his intolerable position: de Trentinian was to be posted back to the Soudan at once; or, if he became inspector-general, a civil lieutenant-governor was to be installed at Kayes; or, finally, the Soudan was to be divided up among the coastal colonies, leaving only two military posts at Timbuctu and Say on the Niger to guard the north. The last appealed to him most.

Voilà la solution vraie, celle qui coupe court radicalement aux dépenses d'occupation militaire et qui permet aux colonies côtières

[1] Ibid. Chaudié to Ministère des Colonies, 6 April 1899. By September 1899, it was estimated that the credits from the State Budget for the Colonies to the Sudan would be over-spent by 3,000,000 francs. The reason given by Acting Lieutenant-Governor Vimard was 'erreurs de calcul lors des évaluations'—especially for the cost of military personnel. Ministère de la France d'Outre-Mer, Afrique Occidentale Française/I/2, Secretary-General, Senegal, to Ministère des Colonies, 19 September 1899.

de prendre l'essor commercial et économique auquel elles peuvent
prétendre.

Pour maintenir l'harmonie entre les diverses parties de cette
fédération, il faut un gouvernement général indépendant de chacune
d'elles, ayant une autorité forte et nettement établie, disposant,
comme en Indo-Chine, d'un budget pour les dépenses d'utilité
générale et commune—A côté de lui un général commandant en
chef organiserait la défense intérieure et extérieure avec les merveil-
leuses ressources que lui donneraient ces pays réunis et avec les
crédits globaux qui ne distingueraient pas les dépenses de chaque
fraction.

Failing acceptance of any of these proposals, Chaudié warned
Binger he would resign.

As a result of this ultimatum, Chaudié and de Trentinian
were summoned to Paris where plans for the reorganization of
the Government General and the Soudan were discussed by a
commission of administrators and officials at the Ministry for
the Colonies in September 1899. Two projects were considered.
One came from Commandant Destenave, who criticized the
weakness of the Soudan military administration, spread from
Senegal to the Volta, and recommended that Senegal be
extended as far as Bamako, and that French Guinea include
the region between Liberia, Sierra Leone and the Niger Basin.
Similarly, the boundaries of the Ivory Coast and Dahomey were
to be advanced north and north-west towards the Kong and
Macina areas. In opposition to this scheme—which was close
to Chaudié's views—Colonel de Trentinian presented a long
report of his own which urged reform of the Government
General, but which left the Soudan intact under military rule.
The basis of the colonel's argument was commercial, and
introduced a new element into the debate—the need for tariff
unification among the coastal colonies.[1] France, he explained,
was a weak competitor for West African markets. The remedy
was to create a federal authority strong enough to introduce a

_____

[1] De Trentinian cited figures to show that between 1892 and 1896
France's share of the total trade of the French West African possessions
was only 36,000,000 fr. (or 47 per cent), while Great Britain's share of
total trade in her West African colonies was 52,000,000 fr. (or 51 per cent).
Eight million francs of the French imports, he noted, were destined for
the French army; and many imported items, valued as French imports,
were of British origin—notably cloth.

preferential tariff system in favour of French imports and to
remove duties on goods destined for the Soudan. This reasoning,
though interesting and important later, carried little weight
at the time—least of all with French traders who preferred to
buy from the cheapest markets the cotton goods France did not
supply and who were anxious, especially in Senegal, to swallow
up the Soudan and avoid internal customs of the kind set up
by Audéoud in 1898.

The final report of the commission to the Ministry for the
Colonies was a summary of the conclusions reached by Chaudié,
Lieutenant-Governor Ballay of Guinea, and Binger: the
authority of the governor-general was to be increased; and the
Soudan was to be dismembered to the advantage of the coastal
colonies. This, their report noted, would put an end to expensive military operations: 'La tendance bien humaine qui porte
l'officier combattant a chercher l'occasion de se distinguer par
une action d'éclat toujours glorieuse mais quelquefois inutile
serait définitivement enrayée'.

A month after these findings were presented, a Decree
reorganizing the administration of French West Africa was
signed. Decrais, in his preamble to the new legislation, recalled
that the French territories—including Dahomey—needed a
central authority in the hands of a governor-general, unimpeded by rival political and military administrations. To achieve
this, the Soudan territory—'manifestement artificiel et provi-
soire'—was to be divided among the other colonies; and the
control of West African forces was to pass to an officer directly
responsible to the governor-general. In short, eleven of the
twenty-two *cercles* of the Soudan were joined to Senegal, sharing
a budget with the military territories to the east, the expenses of
which were laid down by the governor-general; six *cercles* were
attached to Guinea; the Ivory Coast took over a further three;
and the colony of Dahomey was extended into the Soudan
slightly to the north of Say.

Chaudié, who continued as governor-general, made it clear
to the colonies that henceforth the use of armed forces, financed
directly by the State Budget for the Colonies, depended on his
personal discretion. Furthermore, tariffs were to be 'harmon-
ized' and internal customs were abolished. As a further centraliz-
ing measure, a treasury-paymaster was sent out from Paris to

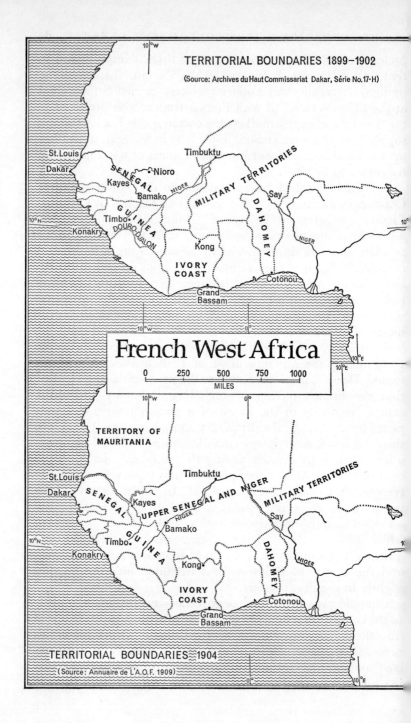

TERRITORIAL BOUNDARIES 1899–1902

(Source: Archives du Haut Commissariat Dakar, Série No.17-H)

St.Louis
Dakar
Timbuktu
SENEGAL
Nioro
Kayes
NIGER
MILITARY TERRITORIES
Bamako
DAHOMEY
GUINEA
Say
Timbo
Konakry
DOURO DJALON
NIGER
Kong
IVORY COAST
Cotonou
Grand Bassam

French West Africa

0   250   500   750   1000
MILES

TERRITORY OF MAURITANIA

St.Louis
Dakar
Timbuktu
SENEGAL
Kayes
UPPER SENEGAL AND NIGER
MILITARY TERRITORIES
NIGER
Say
Bamako
GUINEA
DAHOMEY
Timbo
Konakry
Kong
NIGER
IVORY COAST
Cotonou
Grand Bassam

TERRITORIAL BOUNDARIES 1904

(Source: Annuaire de L'A.O.F. 1909)

administer the finances of the Government General through assistant officials of his own in each of the colonies. Finally, a delegate of the governor-general was posted to Kayes to supervise the territories between the Senegal and the Niger whose administrative services were joined with those of Senegal. Chaudié himself went on tour through the north to see these arrangements were carried out.

The day of the colonels had passed. With the signing of the Anglo-French Convention of 1898 French rule from Saint-Louis to the Chad had been formally recognized. As Destenave summed it up in his influential memorandum: 'C'est le commencement de l'ère réservée aux commerçants et aux ingénieurs.'

7. The development of African politics

BERNARD SCHNAPPER *La Politique et le commerce français dans le Golfe de Guinée 1838–1871* Mouton & Co., Paris 1961; pages 223–6 (In translation)

Territorial aims after 1860 were bound to call into question the native policy, which had been designed only for trading stations. Fortified stations had been set up in the native kingdoms which placed themselves under French protection and surrendered their sovereignty. But this idea of sovereignty was understood in a very limited sense. Surrender of sovereignty meant no more than forbidding the chiefs to make any future treaty with European powers other than France. But care was taken not to touch internal administration. The commandants of the trading stations received instructions not to interfere in the home affairs of the African kingdoms, but to exert over them moral influence and to take action in political matters only if traders were molested or the station threatened. The French government had no desire to exercise full sovereignty in place of the chiefs, contrary to what the wording of the treaty might lead one to believe.

Already the 1863 treaty, establishing a protectorate over

Porto Novo, indicated a new development in the concept of what an African policy was to be. When the treaty had been signed, the head of the naval division and the consular agent, Daumas, set up, on the pattern of English practices in the Niger delta, a commission of European traders which overhauled the customs-system of the state and which was to form a commercial court. Though it did not provide for any garrison or occupation, this treaty constituted a much more marked form of intervention in the home affairs of an African state than those of the pre-1860 period. The 1863 treaty provided for an interventionist protectorate, rather than protection.

Indeed, there began to be doubts about the future of the African states on the Coast. Most of these states had built up their prosperity on the slave trade. The more and more rapid decline of the slave trade dealt them a very hard blow. As a result of his impoverishment, the King of Dahomey was led to make more and more demand on European trade. Some of the slave-trading states had managed to find a valuable source of revenue in legitimate trade, particularly in palm-oil, though it brought in less than slave trading. To secure maximum profit in this trade, they made efforts to prevent traders who were directly dependent on European merchants from penetrating inland. All went well so long as the Europeans were prepared to use the expensive intermediary of independent agents. But a drop in European prices of palm-oil, a rise in its purchase price, and the intervention of new companies taking advantage of the lowering of freight-charges, brought about the collapse of the system of independent agents and a certain political tension between the chiefs—who saw their principal source of wealth slipping out of their hands—and the European traders backed up by the official representatives of their countries.

The head of the naval division was aware of it and Admiral Dauriac expressed this feeling admirably:

On the whole, it is clear that it is not desirable for all these Negro kingdoms on the Coast to continue an independent existence. The general interest required that Europeans, the English since they alone appear to have such aspirations, manage to open up these doors which have been shut for so long, and attract, develop and protect trade.

The outlines of a new policy were emerging; it would be much less favourable to the continued existence of these African states which were becoming more and more a hindrance to European trade and less and less the help which they were thought to be at the time when the trading stations had been set up. In the Gulf of Guinea, France did not wish to have a hand in their breaking up, but merely to add to or fill out her trading posts, or even to take any opportunities that arose for turning to account a possible surrender of the protectorates by negotiation with England.

Knowing that the African states favoured the survival of barbarous practices, the navy wished them to disappear rapidly and was ready to apply a completely new native policy in all those areas where French protection had been promised. Instead of leaving the protected princes to manage freely the affairs of their states, preserve their old customs and dispense justice, the new policy consisted of intervening in their domestic affairs and—in the name of 'exercising sovereignty'—moving on to direct control which took away from the chiefs their most important powers. Not only was the administration beginning to think that it would be a good thing to do away with the states that were still independent, like Dahomey or Porto Novo, but above all that the old treaties of protection ought to be given a new meaning.

Not all the officers were in agreement with such a change. The Gaboon commercial agents used an extremely rigorous security-system in their relations with the people of the interior. They demanded from the sub-agents, to whom they advanced goods and who had agreed to obtain for them ivory and wood for dyes, the delivery of hostages—usually girls. This practice, apart from the fact that it was the next thing to slavery or prostitution, often caused serious political difficulties between M'Pongwes and Pahouins. In 1868, the commandant of Gaboon seized from a chief of Glass a boy and two little Pahouin girls whom he sent to the commandant of an aviso with instructions to send them back to their parents. At the same time, he warned those who received hostages in exchange for their goods that they would be regarded as slave traders and be treated as such. Two months later, after his return to Gaboon, Admiral Dauriac repudiated this move and reaffirmed the most traditional principles of African policy:

The Admiral desires that these domestic affairs of the indigenous peoples should be interfered with as little as possible. If they come to ask for your arbitration, you may grant it them and judge between them; but after that, leave them to accept your decision or not as they wish. Only when our commercial interests are involved must we proceed to any important intervention.

Non-intervention in home affairs was not always easy, for the extension of commercial influence made Europeans more and more often witness to barbarous practices. In 1870, Bony, chief of Half Jack, the village where a customs post had been set up, cut the throats of two of his wives and a child, whom he then had displayed in public. Could French sovereignty adjust to such practices? It was in connection with that incident that Admiral Bourgeois, the new head of the naval division, expressed admirably the choice which lay before the French government:

But I think [he wrote] these days many enlightened minds agree that sovereignty should be accepted only where its duties and rights can be carried out and exercised; the duties—by properly protecting the subject peoples against unwarranted attacks by their neighbours; the rights—by imposing on them the obligation to give up those of their customs which, by being directed against life or human liberty, seriously offend the morality of civilized peoples.

Thus, there was nothing in common between this and the policy that had been followed up to then; no longer protection, but occupation: it was a policy of all or nothing. If the government did not wish to exercise sovereignty, then it had to regard the earlier treaties of protection as mere pacts of friendship. If, for instance, Amatifou had disputes with his Ashanti or Appollonian neighbours, the protection due to him would have to be reduced 'to moral support and good neighbourly action'. Complete non-intervention or full sovereignty; the policy advocated did not have the ambiguity of the *points d'appui* policy. It was up to the Minister to choose.

Translated by Mrs. C. P. Bagle

II. ECONOMIC DEVELOPMENT IN WEST AFRICA

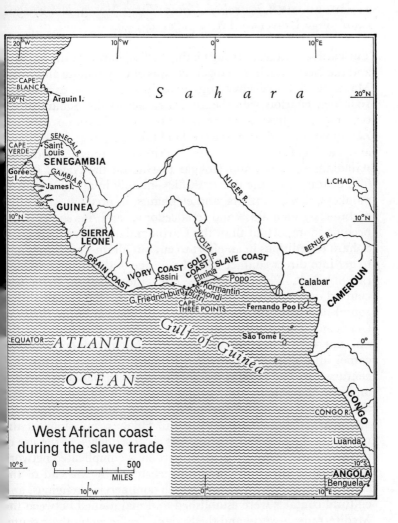

West African coast during the slave trade

0   500
MILES

8. The caravan trade in the nineteenth century

A. ADU BOAHEN *Journal of African History* Vol. 3, No. 2, 1962
Cambridge University Press; pages 349–56

The caravan trade, a strong chain binding Barbary, the Sahara, and the Negro territories together, was of very remote antiquity. Mauny and Lhote have convincingly shown that as early as 1000 B.C. chariots were being drawn across the Sahara along two main routes: a western route from Morocco through Zemmour and Adrar to the banks of the Senegal and the Niger, and a central route from Tripoli through Cydamus (Ghadames), Ghat, and Hoggar to Gao on the Niger. By the fifth century B.C., the desert traffic—mainly in animals such as monkeys, lions, panthers, and elephants, in precious stones like carbuncles, emeralds, and chalcedony, and in slaves—had become so important that 'the Carthaginians began their great Sahara expeditions in an effort to cut out all intermediaries and to get into direct contact with the source of the riches in which they traded'. Three centuries later the Saharan trade was centred on the Tripoli–Fezzan–Bornu route (the Garamantian route) and constituted one of the main sources of the riches of Carthage. The phenomenal development of this desert traffic did not take place, however, until the introduction of the camel into Tripolitania by the Romans probably in the first century A.D. The rapid spread of the camel throughout Barbary and into the Sahara and beyond was begun by the Arabs and the Berbers. The process seemed to have gathered momentum and reached its climax during the Hilalian invasions in the middle of the eleventh century. As a consequence of the use of this singularly endowed beast of burden, a complicated network of caravan routes had come into existence by the end of the eleventh century by means of which commercial, religious, and cultural contacts were established and maintained between the Mediterranean world and the Sudan. Traffic along these routes reached its peak in the period 1490–1590 when the Songhay Empire under the Askias and the Bornu Empire under the Sefuwas dominated the Sahara and Sudan, and maintained such political stability and order as have probably not been known in those areas since that time.

From the end of the sixteenth century, however, the traffic began to decline, and by the nineteenth century it had become concentrated on four main routes. These were the Morocco–Taodeni–Timbuctu route with its important branch, the Mabruk–Tuat route in the west, the Ghadames–Air–Kano and the Tripoli–Fezzan–Bornu routes in the centre, and the Cyrenaica–Kufra–Wadai route in the east. According to Bovill, the greatest of these routes was the Taghaza–Timbuctu route 'pre-eminent in the gold trade and still more important as a cultural high-way'. This might well have been the case in the period up to the end of the sixteenth century. The available evidence for the nineteenth century hardly justifies Bovill's view.

The ebb and flow of traffic on these routes were determined by two main factors, namely, the political conditions in Sudan and the security of the routes in the Sahara. On both points, the odds were heavily against the western route. Bovill himself describes, with remarkable scholarship, the anarchy that followed the overthrow of the Songhay Empire in the early 1590s by the armies of El-Mansur, the Sultan of Morocco, and the failure of the Moroccans to establish any effective administrative machinery in their newly conquered domain. The seventeenth and eighteenth centuries saw rivalry among the Tuareg, the Fulani, and the Bambara for the legacy of the Askias, while in the Sahara the various Arab, Moorish, and Tuareg tribes fought for the control of the western route. These wars continued intermittently throughout the nineteenth century, as is obvious from the reports of the explorers Laing, Caillié, Barth, and Dubois. As a result of these political conditions in the Sahara, the western route became so insecure that traffic along it was confined to the large annual caravans. Indeed, far from being the greatest, the Taghaza–Timbuctu route was the least important of the four principal routes. Nothing illustrates this better than the state of its once famous termini, Timbuctu and Gao. The former, which Leo Africanus described in such glowing terms at the beginning of the sixteenth century, had by the 1820s been reduced to a town of a circumference of only three to four miles. Caillié, who was there in 1827, could not conceal his disappointment. He noted that he found it 'neither so large nor so populous' as he had expected, and was shocked by the inactivity and indolence displayed by the inhabitants. In 1854 Barth found Gao, the famous capital of the Songhay Empire and the main market for the gold of Wangara, 'the desolate abode of a small and miserable population'. Bovill quotes an English merchant who reported in 1638 that 'the golden trade of Gao hath long since been intermitted'. The traffic along the western route never recovered its former greatness but continued to decline as the anarchy and insecurity let loose by the Moroccan conquest increased in intensity. By overthrowing the peace and order of the Askias, the Moroccans killed the goose that more or less literally laid the golden eggs.

The other route which steadily lost its importance in the course of the nineteenth century was the Tripoli–Fezzan–Bornu route. With the fall of the Songhay Empire, the political centre of gravity swung from the Niger to the Chad, from Timbuctu to Birni Ngazargamo, the capital of the Bornu Empire. This Empire remained stable throughout the seventeenth and eighteenth centuries and successfully dominated the regions of the Sahara as far west as the southern boundaries of Fezzan. Though the Fulani rebellion of 1804 and the subsequent wars shook Bornu to its foundations, the friendly relations which El Kanemi, its Sheikh and uncrowned ruler, successfully established with the Pasha of Tripoli and the Governor of Fezzan in the first three decades of the nineteenth century kept the Garamantian route open. In describing the Morocco-Timbuctu and Fezzan–Bornu routes in 1825, Laing stated: 'the latter is a regular trading route along which a child might travel but on this there are many conflicting interests and the Bashaw's influence ends at Ghadames'. Indeed, it seems that from about the beginning of the seventeenth century until the 1820s the Fezzan–Bornu route was the most active of all. The state of prosperity in which Denham and Clapperton found Kuka (or Kukawa), the new capital of Bornu, built in 1814, and Ngornu, the main emporium of the Empire, bears this out. After the death of El Kanemi in 1837, however, wars raged among Bornu, Wadai, and Bagirmi in which Mgornu was destroyed. These wars greatly disturbed the stability of the Chad region. In the north the political revolutions in Tripoli between 1830 and 1842 led to the occupation of Tripoli and

Fezzan by the forces of the Sultan of Turkey, the entire abolition of the Karamanli dynasty, and the mass migration of the
Awlād Sulymān from Fezzan to the northern regions of the
Chad, where they have remained ever since. These developments had a disastrous effect on the traffic along this route. In
the first place, the revolutions brought that traffic to a complete
standstill between 1830 and 1842 and part of it was therefore
diverted into the Wadai–Benghazi and the Sudan routes.
Secondly, the substitution of the feeble Turkish administration,
whose influence did not even reach the southern provinces of
Fezzan, for the oppressive though relatively powerful Karamanli government enabled the Tuareg and the Tibu, the two
great peoples of the Sahara, to revive their traditional raids and
plundering expeditions against each other. As a result of the
wars between the Tuareg and the Tibu, for instance, the road
from Murzuk to Bornu was completely blocked between April
1851 and June 1852. As late as 1906 Hans Vischer, who
travelled from Tripoli to Bornu, reported that the raids were
still going on. These internecine wars and raids were intensified
by the activities of the Awlād Sulymān who, from the time of
their arrival in the basin of the Chad, earned their living solely
by plundering and raiding all and sundry. The activities of the
Turks, the Tuareg, the Tibu, and the Awlād Sulymān rendered
this route so insecure that although the caravan traffic on it
revived in the 1840s it became, as on the western route, essentially an annual affair.

Commercially, it was the Ghadames–Air–Kano route which
was the most important of the routes in the nineteenth century.
Following the Fulani Jihad and the successful establishment
of the twin Fulani Empire of Sokoto and Gwando, the political
centre of gravity shifted once more from Bornu to Hausaland,
from Kuka to Sokoto and Kano. If the western half of the
Empire—the Gwando Empire—was far from stable as a result
of the irrepressibly rebellious spirit of the Goverawa, the
Kebbawa, and the people of Dendina, the Sokoto Empire itself
from the 1830s onwards maintained its equilibrium. The
Saharan sector of that route was by the nineteenth century
under the domination of two of the most powerful branches of
the Tuareg of the Sahara, the Azger and the Kel Owi Tuareg.
As both of them depended for their livelihood entirely on the

caravan trade, they did everything to ensure the security of the route. All the nineteenth-century explorers, among them Richardson, Barth, and Duveyrier, testified to its security and to the honesty displayed by the Tuareg. As a result of the whole-some state of affairs along this route, not only large annual caravans but also small caravans were to be seen on it almost all the year round. Richardson, for instance, was surprised to meet between Air and Ghat a caravan of only two merchants, five servants, and some forty slaves 'all without arms or perhaps with a couple of swords'. The full flood of prosperity in which Clapperton in 1824 and Barth in 1851 found Kano, the main terminus of this route, bears testimony to the swiftness and the richness of the commercial current that flowed along it.

The fourth route, the Cyrenaica–Kufra–Wadai road, which Bovill never mentions at all, became particularly important culturally and commercially during the second half of the nineteenth century. This was mainly due to the introduction of the Sanusi order into Cyrenaica in 1843 by its founder, Sayyid Muhammad b' Ali al-Sanusi, and the ensuing rapid spread of this order into the Sahara and Western Sudan. The number of its branches increased from 22 in 1953 to 143 in 1900; 5 of them were in Morocco, 25 in Fezzan, 45 in Cyrenaica and 15 of the remaining branches were in Wadai, Kanem, Kano, Zinder, and Timbuctu. Not only did the spread of this order give a great fillip to Islam in the Sahara and Western Sudan, but it also, in a number of ways, affected traffic on the eastern route along which most of the headquarters of the branches were concentrated. First, al-Sanusi and his son and successor Sayyid Muhammad Al-Mahdi (1856–1900) were able to win over most of the Bedouin tribes of Cyrenaica, the Zuwaya of Kufra, the Tibu of Tibesti, and the Awlād Sulymān of Eastern Kanem, and to establish and maintain peace and friendship among them. The result was that, during the latter half of the nineteenth century, the eastern route became exceedingly safe. Hassanain Bey, the Egyptian Oxford graduate, who travelled along the route in 1923, met some Bedouins who told him that in the days of Al-Mahdi, a woman could walk from Barca in Cyrenaica to Wadai unmolested; at the end of his trip he concluded that the 'importance of these aspects of the Senussi rule in maintaining tranquillity and well-being of the people of the Libyan desert can scarcely be over-estimated'. Secondly, the *Zawiyas* (lodges or headquarters) of the branches of the brotherhood, which were usually built along the route, served as hotels for pilgrims as well as traders. Thirdly, as each of these *Zawiyas* had to maintain itself from alms, tolls, and its own commercial activities, their governors often became great caravan traders themselves and gave every stimulus to the trade. Al-Mahdi himself dug wells between Kufra and Wadai. Even Duveyrier, the bitter critic of the Sanusi, admits that Al-Mahdi managed 'to establish the ancient commercial relations between Wadai and the Mediterranean'. Indeed by the first decade of the present century, it was the only route along which the venerable annual caravans continued to move. When Hans Vischer visited Murzuk in 1906, he discovered that all the financiers and important caravan traders had abandoned that town long ago and were continuing their trade 'on the one remaining trans-Saharan trade route from Wadai and Darfur through the eastern Borgu and Tibesti to Kufra and the Libyan desert to Bengasi'. The two great French travellers and scholars, Gautier and Chudeau, tell us that, whereas by 1905 the route from Bornu Fezzan was hardly ever used and all traffic along the Morocco–Timbuctu route had been diverted to Senegal, large caravans were still leaving Benghazi for Wadai carrying mainly guns and ammunition to be bartered for slaves. What finally disrupted the last of the ancient links between Barbary and Sudan was the French occupation of Wadai in 1906, Tibesti and Borgu in 1913–14, and the Italian occupation of Cyrenaica in 1911–12.

Each of these routes had in the nineteenth century as in medieval times four main points. These were the northern termini, the rendezvous or 'point de départ au sud', the refreshment centres, and the southern termini. Mogador remained, as it had been through the centuries, the main terminus for the western route. Algiers, Constantine, and Tunis were the termini for the branch route through Tuat. The French occupation of Algeria in 1830, however, reduced the traffic from Tuat to these places to a spasmodic trickle until the 1860s. Tripoli and Benghazi were the termini for the central and the eastern routes respectively.

All the caravans usually assembled at definite centres before they commenced their journey southwards. These centres were normally towns where provisions could be obtained, where beasts of burden, camel drivers, and guides could be hired and where the financiers or their representatives resided. After the destruction of Sijilmassa, the traditional rendezvous for caravans on the western route, in the eighteenth century, Tenduf, the capital of the oasis of El Haha, took its place. Another important 'point de départ'—probably the most important one until the 1850s—was Ghadames. Caravans from the Regency of Tripoli, Tunis, and Algeria assembled there before they departed westwards through Tuat to Timbuctu, southwards through Ghat to Kano, or south-eastwards through Murzuk to Bornu. Ghadames still retained in the nineteenth century the position it enjoyed in the days of Leo Africanus as the home of most of the bankers and wholesalers and the head-quarters of most of the trading firms operating in the interior. Richardson found at least four principal trading firms there in 1845; five years later, Barth described Ghadames as 'the residence of wealthy merchants who embarked all their capital on commercial enterprise and bring home their own merchandise'. Djalo in the oasis of Aujila was, as the British Vice-Consul at Benghazi reported as late as 1875, the main starting point of the numerous caravans to Wadai and Bornu.

After these rendezvous, the next important points on the routes were the refreshment centres, which might appropriately be compared to coaling stations in maritime navigation. These centres were usually situated in fertile oases where food and fresh water could be obtained and camels and guides might be changed. As the caravans remained at these oases for long periods—a fact which differentiated them from the resting places where caravans halted at the end of the day's march—they were often great trading centres. Indeed, some of the traders from the Sudan as well as from the Mediterranean coast often disposed of their merchandise there and returned home. These centres thus served as points where the batons of the trans-Saharan commercial relay were changed. Tuat and Arawan were the main such centres on the western route. In the market of Arawan, for example, exchange usually took place between the 'gold' caravans from the south, and the 'salt' caravans from the north. On the Sudan route, Ghat and Iferuan in Air, which had by the nineteenth century superseded the old centre of Agades, were the main 'coaling stations'. Ghat was also the busiest market centre in the Sahara and the terminus of most of the smaller northern and southern caravans. Richardson, who attended the winter Souk (market) of Ghat in 1845, reported that 'caravans from Sudan including all the large cities but especially from Kano, from Bornou, from the Tibboo country, from Touat, from Fezzan, from Souf, from Ghadames and from Tripoli and Tunis and the north coast visited Ghat Souk this winter'. Both Barth and Duveyrier, who visited Ghat in 1850 and 1860 respectively, found it still an important and thriving commercial centre. Murzuk in Fezzan and El Giof in Kufra served as the refreshment centres for the Garamantian and eastern routes. By the 1860s, however, the former had lost its importance, partly because of competition from Ghat and partly because of the abolition of the slave trade in the Regency of Tripoli in 1857.

The fourth and final important points on the caravan routes were the southern termini. These were Timbuctu, Kano, Kukawa, Wara and Abeche for the western, Sudan, Garamantian, and eastern routes respectively. Some of these were primarily entrepôts, others were mainly market-centres where merchandise was retailed, while some served as both. Timbuctu was a typical example of the first. The exterior of the houses there might wear a look of dilapidation and desolation, but, as Dubois discovered when he entered them, they were filled with goods awaiting transportation southwards and northwards. The goods from the north were conveyed from these warehouses in Timbuctu first to its port Kabara, five miles south, and thence in boats up the river to Jenne, Segu, Sansanding, Bamako, and Bure. Some of the goods were retailed in these places and some were conveyed farther south and west to places like Kong and Bobo-Dioulasso in the Ivory Coast and to Gbeho and Dormaa in the Brong-Ahafo region of modern Ghana. In the markets of the towns south and west of Jenne, it was not unusual, especially before the mid-fifties, to find commodities from Barbary and the Sahara, like salt and calico, competing with similar or identical goods brought in via the Senegal and the west coast. A classic example of the combined entrepôt and market type of terminus was Kano. Both Clapperton and Barth described the market there as 'crowded from sun-rise to sunset every day'. At Kano they met traders from towns as far apart as Tripoli to the north and Salaga in modern Ghana to the south, and from In Salah in Tuat to the north-west and Masena, the capital of Bagirmi, to the south-east. In addition to being a great trading centre, Kano was also an important entrepôt from which trade routes radiated westwards through Gwando and Fada Ngurma to Wagadugu in what is now Volta, south-westwards through Bussa and Nikki to Salaga in modern Ghana, southwards via Zaria, Rabba, Ilorin, Ibadan, and Abeokuta to Badagry in Dahomey, and eastwards through Katagun to Bornu, Bagirmi, and Adamawa on the Benue.[1]

9. Underlying forces and influences[2]

P. J. BAUER *West African Trade* Routledge & Kegan Paul 1963; pages 7–8, 11–21

Difficulties of Adjustment to a Money Economy

. . . Although by Western standards the real income of the population of the West African colonies is still low, and very low in some territories, these economies are not stagnant. In fact, many of their problems arise from the very rapid and necessarily uneven development which has taken place, and especially from the impact and progress of a money and exchange economy. There has been trade between Europe and the west coast of Africa since the sixteenth century, but its character, composition and volume have changed fundament-ally during the last few decades. Until about fifty years ago there were no exports of cocoa, groundnuts, hides and skins or

---

[1] There are two main types of caravans, the large annual ones which could consist of between 500 and 2,000 camels, and the small irregular caravans consisting of from 5 to 100.

[2] Although written with the twentieth century principally in mind, this passage is also relevant to developments that were beginning earlier. Compare this extract with reading 39, p. 379. [Ed.]

timber, and the export of palm products was only a fraction of what it is today. The Ibo, who today play an important part in Nigerian trade, were in an almost savage state as recently as 1910. It would call for anthropologists and sociologists to analyse many facets of the progress and the effects of this rapid transition. But those which bear closely on the present study require discussion here.

The comparatively recent emergence of a money economy explains the presence of institutions and attitudes which are largely unsuited to its requirements. The family system is an example.[1] In West Africa a reasonably prosperous man is frequently obliged to support even distant kinsmen and relatives. A moderately successful man may find that a score or more relatives descend on him, expecting to live off his bounty. Some of the successful Africans probably enjoy the status and sense of power attaching to the support of their relatives, but many admit in private discussion that they dread these extensive obligations.

The system is not without redeeming features. It exhibits elements of real charity and generosity. Moreover, it often results in the pooling of family resources for such purposes as the education of promising children or the setting up of a member of the family in trade or in a profession. In such circumstances it amounts to a circulation of capital within the family. Persons supporting a number of needy kinsmen may themselves have been supported by distant relatives a few years earlier.

The principal weakness seems to be the comparative absence of discrimination in its exercise. Relatives who might be able to support themselves qualify for assistance on much the same basis as those who cannot find employment. Quite clearly the system

[1] The term 'family' includes many more distant relatives and kinsmen than in Europe. The brief discussion of the family system in the text is intended only as a rough outline of those of its features which bear on the structure of West African trade. The information is based on numerous discussions with Europeans and Africans, and on some personal observations of the system and of its results. This seems sufficient for the brief analysis of its effects on the structure of trade, but comprehensive discussion would, of course, require the methods and the training of an anthropologist, by whose standards and for whose purposes the discussion presented here is necessarily amateurish.

is largely the legacy of a subsistence economy.[1] Excessive and indiscriminate hospitality is a feature of subsistence economies where surpluses cannot be marketed, and where it is therefore expected that these should be used for charity, and in particular for liberal entertainment of kinsmen, friends and visitors. . . .

Imperfect Specialization

The economic activities of large sections of the population of West Africa are still partly or largely unspecialized. The preponderance of a few staple exports is compatible with a low degree of economic specialization. Many farmers produce a number of products on a very small scale.[2] Even in northern Nigeria and in the Northern Territories of the Gold Coast many farmers spend a substantial part of their time in non-agricultural activities, or in activities away from their home as migrant labourers or traders. In other parts of these countries, especially in southern Nigeria and the colony area of the Gold Coast, the great bulk of the population has other occupations, generally some form of trading, in addition to their main activity. The lack of specialization becomes more apparent when the economic activities of wives and children are taken into account. Africans frequently do not regard trade as an occupation (especially when carried on by dependants), and would not refer to it as such. They regard it as part of existence and not as a distinct occupation.[3]

[1] The widespread unemployment of unskilled workers is possibly a secondary reason. But the system is so indiscriminate as to make it certain that this is not a major reason.

[2] The cocoa farmers are probably more specialized than the rest of the farming population.

[3] In general the wives and children are independent economic agents as much as dependent relatives. They almost invariably take part in trade, and participate to some extent in the economic life of the country. The wife is expected to make some contribution to the family income. This is no doubt partly because there is very little for her to do in the house. In parts of Nigeria and the Gold Coast a man expects his wife to trade, and he is likely to regard the bride price (which is in fact a dowry in reverse and not a sign of the low social status of women) partly as an investment in a trading concern. In certain parts of the Gold Coast a husband can divorce his wife if she fails more than twice as a trader. On the other hand, women often trade in order to save enough money to return the bride price and thus be able to divorce their husbands. The children also generally trade, as there are few adequate schools and there is little else to occupy them.

The lack of specialization which affects a large section of West African economic life derives from narrow markets which are an aspect of the low level of the local economy. In turn it impedes efficiency and retards economic progress. Thus it is both a symptom and a cause of the low standard of living.

This imperfect specialization and the importance of secondary activities carried on by members of the household greatly diminish the value and relevance of the conventional occupational classifications of statistical compilations. This fact has not been sufficiently recognized. Official reports and standard works state, for example, that five-sixths of the population is engaged in agriculture, and they rarely mention trade among the lists of the economic activities of the population. In fact, in many of these so-called agricultural households the head of the family trades part-time even during the normally short farming season, and more actively outside the season, whilst members of his family trade intermittently throughout the year. It is misleading to ignore these trading activities and to imply that the great bulk of the population is engaged in farming only.

The fluidity of activity extends to personal relations where they bear closely on economic life. A prominent African trader in Lagos, whose children are being educated at expensive residential schools and universities in Britain, told me that his wife was one of his principal customers, and that she bought goods from him both on cash and on credit terms. He did not consider this unusual; indeed, it is not so, as similar commercial relations exist between other prominent Africans and their wives and children. It is not unusual for wives to sue their husbands for commercial debts.

It is well known that many African doctors and lawyers have extensive trading interests. Government employees are also frequently part-time traders. Every servant or driver who worked for me on my two visists to Nigeria was either in trade or asked for my assistance in finding trading contacts for him. Many of these requests were simply advanced to obtain either free samples or else so-called short-supply goods at controlled prices for re-sale at easy and immediate profit. But at least one of my drivers, a full-time employee of a government department, displayed an excellent knowledge of market prices and of market conditions for provisions throughout southern Nigeria, and acted upon it.[1]

Quite apart from this imperfect occupational specialization there is still widespread lack of specialization in trading operations both horizontally (by type of commodity handled) and vertically (by successive stages of distribution). These will be considered when the import trade comes to be reviewed.

The Low Level of Productive Resources

West Africa is generally poor in disclosed and accessible natural economic resources, acquired capital and technical and administrative skills. It is preferable to speak of the low level of capital rather than of its scarcity. The comparative lack of local technical and administrative skill aggravates the effects of the scarcity of equipment; it is not lack of capital alone which retards development. For this reason indiscriminate import of capital, or even substantial capital accumulation in the hands of public organizations, alone would not necessarily improve the situation.

The African communities are very poor in acquired reserves of fertile soil, in accumulated plant, buildings, roads and railways, as well as in stocks of working capital and in liquid assets with which external capital can be obtained. Though the measurement of capital raises conceptual difficulties, it is quite easy to illustrate its low level in West Africa. Nigeria may be taken as an example. The territory has an area of approximately 372,000 sq. miles and a population of about 30 millions. The f.o.b. value of its exports is at present over £100 m. a year. Two of its major export crops originate in the north, 700–1000 miles from the sea. The bulk of the meat supply also comes from that area or even farther north. The volume of the shipborne cargo handled in the ports of Nigeria in 1949 was almost 2½ m

---

[1] The following episode is characteristic of several aspects of economic life and of trade in Nigeria. This driver, when on tour with me, ascertained in Ibadan (112 miles from Lagos) that the price of tins of Horlicks was lower there than in Lagos, where they were originally landed. The difference was 6d. a tin. He decided to buy a dozen tins, gave a deposit of 5s. and on our return to Lagos a few days later sent a relative to collect the goods. The return fare of the relative was 3s. and the gross profit on the transaction was 6s.; the net profit was divided between the driver and the relative.

tons. The capital equipment sustaining this very large trade is extremely small. At the end of 1949 the total track mileage of the Nigerian railway was 1,900 miles. There were only 900 miles of bituminous roads in the country. There were about 11,000 commercial vehicles, almost one-half of which were over ten years old, and the poor roads and inadequate maintenance reduce their effectiveness. There were less than 900 telephone subscribers and about 8,000 instruments.

The low level of fixed capital increases the working capital requirements of the economy by tying up large quantities of resources in the form of stocks and goods in transit. The large accumulation of unrailed groundnuts in Kano is well known, but it is only one instance of a general problem. Part of the Benue, the principal tributary of the Niger, is open for navigation during two months of the year only, and the annual requirements of the substantial hinterland of the upper Benue have to be transported within that short period. Considerable quantities of export produce are evacuated by the Benue, and if they are not shipped in time they may have to wait for almost another year before they can be removed. Similar difficulties also arise in the movement of palm produce from certain areas of the Eastern Provinces. In short, owing to the dearth of fixed capital much larger stocks are required to sustain an even flow of goods than would otherwise be necessary.

The low level of technical knowledge reduces both the life and the efficiency of available capital. Lack of spare parts combined with inadequate repairs result in rapid deterioration of machinery and equipment. The difficulties are aggravated by restrictions on imports from North America; British transport equipment does not stand up to local conditions as successfully as American.

Some financial data also illustrate the low level of capital. Deposits in the Nigerian Post Office Savings Bank increased fifteen-fold between 1934 and 1951, but still totalled only about £3 m. The total currency in circulation in Nigeria in March 1951 was about £40 m., and this included money held for business transactions and for current expenditure on consumption, as well as for savings accumulated over a period. The total volume of bank deposits outstanding was about

£78 m., and these were largely business and government deposits.

In a subsistence economy the low level of capital may be regarded as inherent in the situation. The very rapid progress of the West African colonies beyond the subsistence stage has been so recent that there has been no time to accumulate much capital. The general poverty of these territories, the backward state of very large sections of the population, the social and institutional organization and the rapid growth of population have all enhanced the difficulty of capital accumulation. The substantial increase in the volume of trade and general activity in these territories over the last few decades has greatly strained the stock of capital. Lorries are in service twenty-four hours a day for seven days a week and are generally tightly packed with passengers and freight. The railway is barely able to move the traffic which is offering. By the middle of June 1950 some of the groundnut crop of 1948–9 had not yet been railed, fifteen months after the close of the season; and if the 1949–50 crop had not been a comparative failure an appreciable part of that would also have remained unrailed.

There are in West Africa a number of wealthy Africans, many more than before the war. But there is no substantial local capitalist class comparable to the Chinese and Indians in south-east Asia and in the territories bordering on the Indian Ocean. There were substantial African traders operating in West Africa in the nineteenth century, but their resources and methods were inadequate to meet the great expansion of trade over the last half-century or so, with its increased capital requirements brought about by larger turnover, the extension of trade into the interior and the gradual emergence of cash payments for the services of employees.

The absence of a strong local capitalist class helps to explain certain features of the West African trade. The activities of the European trading firms spread into small-scale wholesaling partly because there were too few local merchants able to handle imported commodities in wholesale quantities.[1] The firms were compelled to carry stocks and take them up-country

[1] This was not the only reason for the development of vertically integrated organizations; considerations of market strategy have contributed toward this development.

to their own stores because the local African merchants were unable to undertake the task. The large firms still experience difficulties in finding Africans willing and able to buy readily and regularly on a wholesale basis.

The extension of the activities of the firms into local selling, as distinct from importing or wholesaling only at ports and central towns, has greatly raised the capital requirements of trading in West Africa compared with, for example, the Far East or South America, where generally speaking the British import merchants are able to turn their capital over fairly rapidly. The long distances, the backward communications, the shortage of equipment and the absence of a local capitalist class have thrown a greater burden on the capital resources of the importer. This in turn has served to strengthen the position of the large firms.

The low level of local capital is reflected in the much-discussed practice by which non-African firms make advances to middlemen (often Africans) for the purchase of export produce on their behalf. The merchant firms frequently advance substantial sums of money for weeks and occasionally even for months for the purchase of a particular crop. Although the risks are often exaggerated[1] much capital is used in this way.[2]

The system has been much criticized in recent years, often without appreciation of the conditions which have brought it about. In essence the system of advances uses foreign capital to assist in the harvesting and movement of local crops. It has grown up largely[3] as a result of the absence of a substantial capitalist class, and it has continued even after the elements of such a class have emerged. These advances are generally given

[1] Many of these advances are not really a credit risk as the firms may hold sufficient security; in other instances the advances really represent moneys entrusted to semi-independent employees who are advantageously placed for the purchase of produce. In accounting language it would be difficult to decide whether to call these advances 'cash' or 'debtors' balances'.

[2] The system differs from that prevailing generally in the Far East where the trading firms buy rubber and copra at prices ruling at the time of delivery from intermediaries who provide their own finance.

[3] But it may be connected with motives of market strategy of the type discussed in Part 3 below. It is in some respects analogous with vertical integration which is a feature of the organization of the large merchant firms.

INA

by the firms to middlemen and distributed by them to their
sub-buyers, through whom they reach the producers. Sometimes the funds are advanced well before the purchase of the
produce; the intermediary often uses the money for the temporary financing of other projects such as the purchase of
transport equipment. He may secure such a substantial return
on this outlay that he may be able to repay much of his loan
before his obligation to deliver produce has matured. Thus
here again European capital finances local enterprises.
Advances are generally intended for the movement and
transport of crops already harvested. Where they reach producers before the harvest, the advances from the firms may serve
partially to finance the collection or harvesting of the crop.

These transactions are somewhat different from advances and
loans given by brokers and other intermediaries to the producers early in the season, which may be used to finance the
planting and growing of the crop or the personal consumption
of the borrower until after the harvest. But the extent of such
pre-harvest loans from brokers to producers is increased
because brokers realize that later in the season they are likely
to receive advances from the European firms.

The low level of capital has been one of the factors militating
against the development of small locally owned estates or larger
peasant holdings. It is true that some cocoa farmers have
acquired several scattered holdings, but this has been exceptional. The absence of such enterprises has retarded the growth
of locally owned capital, especially in the agricultural sector of
the economy.

The curious practice known in Lagos and the Western
Provinces of Nigeria as 'gold-coasting' also illustrates the low
level of local capital. This is the use of merchandise obtained
from the importing firms for the purpose of raising short-term
funds for trade or money-lending. An established customer of
an importing house buys standard lines of merchandise on
credit at the beginning of the month, promptly sells these (if
necessary, even at a loss), and uses the proceeds to finance
internal trade or money-lending. The practice is widespread
and 'to gold-coast' has become a recognized expression. Thus
imported cigarettes are frequently gold-coasted; they are
bought from the firms at £130 a case, immediately resold at

£128 or £129 and the funds so received are used as short-term capital. It is frequently possible to lend the money at a rate of interest of 6*d.* in the pound from market day to market day, which in Yoruba country is generally every fifth day. At even much lower rates than this the gold-coaster can recover his loss and make a substantial profit, as he is expected to settle his account with the firm only at the end of the month. By this process European capital is used for financing trade in local foodstuffs and in the petty retailing of imported merchandise.

With the rapid but very uneven expansion of activity in recent years the low level of capital has made itself increasingly felt. One outward manifestation is the very high rate of interest paid even by sound and indeed financially strong African enterprises for loans of all kinds. In Lagos respectable money-lending institutions can obtain 12–18 per cent on first-class mortgages on unencumbered property, the sale of which in Lagos is not subject to the same restrictions as it is elsewhere. The real return on capital under suitable management in internal trade and transport is so high that borrowers can afford to pay these high rates, while the meagre supply of capital forces them to do so.

This insistent demand for credit is a sign not only of the poverty and improvidence of the local population, but also of the high real return to be obtained locally from the use of capital when directed with a small measure of skill and competence. This raises the obvious question why more foreign capital has not been attracted by the favourable rates of return.

Of course large amounts of capital have been invested in West Africa, and this process has played a major part in the development of these colonies. Part of this capital was imported and part was accumulated by non-Africans who saved part of the incomes they created. Nevertheless, certain obstacles have impeded a heavier inflow of capital. Though the low level of local capital leads to attractive rates of return, it also increases the difficulties of the foreign firm establishing itself in West Africa. The initial capital requirements and risks are high, particularly in view of the necessity of granting advances to African intermediaries, of establishing business contacts and of setting up premises and stores up-country, where capital is turned over slowly. In recent years the difficulties have been

increased by the high cost of buildings and the presence of
various shortages and controls, which again raise capital
requirements. The severe restrictions upon the immigration of
non-Africans (especially Levantines) and the refusal to alienate
land to them act as important deterrents to the inflow and
internal creation of capital. Immigration policy has been a
particularly serious obstacle. These and other difficulties of
entry provide some security for firms already established, and
reduce the pressure on them to seek out and exhaust all profitable opportunities, particularly those provided by medium-
and small-scale activities. This in turn also retards the influx,
growth and application of capital.

Lack of Employment

In West Africa, as in many other comparatively undeveloped
countries, there is widespread involuntary unemployment of
unskilled or poorly skilled manual and clerical workers resulting
from lack of resources, and especially capital, to set it to work.
Unskilled or poorly skilled labour is unemployed owing to lack
of other factors of production to co-operate with it in the
productive process. The term 'unemployment' is now generally
used to refer to another type of unemployment, that is, unemployment of labour in industrialized societies resulting not so
much from lack of co-operating factors of production as from
deficiency of aggregate demand and from various other
influences discouraging investment and enterprise. This study
is concerned only with the unemployment which results from
lack of resources.[1]

Although its presence in West Africa is occasionally denied,

[1] Although it is an aspect of the low level of co-operant factors of production, this type of unemployment and under-employment in under-developed
countries is aggravated by the comparatively high rates (high by comparison
with what can be earned in other occupations) at which wages for hired
labour are maintained in certain occupations in these countries. It is a
striking feature of many under-developed countries that money wages are
maintained at high levels by institutional arrangements (such as international pressure, governmental measures or trade union action), while
large numbers are seeking but unable to find work. This discourages the
growth of activities relying on hired labour and encourages (or actually
enforces on a certain section of the population) the pursuit of activities which
do not use hired labour, or in which these high wages are not enforced,
notably self-employment in agriculture, petty trading and domestic service.

there can be no doubt of the prevalence of unemployment in Nigeria, in Sierra Leone and in parts of the Gold Coast. There is no dearth of general evidence. Notices of 'no vacancies' are ubiquitous. A constant stream of applications for employment reaches the mercantile firms, and this increases several times over when it becomes known that a definite vacancy has occurred or that an extension of activities can be expected. The inclination to trade even when only a few pence a day can be earned, the large internal migrations in both Nigeria and the Gold Coast (which are only partly seasonal), the frequent applications addressed to European visitors by their servants to find employment for friends and relatives and the short notice at which these applicants make their appearance—all these point in the same direction and suggest a widespread lack of opportunities for unskilled or poorly skilled people seeking employment at current wages.

I inquired specifically into this question, partly because of its great importance and serious implications for policy, and partly because its existence has been denied. Here are a few random examples of the results. I asked the manager of the tobacco factory of the Nigerian Tobacco Company (a subsidiary of the British-American Tobacco Company) in Ibadan whether he could expand his labour force without raising wages if he wished to do so. He replied that his only problem would be to control the mob of applicants. Very much the same opinion was expressed by the Kano district agent of the firm of John Holt and Company in respect of their tannery. In December 1949 a firm of produce buyers in Kano dismissed two clerks and within two days received between fifty and sixty applications for the posts without having publicized the vacancies. The same firm proposed to erect a groundnut crushing plant. By June 1950 machinery had not yet been installed; but without having advertised a vacancy it had already received about seven hundred letters asking for employment. The larger commercial firms in Kano usually receive about five or six written applications daily for employment, and in the ground-nut season this might rise to twenty or more a day. The figures of applications are much larger in the south. I did not think it necessary to collect further detailed information, though I learnt that the European-owned brewery and the recently established manufacturers of stationery constantly receive shoals of applications for employment.[1]

Some of these applications are duplications, the same person applying for several posts; others presumably come from people already employed who want to improve their position; but this does not affect the general picture. Similarly, it is not immediately relevant how far these offers of labour are the result of lack of opportunity, and how far they reflect dissatisfaction with the emptiness of life in the bush. In Nigeria and probably in the Northern Territories of the Gold Coast the former is certainly a major factor. The Ibo are greatly attached to their country and would not migrate to distant parts if they had opportunities in their native provinces.

The general lack of employment opportunities is not caused everywhere by the absence or shortage of the same type of resources. In the Eastern Provinces of Nigeria there is an insufficiency of suitable land; in northern Nigeria there is ample land but a dearth of capital and of local technical and clerical skill. Not only are physical resources unequally distributed throughout these territories, but the aptitudes of the different sections of the population differ markedly. In Nigeria the southerners have the advantage in enterprise, thrift, resourcefulness, literacy and ability to perceive economic opportunity; the northerners display greater sense of discipline, endurance and perhaps greater discrimination in the choice or acceptance of leaders. Whatever may be the reasons for these differences they are certain to persist for years and they may even become more pronounced.

This uneven scarcity of suitable productive agents has important corollaries. When internal trade and migration are restricted these scarcities are thereby made more acute and the lack of employment becomes more severe. When the activities of southern clerks and traders are openly or covertly restricted in northern Nigeria, the growth of employment, the formation of capital and the general development of that area are retarded for want of skill and enterprise, while the under-

[1] This unemployment has not, of course, been caused by economic advance in West Africa, but it has been brought into the open by it. In a purely subsistence economy idleness tends to be regarded as part of the nature of things.

employment and overcrowding in the south are also aggravated.

There is a strong tendency towards fragmentation in the West African colonies, both in Nigeria and in the Gold Coast. It is partly the result of xenophobia and partly the result of clamour by interested parties. There is an increasing number of restrictions on the movement and employment of people and on the movement of commodities. Fragmentation of West African economies is certain to aggravate the lack of employment.

The controversial matter of immigration policy is also relevant to the lack of employment. The low level of capital and of technical and administrative skill can only be rectified satisfactorily at present by the introduction of foreign capital and personnel, both European (and possibly American) and Levantine. The former can supply a larger volume of capital and a higher level of skill; the latter can subsist at a much lower cost and on a lower turnover, and they can thus widen the market in the remote areas in which the former cannot operate. Immigrant capital and personnel are likely to be seen in a different light when it is realized that they provide work for the unemployed.

The political implications of this want of employment are far-reaching. The semi-literate or barely literate unemployed are the most inflammable political material. They have nothing to lose in a general disorder, either in the way of property or of employment. They are apt to be undiscriminating as well as poor. Those who are literate have much time available for the reading of inflammatory literature, spelling it out slowly. These are considerations of the greatest importance for official policy covering *inter alia* the framing and administration of immigration policy and the control of internal trade and migration.

10. The slave-trade treaties

K. ONWUKA DIKE *Trade and Politics in the Niger Delta* Clarendon Press, Oxford 1956; pages 81–7, 90–6

The slave-trade treaties, which are more or less well known, were initiated by Britain in 1810 and invariably embodied coercive clauses designed to bring other nations into line with her policy of suppression. An essential feature of these treaties was the right of search conceded to the naval squadron. They were first concluded with Portugal and were later 'multiplied with every power in Europe having a maritime flag; with every power in the Americas, except the United States and one or two others'. Nor were the treaties confined to European nations. Britain had applied them with some success to the suppression of the East African slave trade. In 1817 Radama, king of eastern Madagascar, concluded a slave-trade treaty with Britain and in return for his undertaking to put an end to the traffic the British Government promised to pay him a subsidy of 10,000 dollars a year for three years. Similar treaties were signed with the Imam of Muscat and in 1822 with Seyyid Said, Sultan of Zanzibar. In the late thirties the British Government decided in face of opposition from some quarters to extend the slave-trade treaties to the West African states. Laird, a bitter opponent of these agreements, contended that experience had shown them to be grossly ineffective. Subsidies paid to European nations, such as Portugal and Spain, which amounted to several million pounds, were largely wasted bribes, for in spite of them the trade continued with 'unabated vigour'. He ridiculed the decision to enter into these treaties with African chiefs, declaring: 'The attempt to make Christian Powers adhere to them having failed, seemed to be taken as the strongest proof that Pagan ones would strictly comply with the most stringent conditions of a Slave-Trade treaty.'

There was much justification for the scepticism of the critics. In the eighteenth century, when the trade was legal for all nations, the export was between 70,000 and 80,000 a year. In the nineteenth century, when nearly all the great powers (including Britain and America) had condemned the traffic, the annual export had risen to 135,000. These figures may represent little more than official estimates, but the increase in the nineteenth century was an undoubted fact. In the thirties and forties Cuba and Brazil were the biggest markets; even after the United States had abolished the trade, slavery continued in the southern states and the demand for Negroes increased with the rise of cotton cultivation. It has been estimated that between 1808 and 1860 300,000 slaves were imported into the

U.S.A. In spite of the complicated bi-lateral treaties negotiated between Britain and foreign nations, treaties which filled some 1,529 volumes, little check was put on the traffic. Laird marshalled an impressive array of figures to support his case. He showed that in 1815 Great Britain paid £300,000 for the right to seize Portuguese vessels engaged in the trade, and in the same year 'gave up to Portugal her £600,000 for another treaty' designed to end the Portuguese slave trade. In 1817 a third treaty established the Mixed Commission Courts and the Preventive Squadron. 'In 1823 another treaty was brought forth' and by 1839 Britain had concluded five slave-trade treaties with Portugal. In spite of these solemn agreements, Laird argued, the slave trade of Portugal increased from 25,000 in 1807 to 56,000 in 1822:

and in 1839, 48 vessels, under the Portuguese flag [out of a total of 61 slave vessels] were condemned at Sierra Leone. With Spain we commenced [treaty-making] in 1808; but did nothing until 1814, when we offered the Spanish Government a bribe of £800,000 to abolish the trade. . . . Having more honesty than the Portuguese, the Spaniards refused, and . . . the money was saved. . . . In 1815, we got her to sign, with other powers at the Congress of Vienna, a declaration 'that the slave-trade is repugnant to the principles of humanity and universal morality.' In 1817, another treaty was got on our paying £400,000 for it; and in 1822 a third; yet 'the sea swarmed with slave-ships, carrying on the slave-trade under the flag of Spain'.

Viewed in retrospect the situation which faced statesmen was more complex than the critics would allow. So far as Britain was concerned the West African states were foreign territories. She had no other means of bringing them into line with her policy of suppression. The treaties concluded with the African chiefs therefore embodied clauses stipulating that non-observance of the terms justified Britain in taking reprisals against the offending states. These served more as a cover for the employment of force which suppression tactics necessitated than as a guarantee that the treaties would be observed in their entirety by either Britain or the Delta states. We have shown that Nicolls's earlier attempts at treaty-making along these lines failed because he lacked government support. It was not till 1838 that the authorities were converted to his viewpoint and 'were moved to instruct the Naval Officers on the Coast of Africa to endeavour to dispose the Native Chiefs to enter into treaties' for the abolition of the slave trade.

The first of these agreements was concluded with Bonny on 11 March 1839. 'After a long palaver', Bonny agreed to abolish the trade 'provided they should obtain from the British Government, for five years, an annual present of the value of 2,000 dollars', which they stated was not more than half the revenue which they derived from the export slave trade. This treaty was negotiated and concluded by Craigie on behalf of the British Government. Admiral Elliot wrote to Wood, Secretary of the Admiralty, saying that 'in the hope that the goods alluded to [i.e. the first year's subsidy] may be sent out, I have directed the Senior Officer in the West Coast of Africa to take an early opportunity of acquainting the King and Chiefs of Bonny with the intention of H.M. Government'. No payment, however, was made throughout the first twelve months of the treaty and King Pepple the following year openly carried on the slave trade.

At this point Elliot was succeeded by Commander Tucker, who visited Bonny in September 1840 and reported that a 'constant supply of slaves are sent by canoe through the creeks to the rivers Nun and Brass for shipment. Three hundred and sixty having been taken by a Spaniard previous to my arrival in the River.' He quoted King Pepple as saying that it was impossible 'for him to put a stop to his subjects trading in slaves', and cited as evidence that the old trade was actively prosecuted the fact that 'dollars and doubloons are plentiful in Bonny which is always the case after the arrival of a slaver in the Nun or Brass River, as most of the slaves shipped off from there are purchased at Bonny'. Pepple admitted that between 1839 and 1840 he exported 2,000 slaves and would continue to do so through the Brass creek, where in 1841 he sold 'a great number' to Don Pablo.

To Tucker's constant accusation that Bonny still carried on the slave trade, Pepple could argue that she was free to do so until Britain ratified the treaty of 1839 and paid the subsidies as arranged. This was also the view of the Foreign Secretary, Lord Palmerston, whose protest on naval vacillation on this subject of honouring the 1839 treaty with Bonny called forth the long, but in parts inaccurate, 'Memorandum on Negotiations with the Chiefs of Bonny, April 7th, 1841'. It was his pressure and insistence that led the Admiralty to enter into a new treaty with Bonny the same year.

Lord Palmerston, unlike the Treasury and the Admiralty, held the view that since Britain had authorized these treaties to be negotiated, she was in duty bound to honour her part of the contract. On 31 March 1841 'Palmerston was of the opinion that the presents' to the Delta chiefs 'ought to be sent according to stipulation and should be discontinued in future, if the African chiefs do not keep their engagements'. That was precisely the point. It was no use complaining that the African chiefs still carried on the slave trade when Britain refused to ratify treaties for its abolition and withheld subsidies which alone could make those treaties effective. The truth was that on the British side, Palmerston excepted, few people believed that the treaties could ever be effectively enforced. The Treasury thought it 'inexpedient that any stipulation for the presents should be inserted in the treaty' and were averse to giving subsidies where the slave trade had not been 'actually prohibited'.

In Old Calabar and the Cameroons, where the slave trade was no longer important, Britain, as we shall see, made treaties and honoured them. But however difficult the position at Bonny she had no justification for concluding agreements which were no sooner signed than they were repudiated. The confusion at Bonny serves to illustrate the lack of co-ordination between the government departments. Tucker, who was ordered to negotiate the 1841 treaty, was himself convinced that it would not work as the trade was too profitable to be given up easily by the Bonny people. He was certain that they would use the annual subsidy, if paid, for prosecuting the trade with more vigour rather than for its suppression, and pointed out that means of evading the agreement by Bonny were numerous. He recalled the debt of gratitude which the king owed to Britain: 'Cragie in 1837 firmly established King Pepple on his throne' and the king had since received nearly £4,000 a year by way of tonnage duty levied on British ships. He therefore saw little reason why more subsidies should be paid to the king. In point of fact King Pepple and his chiefs were in no mood for more treaties. Between 1836 and 1839 they had been

called upon to sign four treaties—the one of 1837 excepted—
and none of these had been ratified or honoured. Even the 1837
agreement had not been observed by the white traders in the
river. The king had come to view the business of treaty-making
with disgust and angrily observed to an English merchant:
'One white man come, and make book [treaty] and another
white man come tomorrow and break it; white man be fool,
best treaty is in my head.'

When, therefore, Commander Tucker arrived at Bonny for
another treaty in 1841, his reception was cold. But 'after a great
deal of trouble' he obtained the signature of the king and chiefs
to an agreement for the abolition of the foreign slave trade.
The difference between this treaty and that of 1839 was that
whereas in the latter the subsidy was 2,000 dollars a year for
five years, in the new treaty Bonny demanded and got 10,000
dollars a year for five years. 'I beg to inform your Lordship',
wrote Tucker, 'that the King considered the treaty ratified, and
expected the first payment will be sent to him immediately on
receipt of this.' Pepple would not have signed another treaty
had not Tucker assured him that the treaty was ratified as soon
as it was signed.

But in spite of these precautions the 1841 treaty went the way
of its predecessors. Palmerston, who showed great interest and
sympathy for the suppression movement, had been replaced by
the Earl of Aberdeen, who complained that the new treaty
'differed widely from those proposed in Lord Palmerston's letter
of April 8th, and are not such as should meet with the concurrence of H.M. Government'. He protested against the
greatly increased subsidy and the suggestion that payment be
made, not as originally stipulated, in goods, but in money, 'and
indeed a bill has already been drawn upon Her Majesty's
Treasury [by King Pepple] for the 10,000 dollars in question'.
He urged the Navy to lose no time in informing the Bonny
chiefs of H.M. Government's sentiments, and inducing them to
accept the old treaty of 1839.

The period of treaty-making at Bonny revealed a complete
lack of policy behind British activities towards the Delta states.
Naval officers did their best, but they were birds of passage,
dependent for their advice on Liverpool supercargoes trading
to these parts. Even the traders were dissatisfied with inter-

mittent and confused interference that did no one any good. Captain Midgley, a Liverpool merchant at Bonny, told a parliamentary select committee in 1842 that these treaties were of great importance to trade provided they were honoured. Unless the British were ready to 'act up to' them

with more energy than they have done they had better keep out of the River [Bonny] altogether. First comes a Captain and makes a treaty, and then another comes and says, 'This treaty shall be null and void', and he tears it up. I allude particularly to Bonny. I piloted one vessel up and was party to a treaty, and in the course of a month or two afterwards, another comes and says, 'I have orders from the Admiralty that this treaty shall be null and void'.

Britain's difficulties in pursuing a consistent and well-conceived colonial policy at this time were enormous, nor were they confined to the West African states. In the working out of a policy many government departments were involved besides the Foreign Office. A parallel can be cited in the difficulties experienced by Sir James Stephen and the Colonial Office in having to deal with the Treasury and the War Office on colonial questions. Hence the situation in the Delta was part of the same problem—the out-dated, clumsy machinery of government in Britain which made swift consistent action so difficult. Again throughout the nineteenth century the misunderstanding of the terms of treaties was a common feature of Afro-European relations. This is particularly true of the partition period in the eighties and nineties. Not only were the differing conceptions of 'sovereignty', 'suzerainty', and 'protection' frequent sources of conflict between the two peoples, but such a purely European term as 'ratification' was alien to the traditional diplomatic practice of West Africans. King Pepple could never understand why a treaty must first be ratified before it could become binding on the contracting parties.

Meanwhile treaty-making after the pattern of that in Bonny had spread to the smaller states of the Delta. On the 18 and 19 September 1840 Lieutenant Pollard of H.M.S. *Buzzard* concluded a commercial agreement with the chiefs of the Cameroons. Later a slave-trade treaty was signed when chiefs Aqua and Bell of that place promised that if Britain granted them annual subsidies 'they will not allow their people, nor will they themselves trade for slaves'. In January 1842 this treaty was ratified and the first annual subsidy paid. Here, as in Bonny, the treaties entered into were of two kinds.

The first was designed to protect British property in the rivers and to promote the growth of legitimate commerce. The other was specifically entered into with the object of abolishing the slave trade. Thus at Old Calabar in 1841, although the leading chief, Eyamba, signed a 'Treaty of Amity and Commerce' with the British, he would not conclude any agreement for the suppression of the export slave trade, for, 'although the slave trade there is of no importance', it still paid them to indulge in what little there might be of it. In 1842, however, both chiefs Eyamba and Eyo—rulers of the two leading trading towns of Old Calabar, Duke Town and Creek Town—signed a treaty abolishing the slave trade in return for 2,000 dollars subsidy for five years. Both the senior officer Captain Foote and Lieutenant Raymond who concluded the treaty spoke highly of their friendship, co-operation, and desire for legitimate trade. In every way Old Calabar was a striking contrast to Bonny. The people and their chiefs were, according to Foote, 'more disposed to be civilised here than at any other place I have yet been to'.

The treaty was ratified and the subsidy paid in December 1843. A similar agreement was reached with Bimbia (Cameroons), the only difference being that the subsidy was reduced to 1,200 dollars. City-states like New Calabar and Brass, which were situated away from the sea and so inaccessible to warships, were unaffected until the establishment of the Consulate in the fifties. . . .

The change from enthusiastic defence of British interests to one of indifference by the Navy was defended in a dispatch to the Admiralty by the Commodore in charge of the African Station, Sir Charles Hotham, in 1847. His statement of policy was emphatic in its opposition to naval interference in the Delta. Sir Charles must have been unaware of the old policy of active intervention, judging from his statement that the 'policy of my predecessors has always been never to interfere in commercial matters'. Nevertheless, his reasons for wanting to abstain were sound. Like King Pepple he tracked down the sore point of Anglo-African relations to the 'trust' or credit system

By a clever manipulation of this system the British merchants derived fabulous profits, yet the disorder and dishonesty which accompanied it made for an unsettled and corrupt community. That was why the king demanded its abolition in 1838 and the white traders, aided by the Navy, opposed it to a man.

'The trade of Africa', declared Sir Charles, 'is formed on credit', and until the basis of that trade was altered it was little use trying to mediate between Africans and Europeans. Even in the imperfect state of trade 'the ignorant black adheres to all the stipulations, and performs his part creditably and well: there may be exceptions, but, on the whole, their behaviour will stand a favourable comparison with that of more civilized nations'. He put the blame for the disorders squarely on the shoulders of the white traders and condemned any attempt to use the warships in defence of those who were in the wrong. 'To lead the [British] merchants to believe that their specula-tions would be backed by military power' was a measure he would not support.

To a petition from Bonny merchants asking for protection, Hotham replied that he was prepared to protect British lives and property where right and necessary, but if by protection they meant 'influence, either moral or physical, to recover your debts, I am bound to tell you that it will be denied. To adopt such a course might benefit the owners of ships at present in Bonny, but would for ever affect the interests of those who will succeed you, and sap the foundations of legitimate trade.' He might have painted a too favourable picture of the Delta middleman, and although a good deal of the upheavals could be traced to quarrels over the credit system yet there was also much discontent over Britain's unwillingness to honour the treaties.

Palmerston, now back in office, could not be expected to share Hotham's view considering the volume of letters and petitions which reached him from British merchants and owners of ships at Bonny, from the African Association of Liver-pool, and others with interests in the Delta trade. Eleven supercargoes had petitioned early in 1847 stating that they were 'under a thorough conviction of the extreme insecurity of both life and property' in the river. They asked that their rights and privileges 'as subjects of Her Britannic Majesty may be enforced by the only power we consider ourselves entitled to call upon, namely, "Her Britannic Majesty's Vessels of War", cruising upon this part of the coast'. In face of the wide publicity which the Bonny events received in Britain, Lord Palmerston decided to intervene.

A Board of Trade inquiry satisfied him that the amount of property at stake was considerable. Palmerston therefore informed the Admiralty 'that Sir Charles Hotham ought to be instructed to compel King Pepple and the Chiefs of Bonny, by force, if necessary, to respect the lives and property of Her Majesty's subjects, and that the Commodore will be justified in enforcing the payment of debts due to British Subjects'. On receipt of this instruction Hotham did not fail to point out that if it was made known to the merchants at Bonny, indiscriminate giving of 'trust' would be the result, making the task of recovering debts doubly difficult. Palmerston concurred and left much to the discretion of the commodore. Sir Charles entrusted the mission to one of his subordinates, Commander Birch, an officer who shared Palmerston's enthusiasm for action. One of his first acts was to put an end to the terrorism inspired by Awanta against British persons and property, a movement which had led to the loss of many lives in the river. King Pepple was powerless to intervene, as according to the laws of the country the High Priest was a sacred person and therefore above the law. Pepple explained that if he touched the person of Awanta, his action would bring disaster to the kingdom: such was the current belief. He indicated that the British would be given permission to capture and take him away if they so desired. Birch, who knew that Awanta's capture was necessary for the safety of the British traders, did not scruple to use force to secure his arrest, and although his act was not openly condemned by Hotham the commodore nevertheless warned against imprudent acts which might antagonize the natives and injure future relations.

With Awanta imprisoned on board a man-of-war, the Foreign Office soon discovered that all sorts of legal tangle would be involved in his trial as he was not a British subject. Palmerston decided to avoid these difficulties by sending him 'to Norfolk Island, both as a punishment for his crimes and as a security against repeating the offence'. But Lord Grey of the

Colonial Office had a different idea. He was 'inclined to direct the Commodore to set this murdering High Priest on shore somewhere on the Coast of Africa as far as possible from the Bonny . . . leaving him to take his chance'. With the execution of this order Awanta disappeared from Bonny and nothing further was heard of him.

There is little doubt that the Awanta terrorists were religious fanatics who fought to rid the country of the foreigners. The king secretly exploited this emotion to direct one wing of his anti-British measures and to lead his attack on New Calabar, the only city-state that defied Bonny supremacy in the eastern Delta. It had always been the policy of the Pepples to conquer and annex New Calabar. Thus the terrorist activities were concentrated on the sixteen-mile stretch of river linking New Calabar with Bonny, depriving the British of access to their trade and property there, and denying the New Calabar Africans of their only means of livelihood, which consisted in trade with the Europeans. It was on this river that most of the murders were committed and the 'masked men' operated, boarding boats and destroying property.

To put an end to these attacks Birch insisted on the inclusion, in the 1848 treaty, of a guarantee by Bonny 'to afford every protection in our power to the persons and property of British subjects trading in the River', and 'to send two trusty men, our subjects, in each boat trading between River Bonny and New Calabar for the purpose of guarding the said boats from attacks made on them by our people, but without our knowledge or approbation'. It was also stipulated that trading boats should not leave Bonny for New Calabar or vice versa, except by daylight, and that masters of British oil ships were at liberty to accept or reject the protection of Bonny guards, but that Bonny could not be held responsible for acts of piracy and murder incurred by ships without guards unless incontrovertible evidence of the identity of the attackers could be produced. This commercial treaty was followed by the slave-trade treaty of 1848 in which King Pepple was induced to accept the 2,000 dollars subsidy of 1839 in place of the 10,000 dollars of 1841.

During his mission to Bonny and throughout the negotiations which led to the conclusion of the 1848 agreements, Birch pointed out that King Pepple 'more than once referred to the bad faith the English Government had kept with him, and at last accused it of defrauding him of 50,000 dollars', the amount of compensation agreed to be paid to him by the treaty of 1841. The king 'declared most solemnly Captain Tucker informed him that immediately the Treaty was signed by him . . . it was in full force, never explaining that it had first to be ratified by our Government'.

The lessons learnt from these upheavals were not lost, and although the events described belong to Delta history their influence on British foreign policy had a West African significance. Palmerston came to realize that the Government had no clear policy towards the Delta states and that the amount of British property involved was large enough to warrant the appointment of a resident official, since the intermittent 'gunboat rule' provided by officers of the naval squadron was clearly inadequate. That this need was urgent can be seen from the fact that between 1844 and 1849, the date of Palmerston's appointment of the first British Consul to the Bights of Benin and Biafra, the naval authorities had themselves employed on nine different occasions the services of an English merchant, John Beecroft, who had unrivalled experience of local affairs, to aid them in their political work. In May 1844 Beecroft accompanied Lieutenant Blount to Old Calabar to ratify the treaty made with that city-state. In June of the same year he followed Commander Brisbane to Bimbia on a political mission to the chief of that place. During 1845 he was employed on three occasions, first with Commander Gooch 'to visit the Chiefs of Calabar, Bimbia, Cameroons to see that they were fulfilling the treaties they had entered into for the suppression of the Slave Trade'. On the second occasion, 'in consequence of the report that the Chiefs of Bimbia were carrying on the Slave Trade an expedition composed of H.M. Frigate *Actaeon*, and Her Majesty's Steam Vessels *Hydra* and *Styx* were despatched there, at the request of Captain Mansell, I accompanied him to investigate charges which were proved groundless'. During 1847 Hotham instructed him 'to accompany Captain Mansell . . . to the mainland for the purpose of communicating and making treaties with the native chiefs', and in August of the same year he diplomatically prevented the French from concluding any treaties with Old Calabar 'having witnessed in the

River Gaboon the prejudicial effects to British Commerce of the interference of the French authorities'. For his work as a political agent John Beecroft received fees totalling £477 from the Government.

When, therefore, in 1849 Palmerston decided to appoint a consul the need for such an official was clearly overdue: there was, moreover, little doubt whom the official would be. John Beecroft had become something of an institution in the Bight of Baifra. His connexion with the Delta began in 1829 when Nicolls, Governor of Fernando Po, brought him out to take charge of the Department of Works. Beecroft stayed on after the settlement was evacuated in 1834 and was connected first with the firm of Messrs. Tennant & Co., of which he was a partner, and when that business went bankrupt in 1837 he was employed by Robert Jamieson of Glasgow on various scientific explorations up the Niger in the steam vessel *Ethiope*. In 1836 he had explored the Delta above Abo and was well known to African chiefs beyond the northern Delta. Between 1841 and 1843, when the controversy over the ill-fated Niger expedition brought the Delta and the Niger valley to the notice of Europe, Spain was careful to reassert her sovereignty over Fernando Po, and it is a measure of Beecroft's influence and ability that Spain appointed him Governor of the island. Among Africans his reputation was great and it was mainly owing to his friendship with the chiefs of Old Calabar that that city-state remained consistently pro-British throughout the thirties and forties. On the whole, then, the first Consul was a fortunate appointment. Throughout the Delta, wrote a contemporary, 'he is well-known, highly respected, and possesses influence such as no man on the coast has ever obtained'.

On 30 June 1849 Beecroft was officially appointed Her Britannic Majesty's Consul for the Bights of Benin and Biafra, an area covering not only the Niger Delta and Lagos, but also the kingdom of Dahomey. It is interesting to note that the following paragraph which denied any territorial ambitions on the part of Great Britain in making this appointment was crossed out in the original draft in Palmerston's own hand: 'H.M.'s Government, in establishing this Consulate in the Bights of Benin and Biafra, have no intention to seek to gain possession, either by purchase or otherwise, of any portion of the African continent in those parts, nor of any neighbouring Islands.' During this period Palmerston was the only Foreign Secretary who appeared to have an intelligent grasp of the meaning of events in the Bights of Benin and Biafra. He was convinced that with the growth of equitable traffic British interference could no longer be delayed. It was he who had attempted to purchase Fernando Po after its abandonment in 1834, had urged the payment of slave-trade subsidies to Bonny, and two years after making his appointment of the first Consul to the Bights in 1849 had ordered the occupation of Lagos.

His purpose in pressing for the payment of slave-trade subsidies was to make effective treaties which alone could give legality to energetic measures pursued towards the African states. He stood for action in this area where a semblance of non-interference could no longer be maintained. Between the months of February and May 1850 more than half a dozen new major projects for furthering British political and economic interests in West Africa were brought to the notice of the Consul with instructions to aid them actively. On 12 February Beecroft was instructed to lead a mission to Dahomey to induce its powerful potentate to establish 'commercial relations with the British Government and abolish the slave trade'. On the 25th of the same month he was directed to forward a report on the recently founded republic of Liberia, giving details of its population, the extent of its authority, and the state of its agriculture and commerce. In another dispatch of the same date, Lord Palmerston proposed that he undertake a mission to Abeokuta, the chief city of the Egbas (50,000 inhabitants) which was connected by the River Ogu to Lagos. 'The establishment of commercial relations with the Interior of Africa through the Yoruba Tribe would materially contribute to the suppression of the slave trade', and if he could make navigation of the Ogu 'free and safe' a vital link between the sea and hinterland would be forged.

Three months later Palmerston wrote to Beecroft.

I have to inform you that several eminent Mercantile and Manufacturing firms in this country have combined for the purpose of testing by practical experiment the possibility of procuring a supply of cotton from the West Coast of Africa and that the parties in question have purchased two vessels, the *Firefly* and *Georgiana*, and are about to

send them out from Liverpool. . . . I have to instruct you to give
every assistance in your power to this Expedition, and to promote,
by exerting your influence with the King of Dahomey and other
Native Chiefs, the object which it has in view.

These instances serve to illustrate the responsibilities thrown
on the Consul and the Palmerstonian attitude to West African
affairs which cannot be described as that of an absent-minded
Minister, even as early as 1850. The Foreign Secretary was
prepared to face to the full the implications of legitimate commerce. His support of missions to establish direct trade contact
with the interior was proof that he saw the Niger Delta in true
perspective—as the key that would open the door to West
African trade.

11. Sources of the nineteenth-century Atlantic slave trade

PHILIP D. CURTIN and JAN VANSINA *Journal of African
History* Vol. 5, No. 2, 1964 Cambridge University Press;
pages 185–91

The Atlantic slave trade was the most important link between
Africa and other continents for at least two full centuries from
1650 to 1850, yet relatively little is known about the sources of
the trade, its commercial organization within Africa, or the
overall consequence for African societies. Estimates of the
number of slaves exported each year or decade are mainly
educated guesses. For certain periods it is relatively easy to
determine the number of slaves carried by the ships of one or
other of the European maritime powers, but many different
nations participated in the trade. Statistical information is
widely scattered in a dozen different archives, and historical
demographers have not yet attempted a systematic exploration
of these diffuse sources of information. The national origins of
slaves have also been studied at the receiving end, within the
national context of a single American country. While this kind

of investigation is important for the history of Mexico or Brazil, no country in America received a true sample of all slaves entering the trade. The sources of the trade were, indeed, subject to change from time to time, and the distribution of the slaves in America shifted constantly in response to all kinds of political and economic changes in Europe and in the Americas themselves.

The British attempt to suppress the slave trade of the early nineteenth century, however, produced data about the European slave trade as a whole. When the British attempted to capture slavers at sea, they also captured the slaves in transit. From 1808 to 1842, the great majority of these recaptives, or 'liberated Africans', as they were usually called at the time, were landed and settled in Sierra Leone.[1] To the degree that the Royal Navy captured a random sample of slaves entering the trade, the national origins of the population of Sierra Leone in the 1840s will reflect the range of national origins for the Atlantic slave trade as a whole.

Fortunately there are some excellent qualitative data about origins of the Sierra Leone population, and some quantitative data as well. These are contained in two separate surveys of the later 1840s. By far the most detailed was the work of Sigismund Wilhelm Koelle, who spent five years (December 1847 to February 1853) in Sierra Leone as a linguist employed by the Church Missionary Society. One aspect of his research, mainly carried out in 1849, was the collection of sample vocabularies of African languages spoken by the liberated Africans and other visitors to the colony. In all, he collected some 160 languages,

---

[1] Statistics about the liberated Africans are notably unreliable. (See discussion by R. R. Kuczynski, *Demographic Survey of the British Colonial Empire. Volume I, West Africa* (London, 1948), 95–150.) The Navy's figures for slaves recaptured and landed alive between 1810 and 1840 indicate a total of 94,703. The colonial statistics for the numbers liberated in Sierra Leone over the same period show 70,809. (C. Lloyd, *The Navy and the Slave Trade* (London, 1849), 275–6; *Parliamentary Papers* (1842), xii (551), 248–9.) The British West Indian colonies received a total of 3,212. (G. W. Roberts, 'Immigration of Africans into the British Caribbean', *Population Studies*, VII (1953–4), 235–63, 259.) Some (but probably not a majority) of the remaining 20,000 were also landed elsewhere. Slaves landed from the slave ships were usually in very bad health; the death rate between landing and liberation through action of the courts was normally very high.

occasionally with a number of dialectical variants. These were ultimately published in the great *Polyglotta Africana*. The value of the work is more than linguistic. Since he tried to make his survey as exhaustive as possible, his list of languages represents very nearly all of those spoken by the liberated Africans in Sierra Leone. Koelle also kept very careful notes about his informants, giving the name, the country of origin, the date of departure from that country, and the number of each informant's fellow countrymen present in the colony.

The second survey was the Sierra Leone census of 1848, which included data on 'tribal origins' for Freetown and vicinity. The census's 'tribal' categories were not the same as those of Koelle, but the enumeration fills the most important gap in Koelle's quantitative data. Koelle's informants could report the numbers of their fellow countrymen accurately enough when they were very few, but they could not supply quantitative data about the very large groups, like the Yoruba or Ibo. Thus, while Koelle gives a list of groups present in Sierra Leone, and reasonably accurate statistics about the size of the smaller groups, the census figures give the broader picture of regional origins. The two together thus present a reasonably full and complementary picture.

While the two surveys together reveal the broad patterns of the nineteenth-century slave trade, they have certain limitations. First of all, the Sierra Leone population of 1848–9 was not completely representative of the liberated Africans as a whole. About three-quarters of all slaves recaptured by British ships between 1808 and 1840 were landed in Sierra Leone. Thereafter, about half were taken to the West Indies instead.[1] Furthermore, the surveys conducted at the end of three decades necessarily contain an age bias and an emigration bias. That is, they will certainly under-represent the older people among those captured early in the century. They will also

[1] The Navy's figure for recaptives landed alive between 1840 and 1849 is 41,222. The number of recaptives who immigrated to the British West Indian colonies over this period was 23,206. (Lloyd, *The Navy and the Slave Trade*, 275–6; Roberts, 'Immigration of Africans', 259.) Other evidence also indicates that about half of the recaptives landed in Sierra Leone after 1840 were induced to emigrate to the Caribbean. (Kuczynski, *Demographic Survey*, p. 141.)

under-represent groups from the hinterland of Sierra Leone or other coastal regions to which it was relatively easy to return.

The distances these liberated Africans could travel are sometimes surprising. Koelle's Wolof informant makes it clear that virtually all of the Wolof in Sierra Leone returned to Senegal. Some of the Yoruba recaptives returned by sea to Badagri and Lagos during the 1840s, and more were to follow. Discrepancies between the number of liberated Africans landed in the colony and the total colonial population are probably accounted for by emigration of this kind. By 1841, 70,000 recaptives had been landed, while the total population of Sierra Leone was only 37,000.

A second weakness in the data comes from the fact that the Navy patrolled some parts of the coast more frequently than others. It concentrated on West Africa, from the Gambia to the Cameroons. The sample of recaptives from this region is therefore the most nearly representative of Africans entering the trade. Even for this region, however, the operations of the cruisers would not have produced a perfectly random sample. Freetown was the most important British base in tropical Africa between 1808 and 1827. During this period, cruisers patrolled most frequently along the 'Windward Coast' on either side of Sierra Leone. Then, from 1827 to 1832, the British established a base at Fernando Po, and even after this base was withdrawn they used Fernando Po informally and patrolled more frequently in the Bights of Benin and Biafra. The sample may therefore be expected to represent the western section of the coast more accurately from 1810 to the mid-1820s, and the eastern section from the mid-1820s onward.

The sample may also be biased by the legal niceties of the blockade. French and American ships could not be captured legally by British cruisers, though they were occasionally captured by the naval patrols of their own nationality. Illegal French slavers probably operated more frequently off the coasts of Senegal. Groups from the Senegambian interior may therefore be under-represented. Not enough is known about the geographical range of illegal, American-flag slavers to predict the possible influence of their operations.

The influence of changing blockade tactics is also difficult to assess. The number of ships on station varied from time to time, and so did the number of slaves recaptured. It was less than 500 in 1820 and more than 8,500 in 1837. Blockade tactics also varied according to coastal conditions of wind and current. Along the coast between Cape Palmas and the Cameroons the prevailing wind and current are both westerly. Ships inbound from the Americas therefore tended to follow the coastline. Once the cargo was loaded, however, they dropped south of the equator to find the south-east trades and avoid the contrary currents off the coast. The usual naval procedure until after 1839 was to wait well off shore in the hope of catching a loaded slaver making off for the south, as they all had to do if they were to reach the Americas. This tactic was forced on the Navy by the fact that the courts would not condemn slavers unless slaves were actually found on board. In 1835, however, a new treaty with Spain made it legal to capture ships equipped for the slave trade (and, for the first time, to capture Spanish ships south of the equator). The same provisions were extended to Portuguese ships by an Act of Parliament in 1839. From then onward, a close blockade was possible. Ships inbound down the coast were searched for the equipment of the slave trade, and the blockade was supplemented from time to time by raids against the shore installations of the slave traders. Of the two modes of operation, off-shore crusing was more likely to yield a random sample of slavers in the trade. The sample from the Bights of Benin and Biafra is probably more nearly representative than that of the Windward Coast hinterland. The sample from any part of the coast before 1839 will also be more accurate than that of the 1840s. By then, it was possible to make a strategic decision to clean out the slave trade from one section of coast at a time.

But these considerations apply only to West Africa. South of the equator the anti-slavery operations were quite different. The sample from southern areas is smaller (relative to their total slave trade) than the West African samples. The legal position of the Navy was not assured against the Spanish slavers south of the equator until 1835, against the Portuguese until 1839, nor against the Brazilians until 1845. Naval patrols on the Congo and Angola coast, or northward from Cape Town to the Mozambique Channel, began only in the 1840s. Most of the earlier Brazilian slave trade was therefore absent from the Sierra Leone data, and slavers bound for North America and the Caribbean were not likely to be captured until they had reached American waters. Koelle's list of Central African peoples entering the slave trade is nevertheless the most comprehensive we have for any period before the 1840s.[1]

With all these qualifications, the data still throw some light on the sources of slaves entering the trade. In Central Africa, for example, the evidence confirms what was already suspected on other grounds. Thus most of the slaves shipped from the west coast came from the immediate hinterland of Luanda—from such groups as the Ambundu—or else from the hinterland of the slave-trade ports north of the Congo mouth—from such groups as the Vili, Yombe, Boma, Nsundi and Kongo. The numbers finding their way into the trade decreased with increasing distance from the coast. The inland sources were also predictably those living along the principal trade routes into the interior. One route ran from the Congo-mouth harbours to Stanley Pool, and thence up the Congo, with a branch to the upper Ogowe and the Teke and Tsayi country. A second ran from Luanda to Cassange and Lundaland, and a third ran from Benguela to the Ovimbundu country.

The most striking pattern of the east-coast trade is the absence of slaves from the Swahili coast and its hinterland. The trade apparently divided in the vicinity of Cape Delgado, the northern segment flowing to Zanzibar, the Red Sea and the Persian Gulf, while a southern, Portuguese segment flowed both to the islands of the Indian Ocean and to the Americas. The Mozambique slaves, however, came mainly from the immediate hinterland of Inhambane, Quilimane, Mozambique and Tete, with an extension along the Yao-operated trade route from Lake Nyasa to the coast. This route, incidentally, explains why Koelle's Medo informant was also able to speak Yao.

The pattern of the West African slave trade was more complex, and it was more clearly associated with recent political events. Its most striking feature is the apparent absence of the trade from the Ivory Coast and its hinterland.

[1] Certain groups, such as the Bobangi of the upper Congo, known to have been common in the slave trade as early as the 1780s, are, however, missing.

In the 1680s this region had been considered the most profitable area in the whole slave trade of the Royal Africa Company. The causes of its neglect in the nineteenth century were mainly geographical. The long unbroken coastline was dangerous for shipping in the best of circumstances. Cargoes had to be landed across a steeply shelving beach with a heavy surf. In earlier centuries it was reckoned to be useless in time of war. Privateers and commerce raiders could all too easily sweep down a coast so nearly free of any chance for concealment. The same conditions made it dangerous for illicit slavers, and they apparently left it alone in favour of better conditions to the east or west.

The Windward Coast from the Gambia to Cape Palmas was far better suited to illegal slave trading. Hiding places were plentiful in the river mouths or in the maze of creeks and channels of Guiné. The Gambia itself, however, was now effectively closed to slavers by the British post at Bathurst, just as the Senegal was closed by the French post at Saint-Louis. Slaves were still taken in the Senegambia, but they were no longer brought down the rivers. Instead, they were carried overland to various points on the open coast. This may account for the fact that few slaves of the sample originated at any great distance from the coast, whereas in the eighteenth century a long-distance inland trade had brought slaves from the Bambara country near the upper Niger, first overland and then down the Senegal or Gambia by boat.

The real heart of the nineteenth-century slave trade lay behind the stretch of coast from Popo on the west to Douala on the east. From the later seventeenth century, the western section of this coast—the 'Slave Coast', roughly the shores of the present Togo and Dahomey Republics—had been a centre for the slave trade, drawing in prisoners of war and other people from the ill-organized segmentary societies of northern Togo and Dahomey. This westward extension of the Nigerian 'middle belt' was still well represented in Koelle's sample, but the early nineteenth century also saw the collapse of Oyo as a political entity and the rise of the Fulani domination in northern Nigeria.

Koelle's informants also confirm our knowledge of the West African slave-trade routes in this period. The Yoruba slaves were brought directly to the coast and sold, either at the older slave-trading port of Whydah, or at newly developed Badagri and Lagos. The captives of the Fulani, however, arrived at the coast by a variety of routes. The Niger and the Benue provided a water route for carrying canoe-loads of slaves to the ports of the Niger delta, such as Brass or Bonny. There were also well-used overland routes. One led from the Niger in the vicinity of Rabba, through Yorubaland to the slave posts on the Bight of Benin. Another led directly south from the lower Benue, overland to Bonny. A third left either the upper or middle Benue for the slave markets of Old Calabar on the Cross river.

When the Fulani led long-distance raids to the south of their own territory, they did not necessarily take the slaves back to the north with them. The captives of the great Fulani raids southward from Adamawa in the 1820s, for example, were mainly sold to other peoples in the vicinity, and thus passed from hand to hand until they were finally sold to the Europeans in Old Calabar. Other captives, however, were taken back into the heart of the Fulani empire before being sold down whichever route was convenient at the time. Thus the Wute informant made a journey of well over a thousand miles before being sold to the Slave Coast via Yorubaland, even though his home country was less than five hundred miles from Douala.

As in East Africa, there was a division between the Muslim and the Christian slave trade. Some West African slaves were shipped north to the Maghrib or Egypt, while others went south to the European dealers on the coast. The Sierra Leone sample throws some light on this division, if only through its *lacunae*. The Fulani *jihad* in Massina, for example, must have produced a body of war prisoners from the Niger valley just above the great northern bend of the river. Some merchants from this region were represented in Sierra Leone, but no slaves appear. Apparently these prisoners were either retained for local use or sold to North Africa. In the same way, prisoners taken in the fighting associated with the stabilization of Bornu under Muhammad al-Kanami apparently were sold to the north, rather than to the Europeans. Kanuri prisoners captured by the Fulani during the Holy War of 1804–30, however, were sent to the coast in at least some proportion. Although only thirty Kanuri remained in 1849, Koelle's informant reported that there had formerly been about 200 in Sierra Leone. The large number of Hausa is a further reflection of the Fulani *jihad* in northern Nigeria. Even the Habe of Gobir, to the north of the Fulani empire, appear to have sold at least a part of their prisoners to the coast. Three Hausa and Fulani informants had been slaves of the Gobirawa before they were sold to the foreign slave trade. . . .

12. Change in the Ivory Coast

ARISTIDE R. ZOLBERG *One-Party Government in the Ivory Coast* Princeton University Press 1964; pages 23–9

Economics

Until about 1925, the Ivory Coast's main contributions to the French economy continued to be timber and palm oil. But as the result of Governor Angoulvant's efforts, cocoa soon was added to this list. European *colons*, who had been encouraged to settle after World War I, and Africans, especially those living in the south-east, produced about 1,000 tons of this commodity in 1920. During the next decade, as Table 1 indicates, production of cocoa was much more substantial. By 1930, however, the Ivory Coast and other colonies produced more cocoa than France could absorb. On the other hand, because France imported most of its coffee from other monetary zones, coffee growing was encouraged by means of premiums and preferential prices. At the close of World War II, it had by-passed cocoa and has continued to expand greatly.

The further growth of commercial agriculture after World War II was reflected in the increase of the total area of land devoted to this purpose from 337,000 hectares in 1950 to 588,700 in 1956. During the same period, European production of coffee and cocoa decreased from 11 and 12 per cent of the total to 3 and 2 per cent respectively. This was therefore essentially an African phenomenon, the result of the entrance

TABLE 1

Exports of Major Commodities
(in metric tons)*

Commodity	1928	1938	1948	1958
Coffee	248	14,076	55,391	113,500
Cocoa	14,493	52,714	41,220	46,300
Timber	(†)	42,887	73,101	415,600
Bananas	1	12,271	13,447	46,000

* Figures for 1928 and for 1938 are from: Ivory Coast, *Service de l'Agriculture, Rapport Annuel: Année 1938*, pp. 14–20. Data for 1948: Ivory Coast, Ministère du Plan, *Inventaire . . .*, pp. 34–90. For 1958: Ivory Coast, Ministère du Plan, *Supplément trimestriel au bulletin mensuel de statistique* (1er trimestre, 1959), p. 24.

† Quantity unknown.

of many new farmers into the commercial circuit rather than of the expansion of existing holdings. There were about 40,000 cocoa and coffee farms in 1944, 120,000 in 1956, and an estimated 200,000 in 1959.[1] Before the war, most of them had been concentrated in the south-east, but in recent decades, as Table 2 shows, commercial agriculture has spread throughout the southern half of the country and penetrated even into the marginally suited districts of the centre. By 1957, each of the three geographical areas produced approximately one-third of the total.

This growth was accompanied by the development of transportation, communications, and electrical energy. Between 1947 and 1956, the total network of roads increased by 54 per cent; the number of vehicles in circulation grew from 2,097 to 19,064; and the consumption of electrical energy rose from 1.7 million kilowatt-hours to 19.9 million. But the Ivory Coast was still essentially an agricultural country. Industries remained rare and were entirely in the hands of European concerns. In 1959 there were only 85,000 non-agricultural wage earners, of

[1] The figure for 1956 was issued by the government and reported in Agence France-Presse, *Bulletin quotidien d'information*, 7 January 1956 Estimates for 1944 and for 1959 were obtained from officials of the Chamber of Agriculture of the Ivory Coast.

TABLE 2

Decentralization of Cocoa and Coffee Production

Region	1942*		1951*		1957†	
	Tons	Per Cent	Tons	Per Cent	Tons	Per Cent
South-west	21,920	25	30,610	27	43,825	35
Centre	19,600	22	42,500	36	38,709	31
South-east	46,100	53	43,500	37	41,749	34
Total	87,620	100	116,610	100	124,283	100

* Computed from data obtained from: Ivory Coast, *Rapport présenté à la session budgétaire de l'Assemblée Territoriale* (Abidjan: Imprimerie du Gouvernement, 1952), pp. 22, 31, 32. The 1942 figure for the south-west includes a large proportion of European production.

† Data obtained from: Ivory Coast, *Rapport sur l'activité générale pour l'année 1957* (Abidjan: Imprimerie du Gouvernement, 1958), p. 273. These figures include African production only. The total differs from exports for that year because of unsold stocks.

whom 25,000 were employed by various government agencies. Of those in the private sector of the economy, the bulk were in commerce or in transportation, activities related to the import and export of commodities. However, these figures do not show that a large number of Africans were involved in trading. The dividing line between farming and trading is an easy one to cross; during a good year, a successful farmer may buy a truck and become a businessman; during a bad year, he may return to his farm when he loses his truck by defaulting on time-payments.

Commercial agriculture fostered the growth of a stratum of Africans who shared similar concerns and who were affected in the same way by colonial policies, competition with European *colons*, and cyclical fluctuations in the world market for primary commodities. Commercial communications among them channelled a greater awareness of their common situation and fostered the organization of economic defence associations among cocoa and coffee growers. This was the beginning of African political participation in the Ivory Coast.

It is more difficult to determine to what extent agricultural change has resulted in a new pattern of social stratification. It is sometimes suggested, in order to explain the relatively conservative politics of the Ivory Coast regime in recent years, that the P.D.C.I. based its strength on a sort of planter *bourgeoisie*, and that this new class now dominates Ivory Coast society. Many of the founders of the party, including Houphouet-Boigny and Auguste Denise, do control sizeable landholdings. Nevertheless, it seems an exaggeration to speak of a landed class in the Ivory Coast. For the country as a whole, it has been estimated that of those who exploit commercial farms, 74 per cent have less than 5 hectares; only 10 per cent have over 10.[1] In the south-east, farms tend to be larger, and farmers tend to hire more manpower outside their own family than in the south-west and the centre. But within any given region, age is the most important determinant of the size of an agricultural holding. This can be explained by the inheritance system, which works in chain-letter fashion, with an accumulation in the hands of the oldest survivor in a given lineage and a further redistribution after his own death. There is no evidence of inter-generational transmission of concentrated landholdings, except in a few rare cases where the land has been registered under the French civil-code system. Furthermore, there is no agricultural proletariat to speak of in the Ivory Coast proper. In Bongouanou, for example, 35 per cent of the farmers had hired help; of a total of 100 workers, only 18 were from the Ivory Coast; the remainder came from neighbouring territories, especially from Upper Volta. Finally, since land continues to be held mostly by extended families, wage earners outside agriculture are not cut off from revenue from the land.

The most significant economic differentiation is the one which has developed between regions. The south is much richer than the north, and the gap between them has grown; in the south, easterners are richer than westerners; the centre is somewhere between the two extremes. These differences between regions correspond generally to the culture circles discussed earlier and are summarized in Table 3. Traditionally,

[1] Detailed studies of particular regions have shown a range of 60 to 70 per cent in the less-than-5 ha. category, and of 6 to 12 per cent above 10 ha. Ivory Coast, *Enquête agricole à Bongouanou* (Abidjan: Imprimerie du Gouvernement, 1956), p. 51.

the several regions were economically self-sufficient, although as we have seen, there was some exchange between them. Per capita revenue in agriculture, which includes the sub-sistence sector, shows a range of 2 to 1 for the entire country.

TABLE 3

Income Differentiations in the Ivory Coast by Regions*

Region	Estimated Population	Per Capita Revenue in Agriculture†	Per Capita Cash Income in Agriculture	Per Cent Sub-sistence
Forest East	905,000	31,750	11,800	63
Forest West	980,000	15,750	7,400	56
Centre	360,000	27,600	5,900	82
North	995,000	21,350	2,000	91
Country	3,220,000	22,750	6,500	78

* Computed from data contained in: S.E.R.E.S.A., 'Rapport d'enquête dans le secteur agricole' (Abidjan, 1959), pp. 22–8. The figures are for 1957 and are expressed in C.F.A. francs. One dollar equalled about 245 frs. C.F.A. in 1959.

† The report computed these figures on the basis of the value of subsistence crops when marketed locally; per cent subsistence equalled per capita revenue in agriculture minus per capita cash income in agriculture.

But per capita cash income varies in the ratio of 6 in the richest region to 1 in the poorest. According to another estimate, income in the south-east, for a family of 8, is 100,000 C.F.A. fr. per year, but only 15,000 C.F.A. fr. in the north. Because the largest part of this cash income is spent on consumption goods, variations in income are clearly visible in the daily lives of the inhabitants of the regions. Nowhere in the Ivory Coast is there great misery. In the north, Sénoufo farmers meet their basic needs in food, shelter, and clothing from traditional economic activities. But the implements of modern living are rare; the arrival of an automobile in a village is an unusual event; many Sénoufo wear imported cotton cloth only as their shroud; few can afford to send their children to school. In the south-east, among the Agni or the Abouré, for example, many individual farmers live in houses built of permanent construction materials; modern means of transportation, including bicycles, motor bikes, or even automobiles, are common; children who do not earn government scholarships can be sent to school at their family's expense. Although it is incorrect to speak of economic classes, economic differentiations coincide with traditional cleavages; there are now rich and poor tribes in the Ivory Coast.

III. POLITICS IN THE MAGHREB

13. Diplomatic attack on the trans-Saharan slave trade

A. ADU BOAHEN *Britain, the Sahara and the Western Sudan*
Clarendon Press, Oxford 1964; pages 136–44

... By 1840 then, the abolition of the northern branch of the
African slave traffic had become a national concern and could
no longer be treated in a cavalier manner. Thus, as a result of
the perseverance of Warrington and pressure from Buxton and
the humanitarians, the attack on the oldest branch of the
African slave trade belatedly began, and from 1840 onwards
was carried on simultaneously in Tripoli, Morocco, and
Turkey.

On the strength of the instructions from the Foreign Office,
which were reiterated in May 1841, Warrington invited Abd
al-Jalīl, who was then in Murzuk, to a meeting somewhere in
the district around the Gulf of Syrte. Nothing was heard from
the Sheikh until January 1842, when he wrote to apologize
for his long silence and agreed to meet Warrington at the
appointed place. Three months later the long-expected meeting
took place. This palaver came off successfully. In a letter to the
Colonial Office, the Sheikh agreed to abolish the slave trade
and slavery, promote legitimate commerce, and persuade the
rulers of the interior to do the same. But in return he demanded
free access to the coast, and especially to the port of Benghazi,
and his recognition by the Porte as the Bey of Fezzan. On the
advice of Warrington, the Sheikh also wrote a letter to the
Sultan of Turkey in which he professed his allegiance and asked
him to appoint a commission to investigate the anarchy
prevalent in Tripoli. The Consul-General forwarded all these
letters to the Foreign Office with the recommendation that they
should be transmitted to the British ambassador at Constantinople for prompt action.

Warrington felt highly elated about this palaver, and
justifiably so. As Abd al-Jalīl controlled Fezzan and was then
widely known in Bornu (he married the sister of the Sultan of

Bornu in 1835), his services would have been invaluable in the enforcement of regulations against the slave trade and the development of legitimate traffic. With the overwhelming influence of the British Government over the Porte at the time, it seemed that the Sheikh's demands could be easily granted. Indeed, in May 1842 Sir Stratford Canning, then British ambassador in Constantinople, informed Warrington not only that he had obtained the recall of Askar Ali, the Turkish Governor of Tripoli—a step which the Consul-General had been pressing for since 1840—but also that the Sheikh's petition declaring his allegiance and asking for peace had been favourably received by the Turkish ministers and that the new Governor being posted to Tripoli would be accordingly instructed. Unfortunately, even before reports of the interview reached England, and before news of the removal of Askar Ali arrived in Tripoli, the benevolent Sheikh was murdered, in May 1842. Askar Ali was a great slave trader himself, and Warrington's view that Ali redoubled his efforts to vanquish the Sheikh on hearing of the latter's promise to abolish the slave trade might well be true. Considering the favourable view that the Porte was reported to have taken of the Sheikh's petition, no event could have been more unfortunate for the abolition of slavery and the opening up of the routes into the interior than Abd al-Jalīl's death. With the effective occupation of Fezzan by the Turks, any further efforts for the abolition of the trans-Saharan slave traffic through Fezzan and Tripoli had to be made in Constantinople.

While Warrington was frantically exerting himself in Tripoli, Sir Thomas Reade, the British Consul in Tunis, was negotiating with the Bey for the abolition of the hideous traffic. Here the campaign was, diplomatically, an immediate and resounding success. From his very first interview with the Bey on the subject in April 1841, Reade came out with a copy of an order prohibiting the export of slaves from the Regency. This was accompanied by a firm promise by the Bey to do everything in his power to abolish the slave trade and the institution of slavery itself as soon as possible. This order would probably not have been taken seriously had the Bey not followed it up with the liberation of all his slaves.

Incredible and inexplicable as Reade's achievement is when

it is viewed in isolation, this and the subsequent measures become less mysterious when viewed against the background of the political situation in Tunis. In 1837 the French had occupied the province of Constantine on the western frontier of Tunis and had begun to cast envious glances eastward. East of Tunis, the Sultan of Turkey had by that date made good his occupation of the coastal districts of Tripoli, and people in Turkey were openly speaking of repeating in Tunis the successful operation in Tripoli. Flanked on both sides by these ambitious powers, the Bey perceived that it would stand him in good stead to obtain the support of another great power. The obvious choice was Britain. With her eyes on the trade routes to India and the markets of Greece, Turkey, and the Levant, Britain herself was as interested to prevent the Mediterranean from becoming a French lake as were the Sultan of Turkey, the Bey of Tunis, and the Sultan of Morocco. There was also another side to the coin. After the vacillations of the 1810s and 1820s, British foreign policy towards the Ottoman Empire had by the late thirties crystallized into one of maintaining its integrity. While Czar Nicholas was speaking of the Sultan of Turkey as the 'sick man of Europe', Palmerston described as 'pure and unadulterated nonsense' all talk about the decay of the Turkish Empire. His aim was not merely to maintain its integrity, but 'by reforming it to make it more capable of resisting its enemies and able to play its part in the balance of power in Eastern Europe'. As Tunis was always regarded in theory as an integral part of the Ottoman Empire, Britain would not see the Regency appropriated by the French or even recognized as a completely sovereign state. Either development, it was feared, would have been taken as the signal for the death of the 'sick man' and would have encouraged Russia or Egypt to nibble at that Empire. On the other hand, if the Sultan were allowed effectively to occupy Tunis, France would have demanded some compensation or probably declared war on Turkey. The obvious answer to the diplomatic situation was the maintenance of the *status quo*, and precisely this became the object of British foreign policy towards the Barbary States and the Ottoman Empire until the seventies.

Thus, when in 1837 the Bey became alarmed by French expansion eastward, Palmerston promptly allayed his fears.

He assured him of Britain's full support and assistance so long
as he remained true to the Sultan, 'according to the relations
now subsisting between him and the Porte', and promised to
take steps in Paris to protect the Regency from any unprovoked
aggression from France. Granville, the British ambassador in
Paris, was accordingly instructed to inform the French Government that 'Great Britain could not see with indifference any
attempt of France so to encroach upon the territory of Tunis
as to alter the political relations which now connect the Bey of
that Regency with the Porte'. On the other hand, when in 1841
the Sultan of Turkey attempted to reduce Tunis to a mere
province by demanding payment of annual tribute and control
of her finances as well as her foreign policy, Reade supported
the Bey in his appeal to the Foreign Office. Palmerston acted
with dispatch in this case also. Ponsonby was asked to warn the
Porte not to attempt to make any change 'in the relations which
had hitherto subsisted between the Bey of Tunis and the
Sultan'. Thus from 1837 onwards the position of the Bey
depended largely on Britain's policy of maintaining the *status
quo*. Consequently, until that policy was abandoned in 1878, it
became the aim of the Beys of Tunis to win the goodwill and
friendship of Britain, and sometimes to buy it at any price. In
the light of all this, it is hardly surprising that the Bey should
have acted so promptly when Reade informed him that nothing
would be more 'gratifying not only to the British Government
itself, but to the British nation generally', than the abolition of
the traffic in slaves and slavery itself.

The reaction of the Foreign Office to the first anti-slavery
measure introduced by the Bey was such as to spur him on.
Reade was instructed to express to him the appreciation of the
British people and to assure him that 'nothing could tend to
interest the English nation in his favour so strongly as a con-
tinuance in this course and as the complete abolition of slavery
in the Regency of Tunis'. The Bey was also asked to rely upon
the friendship and good offices of Britain 'to dispose the Sultan
in his favour as long as he pursues the wise and prudent course
which he has hitherto followed'. So inspirited was the Bey by
the British Government's remarks that only the fear of precipi-
tating an internal revolution compelled him and Reade to take
the politic decision to proceed by stages. Five months later the

Bey issued another proclamation abolishing slave markets and prohibiting the public sale of slaves. This again was followed by immediate practical steps. The public slave markets in Tunis and other towns were razed to the ground.

This measure was given an even warmer reception in Britain than the first. The British and Foreign Anti-Slavery Society sent an address of congratulation to the Bey. Its agent in Malta, James Richardson, presented him with 'a testimonial of gratitude' on behalf of British residents in Malta, Gibraltar, Leghorn, Florence, Naples, and Tripoli, who expressed their admiration of his action and the hope that it would incite other Muhammedan and Christian sovereigns to follow his example.

Feeling highly flattered, and anxious to ingratiate himself even more with the British Government and public, the Bey only waited for an opportune moment to strike another blow at the traffic. This seems to have arrived eight months later, after the storm of protests raised by the first two measures had settled down. In April 1842 the third order was issued, which completely abolished the importation of slaves into Tunis by land or sea. It also ordered that any slave who set foot on Tunisian soil after 27 April automatically became free. After another eight months' delay, the Bey issued a new order declaring free all children born of slaves after 8 September. Only the lack of funds for the payment of compensation to slave owners prevented him from abolishing slavery outright. But that inevitable step was taken four years later. In January 1846 a proclamation was issued liberating every slave in the Regency and declaring the institution of slavery illegal. In his letter informing Reade of this final step, the Bey stated significantly that he took it because 'we know it is also an object of attention to the great and illustrious British Government, and we pray the most High that our opinions be always in unison with their own on every point'. This final act was naturally received 'with great satisfaction' by the British Government, and as a demonstration of their gratitude, they presented to the Bey a carriage with harness for six horses and seven British carpets of various sizes.

The proclamation of January 1846 brought to a victorious conclusion the diplomatic campaign against the slave traffic in Tunis. The various measures were enforced with every sincerity. Commissioners were sent out even to the remote provinces of the Regency to issue *tiskeras* or papers of freedom to every slave who presented himself. Indeed, a missionary who toured the Regency in March 1846 concluded that 'it may now be safely declared that slavery is abolished in the Regency of Tunis'. It is true that slaves were smuggled into the Regency, especially in the fifties and sixties, but all those who were detected were promptly liberated by the Bey. The ease with which this victory was accomplished was certainly owing to political conditions in Tunis as well as to the skilful diplomacy of Reade and his great interest in abolition. Though the exigencies of British foreign policy and fear of French occupation of Tunis would have compelled Britain to interest herself in the fate of the Bey, there is no doubt that these bold and humane measures raised his prestige in the eyes of the Government and people of Britain and won him their ungrudging support.

Meanwhile the attack on the slave trade was being waged in Morocco also. Hay, the British Consul-General there, did not move until he received the circular of December 1841 asking for copies of the laws passed in connexion with the slave trade. This circular was communicated to the Sultan. In reply, the Sultan stated that he was not aware that the traffic in slaves had been prohibited 'by the laws of any sect', and that it was a matter on which 'all sects and nations have agreed from the time of the sons of Adam . . . up to this day'. This reply touched off a lively exchange between the Consul-General and the Sultan, in which Hay tried to persuade the Sultan to abolish the slave trade. In his long dispatch, Hay first of all proved to the Sultan that he was wrong in his view that no sect or nation had abolished that traffic by reviewing the progress that had been made in that direction during the preceding thirty-four years. He mentioned the lead taken by Britain, the countries that had followed her example in Europe, and the fact that even 'rulers of several Moslem states' such as Muscat, Tunis, and Egypt, were also issuing orders against the traffic. He then concluded with a passionate appeal for his co-operation.

Hay's brilliant dissertation elicited only a more positive refusal from the Sultan. He pointed out that as the 'making of slaves and trading therewith' were sanctioned by the Koran, which 'admits not either of addition or diminution', to abolish the trade or in any way impede it was completely out of the question. The Consul-General became so convinced of the hopelessness of the attempt to convince the Sultan that he abandoned it. But he salved his own conscience and that of the Foreign Office by pointing out that slaves in Morocco were not numerous, that they were exceedingly well treated, and that for the past thirteen years not a single slave had been exported from that country.

Though Hay's observations about the slave traffic in Morocco were true, they were not enough to cause in British humanitarian circles the same feeling of complacency as in the British consulate in Morocco and in the Foreign Office. Hence, a year after these official exchanges, the Anti-Slavery Society sent Richardson from Malta on a mission to the Sultan. In an address to be presented by Richardson, the Anti-Slavery Society appealed to the Sultan to abolish the slave trade and slavery on the ground that as God had made all men equal, it was sinful to enslave fellow human beings. Richardson arrived in Tangier in December 1843.

For reasons to be dealt with presently, Hay was instructed by the Foreign Office to assist Richardson 'unofficially'. On Richardson's departure for Mogador, however, Hay gave him a letter of introduction to Willshire, the British Vice-Consul there, asking him to request permission from the Governor there for Richardson to proceed to the Sultan's Court. Willshire had already gone to Morocco when Richardson reached Mogador. When the Vice-Consul returned he brought the rather disheartening news that the Sultan had already got wind of Richardson's mission, and had not only refused to receive him, but had ordered him to leave the kingdom immediately. This was too bitter a pill for Richardson to swallow. He informed Willshire that the Anti-Slavery Society would not consider that he had discharged his duty until he had left no stone unturned for the accomplishment of his mission. With the co-operation of the Vice-Consul, Richardson obtained an audience with the Governor of Mogador. At this interview he pleaded that the address of the Anti-Slavery Society should be received by the Sultan. But in reply the Governor merely repeated the Sultan's former view that the demand for abolition was against the

Muslim religion, and refused even to touch the address. Like Hay in 1842, Richardson had to admit defeat. He left Morocco in April 1844.

Though these attacks failed, the question of abolition disappeared completely from the correspondence between the British consuls in Morocco and the Foreign Office until 1857. In that year the Consul-General was suddenly asked for information about the traffic and the attempts which had been made to abolish it. He replied quite frankly that after the correspondence that took place 'in the time of my predecessor' (i.e. 1842), he did not think that any beneficial results would be obtained as long as the same Sultan continued to reign in Morocco. Like his predecessor, he also tried to minimize the gravity of this failure by pointing out the paucity of slaves in Morocco, and the leniency with which they were treated. Though the Consul-General ended his note with a promise not to lose any favourable opportunity that might present itself to bring up the question, it seems this opportunity never arose. Indeed the next attack on the Moroccan slave trade was not made until 1885, when the Anti-Slavery Society sent out its Secretary and Treasurer on a mission to Morocco. But although the Society continued to send petitions and addresses to the British Government, it was not until the French occupation of Morocco in 1912 that the hideous traffic and the institution of slavery were abolished.

It is obvious then that while the campaign in Tunis was a glorious success, that in Morocco was a deplorable failure. As in Tunis, this failure and the reluctance of the British Government and Consuls to raise the question with any frequency were due primarily to the diplomatic situation in the Mediterranean in general, and to British relations with the Sultan in particular. . . .

14. Algeria

DOUGLAS JOHNSTON *Journal of African History* Vol. 5, No. 2, 1964 Cambridge University Press; pages 232–42

... To begin with, it must be remembered that, unlike settlers in other parts of the world, the French in North Africa could always preserve their links with France. The dossiers of those settlers who were brought to Algeria under official schemes show that many of them retained some property in France. The very existence of such official schemes suggests that many settlers were dependent on the government and the administration, and that, being expectant of help, they devoted much of their energy towards policies of recrimination and protestation. During the Second Empire, a hostile observer noted, 'les colons sont dans leur rôle et obéissent à un mot d'ordre en criant toujours, en mentant et en critiquant toujours. . . . Ils critiquent avec fureur pour obtenir une satisfaction; à peine les a-t-on satisfaits que leurs clameurs s'atteignent à un autre point. Après nouvelle satisfaction, ils ont une troisième trompette à faire éclater. . . .' Under the Third Republic, Jules Ferry commented in 1892, 'le colon d'Algérie a beaucoup de défauts, il est particulariste, il ne demande pas mieux que d'exploiter l'indigène et la métropole. Son niveau moral et intellectuel est peu élévé au-dessus de l'horizon journalier', and again, 'les colons se préoccupent peu des intérêts généraux de la colonie et de la France. L'esprit public n'est pas encore majeur.' Historians describe these non-Muslim populations 'enfermés dans le ghetto colonial, les colons réagissent avec la violence engendrée par la claustrophobie et ne visent qu'un but: le profit maximum, contre-partie nécessaire de leur exil'. Settler politics have been violent and personal, rejecting theories and principles, directed towards a source of power outside Algeria, adept for negotiation and recrimination, the expression of a basically uncertain position, that of 'le colon glorieux et humilié'.

French settlers during the nineteenth century came mainly from the south of France; in 1896 the most important departments for furnishing immigrants were Corsica, the Bouches-du-Rhône, the Hérault, Gard, Pyrénées-Orientales, Var and Haute-Garonne. But many settlers came from Spain, Italy, Malta and, during the early years of colonization, from

Germany. When Bugeaud left Algeria in June 1847, out of a European population of 109,400 some 62,126 were said to be non-French. The immigration from Spain, which was particularly important in the regions of Oran, Sidi-bel-Abbès and Algiers, and the immigration from Italy, particularly to the regions of Constantine, Bône and Philippeville, continued well after the First World War. If the law of 1889 had not permitted easy naturalization, it seems as if some of the more important towns would have been dominated by populations which were not French. Immigration from France frequently coincided with particular crises on the French side of the Mediterranean. In 1848 some 12,000 workmen, the unemployed of the Second Republic, were transferred by the government to a number of Algerian agricultural centres; with the Second Empire, a large number of political prisoners were transferred; after the Franco-Prussian War it was inhabitants of Alsace-Lorraine wishing to avoid German citizenship. The disease of phylloxera in the French vineyards, and crises in the French silk and dyeing industries, caused further movements of immigration into Algeria. If it is an exaggeration to say that 'chaque crise historique . . . a déposé sur le rivage algérien des alluvions humaines qui n'avaient en commun . . . que leur inadaption', it remains true that this population, coming largely from poor regions in Europe, had difficulty in conceiving its unity. Whenever one can examine non-Muslim political life in any detail one is struck by its divisions. The differences between Algiers and Paris, between the army and the settlers, between the settlers and the administration, between the Jewish populations of Algeria and anti-Semitic leaders, between the Church and the administration, between the supporters of 'colonisation officielle' and 'colonisation libre', between east and west over specific issues such as that of the 'rattachements', differences between different social classes—all these differences are, as it were, confirmed by a geographer's recent study of modern Algiers, where he stresses the different aspects and different rhythm of life in the various parts of the European town, commenting 'peu de cités ont des quartiers dont la personnalité est aussi grande'.

The economic history of European settlement in Algeria is, in many ways, a succession of crises. Agriculturists, short of credit, short of labour, often short of irrigation, sought for a crop which would be successful and which could not offend the interests of metropolitan France. They tried unsuccessfully to grow sugar cane, cotton, tobacco, linen, tea, mulberry, to mention only some of the best-known ventures, in addition to cereal crops. The great crises of 1845–50, of 1858–64 and of 1866–70, when catastrophic local conditions were affected by economic events in Europe, weakened French settlement. Only in the years after 1871, when an influx of European population, the revival of Mediterranean activity with the opening of the Suez Canal, and the possibility of Algeria producing wine and being 'bein réellement le pays de la vigne', did there seem much possibility of optimism.[1] But there was a financial and economic crisis, particularly in the Constantinois, in 1875; a series of bad harvests in the 1880s and 1890s; the spreading of phylloxera to Algeria and the recovery of the French vineyards; transport and credit difficulties; and the repercussions on the Algerian economy of Europe's twentieth-century economic crises. All these ruined many European settlers and gave an atmosphere of insecurity and speculation to much European economic activity.[2]

The limits of settlement were determined by natural causes as well as by the shortcomings of settler equipment or effort. Consequently, French settlement became predominantly urban. It had always been partly urban, and in the early days of colonization some people had criticized it for not being more clearly agricultural. Algiers, for example, had rapidly gained a European population, and in 1956 the urban population of the department of Algiers was slightly more than the rural population. The increase of immigrants into Algeria after 1872 benefited the towns more than the countryside, in spite of the

---

[1] Wine production had earlier been limited because the interests of the French Midi had to be protected (Moll, *Colonisation et agriculture en Algérie* (Paris, 1845), II, 441). For twenty years French settlers had not been able to export their products to France at all. Cobden, for example, had commented on the inactivity of Algiers as a port and had explained it by the French protective legislation. Cobden to Arlès Dufour, 1 January 1861, Cobden Papers, British Museum Add. MSS, 43666.

[2] One should remember the formula suggested by one historian, 'misère chez le colon = famine et mort chez l'indigène' (Yacono, *La colonisation des plaines du Chétif*, II, 176).

fact that this was the period of viticulture and of new cereal farming. From 1886 to 1911 the proportion of the European population which can be described as 'agricultural' declined from 38 to 27 per cent. European agricultural holdings became more concentrated, and there were already examples of Europeans selling their lands to Muslims. It is estimated that after 1926 the movement of Europeans from the countryside into the towns became even more marked, and that 1926 marks the maximum for European rural settlement. By 1954 the urban population constituted 79.4 per cent of the European population as a whole.

This change brought about a considerable modification of the picture of the European settler. It became necessary to stress the non-agricultural side of European life. '. . . Ouvriers spécialisés, fonctionnaires, employés, chauffeurs de taxi, des standardistes, des manœuvres, des ingénieurs, des commerçants, dont l'ensemble représente vraisemblablement plus des trois-quarts de l'infrastructure': or, as another analysis puts it, out of an active non-Muslim population of 354,500, agriculture accounted for less than one-tenth, whilst more than one-half was represented by small wage-earners. It is difficult to judge how correct are those statements which claim that 'l'immense majorité des Français d'Algérie est composée de prolétaires ou de petits bourgeois . . . qui ont eu et ont encore la vie difficile d'un sous-prolétariat européen', but it is certain that the influx of Europeans into the towns swelled the tertiary sector of the Algerian economy beyond all measure, 44 per cent of the active non-Muslim population being engaged in transport, commerce and services (as opposed to 30 per cent in France). By 1954 more than half of the non-Muslim population lived in the agglomerations of Algiers and Oran, typifying European concentration in the west and centre rather than in the east.

This concentration of the non-Muslim population, both in towns and in regions, did not endow it with a greater sense of security. The proliferation of small employees, the importance of exports such as wine (especially for a town like Oran which had no industry and, until the growth of Saharan petrol production, no raw material to export), the abnormal growth of the Algiers region, all increased rather than diminished European dependence upon metropolitan France. The expecta-

tions of European population growth were not being fulfilled
(although Peyerhimoff's estimate of a European population of
1,200,000 by 1950 was not very wide of the mark, since the 1954
census recorded a non-Muslim population of 1,042,409) and
the self-consciousness of European insufficiency was intensified
by the influx of Muslims into the towns. By 1954, although as
has been said the European population was essentially urban,
there were only three towns where the Europeans were in a
majority (Oran, Perrégaux and Philippeville). Nor did this
concentration of the non-Muslim population make for easier
understanding between the communities. In the countryside
Europeans tended to be isolated, with a mechanized agriculture
which did not require a large labour force, producing for
external rather than for internal markets, often investing their
profits and their leisure away from their holdings in the nearest
big town, in Algiers or in France. In towns such as Algiers, the
populations were effectively isolated from each other. All this
was a long way from some of the characteristics of early French
settlement, when classes in Arabic were organized for the
children of even humble French settlers and officials, or when
the administration encouraged with bonuses those Europeans
who sold their produce in the native markets. It has been
estimated that only a minority of the Muslim population has
aquired a knowledge of French.

One observer has claimed to have discerned a mutual
influence between non-Muslims and Muslims in the rural areas,
the non-Muslims becoming more fatalistic and nonchalant,
whilst the Muslims became more dynamic and businesslike.
But this sort of mutual influence, if it existed, must have become
rarer as the non-Muslim population became more concentrated. French settlement showed itself to be tenacious and in
many ways to be efficient and technically successful. But
Peyerhimoff's boast that it was the French who were best suited
to accomplish the tasks of colonization, since they possessed
'une puissance, certainement unique dans le monde, d'assimilation, d'attraction, de séduction', has not been borne out. It is
the contrary which is true. The French largely failed to inte-
grate themselves or their economy to Algeria. They behaved
as if they believed one of the ideas of the 1840s, that Algeria
naturally had a European rather than an African destiny.

Algerian nationalism was in many ways a contradiction of this assumption and a response to this situation.

Many historians who have considered Algerian reactions to French rule have insisted on the permanence of protest, whether in the form of the great insurrections or in the form of political organizations. Some have seen in this the expansion of a long-standing Algerian patriotism, and it has been recalled that Bugeaud himself had insisted that his task was to overthrow 'la nationalité arabe'. Other observers emphasized the apparent ease with which insurrectionary movements could be launched. But most French writers have believed that this hostility was to be explained by Islam and by the religious fanaticism of the Muslim inhabitants of Algeria. Against all rational calculation, there would be a desperate revolt, urged on by leaders of the 'confréries', or religious brotherhoods, who were invested with supreme authority; movements such as those of 1864 were preceded by a revival of piety and religious fervour; native society was in a state of perpetual conspiracy against the French because the Algerians were but a small part of the Muslim world, which was nourished in the hatred of Christianity; the very simplicity and clarity of Islam was said to endow it with an insurmountable force.

It is difficult to accept these assertions at their face value. Few historians can accept the idea of a fundamental hostility between Christianity and Islam without wondering whether their differences are essentially religious, or whether one should not rather see the religions as merely giving form and stability to different ways of life and to different cultures. It is necessary, if one's understanding of Algerian history is to move forward, to try and identify some of the main themes of Algerian politics. To begin with, it seems that much of the activity amongst the Muslims during the first decades of the conquest has to be explained mainly in Algerian terms. It is French publicists who first gave an undue importance to Abd el Kader as a national leader, carrying on a holy war against the Christians. Just as Bugeaud set about dismantling Abd el Kader's political organization tribe by tribe, and area by area, so in the first place had Abd el Kader built it up. And it does not seem as if the principle of its construction was one of essential hostility to Europeans and Christians. On the contrary there is ample evidence that

Abd el Kader showed no inveterate hostility to Christians, and it can even be argued that he was anxious to avoid an armed clash in 1839. The main principle of Abd el Kader's state was rather one of hostility to the privileged groupings of the Turkish *makhzan*. In this sense he was rather the last of the old *ra'īya* patriots than the first of the new national patriots, in spite of his attempts at imposing a unity. And this being so, one is as much struck by the opposition to Abd el Kader from other Muslim groupings as by the extent of his empire, and if one is impressed by the emir's skill in organizing resistance to the French, one must also note Bugeaud's success in detaching various tribal dignitaries from amongst his supporters. The elements of Abd el Kader's state are complicated: the hostility of former *makhzan* groupings, the enmity and suspicion of certain of the religious brotherhoods (Tidjaniyya, Darquwiya, Taïbya), the reliance on marabouts and maraboutic families rather than on the *juwād*, or 'noblesse d'épée' (again in contra-distinction to Turkish policy), the heavy rate of taxation and the resentment it caused, the diplomatic skill of the emir's early negotiations with the French, his strength in the west rather than in the east. It is an over-simplification to describe him simply as a national Islamic leader. In the history of the pacification of Grande Kabylie, one can see how Kabyle rivalries and politics continued, and how the arrival of the French provided a new element, with its own variety of compli-cations and opportunities. This was not always realized in Algiers, where the in-and-out nature of Kabyle politics was not appreciated; the rallying of former enemies was often hailed as the sign of pacification, but it was frequently accompanied by the consequent defection of former allies.

Many of the pre-1830 issues continued within the different sectors of Algerian society and did not cease to exist because of the presence of Europeans. The antagonisms between tribes, fractions, *çoffs*, the *chicayas* which could divide families, and the ancestral rivalries which opposed family to family in long-stand-ing feuds and which have been described as 'une donnée de la nature comme la religion et comme la misère', all continued. But within these traditional movements one can discern particular responses to the French presence, and responses which are very different from the fanatical religious hatreds

MNA

which have often been described. When one examines insurrectionary movements, then one finds a variety of causes for the unrest. There are causes which are particular and local, such as a quarrel over property or between notabilities; there is often uneasiness concerning food supplies, drought or fear of drought; there are frequently agitators, with claims to religious authority, who incite the population against the French and who call attention to the seizure of religious foundations and the destruction of mosques; but most often and most significantly there is resentment against French-imposed taxation and fines, protest against the loss of land and fear of further deprivation. Whenever a road was opened, the Muslims feared for their lands. On numerous occasions, French officers reported that what appeared to be a revolt inspired by some religious fanatic was in reality caused by the progress of colonization. It is true to say that for several years most of the Kabyles showed themselves indifferent to the French conquest; there had been no mass attack on Europeans. But by 1850 the Kabyles realized that the French had conquered most of Algeria. Once they became apprehensive for their land and for their independence, then they became more sensitive to the *sharīf* who preached holy war against the French. During the Second Empire, Muslims preferred to be in military territory rather than in civil territory, with the 'bureaux arabes' rather than in areas where the settlers were dominant, and this preference is undoubtedly an important element in Mokrani's revolt of 1871. It has been customary to suggest that this movement can be explained by hostility to the Crémieux laws which naturalized Jews, and by the action of the religious brotherhoods. Both these responses would be of the unthinking fanatical kind. But it seems more likely that the rising was a product of particular reasons (Mokrani's own financial embarrassment) and the fear of what would happen when the military institutions of the Second Empire gave way to more direct settler control.

It seems likely therefore that one must treat with some suspicion the reports of French officers who explained the insurrectionary movements as the work of the religious brotherhoods, and one notices the report of a French observer who in 1842 commented that the inhabitants of Algeria were in general less fanatical than many others in southern Europe, and that peace was more venerated amongst them than holy war. It is more important to stress the destructive nature of French rule. Bugeaud, for example, did not believe that French rule could be firmly implanted unless it had been preceded by a successful campaign. He resented the suggestion that the province of Constantine could be considered pacified without 'une guerre énergique et prolongée', and until that had taken place he regarded Constantine as in a 'situation incomplète', and many officers followed in his tradition. Politically the French endeavoured to construct their domination upon the collaboration of a local aristocracy and on the belief that the tribe was to be identified with a tribal chief or leader. This meant attaching their administration to an institution which was already of doubtful solidity; successive land laws, military destruction and confiscation, natural disasters and the growing use of money with its consequent complications, all contributed to depreciate the position of this aristocracy. Nor were the devices of the French administration, the division of the country into departments, arrondissements and communes, likely to create any meaningful construction around which the Muslim populations could associate themselves with French rule. This being so, it was only possible for these populations, whose economy and social structure had been shattered, to discover political sense in contrast to the French connexion. The consciousness of the dualism of the Algerian situation, the realization of the separation between non-Muslim and Muslim and of the cleavage between the communities, arose naturally and easily because the French had failed to create any structure into which political activity could fit otherwise. It is true that this sentiment of difference, of 'altérité' as it has been called, could give rise to a desire for assimilation, to the ambition of becoming properly French, so that a certain ambivalence is to be found in the evolution of many Algerian intellectuals. But the impossibility of becoming French, that is, of attaining a position of political and economic privilege, only served to confirm this sense of alienation.

The evolution of Algerian political parties has been outlined by a number of writers. The connexion between Muslim leaders in Algeria and those from other parts of the Islamic world has been to some extent described. Some of the conditions peculiar to France and Algeria are clear enough: the confusion of metropolitan French politics which sometimes provided a lever for Algerian politicians, the presence in Algeria of Frenchmen who were anxious to promote change (such as Victor Spielman, who directed the newspaper *Tribune,* or countless French school-teachers), the influence of the 1930 centenary celebrations, the 1940 French defeat, the allied landings in North Africa and so on. But what the historian needs to do is to try and determine at what moment and how this sentiment of a break between the communities, which is fundamental in the evolution of Algerian nationalism, became generalized. The nationalist leaders themselves are not very helpful. Ferhat Abbas, who dates the change from about 1941, attributes it simply to popular instinct, and quotes Anatole France, 'C'est toujours à l'insu des lettrés que les foules ignorantes créent des dieux.' The Kabyle writer, Mouloud Feraoun, notes a changed attitude amongst certain of his compatriots as late as 1955. Perhaps all one can try to suggest at present are four aspects of Algerian history which help to explain the acceleration of Algerian political consciousness and the Algerian revolution.

First, there was the spectacular increase in the Muslim population, passing from 2,496,067 in 1856 to 9,529,726 in 1954, with one of the highest birth-rates in the world. It has been suggested that the increase of the birth-rate, which was noticeable from about 1916 onwards, was due to a rise in the standard of living. There seems to be little evidence to support this. At all events it seems certain that within a short time, by 1930 or 1935, the population had outstripped the food resources of the country; the smallholdings of Muslim peasants became insufficient to meet the needs of their families. Secondly, these populations began to move into the towns, thus beginning what has been called the 'clochardisation' of the Algerian, emphasizing his consciousness of deprivation and placing him at the disposition of a mass organization, as well as encouraging emigration to France. Thirdly, the sense of cleavage between the two communities was accentuated by the importance in Algeria's economy of wine production. From 1929 to 1935, when population growth was placing Algeria's economy in a state of crisis, viticulture underwent a new period of boom.

This prosperity, which was intrinsically precarious, since it depended upon the goodwill of the metropolitan government, has been described as a 'façade menteuse', since it brought activity only to certain regions of the country and profit mainly to the non-Muslims. It was an economic activity which was segregationist in most of its features, and it can be argued that by perverting the economic growth and commerce of the country it provided the symbol of Algeria's colonial status necessary to the achievement of a national self-consciousness. Fourthly, once the Algerian revolution had started in 1954 and 1955, the action of the French army, with its regrouping of populations, its establishment of forbidden zones, its attempts to form new centres of habitation and new structures of political control, accelerated the decline of traditional societies and made them increasingly receptive to new forms of political activity. . . .

In conclusion, the importance of historical studies may perhaps be stressed. There can be little doubt that had the real conditions of the French position in Algeria been understood, then the French populations, both in France and in Algeria, might not have experienced the disappointments and bewilderments which have been theirs.

IV. EGYPT AND THE NILE VALLEY

15. Impact of the West

PHILIP K. HITTI *History of the Arabs* Macmillan 1964; pages 749–51

. . . Ibrāhīm's invasion of Syria and Napoleon's invasion of Egypt produced in a sense the same results: they closed the ancient order of decentralized authority in both lands and ushered in a new era of centralized dependence. More than that, they threw these lands into the cockpit of foreign imperial machinations. The expansionist trends of the Great Powers began to clash there as nowhere else. Especially keen was the rivalry between England and France, each endeavouring to obtain for herself a preponderating influence in Egyptian and Syrian affairs for the same reason: securing the fullest measure of advantage for her trade with India and the Far East. Many of the wars of the nineteenth century may be traced to some origin in the Near East. The Crimean War (1854–6) had as one of its causes conflicting claims on the part of France and Russia for the protection of the holy places in Palestine.

The opening of the Suez Canal in 1869 enhanced the strategic importance of these lands and accelerated their re-entry upon the scene of world trade and world affairs. The canal soon became an integral part of the life-line of international communication and compensated for the loss sustained through the discovery of the route around the Cape of Good Hope. The digging of the canal, a hundred miles long, cost about £20,000,000, most of which was raised by public subscription in Europe, chiefly in France. The khedivial shares were 176,602 at £20 each, which in 1875 were purchased by the British government.

In Egypt the extravagance of Ismā'īl, in whose reign the canal was opened, led to state bankruptcy and eventually to European intervention. In consideration of Ismā'īl's generous offer to double Egypt's tribute, the Porte bestowed upon him (1866 and 1873) the right of primogeniture for his family and the title of khedive, which amounted almost to an acknowledgment of sovereignty. In 1879 a dual control by England and France was established over the land, and the khedive was deposed. Meantime the grievances of the army, which was officered mostly by Circassians, and of the peasantry, which suffered under heavy taxation, conscription and a system of *corvée* by which the government could force any able-bodied male to work for little or no pay on public projects often of doubtful utility, found a champion in an army officer, Ahmad 'Arābi, who was himself of peasant stock. The insurrection was brought to a sudden end by the British victory at al-Tall al-Kabīr (Tell el-Kabir) on 13 September 1882, and the banishment of 'Arābi. The occasion provided the British with a chance to occupy the land which, however, remained under nominal Turkish suzerainty until shortly after the outbreak of the first World War, when England declared a protectorate over Egypt. The Khedive 'Abbās Hilmi was then deported and his uncle Husayn Kāmil, with the title of sultan, succeeded. Fu'ād, who in 1917 followed his brother Husayn, was proclaimed *malik* (king) in February 1922, at which time the protectorate was terminated, Egypt was declared independent and a constitution was promulgated. The constitution made Islam the religion of the state and Arabic the official language. It served as a model for the later constitutions of Syria and al-'Irāq. This concession on the part of England was not made without struggle on the part of the natives. The nationalist leader, Sa'd Zaghlūl, was a follower of 'Arābi and, like him, the son of a peasant, but more capable and more highly educated. In 1919 this fiery lawyer, a pupil of Jamāl-al-Dīn al-Afghāni and a former editor of *al-Waqā'i' al-Misrīyah* under Muhammad 'Abduh, sought permission from the British to leave the country with a delegation (*wafd*) to plead its cause before the Peace Conference in Paris and in London, but was rebuffed and sent to Malta, an act which immediately made a national hero of him. His and his party's efforts were crowned with success when, in 1936, an Anglo-Egyptian treaty was signed stipulating the withdrawal of the British troops of occupation to the Canal zone, the relinquishing of British responsibility for the life and property of foreigners in favour of the Egyptian government and the rendition of reciprocal aid against enemies involving the use of ports, aerodromes and means of communications. The capitulations were abolished but the question of the Sudan sovereignty was held in suspense. . . .

16. The founder of modern Egypt (i)

HENRY DODWELL *The Founder of Modern Egypt* Cambridge University Press 1931; pages 205–8, 237–40

. . . The most interesting aspect of Muhammad 'Ali's rule is certainly the pains he took to develop and enlarge the practice of discussing public business before proceeding to any action. In 1819 he set up a council or divan of seven persons to manage and discuss transactions between the Treasury and European merchants, and this system of official deliberation was applied to all departments of the central government. Every matter was to be maturely discussed before being remitted for the pasha's orders. Then in 1829 the principle was more widely extended. Ibrahim Pasha presided over a gathering of 400 persons specially convened, comprising the chief civil and military officers, the mudirs, and even a number of village shaikhs, to discuss the best way of correcting abuses and improving the condition of the peasants. It sat every night for some time, and the members were sworn to secrecy. In 1832 a similar plan was tried in Syria. A small body of Grand Notables, twenty-two in number, was convoked to deliberate on the affairs of the people. In 1834 the shaikh of the Al Azhar mosque and the shaikh of the merchants' guild were directed to nominate suitable ulema and merchants to sit in the Superior Council, and at the same time the mudirs were ordered to convene in each *mudirliq* an assembly including cultivators, the village shaikhs, and others, to choose two village shaikhs to represent the cultivators of the *mudirliq* in the council. These things were generally misconceived and misrepresented by the tourists whose information gave the tone to European opinion. On the one side was the young Disraeli representing the pasha as saying he would have as many parliaments as William IV but would take care to choose them himself. On the other were

Philosophic Radicals and Saint-Simoniens who claimed Muhammad 'Ali as a convert to western democracy. The one suggests that the pasha's experiments were mere tricks designed to impress European opinion; the other that they meant the establishment of representative government. Of course they were neither one nor the other. Ordinary public business in the East had always been decided by a group of officials—a divan or dubar—presided over by the pasha in person, or some superior official, and sitting virtually in public, with a constant succession of petitioners and spectators. As Bartle Frere once said, important as is a knowledge of public opinion in a western country, its importance is even greater in the East. The oriental ruler needed urgently to know what men were saying in the bazaars and caravan-sarais. In part he could depend upon his spies—the most permanent of all instruments of government in Asia. But another side perhaps could be revealed by the assemblies which Muhammad 'Ali from time to time convoked. He was much too shrewd to dream of borrowing wholesale from western practice. But he was also much too shrewd not to see that a discreet borrowing of western ideas, adapted in such a way as not to disturb accustomed forms, might prove very beneficial to his government. He must have been influenced too by another motive. A man with so strong and clear a sense of the value of knowledge can hardly have been unaware that his tentative assemblies were instruments not only of government but also of political education. Had chance but provided Egypt with an heir to Muhammad 'Ali's talents as well as to his dominions, the country would have afforded to western nations an example of political reform as remarkable as that of Japan. But a single life, largely spent in building up a political dominion, cannot conceivably do more than plan the outline of institutional development.

His financial management was extraordinarily successful. Onlookers were always anticipating his financial ruin and declaring that his wars and internal projects would ruin him and the country alike. In 1827, for instance, when he was burdened with the cost of the war in the Morea at the moment that his resources were straitened by two successive failures of the Nile to attain its usual height, he still went on building factories and constructing a mole and dockyard at Alexandria.

Four years later he was contemplating projects ten times as great. He kept out of the hands of European moneylenders. In 1837 it was thought that the fall in the price of cotton (of which he exercised a monopoly) would hit him hard: and yet he managed to pay off the arrears due to his troops. Barker thought he really must have found Aladdin's lamp.

But his magic lay merely in prudence and attention. The public accounts, when he obtained the government, were kept by Copts, who made them a perfect model of intricacy. This had two advantages—it made their services indispensable and it hid their defalcations. The public accounts were not centralised. Various taxes would be assigned to various services according to the approved Turkish mode. There was no budget nor any possibility of one. Here as elsewhere the pasha was willing to learn and borrow from the European. He directed Boghoz Bey, the Armenian, the most trusted and the most trustworthy of all his servants, to obtain a scheme of accounts as used in public offices in Europe; and the Frenchman Jomard was employed to frame a new system. But that still left untouched the vicious method of apportioning

different districts . . . to different ministers to provide for their expenses instead of sending their revenue to a common treasury. The present state of things leads to great abuses, as every minister has a treasury of his own, and seven doors are opened (those are the different ministries) to fraud and abuse, when one in a country like this is already but too many.

When Bowring visited Egypt in 1838 the pasha sought his advice in the matter of accountancy. All the public accounts were produced for inspection, and Bowring made a number of recommendations for their improvement. First came the introduction of a budget of receipts and expenditure at the beginning of each year; then the payment of all revenues into the central treasury; the complete separation of the power to receive and issue public money; the establishment of the power in the Finance Minister to sanction or reject proposed expenditure; and finally provision for the prompt payment, balancing and audit of all public accounts.

The fragmentary evidence as yet available does not permit of any full or exact narrative of the pasha's financial history. But

he seems usually to have succeeded in keeping his expenditure
well below his revenue. . . .

But his educational measures afford the most remarkable
evidence of his policy of reform. Cairo was of course one of the
great centres of Islamic culture. To its great university housed
in the old Al Azhar mosque came students of all the nations of
Islam. But its organisation and studies were alike medieval.
It bred theologians and ecclesiastical lawyers. It did not breed
men of affairs and administrators. All western knowledge was
completely excluded. New schools were needed to provide the
wider outlook which the pasha's administrative ideas required.
While Muhammad 'Ali continued to protect and maintain the
ancient university, he set up beside it a whole series of institutions designed indirectly to modify and modernise the popular
mind. An English contemporary well summed up his purpose
and attitude. Whereas Sultan Mahmud, he says, by his sudden,
violent reforms had weakened the allegiance of the Turks,
Muhammad 'Ali had always maintained a high character
among Muslims

by adopting the only wise course to be pursued with a nation in so
low a scale of civilisation. By a system of gradual ameliorations,
without violating religious prejudices, he has laid the foundation of
a permanent reform in the institutions of the nation, trusting to the
progress of knowledge from the general establishment of public
schools throughout his government for the final establishment of his
plans of reform.

This policy seems to date from about 1820 and was in origin
the natural corollary of the reform of the army. The introduction of European methods of organization and training clearly
demanded officers capable of studying European military
science, engineering, mathematics. The first indication that
this was recognised seems to be the establishment of an Italian,
Costi by name, in the citadel of Cairo, to teach drawing and
mathematics. Then come orders for the teaching of Italian—
the *lingua franca* of the Levant—and demands for teachers of
French and Turkish, and a capable engineer. From this simple
beginning arose schools designed to train officers for the five
branches of the pasha's service—the artillery, engineers,
cavalry, infantry, and marine—under European direction.

In order to broaden the basis of instruction, a considerable number of young Egyptians were sent to France, and a few to England, to be educated at the pasha's expense. The fruits of this were seen in 1833 when a Polytechnic School was established as a training school for the officers' colleges. The teaching staff included two Europeans only, one for chemistry and one for mathematics. Beside them were four Armenians, one of whom had spent ten years at Stoneyhurst, and six Muslims, three of whom had been educated at Paris and three in England. This expansion was followed up by the establishment of several primary schools in each *mudirliq*, with two large 'preparatory' schools, one at Cairo and one at Alexandria, designed to feed the Polytechnic School. Admission to the schools was in effect reception into the pasha's service. The pupils were fed, clothed, and lodged at the public charge, and received besides small monthly allowances, rising in amount as the boys passed from class to class. Their future career, the branch of service into which they were drafted, the technical training which each received, was a matter for the determination of the pasha or his officials. Egypt was the first oriental country in which anything like a regular system of westernised education was established. Bowring was right in criticising the scheme as founded on too narrow a basis of primary education, and as designed to secure superior education for the few instead of providing a universal system for the many. But the pasha cannot reasonably be condemned for not adopting a system which the most advanced western nations had not yet adopted.

This foundation of schools and colleges was accompanied by the establishment of printing presses and the appearance of a newspaper and a gazette. By the end of 1837 seventy-three oriental works had been printed at the press set up at Bulaq, then the suburb of Cairo abutting on the Nile. These included translations of a good many technical works for the use of the new schools. The pasha projected a newspaper to be printed in French and Arabic. The *European Press* existed at Alexandria in 1824, and in that year printed a descriptive poem by Salt, the consul-general. At the same time the position of the European and the Christian were transformed. Before Muhammad 'Ali's rise to power native Christians had been subject to many disabilities. They were obliged to distinguish themselves by the colour of their dress. They were forbidden to ride horses. They were forbidden during the month of the great Muslim fast to eat, drink, or smoke in the streets by day, so as not to remind the true believer of his compulsory abstinence. The Frank inhabitants of Cairo and Alexandria lived in separate quarters with guarded entrances, and, when they went abroad, wore Turkish dress in order to avoid insult. 'As is known to every prudent person,' ran the Turkish declaration of war on Russia in 1827, 'every Muslim is by nature the mortal enemy of infidels, and every infidel the mortal enemy of Muslims.' But under the pasha's rule the spirit of the government was transformed, and that of the people sensibly modified. . . .

17. The founder of modern Egypt (ii)

HELEN A. B. RIVLIN *The Agricultural Policy of Muhammad Ali in Egypt* Harvard University Press 1961; pages 75–8, 250–4

Administration of Egypt under Muhammad 'Alī

The *Qānūn-nāmah* promulgated by Sulaymān the Magnificent after the Ottoman conquest of Egypt in the sixteenth century established the basis by which Egypt was to be ruled for the three centuries which preceded Muhammad 'Ali's reign. The general outlines of the administrative and financial machinery established by Sulaymān remained clearly recognizable throughout this period, although, in the course of time, the *Qānūn-nāmah* was modified, arbitrary interpretations were given to its decrees, new practices were evolved, and control of the Egyptian administration by the central government at Istanbul practically disappeared.

By the eighteenth century, the Mamlūks had emerged as the new ruling class, usurping effective control of the country, while the Turkish pasha appointed by the sultan had become only a phantom administrator subjected to their whims, their caprices, and their tolerance. The Arab historian, al-Jabartī, describes with what regularity these pashas were compelled to descend the Citadel at the insistence of the Mamlūks to make way for new appointees from Istanbul. The Mamlūks also neglected the duties and responsibilities owed to the Turkish sovereign and even ceased to pay the annual contribution to the Sultan's private Treasury. Finally, in the last decades of the eighteenth century, the Turkish government decided to reassert its power over its Egyptian province. First, the Turks accused the Mamlūks of rebellion against the Sultan and then took advantage of the internecine struggle between the Mamlūk factions to play one group off against the other. They were unable, however, to win any decisive victory over the Mamlūks before the French invasion of Egypt called a halt to the struggle. No sooner had their troops landed in Egypt when the French, professing great friendship for the Sultan, sent assurances to him that the object of the invasion was to aid him in his struggle against the rebellious Mamlūks. The Sultan, however, was not to be so easily duped and cooperated instead with the British in expelling the French from Egypt. As soon as the French troops were withdrawn, the struggle between the Turks and the Mamlūks for the control of Egypt was resumed with new vigour. It was this renewed struggle between the Turks and the Mamlūks which gave Muhammad 'Alī his opportunity to capture control of Egypt for himself. During the course of this conflict, Muhammad 'Alī shifted from one side to the other as it suited his own interests, at the same time cultivating the good will of the Egyptian notables. He finally succeeded in obtaining the support both of the Egyptian notables and of the Sultan for his candidacy for the office of *walī* (governor) of Egypt by promising the former that he would adopt no new policy without their consent and by promising the latter that he would accept the duties and responsibilities owed to him, including the payment of the annual remittance to Istanbul. In 1805 he was appointed *walī* and his appointment was renewed each year thereafter. Muhammad 'Alī thus emerged as the governor of Egypt, a country which had passed through civil wars and foreign occupation, had served as the battlefield for the French, British, and Turkish armies, would continue to be the scene of struggle between the Mamlūks and Muhammad 'Alī's troops for several years, and finally in 1807 would suffer a British invasion.

Despite political upheavals in Egypt during this entire period some measure of continuity in the administrative and financial machinery of the government persisted. Even during the French occupation, when the Mamlūks and the higher officials in the old bureaucracy were dispersed, those who were willing to collaborate with the French were permitted to remain in government service. The Copts, in particular, were at first given posts of greater responsibility than they had formerly enjoyed. The key positions, however, were held by Frenchmen. After the French withdrawal from Egypt the Turkish government appointed its officers to serve in the administration, but the Copts, who had already lost their position of favour, continued to function at the lower levels. The administration now appeared, however, to be on the verge of collapse, not only because of the ineptness of the Turkish officials who were appointed to govern the country but also because of the struggle for power involving the Turks and the Mamlūks as well as the various groups of soldiers imported into Egypt by the Turks. This struggle was reflected most strongly in the chaotic system of tax collection. The country was devastated by arbitrary and frequent tax levies by competing groups of soldiers; the suffering of the people was so great that Colonel Missett, the British agent in Egypt, reported to his government that he felt the breakdown in the system would cause the people to welcome the occupation of any European power to protect them against the Mamlūks, Albanians, and 'Uthmānlīs. This apparently anarchic situation prevailing at the moment when Muhammad 'Alī became governor of Egypt, however, disguised the essential fact that there still existed an administration, a minor officialdom, and a body of regulations and customary usages upon which the new Pasha could base his future government. His immediate problem, therefore, was not to reorganize the government but to make it an effective instrument by which he could control the country, collect the taxes he urgently needed, and consolidate his own position so that he could remain in power.

The system of government which was gradually evolved was highly centralized compared to the former regime under Mamlūk domination; once again a Turkish-appointed *walī* was in complete control, although under circumstances vastly

different from those envisaged by the *Qānūn-nāmah* of Sulaymān. The business of the central government was now
conducted on two levels, by means of one or more deliberative
councils (sing. *majlis*) presided over by *nāzirs* and by
bureaucratic departments (*dīwaāns*) also headed by *nāzirs*.
The *majlises* and *dīwāns* were reorganized periodically and
varied in number to meet administrative requirements.
Although public business was discussed in deliberative councils
(similar in character to those established by the *Qānūn-nāmah*
and maintained during the period of Mamlūk and French
domination) and decisions were made by majority rule as
stipulated in an official regulation dated Rabī' ath-Thānī,
A.H. 1233 (February–March 1818), these councils had no
authority to act without the concurrence of the Pasha; their
recommendations had first to be presented to Muhammad
'Alī for his approval, and final authority always rested with
him. In 1240/1824–25 two principal councils were organized:
(1) *al-Majlis al-'Alī al-Malakī* (or *al-Majlis al-'Alī*) for civil
affairs and (2) *Majlis al-Jihādīyah* for military affairs. The
former, referred to as the Council of State, was dissolved in
1837 and reformed as *al-Majlis al-Kabīr* the Great Council or
the Great Council of Ministers. *Al-Majlis al-Kabīr* was in turn
disbanded in 1254/1838–39; at least, it no longer existed in
1258/1842–43. *Dīwāns* were also established as their need arose,
but six principal *dīwāns* carried the burden of administrative
functions: (1) interior, (2) treasury, (3) war, (4) marine, (5)
public instruction and public works, and (6) foreign affairs and
commerce. In addition to numerous departments of secondary
importance there were two important *dīwāns* which performed
functions belonging rightfully to that of the interior (*Dīwān
al-Khidīwī*): (1) *Dīwān al-Katkhudā* (*Kikhyah*), *dīwān* of the
lieutenant of the Pasha and (2) *Dīwān 'Umum at-Taftīsh*,
dīwān of general inspection. . . .

   The Ottoman Empire, which had begun to decline in the
sixteenth century, was in a state of crisis by the eighteenth.
Internal and external enemies alike were undermining the very
foundations of the state, and the need for basic reforms of
Ottoman institutions was becoming imperative. This need was
clearly recognized by Sultan Salīm III; consequently he introduced the *Nizām Jadīd* in 1792 by means of which he hoped to

create a modern army capable of defending the Empire from
its enemies. The Sultan, far in advance of Ottoman public
opinion, eventually became a martyr to the cause of reforms,
for he was murdered by the adherents of the extreme reac-
tionary party which had failed to grasp the significance of his
programme of reform, viewing it simply as a threat to its own
prerogatives.

Salim was dead but his ideas survived, for before his death he
had instilled in his nephew Mahmūd the conviction that the
Empire must change or perish. Therefore, when Mahmūd
became the new Sultan, he ascended the Ottoman throne as an
ardent exponent of reform and throughout his reign laboured to
achieve it and safeguard the integrity of his Empire. Although
his objectives were clear from the outset of his reign, Mahmūd
II had to proceed cautiously, for the obstacles which stood in
his way appeared almost insurmountable. He was not to be
deflected from his course on this account, however. Slowly but
steadfastly he moved in the direction of his goal, welcoming
in the meantime whatever assistance he could get towards the
attainment of the ends for which he was striving.

Muhammad 'Alī, an obscure Albanian officer who had
insinuated himself into the important post of Pasha of Egypt,
appeared at first to be a willing tool in the accomplishment of
the Sultan's larger objectives. He rid Egypt of the Mamlūks, a
rebellious military caste, who had long ignored their obligations
towards the central government at Istanbul and whose
disregard of the Sultan's authority had added to the centrifugal
tendencies which were disrupting the Empire from within while
it was being ruthlessly attacked from without. Muhammad
Alī also assisted the Sultan in the conquest of the Wahhābīs
in Arabia who had challenged the Sultan's position as the
guardian of the Holy Cities and, finally, he played a significant
role on behalf of his sovereign in the Greek War of Independence. Moreover, Muhammad 'Alī had drawn the same conclusions from the humiliating defeat of the haughty Mamlūks
by Napoleon's army as Sultan Salīm had drawn from the defeat
of the Ottoman armies by the Russian troops of Catherine the
Great. He recognized, first of all, that the once invincible
Ottoman armies were incapable of withstanding the modern
armies of Europe which had profited from the technological

advances made by the West during the seventeenth and eighteenth centuries while the Ottoman Empire had remained complacent. Second, it was perfectly clear to the Pasha that the ability of the Ottoman Empire to meet the challenge of the West would depend upon Turkey's capacity to absorb new ideas and the speed with which the Ottoman armies were modernized. As a result of these conclusions, Muhammad 'Alī became an ardent proponent of reform and was, in fact, the first Ottoman official to introduce the *Nizām Jadīd* into his province with any measure of success.

Indeed, had Muhammad 'Alī been merely a patriotic Ottoman officer satisfied with playing the role of chief supporter of his sovereign's reform programme, the Ottoman Empire might possibly have recovered its former position as a Great Power. Instead, the Egyptian Pasha, consumed by his own ambitions, used Ottoman patriotism as a stratagem for furthering his own private ends and his reform programme as the means for achieving his objectives. Instead of safeguarding the Ottoman Empire, Muhammad 'Alī, in fact, insured its demolition. Perhaps the demise of the Empire was inevitable and the factors making for its dissolution already too firmly entrenched for the trend to have been reversed. Perhaps, also, Muhammad 'Alī was a prophet of nationalism who favoured bringing to an end the outmoded supranational Ottoman Empire. But if he was such a prophet, his conversion to the ideals of nationalism was certainly not a conscious one, for Muhammad 'Alī was no nationalist in the modern sense and above all no Egyptian nationalist. He considered himself a Turk if anything and thought of Egypt simply as a private preserve to be exploited for his own and his family's benefit. His struggle for independence, therefore, was not a struggle for Egyptian independence but rather an attempt to leave to his descendants a secure inheritance. He achieved his goal and thus quite unintentionally launched Egypt upon the road to national independence; at the same time, he delivered the fatal blow from which the Ottoman Empire never recovered.

Muhammad 'Alī's career may be divided into four phases: his struggle for power, his retention of power, the expansion of his power, and the transference of power to his heirs. In each of these stages he required both a strong army and an inexhaustible supply of revenue. Consequently he formulated a military policy and a fiscal policy which were designed to supply him with both. It is with his fiscal policy that this study has been primarily concerned, for it was intimately connected with agriculture, the source of wealth in Egypt. In fact, insofar as Muhammad 'Alī possessed an agricultural policy at all, it was merely as one aspect of his fiscal policy and inseparable from it. At the same time, his military policy has also been taken into account, for it impinged upon Muhammad 'Alī's fiscal policy by draining the resources of the country and by exhausting the agricultural manpower of the nation through excessive conscription. Consequently, the assessment of the much narrower problem of Muhammad 'Alī's agricultural policy requires an analysis of the broader fiscal policy and a consideration of the effects of the military policy on the economy of the country.

Muhammad 'Alī's fiscal policy centred around the problem of increasing his sources of revenue to meet the insatiable demands of the army. To this end he reorganized the system of landholding, consolidated taxes, improved the system of tax collection, and organized a civil administration capable of executing his orders effectively. Furthermore, he introduced a important new crop, long-staple cotton, and attempted to improve all agricultural procedures. He improved irrigation, introduced *sayfī* canals, and reclaimed land; he engaged in commerce that was dependent primarily upon agricultural produce; finally, he introduced industry with an eye to utilizing the raw agricultural materials produced in the country and to supplying his army with some of its equipment. The consequences of these measures had both positive and negative results.

On the positive side, Muhammad 'Alī provided capital for the cultivation of money crops, transforming Egyptian agriculture from a subsistence economy to a cash crop economy; he introduced *sayfī* canals, thereby pointing the way to perennial irrigation upon which the prosperity of modern Egypt is based; he centralized marketing facilities, enabling large quantities of Egyptian agricultural produce to enter the lucrative European market and establishing new horizons for Egyptian trade and a source of great wealth for the country; he attracted large numbers of European merchants who brought with them many Western techniques, Western ideas, and Western customers. These innovations changed the entire pattern of Egyptian trade; henceforth Egyptian commerce was to be linked up closely with Europe. By bringing Egypt within the orbit of European trade Muhammad 'Alī brought the country inevitably within the sphere of European civilization, although, unfortunately, on the most superficial level. By opening Egypt to European influences, by stimulating commerce and encouraging the growth of Egyptian cities and towns, by developing an Egyptian bureaucratic class and an Egyptian military class, and by establishing a hereditary dynasty, Muhammad 'Alī laid the foundations of the Egyptian national state. These are undeniable achievements which have proved of paramount importance in the development of modern Egypt.

On the other hand, he undermined the Ottoman Empire and opened the way to Western colonial penetration. His Western orientation of Egyptian trade increased the country's dependence upon European markets and made it susceptible to fluctuations in the European economy. The influx of European merchants made Egypt more vulnerable to European interference in the internal affairs of the country on the pretext offered by the European governments that they were entitled to protect their traders and their commercial interests under the terms of the Treaties of Capitulations. Furthermore, by depriving the religious class of its independence, Muhammad 'Alī immobilized the only class capable of exercising a restraining influence over the excesses of the ruling class. At the same time he destroyed the institutions which for centuries had served to protect the people against unlimited oppression. Thus, he weakened the leaders of the people and destroyed the protective institutions without providing simultaneously for the development of new leadership and new institutions upon which a healthy society in Egypt could be based. His policy towards the religious class and the cutting off of revenues from the religious institutions injured Egyptian education, for, restricted as the traditional system of education had been, it had offered some intellectual training to Egyptian children. Muhammad 'Alī' government schools and foreign missions could never substitute for an elementary school system and this the Pasha never pro vided for. In fact, he abandoned his government schools almost completely after 1841. The intellectual dislocation resulting from Muhammad 'Alī's truncated educational policy is impossible to measure, but its effects are unquestionably still being felt in Egypt today.

Muhammad 'Alī also destroyed the native merchant class and the native artisan class, inhibiting thereby the development of an Egyptian middle class and Egyptian industrial growth. His own industrial experiments failed miserably; his factories were abandoned, the workers were sent home to their fields, and the development of a skilled industrial proletariat was indefinitely postponed. Moreover, the Pasha created a class of landholders composed of members of his family, his retinue, and his favourites, after European military interference had confined him to Egypt and European diplomatic pressures had forced him to abandon his monopolies. In this way Muhammad 'Alī established a pattern of large-scale landholding which prevented the emergence of an independent and responsible class of small farmers. Under Muhammad 'Alī's regime the national income rose; yet he failed to improve the conditions of the *fallāḥīn*. It is true that he spoke often of his concern for the welfare of the people over whom he governed, but when this social consciousness was translated into action it invariably took the form of new burdens and crushing exactions. While Muhammad 'Alī laid the foundations of the Egyptian national state on the one hand, he thus also laid the foundations on the other for many of the economic and social problems with which Egypt is still grappling.

In short, Muhammad 'Alī's contribution to Egypt would undoubtedly have been more impressive had he curbed his private ambitions and had he, instead, devoted his energies to the improvement of the conditions of the people over whom he ruled and to the development of sound institutions to replace those which he so ruthlessly destroyed. He would also have been better advised to have assisted the Ottoman Sultan in the struggle against Western encroachment instead of betraying him and providing the European nations with the opportunity of deciding the fate of the Empire. This was a most dangerous precedent and one which set the pattern for the future. To be sure, the Egyptian Pasha achieved his objective by establishing a hereditary dynasty in the family of Muhammad 'Ali, but he also opened the door to European interference before Egypt had evolved institutions that could have aided the Egyptians to meet the challenge of a new age and thus defend their independence against the attacks of predatory European nations.

V. EAST AFRICAN EMPIRES

18. Somali conquest of the Horn of Africa

I. M. LEWIS *Journal of African History* Vol. 1, No. 2, 1960
Cambridge University Press; pages 214–16, 218–28

... Today the Somali number at least two and a half million[1]
and dominate the Red Sea and Indian Ocean coasts of
Ethiopia, from the Gulf of Tajura in French Somaliland to the
Northern Province of Kenya. They are essentially a pastoral
people, as they have been for centuries, following a restricted
nomadism in which the average pastoralist moves widely but
with a certain regularity with his herds of camels, flocks of
sheep and goats, and in suitable regions, cattle. Agriculture is
most developed and has a tradition going back several centuries
in the more favourable regions between the Shebelle and Juba
Rivers of southern Somalia. Here it seems to have been adopted
by nomadic Somali settlers from their Bantu predecessors. In
northern Somaliland, while there are indications that terraced
agriculture was practised in the past near what are now ruined
towns, here in its present form cultivation, chiefly sorghum, is
recent, restricted mainly to the west of the British Protectorate
and Harar Province of Ethiopia, and the techniques involved
have been directly borrowed from the neighbouring agricultural
Galla of Ethiopia.

Thus there is a general geographical division between the
dry north and the better watered areas of southern Somalia.
To some extent the primary division of the Somali nation into
two great congeries of clans—the Samāle or Somali proper, and
the Sab—coincides with this geographical division. Most of
the Samāle are pastoralists moving over the arid terrain of

---

[1] French Somaliland has a population of about 28,000 Somali (as well as
26,000 'Afar or Danakil, a closely related Hamitic people); the British
Protectorate has an estimated 640,000 Somali; Harar Province of Ethiopia
about 500,000 Somali; Somalia has between a million and a quarter and
two million Somali; and the Northern Province of Kenya about 80,000.
Other immigrant Somali populations are found elsewhere in East Africa
and in Aden.

northern and central Somaliland, but also spilling over into the scarcely less hostile conditions of Jubaland and the Northern Province of Kenya. The Sab on the other hand are chiefly cultivators and occupy the more fertile regions between the Juba and Shebelle Rivers in southern Somalia.

Each community is divided by patrilineal descent into a number of large agnatic groups which may conveniently be called 'clan-families'. These range in population from about a quarter of a million to one million persons. The Samāle, who considerably outnumber the Sab, have four main clan-families —the Dir, Isāq, and Hawiye, and the Dārōd who strictly are only related to the others on their maternal side. The Sab, with a total strength of about half a million, comprise only two clan-families—the Digil, and Rahanwīn. I mention these groups here by name since it will be necessary to refer to them individually in the account which follows. Each clan-family, whether of Samāle or Sab, is further segmented into what can only be described as a vast series of clans and lineages. And it is necessary to point out here that every Somali group has a genealogy which has some historical content, and which also represents the way in which contemporary groups combine and divide in the present political structure of Somali society. I do not discuss the historical content of genealogies further here or the way in which they appear to be foreshortened over the generations since no extensive use of genealogical chronologies is made in this paper.

The Samāle and Sab communities differ not only in economy and technology but also in culture and social organization. In language their speech differs perhaps to much the same degree as French differs from Italian. In their social organization and social values the Samāle pastoralists can be loosely characterized as democratic almost to the point of anarchy; they have clan-heads, often styled 'Sultan', but these have little authority and there is no formal hierarchy of chiefly offices—in short no instituted government. The southern cultivating Sab, on the other hand, are less bellicose and have a more hierarchical political organization in which there is respect for authority. Again, the political units of the Sab are generally founded on territorial interests and geographical propinquity, while amongst the pastoralists the lineages which are their political units are not rigidly associated with specific localities, but widely dispersed in the pastures and only mobilized when they are threatened by hostile groups. These differences, indicated here very generally, can be seen to conform to the contrasting environments in which the two communities live. They also reflect the ethnic history of Somaliland and its different characteristics in the two areas.

In Somaliland as a whole there have been three distinct ethnic movements. Before the incursions from the north of the Hamitic Galla and Somali, southern Somalia, at least between the rivers, was occupied by a mixed negroid or Bantu population which seems to have contained at least two main cultural elements and which was known to the early Arab geographers as the 'Zengi' (Blacks). The major element consisted of negroid and partly Bantu cultivators living as sedentaries along the Juba and Shebelle Rivers and in fertile pockets between them. They figure in Galla and Somali traditions, especially in the folk traditions of those Digil and Rahanwin peoples who entered this area from the north and settled amongst the 'Blacks' as an aristocracy. Something of their life and social organization is preserved in a late Arabic compilation (the 'Book of the Zengi') found in the possession of the Kadi of Kismayu in 1923 and recently published by Cerulli. This document, the work apparently of a series of hands at different periods, is probably also largely based on folk-traditions, but provides more detailed information than the latter today offer. These sources are confirmed by more tangible evidence. Remnants, partly Swahili-speaking, reinforced by ex-slaves from further south, survive today in five distinct communities along the Shebelle River and in two on the Juba. Others today are found at Baidoa in the hinterland between the rivers, and also in Brava district: indeed in the ancient town of Brava itself a Swahili dialect, Chimbalazi, is still spoken.

The second pre-Hamitic population, less numerous than the riverine cultivators, was a hunting and fishing people living an apparently nomadic existence. Their present-day descendants, much modified by Hamitic influence, survive in scattered hunting groups in Jubaland and southern Somalia where they are generally known as Ribi (or WaRibi) and as Boni (or

WaBoni). Physically it has been suggested tentatively that they contain Bushman-like elements. But their physical character-istics have not been intensively studied. They appear to have been politically and economically linked to the Bantu seden-taries, and still today small hunting communities of this stock are found living under the tutelage of more powerful negroid groups in southern Somalia.

Today the descendants of this mixed Zengi population contribute some 80,000 persons to the population of Somalia and are in no sense an insignificant element. It is impossible, however, to estimate their numbers before the Galla and Somali invasions. Nor is it possible to determine their early distribution with any accuracy. By about the tenth century it seems that these pre-Hamites did not extend north of the Shebelle, and were there in contact with the Galla who in turn were under pressure from the expanding Somali concentrated in the north-east part of the Horn. This distribution deduced from oral tradition finds support in the records of the early Arab geo-graphers who refer to the Hamitic peoples of the north by the classical name Berberi, and distinguish them in physical features and culture from the Zengi to their south. . . .

About the tenth century when these coastal centres were developing it will be recalled that much of southern Somalia was still occupied by the pre-Hamitic Zengi while to the north lay the Galla and Somali. It has generally been assumed that the Galla occupied much if not all of northern Somaliland prior to the Somali. And recent research has lent firm support to this view. The best evidence for this depends upon Somali oral tradition, upon the presence today of residual pockets of Galla amongst the northern Somali—especially in the west and Ogaden region—and the fact that a number of place-names in the British Protectorate are almost certainly of Galla origin. It appears, however, that by about this time the Dir Somali—universally regarded as the oldest Somali community—were already established as a small Somali nucleus along most of the northern coastal strip and were pressing upon their Galla neighbours inland.

But the first major impetus to Somali migration which tradi-tion records is the arrival from Arabia of Sheikh Ismā'īl Jabarti in about the tenth or eleventh century, and the expansion of his descendants, the Dārod clan-family, from their early seat in the north-east corner of northern Somalia. It is impossible to date this movement absolutely but from subsequent events it seems most likely that it should be ascribed to this period. This was followed, some two centuries later, by the arrival, also from Arabia, of Sheikh Isāq, founder of the Isāq Somali who settled a little to the west of the Dārod in what is today Erigavo District of the British Protectorate. Sheikh Isāq made his capital the ancient city of Mait where his domed tomb stands today, and, like his predecessor Sheikh Dārōd, married with the local Dir Somali. Today in northern Somaliland the Dir, although in contact with the Isāq on their western fringes, have little effective contact with the Dārōd, yet the affinal connexions of the three peoples are preserved in their genealogies. It is also possible to establish some sort of chronological relationship between Isāq and Dārōd from the fact that the founding ancestors of some Dārōd clans married daughters of Sheikh Isāq and this evidence corresponds well with a gap of about two centuries between the two Sheikhs.

The folk traditions describing the life and works of these two founding ancestors, today venerated as saints, have been collected with hymns in praise of them in a number of manuscript and published hagiologies. This is not the place to discuss these in detail. It is sufficient to say here that they embroider the folk traditions considerably and, with a wealth of unlikely circumstantial detail, link Dārōd and Isāq with Arabia. Indeed, one recently published Dārōd hagiology claims a connexion between Dārōd and a well-known Arabian saint which is almost certainly false, and which since the Arabian saint in question died in 1403 contradicts the burden of oral tradition on the chronological precedence of Dārōd over Sheikh Isāq. No Arabist, I think, would accept the particular pedigrees claimed for Dārōd and Isāq, at least not as set forth in their published hagiologies. Yet the fact remains that Arabians such as Isāq and Dārōd did over the centuries settle in Somaliland and found local Somali lineages. As the matter stands at present I believe that the Dārōd and Isāq legends, however doubtful their precise historical content, nonetheless represent the growth and expansion of the Dārōd and Isāq peoples about the time claimed for the arrival of their founders in Somaliland.

If this is accepted we can conclude that about the twelfth century the Dir and Dārōd, and later the Isāq, were pressing upon their Galla neighbours and the great series of movements which finally disestablished the latter can be said to have begun. Folk tradition today offers little information as to the causes of this Somali movement. One can conjecture that climatic conditions—a series of severe droughts, for example—may have stimulated a general movement in search of new pastures. Almost certainly also, increased immigration from Arabia was a contributory factor. For in an arid country, where there is always a very precarious balance between sufficiency and famine, small increases in population can exert a marked effect. But however uncertain the causes of this migration are, there can be no doubt of its general direction. An analysis of clan traditions shows that in their advance south the Somali followed two main routes, moving either down the valley of the Shebelle River and its tributaries, or along the line of coastal wells on the Indian Ocean coast.

This Somali movement immediately led the Galla to push westwards towards Ethiopia where, as Huntingford suggests, they seem to have already begun their penetration of the Harar Highlands in the twelfth century. An Arabic chronicle of the rulers of Zeila[1] makes it possible to refer a local tradition of Somali conflict with the Galla in the Hargeisa region to the same century. Thus at this time it appears that the Galla still occupied much of the hinterland in the centre of what is today the Protectorate. And from similar traditions of conflict with the Dārōd, the Galla were still also in the east of northern Somaliland, but in both areas losing ground to the militant and recently converted Muslim Somali.

In their turn the Dir vacated north-eastern Somaliland, leaving there the few residual communities which provide evidence of their earlier occupation. They moved westwards behind one flank of the Galla, always according to tradition struggling

---

[1] There are several versions of this chronicle; one has been published by Cerulli, *Documenti Arabi per la Storia dell'Etiopia* (Rome, 1931), 4–15. The document refers to Sheikh Aw Barkhadle, one of the ancestors of the Walashama' dynasty of Ifāt who settled near Hargeisa teaching Islam. He is regarded as one of the Fathers of Somali Islam and his tomb is a famous place of pilgrimage.

with them, and eventually established themselves in the west of the Protectorate and French Somaliland where the 'Ise and Gadabūrsi clans are their strongest representatives today. Further evidence for this reconstruction of their movements comes from the distribution of the graves of the 'Ise and Gadabūrse clan ancestors. These lie close to Sheikh Isāq's tomb at Mait in Erigavo District, several hundred miles from the grazing areas of the two clans today. Folk tradition also records the movement of other Dir groups from the east into the Harar-Jigjiga region of Ethiopia where they are today. Other Dir thrust south. This general movement seems by the sixteenth and seventeenth centuries to have proceeded to a point where the Dārōd and Isāq had taken over much of northern Somaliland and the Ogaden Province of Ethiopia. So that almost certainly by the seventeenth century the distribution of clans and peoples in northern Somaliland had become much as it is today.

In step with these Somali movements in the north the Galla were increasingly thrust westwards and south and ultimately into Ethiopia where, however, their main invasion was delayed until the sixteenth century. As they withdrew, their predecessors, the negroid Zengi, were thrust further into Kenya. At the same time, the Somali were continuing their drive south, in the early stages, to some extent by-passing the established Galla.

We owe most of our knowledge of this southerly Somali expansion to the painstaking research of Dr Enrico Cerulli. According to Cerulli's examination of folk traditions in the south, the earliest Somali to enter this area were the Jidu, who having pressed south settled for a time on the Shebelle River, and then thrust across it towards the coast near Merca. When this took place is not clear. Tradition in the Mogadishu-Warsheikh area refers to the arrival of the first Somali settlers from the north in three waves: first the Jidu, then the Ajuran, and finally the Abgal. The last two clans are of the Hawiye clan-family or closely associated with it. The Arab geographer Ibn Sa'īd records that in the thirteenth century the land lying round the Arabian settlement of Merca was occupied by Hawiye, so that although it is impossible to deduce the time of their arrival or of their predecessors, the Jidu, it seems that by this century the local distribution of peoples was as follows:

the Hawiye Somali in the coastal region between Itala and Merca; further south and towards the interior the Jidu; and finally to the west the Galla.

In this area local tradition has most to say of the Ajurān, a group tracing descent patrilineally to a noble Arabian immigrant on the same pattern as the Dārōd and Isāq and derived maternally from the Hawiye. Under a hereditary dynasty which may have had its seat at Meregh the Ajurān consolidated their position as the masters of the fertile reaches of the lower Shebelle basin and established a commercial connexion with the important port of Mogadishu. It seems likely that the commercial fortunes of the Ajurān sultanate and Mogadishu were very closely intertwined, and that the Ajurān reached the peak of their power in the fifteenth century when the evidence from local inscriptions and documents indicates that Mogadishu had reached her greatest prosperity.

Of greater importance as far as the Somali movements of expansion are concerned were the campaigns of the sixteenth century when after more than a hundred years of fairly peaceful relations with Abyssinia Adal had recovered sufficiently to re-enter the conflict. It is possible, as has been suggested, that some impetus for the new Muslim onslaught came from a Somali movement of expansion at the time. However likely, this is impossible to establish; what is clear is that in Imām Ahmad Ibrāhim al-Ghāzī (1506–43) the Muslims had at last found the charismatic leader they lacked.[1] Resounding Muslim victories were won, and the Imām's armies, equipped with cannon imported from Arabia through Zeila, penetrated into the heart of Ethiopia after a series of savage battles the memory of which is still preserved today.

Somali forces contributed much to the Imām's victories. Shihāb ad-Din, the Muslim chronicler of the period, writing between 1540 and 1560, mentions them frequently. The most prominent Somali groups in the campaigns were the Geri, Marrehān, and Harti—all Dārōd clans. Shihāb ad-Din is very

---

[1] The Imām is known popularly to Somali as Ahmad Guray (in Amharic, Granhe)—Ahmad the left-handed. His origins are virtually unknown, and both the Ethiopian and Arab chroniclers throw little light on his ancestry. In Somali tradition he is often confused with one of his Somali generals also called Ahmad Guray.

vague as to their distribution and grazing areas, but describes the Harti as at the time in possession of the ancient eastern port of Mait. Of the Isāq only the Habar Magādle clan seem to have been involved and their distribution is not recorded. Finally, several Dir clans also took part. The effective participation of these pastoral nomads, renowned 'clutterers of roads', in the Muslim victories indicates something of the power of leadership, spiritual as well as temporal, of the Imām; for the Somali were certainly unaccustomed to joining together in common cause and did not take easily to military discipline on so wide a front. Certainly there can be few occasions in Somali history when so many disparate and hostile clans combined together, even for a short time, under one banner.

This extraordinary outburst of Muslim enterprise, as might be expected, was not long sustained. In 1542 the reigning Emperor of Abyssinia Galāwdēwos, with Portuguese support, routed the Muslims near Lake Tana. The Imām was killed and Galāwdēwos' victory marked the final extinction of the Muslim threat and decided the fate of Abyssinia in favour of the Christian kingdom. Although the Muslims, with Harar as their new headquarters, continued the struggle, hoping to reverse the Christian gains, they were unsuccessful and the glorious victories of the Imām were never repeated. Adal declined rapidly, and from Harar the capital was transferred in 1577 to the oasis of Aussa in the scorching Dankali deserts where it was thought to be secure from further Abyssinian attack. Here, however, it was regularly harried by the Galla and ultimately overthrown by the nomadic Danakil, its ancient dynasty disappearing towards the end of the seventeenth century.

Adal's confines have thus a shifting and fluid history and although Somali played an important part in the sixteenth-century conquest of Abyssinia it is not yet clear to what extent they formed part of the Muslim state at other periods. Here it is important to note that Zeila, Berbera, and Mait were not the only Muslim towns associated with Adal. At least twenty other Muslim centres flourished in the hinterland of what is today the British Protectorate and Harar Province of Ethiopia, and it seems that, in the sixteenth century at any rate, they formed part of the state of Adal. The excavation of these sites, some of which include the remains of extensive waterworks, is urgently required, not only for the light this should shed on Somali history and tribal movements but also for its contribution to the fuller understanding of Ethiopian history. A preliminary survey of the majority of the ruined towns made some twenty years ago by Curle led to finds of pottery, beads, and coins, which have been dated and which show that these Muslim centres flourished in the fifteenth and sixteenth centuries at the time when Zeila also reached her greatest prosperity.

Ahmad Granhe's victories and their reversal by Galāwdēwos had at least two important effects for the movements of the Galla and Somali in the Horn of Africa. Ahmad's attacks led to a concentration of Abyssinian forces in the north and apparently to a corresponding weakening of Abyssinian resistance in the south-west where the Galla, pressed by the Somali, were able to penetrate in very large numbers early in the sixteenth century. Subsequently, the recovery of Abyssinia appears to have closed the gateway to further Somali expansion in the north-west, and to have led the Somali to press increasingly upon the Galla in southern Somalia, thus maintaining the Galla thrust into south-western Abyssinia. By this time, however, according to oral tradition certain Dārōd groups which had formed part of the Imām's armies had already established themselves in the Harar-Jigiiga regions where they are today. So that despite the ultimate failure of the Muslim cause the movement of the Imām's armies was accompanied by some new Somali expansion in the north-west.

In the south as the Galla withdrew, northern Somali settlers gathered in increasing numbers. New groups of Hawiye immigrants found their way to the Shebelle and began to challenge the ascendancy of the Ajurān, eventually overthrowing them. Hawiye oral traditions collected by Cerulli connect the defeat of the Ajurān with the penetration of Mogadishu by new Hawiye settlers and the collapse of the city's Mudaffar dynasty. A provisional date of 1624 can be assigned to the latter event since it is recorded in a letter written by the Jesuit missionary Father de Velasco, who in that year visited Pate and Malindi. This suggests that the Ajurān lost their influence in southern Somalia to new Hawiye settlers early in the seventeenth century. It appears however from local tradition that at that time the zone between the Shebelle and

Juba Rivers to the south of Bur Hacaba was still in the hands of the Galla.

About the same time, again from the evidence of tradition, the Rahanwin Somali who had descended from the north down the valley of the Shebelle began to make their presence felt in these regions. They thrust into the Baidoa plateau, overcoming its previous occupants, and began to press northwestwards towards the Galla at Bur Hacaba. Thus it appears from the folk traditions of this area that early in the seventeenth century the regions from the coast near Mogadishu westwards in the direction of the present Ethiopian frontier were occupied first by the Hawiye, then by the Galla, and finally by the Rahanwīn. This inferred distribution is confirmed by a Portuguese document of 1625 describing the caravan route from Mogadishu to Abyssinia.

The Rahanwīn continued their progress and apparently before the end of the century had dislodged the Galla from their stronghold at Bur Hacaba, forcing them to withdraw to the south-west and eventually over the Juba River to its right bank. This brought further Galla pressure to bear on the Zengi whose traditional capital, Shungwaya, was in the seventeenth century, according to the 'Book of Zengi', in the Juba region. Thus by the end of the seventeenth century the Galla, whose strength must have been very considerably reduced by their great thrusts into Ethiopia, had lost to the Somali all their former territory as far south as the Juba. But they left behind them secure evidence of their former presence in the many Galla minority groups today found amongst the Rahanwīn and Digil Somali of the Shebelle and Juba regions.

Finally, groups of Dir Somali, whose displacement from northern Somaliland by the Dārōd and Isāq was by this time almost complete, reached the south. The most important of these new immigrants were the Bīmāl clan who came into conflict with the already established Digil, conquered them, and eventually settled near Merca where they are today. Thus by the eighteenth century southern Somalia as far south as the Juba River had assumed its present ethnic composition.

But the Somali advance did not stop at the Juba. Dārōd from the north and the Ogaden continued to push south in spite of considerable opposition from those clans which had preceded them. Eventually they reached the Shebelle and began to press upon the Digil early in the nineteenth century. They were halted, however, by the Rahanwīn under the strong leadership first of the Gassar Gude, stationed at Lugh Ferrandi on the Juba, and, from about 1840 onwards, of the Geledi based on the Shebelle. This forced the new Dārōd immigrants to move up to the Juba and brought them into contact with the Galla on the right bank of the river. Although they had lost so much territory, the latter were still fighting a rearguard action, and from their centre at Afmadu made occasional raids across the river into Somali territory. Even the religious settlement of Bardera, founded in 1820, on the middle reaches of the Juba, was occasionally threatened. Thus the Dārōd were faced with a formidable neighbour whom at this stage they found it more expedient to appease than to provoke. Having gained their protection, parties of Dārōd managed to cross the river as clients and allies of the Galla, who at the time were subject to occasional attacks from the Akamba to their south-west and the Masai to their west, and welcomed Somali support.

Further Dārōd immigrants entered the area, sought alliance with the Galla, and crossing the river joined their kinsmen there. Some of these had come by sea in dhows from northern Somaliland. This situation of Dārōd-Galla alliance lasted for some time, and is that described by Guillain when he visited the southern Somalia coast in 1847. About 1865, however, the Galla were stricken by an epidemic of smallpox, and this provided an opportunity for the new Dārōd immigrants to turn the tables upon their Galla masters. In fact almost immediately the Galla were attacked from all sides and suffered very heavy losses. The few who survived fled southwards; and by the turn of the century most of the southern Galla had been cleared from the area, maintaining a foothold only at Wajir and Buna. The Somali pressure continued—partly stimulated by Ethiopian military expeditions in the Ogaden—and in 1909 groups of Dārōd reached the Tana River with stock estimated to number as many as 50,000 head.

In 1912 when administrative and military posts were opened by the British in the area the situation was still fluid. The Dārōd were still on the move and now seeking the complete domination of the region from Buna in the west through Wajir to the Tana River in the south-east. Many of the pre-Hamitic WaBoni who survived had become serfs to the 'Abdalla Dārōd, and most of the Warday Galla had to be moved across the Tana to prevent their extinction by the Somali. A good number, however, remained amongst the new Dārōd immigrants as their clients, thus completely reversing the earlier position when the Galla dominated the river. To the west the once powerful Ajurān, who had earlier, about the seventeenth century, been forced south by later Somali immigrants, were being infiltrated by the Digodia Somali, and the southern Galla Boran were being increasingly driven to the north-west. By 1919 feeling between the Dārōd and those Warday Galla who had been moved across the Tana and those who had remained amongst the Dārōd reached such a pitch that it was again necessary for the Kenya government to intervene. This led to the Somali-Orma (Galla) agreement which allowed the Galla who remained with the Dārōd on the left bank to choose between accepting the formal status of serfs or moving across the river to join their free kinsmen. Those who opted to cross the Tana were obliged to leave behind them with their Somali patrons half the cattle which they had acquired during their bondage. In fact, however, few of the Warday Galla moved.

About twelve years later there was further unrest amongst the Galla subjects of the Dārōd on the Tana and a rumour that the Somali were about to disregard the 1919 agreement gained wide currency. Whether as a direct result of this, or from other causes, about eight hundred Galla dependants with about ten times that number of livestock made a singularly unsuccessful bid for freedom, moving towards the Tana River at the height of the dry season. Nearly half their number are thought to have perished, and the remainder were ignominiously returned to the left bank of the river. In 1936 the agreement ended and the government of Kenya tacitly recognized that except for those on the right bank of the Tana, the Warday Galla had been finally absorbed by the Somali.

Thus, although the establishment of administrative posts in Jubaland, about 1912, marked the final stages of the great Somali migrations which had lasted almost ten centuries, Somali infiltration southwards still continued and still continues today. Now, however, the movement is more peaceful, and as merchants and traders Somali immigrants have penetrated as far south as Tanganyika, and in a few cases even reached the Rhodesias and the Union of South Africa.

Those movements had of course far-reaching social repercussions. They led to the present distribution of peoples in the Somalilands and contributed to the Galla invasion of Ethiopia, where today Galla make up perhaps half the total population. Similarly the pre-Hamitic Zengi peoples were driven south into the East African coastlands except for the few residual communities which still survive in southern Somalia and in the Northern Province of Kenya. At the same time the Somali themselves were profoundly modified in the process. All the immigrants from the north were nomadic pastoralists, but when they reached the more fertile regions of southern Somalia some adopted cultivation and to varying degrees combined it with pastoralism. Through intermixture with negroid and Galla peoples in southern Somalia, the present Digil and Rahanwīn confederations emerged with their distinctive characteristics. From the negroid sedentaries they adopted cultivation, and from the Galla temporarily copied their system of age-grades as the Jubaland Dārōd also did later and also finally discarded. From their mixed origins and new economy the Digil and Rahanwīn evolved their hierarchical political system which differs considerably from that of the northern pastoral Somali. And while their new political system was not that of a state, it does bear some resemblance to the Hamitic conquest states of East Africa.

Before, however, pursuing the further advance of the Somali, of whom a medley of clans now made their presence felt in the south, it is necessary to return briefly to events in northern Somaliland, and to the struggle for supremacy between the Muslim emirate of Adal and the expanding Abyssinian kingdom. Here there are written records available for the reconstruction of the past, though many are not so much contemporary accounts as later compilations of oral tradition. These show that by the thirteenth century the Muslim state of Ifāt, which included Adal and the port of Zeila, was ruled by the Walashma', a dynasty then claiming Arab origins. By this time the rival ambitions of the Muslims and Christians had reached a point where serious strife was inevitable. The initiative was first taken by the Muslims. Early in the fourteenth century Haq ad-Dīn, Sultan of Ifāt, turned the sporadic and disjointed forays of his predecessors into a full-scale war of aggression and, according to an Arab chronicle of Zeila in my possession, for the first time couched his call to arms in terms of a religious war against the infidels.

At first the Muslims were remarkably successful. Christian territory was invaded, churches were razed, and Christians forced to apostatize at the point of the sword. In 1415, however, the Muslims were routed and the ruler of Ifāt, Sa'd ad-Dīn, was pursued and eventually killed in his last stronghold on the island off the coast of Zeila which to this day bears his name. From this period Arab chroniclers refer to Adal itself as the 'Land of Sa'd ad-Dīn'. This crushing defeat and Sa'd ad-Dīn's martyrdom, for his death soon came to be regarded in this light, took place in the reign of the Abyssinian Negus Yeshāq (1414–29), and it is in songs celebrating his victories over the Muslims that the name 'Somali' is first recorded.

The Abyssinian victories and the occupation of Zeila virtually extinguished the Muslim kingdom of Ifāt; Sa'd ad-Dīn's sons fled to Arabia where they sought refuge with the King of Yemen. They were able, however, to return a few years later, and the Walashma' dynasty then took the title of kings of Adal and transferred its capital to Dakar, a centre probably situated to the south-east of Harar further from the threat of Abyssinian attack. These consequences of Sa'd ad-Dīn's defeat are clear. The effects of the Abyssinian victories on the Somali, however, can only be conjectured. It seems likely that the 'Ise and Gadabūrse clans which by this time were in the vicinity of Zeila felt some effects from the conquest, especially since a local Gadabūrse chronicle refers to the clan's founding ancestor Imām 'Ali Si'id (d. 1392) as one of the Muslim leaders fighting on the Western flank of Sa'd ad-Dīn's armies.

In northern Somaliland the Somali seem to have been little affected by contact with the Galla and it is only recently, and not as a direct result of their former migrations, that they have in the west begun to borrow items of Galla culture associated with the adoption of agriculture. In the south the mixture of peoples was more heterogeneous, and the residual Galla and negroid communities, while contributing to the new culture and social organization of the Digil and Rahanwīn, were also themselves profoundly modified by contact with the Somali. The riverine negroids have preserved certain ritual and cultural features of their own, but have adopted Islam, and in most things tend to conform to the ways of the conquering Somali. At the same time the infusion of negroid blood amongst the Sab of southern Somalia has heightened the contempt which the northern pastoralists traditionally exhibit towards cultivators; and people of negroid features are stigmatized as *bon*, subject peoples, not pastoral aristocrats (*billis*). This if anything has strengthened the primary schism in the Somali nation between the sedentary Sab and nomadic Samāle, and has helped to perpetuate a line of division which, despite the strength of pan-Somali nationalism today, is still to some extent reflected in modern party politics. . . .

19. Seyyid Said

REGINALD COUPLAND *The Exploitation of East Africa 1856–1890* Faber & Faber 1939; pages 1–7, 10–13

In the second half of the nineteenth century the Colonial Powers of Europe took possession of almost all mid-Africa—the tropical belt between the Sahara and the Zambesi. East and West, it was an equally easy achievement. Nowhere were there any forces, other than those of Nature, which could offer serious or sustained resistance to the wealth and equipment of European nations. Their only substantial difficulty arose from their own rivalry, from quarrels, flaming up nearly at times but never quite into war, about their respective shares of African soil. But, if it was roughly the same story everywhere, there was one great difference in the way it was unfolded in East Africa and in West. On the west coast Europe had only Africans to deal with. On the east coast she found that Asia had forestalled her and was already in possession. She was confronted with the Arab state of Zanzibar.

This state was the creation of a great Arab, Said-bin-Sultan.

In 1806, when he started his remarkable career by usurping the sovereignty of Muscat, mid-East Africa was almost unknown outside the orbit of the western Indian Ocean. Arabs and Indians had traded there from the dawn of history, and the Arab colonies planted along the coast from the beginning of the eighth century A.D. onwards had once been thriving little 'city-states', exporting African products to Arabia, Persia and India and importing manufactured goods therefrom. But their prosperity had been blighted in the sixteenth century by subjection to the political control and economic monopoly of the Portuguese; and when after some hundred and fifty years of decline and decay the Portuguese Empire in the East collapsed, they had regained their independence north of Mozambique but little else. Ruined walls and forts and mosques, deserted sites of once populous towns now fast going 'back to the jungle', bore witness to a standard of wealth and civilisation that was lost beyond recovery. Never again would Arab travellers write, for all the learned world to read, about the fine houses and gardens, the crowded harbours, the gold and silver and silken garments of Arab East Africa. Even the independence of the Arab colonies was not quite as complete as it once had been. The Imām of Muscat who, backed by the fierce sea-faring folk of Oman, had taken the lead in their deliverance from the Portuguese, had asserted his own overlordship and levied tribute as the price of his protection: and his successors had claimed, though they had not effectively or regularly exercised, the same rights of suzerainty.

It was by enforcing these rights that Said acquired his East African 'dominions', as they were termed in the language of international diplomacy. Having spent the first half of his reign in securing his position in south-east Arabia—as far as it was possible to secure it against such militant or predatory neighbours as the Wahabi of the desert or the Jawasmi of the Persian Gulf—he spent the second half in establishing a new political and economic system in East Africa. By force or guile he obtained the submission of all the Arab towns along the coast and on the adjacent islands between Warsheikh in the north and Cape Delgado in the south. At the more important of them he appointed Governors as his personal representatives, supported by little garrisons from his small mercenary army. But the rights of intervention or control implicit in Said's overlordship were never defined, and in practice the Arab townsmen were allowed as a rule to manage their local affairs under their own traditional sheikhs or sultans. Apart from an occasional interference in disputes or a reference to Said's ultimate judicial authority, the Governors did little more than collect the quota which Said levied on the customs-dues collected at each port. But the substantial measure of autonomy thus conceded was only local. Just as Said's overlordship protected the Arab towns from external attack, so it precluded them from any independent relationship with foreign States.

Except in the north, in Somaliland, the subjects of this overlordship, the townsmen of the coast, were Arabs or Swahili—the name of the mixed Arab and African race, which now far outnumbered the dwindling remnant of pure Arabs, and of the similarly mixed language which had long taken the place of Arabic along the maritime belt. But in the north, at Barawa, Merka and Mogadishu, the original Arab colonies had been dominated and in course of time absorbed by the warlike Somali tribesmen of the countryside. In blood and speech, custom and character, their inhabitants in Said's day were predominantly Somali; and among such martial and free-spirited folk the acceptance of Said's suzerainty was more a matter of acquiescence or convenience than submission: he could never have enforced it. But the Somali and their southern neighbours, the Galla, were, broadly speaking, the only formidable African peoples on the coast. The dreaded Masai dwelt near Mounts Kenya and Kilimanjaro on the western side of the Nyika, the arid thorn-covered wilderness which lies between the maritime belt and the interior. The primitive Bantu tribes along the coast, amongst whom the blood and speech and Moslem faith of the Swahili were steadily spreading, had never been strong enough to question the right of Asiatics from overseas to invade and colonise their country. The Arabs for their part made no attempt to govern them. They sold cloth and wire and beads to them and bought their foodstuffs. They employed them as porters for their caravans. Otherwise they left them more or less alone, since most of their need for labour was met by slaves obtained from the interior. Only one tribe or group of tribes had sufficient political coherence and organisation to deal with the Arabs on anything like equal terms. In the course of its expansion the kingdom of Usambara, centred in a range of mountains some fifty miles from the sea, had extended its control over the people of the coast opposite Pemba island. A conflict between African and Arab might well have resulted: but neither Said nor Kimweri, the capable paramount-chief of the Shambaa at that time, desired to exercise complete sovereignty over that small area. By tacit agreement Kimweri appointed his officials and tax-collectors for the villages and Said his customs-officers at the ports.

Government, in fact, was only a secondary factor in Said's East African *régime*. He was a brave but unsuccessful soldier. His methods of administration were of almost patriarchal simplicity. It was to commerce, to the enrichment of himself and his realm, that he gave most of his subtle and sagacious mind: he was, above all else, a merchant-prince. He attempted, therefore, to exercise over his dominions only that minimum of political control which was required for the maintenance of his economic system. The success of that system, far more than any triumphs of diplomacy or statesmanship, won him the place he holds in history.

There were six main threads in his economic policy. In the first place he amplified the monetary system by the introduction of a small copper coinage from India to supplement the existing silver currency—'Maria Theresa' dollars and Spanish crowns.[1] Secondly, he simplified the customs system. All imports into his African dominions were charged a regular duty of 5 per cent. There were no export duties, and practically no other form of taxation. Thirdly, he exploited the high fertility of Zanzibar and Pemba islands by encouraging, almost indeed enforcing, the plantation of cloves. Fourthly, he revivified and greatly extended the old Arab caravan-trade with the African interior by means of which African products, especially ivory and slaves, were obtained, partly, as in the case of slaves, to supply the local demand at Zanzibar and the Arab coast towns, but mainly for export at a high profit overseas. Fifthly, he warmly welcomed the first incursions of the western business-world into the East African backwater it had consistently ignored and avoided since the early days of the Portuguese

[1] Exchange value from $4\frac{1}{2}$ to $4\frac{3}{4}$ to the pound sterling.

Empire. He concluded commercial treaties with the United States in 1833, with Great Britian in 1839, and with France in 1844, which, except along a stretch of the coast opposite Zanzibar known as the Mrima, granted to the merchants of those countries the same freedom of trade at all Said's African ports as that enjoyed by his own subjects and provided for the establishment of consulates at Zanzibar. Similar encouragement was given to German enterprise, though a commercial treaty with the Hanseatic States was not concluded till after Said's death. Last, but not least, he fostered the growth of the Indian community at Zanzibar not only by giving them complete religious, social and economic freedom but also by personal relationships with some of their ablest men and the use of their services in administration and finance. And this he did for the good reason that the Arabs in general lacked the aptitude and the industry needed for the management of business. Indeed in Said's day, and probably for many generations before it, nearly all the business of Arab East Africa—the banking, the financing of commercial enterprise, the wholesale and even most of the retail trade—was in Indian hands.

Such in outline was the policy which Said pursued in East Africa between 1830 and 1856. Its results were impressive. His primary objective was triumphantly attained: he multiplied his African revenue ten times. Zanzibar grew from an insignificant little town, rarely visited by shipping except for taking in water and provisions, to be the principal port on the western shores of the Indian Ocean, the chief *entrepôt* for Afro-Asiatic trade, the source of almost all the world's supply of cloves, the place where more ivory and gum-copal could be bought than anywhere else, the biggest slave-market in the East, a focus, finally, if only as yet in a minor degree, of international interest where the consuls of three great western peoples flew their flags and the merchants of four maintained their houses of business. This growth of Zanzibar in wealth and importance was not, of course, the outcome, except as regards the clove-trade, of its own insular resources. It was mainly due to the rapid and far-reaching penetration of the African mainland. The old trade-routes into the interior had been extended farther westwards and new ones opened up. By 1856 Arab caravans, much more numerous now and larger and better equipped, had reached the Great Lakes—Nyasa, Tanganyika and Victoria Nyanza; and adventurous traders were pressing on beyond them in quest of ivory or slaves towards the upper reaches of the Congo and the Nile. Since expeditions of such length meant an absence of two years or more from the coast, little inland settlements had been established at central points or crossways of trade. On the great route from Bagamoyo to Lake Tanganyika there was a regular Arab colony or township at Tabora, substantial permanent trade-posts at Masansa and Ujiji, and lesser ones at intervals on the way up from the coast. All this meant a wide extension of Said's authority. The itinerant Arab merchants did not annex the country they passed through. As on the coast, so in the interior, their relations with the Africans were primarily commercial. They might make friends with a tribe in order to buy ivory and slaves from it or attack a tribe in order to enslave it; but otherwise they left the natives to their own devices. Nevertheless, armed as they were with muskets, they were usually, if not quite always, the masters of the country through which they marched or in which they set up their trade-posts: and, since they all acknowledged allegiance to their overlord at Zanzibar, it might be held that Said had extended his dominions, in this somewhat tenuous and elastic manner, from the maritime belt to the Great Lakes. It was significant, for example, that the European explorers and missionaries, who in Said's later years were just beginning to invade the East African *hinterland*, invariably asked for Said's blessing on their ventures and obtained from him what was virtually a passport—a letter of recommendation to ensure, as it always did ensure, that the bearer was welcomed and aided on his way by all Arabs or Swahili he might meet inland.

As the result of this highly successful essay in 'economic imperialism', Seyyid Said became one of the leading figures in the Arab world. But his power was not as great as his prestige. The stronger he had grown in East Africa, the weaker he had grown in Oman. To maintain his authority in both fields at the same time was a difficult task, especially since the voyage between them, one way for half the year and the other way for the other half, was made almost impossible for sailing ships by the prevailing winds. He had seen the difficulty at the outset and chosen to face it. So determined was he to pursue his African ambitions that, for that reason first and foremost among several, he had actually shifted his seat of government from Muscat to Zanzibar. That was in 1840, and by 1856 the result was plain. In East Africa his authority was normally unquestioned, but in Oman his long absences had consistently meant trouble. At regular intervals he had been summoned back from Zanzibar to save his throne and homeland from external attack or internal intrigue and disaffection. More than once, indeed, he would not have saved them if the British Government in India had not come to his help; and when he did recover his grip of Oman unaided, it was more by prestige than power: his personal authority was unique; and it may well have been his realisation of that fact that determined him to arrange for the partition of his swollen realm at his death between two of his sons. Which section he himself preferred was obvious enough. Before he died Said was already much more Sultan of Zanzibar than of Muscat. . . .

The price which Said had to pay for British friendship, which meant in the last resort the safeguarding of his realm and independence by British sea-power, was his submission to British demands for the restriction of the Slave Trade. By means of this traffic some thousands of Africans were obtained every year from the interior and sold into slavery at Zanzibar and the Arab coast towns or in Oman and the neighbouring parts of Asia. But a brief account must be given here of the manner in which Said had become involved in the extension of 'the unweary, unostentatious, and inglorious crusade of England against Slavery' from Europe and the Atlantic to Asia and the Indian Ocean. By the abolition of Slavery in the British Isles in 1772-4, of the British Slave Trade in 1808, and of Slavery in the British colonies in 1834, by cajoling, badgering and bribing other European nations to enact laws against the Slave Trade and to enforce, or allow Britain to enforce, their execution, and by maintaining naval patrols for the prevention of slave smuggling on both sides of the Atlantic, the British people —and from 1790 onwards it was a genuinely popular movement—had done all they could do to destroy the slave system in the West. In the East it was more old-established, more widespread and more difficult to combat; but from 1807 onwards a series of attacks had been made on it. The prohibition of the

Slave Trade was enforced in British India, and the protected
Indian rulers on the north-west coast induced to follow suit;
treaties for the suppression of the Trade were concluded with
Persia and the Arab tribes of the Persian Gulf; and in 1843 the
legal status of Slavery was abolished in British India. But these
repressive measures were only concerned with the countries
into which slaves were imported; and no efforts to end the
Trade could succeed unless measures were also taken in the
countries of export. As long, in fact, as slaves were obtainable,
somehow or other they would be obtained, at any rate in countries less amenable to British control than India, whatever
treaties might be signed or orders issued by their signatories.
That at once brought Said into the picture; for the vast bulk
of the slaves were Africans; the main field of supply was the
area of the Great Lakes; and while some of the slaves obtained
therefrom came down to the coast of Portuguese East Africa,
most of them emerged at the sea-ports of Said's African
dominions. Portuguese and French slave smuggling from Portuguese territory was gradually suppressed by diplomatic pressure
on the Governments concerned and the vigilance of British
cruisers. But that, though a difficult task, was far less difficult
than the task at Zanzibar. France and Portugal had not only
outlawed the Slave Trade: they were not Slave States. Though
something akin to Slavery was introduced for a time in Réunion
under the guise of the 'Free Labour Emigration System', they
could not plead that Slavery was an essential part of their
social system. Therein, on the other hand, lay the strength of
Said's case. The abolition of the Trade would not only involve
the loss of the biggest item in his customs revenue and of the
most lucrative source of livelihood open to his subjects, it would
lead in course of time to the disappearance throughout his
realm, in Oman as in Africa, of an institution on which Arab
society had been based from the dawn of history. In Said's
day, indeed, all Arabs took Slavery as much for granted as
the Prophet had taken it for granted in the Koran. Individual slaves might be freed and their owners acquire merit
thereby, but that all slaves should be freed, that the institution of Slavery itself should ever come to an end was almost
inconceivable.

Fortunately for Said the abolition of the whole slave system in East Africa was necessarily a gradual business. However high-handed British Governments might be, they could not destroy the Slave Trade and Slavery at one stroke. But Said had to bear the first impact of British humanitarianism on his remote old-fashioned corner of the world. It began gently when in 1812 and again in 1815 he was invited by the Government of Bombay to co-operate in the suppression of the Slave Trade. 'Your acquiescence in this proposition', he was told, 'will be extremely gratifying to the British Government.' But Said, of course, was not going to acquiesce unless he must. So stronger pressure was presently brought to bear by the Governments of Bombay and Mauritius in combination; and in the Moresby Treaty of 1822 Said yielded half of what was asked of him. He declared it quite impossible to abolish the 'internal' Trade between the various African and Asiatic parts of his dominions since the maintenance of Slavery throughout his realm depended on it; but he agreed to prohibit his subjects from engaging in the 'external' Trade between his ports and any country to the south of Cape Delgado or to the east of a line drawn from Diu Head to a point sixty miles east of Socotra. It was a costly concession and fiercely resented by Said's subjects, but, having given his word, Said kept it. Despite, however, his genuine attempts to get his prohibitory edict obeyed, the fact that slaves were still allowed to be shipped from Zanzibar and the African coast northwards to Oman made it all too easy for them to be smuggled up the Red Sea and the Persian Gulf and along the Baluchi coast. In 1845, therefore, the pressure on Said was resumed, and another treaty obtained from him which engaged him to forbid all export of slaves from his African dominions. Thus, while slaves could still circulate between Zanzibar and the Arab coast-towns, they could not legally be shipped to Oman.

'You have put on me', Said constantly complained, 'a heavier load than I can bear.' That he did bear it was largely due to the trust that he had learned to place in the sincerity of Captain Hamerton, the British consul and political agent at Zanzibar from 1841 to 1857, whose task it was to convey to Said the desires and intentions of his Government. When Hamerton told him that Britain wished to preserve the integrity of his realm, he believed it. When Hamerton told him that

Britain meant to destroy the Slave Trade and sooner or later would destroy it, he believed that too, however little he might understand the reason for it. And so he did what he was asked to do. It meant, as has been said, a serious loss of revenue; and it provoked such bitterness and anger among the Arabs of East Africa that only a ruler as venerated as Said was in his later years could have brooked it. Arab society throughout its history has always been rent by faction, and even at Zanzibar there was a recalcitrant minority, headed by the arrogant el-Harthi tribe, which questioned Said's authority and criticised his policy. There had always been Arabs, moreover, at Zanzibar as in earlier days at Muscat, who favoured France rather than Britain; and the French Government, it was understood, was not itching like the British to meddle with the Arab Slave Trade. So Said's surrender united two strains of opposition. When the harsh restrictions of the second treaty began to make themselves felt, there was talk of a *coup d'état*, of appealing for French intervention, even of satisfying the known French desire for a foothold on the African coast, if only British interference with Arab customs and Arab money-making could be stopped and the old freedom of the Slave Trade recovered. But Said did not waver. Because he put the independence of his realm above all else, he clung to British friendship to the end. As he lay half-conscious on his deathbed, he called again and again for Hamerton.

20. The Arab slave trade

REGINALD COUPLAND *The Exploitation of East Africa 1856– 1890* Faber & Faber 1939; pages 134–41

The Arab Slave Trade was as old as the Arab connexion with East Africa. Our earliest description of that country, the Greek *Periplus* or guide for navigators, written about A.D. 80, tells of Arabs trading down the coast and of 'slaves of the better sort' being exported from Somaliland to Egypt. How long before that date the Slave Trade had begun it is impossible to say, but after that time presumably it continued up to the period of the Arab colonisation of the coastland which started about A.D. 700. Thenceforward a steady supply of slaves was obtained from the interior both for the domestic use of the Arab colonists and also, and in greater volume as time went on, for export overseas to Arabia, Irak, Turkey, Persia and India. Slave armies were maintained in Irak in the ninth century and in Bengal in the fifteenth. Between 1486 and 1493 the latter kingdom was ruled by two African slave soldiers. African slaves were shipped to the East Indies and were even to be seen as far east as China.

This business of robbing Africa of Africans had thus been carried on by Asiatics for fourteen hundred years and probably a good deal longer before Europe took a hand in it. During their occupation of the coast from Sofala to Mogadishu the Portuguese exported slaves, partly eastwards to their settlements in India and the Indies, but mainly westwards round the Cape and over the Atlantic to Brazil. Spaniards and Frenchmen also took part in due course in this trade from Mozambique—the latter needing slaves not only for the plantations of the French West Indies but for those of Île de France and Bourbon. British 'slavers', content, no doubt, with their major share in the West African trade, neglected the East African field; and the entry of the British into East African waters—their naval mastery of the Indian Ocean and their annexation of Cape Colony, Mauritius and the Seychelles—coincided, as it happened, not only with the complete suppression of their own Slave Trade but also with the initiation of their attempt to stop it being carried on by any other people. From 1815 onwards British diplomacy, backed at need by financial inducements, was continuously exerted to persuade the governments concerned to legislate against the Trade and—what proved to be of more practical value—to conclude treaties enabling the British navy to assist on a nominally reciprocal basis in the execution of the law. To some extent these efforts had proved successful by the end of Seyyid Said's reign. Something had been done at the import end of the Trade by prohibitive measures in British India and by treaties with Persia and the Arabs of the Persian Gulf. More had been done at the export end, i.e. the East African coast, by treaties with Spain, Portugal and France and with King Radamá of Madagascar. By 1852 the shipping of slaves from Mozambique across the Atlantic had been reduced to a small fraction of its earlier volume. In the early 'sixties it dried up altogether. The local need for labour, on the other hand, in Réunion (as Bourbon was renamed in 1848) and in the islands of Nossi-bé and Mayotta acquired by the French in 1840–43, was still being met by a process not very different from the Slave Trade. The French planters of Mauritius, being now British subjects, had been able to replace slave labour with that of 'coolies' from British India; but the Government of India had forbidden the engagement of Indians from the territories under its control for service on foreign soil; and since their possessions in India were far too small to provide the requisite labour, the French authorities determined to obtain it from Africa. In 1843 a system, known as the 'Free Labour Emigration System', was introduced, under which slaves were purchased by French officials from Arab traders, mainly at Kilwa, formally set free, and then engaged as 'voluntary' emigrants to work for a period of years at Réunion, Mayotta or Nossi-bé. This new demand inevitably stimulated Arab slave raiding in the interior. In 1854, moreover, the Portuguese Government were induced to permit the extension of the 'system' to Mozambique with the result that, as Livingstone found on the Zambesi Expedition, the old traffic from Lake Nyasa to the Portuguese coast, which had been reduced to a minimum in the course of the preceding decade, was briskly revived. The British Government strongly and repeatedly protested; but French Ministers made it clear that, as long as 'free labour' from British India was denied to their colonists, they would continue to obtain 'free labour' from East Africa. In 1861 the British Government conceded the right to hire British Indian 'coolies', and in 1864 the 'system' was abolished.

There remained the purely Arab Slave Trade—the trade that was not only fed, like the European, by Arab raiders but directed overseas in Arab ships to Arab and other Asiatic markets. That the system of treaties and naval patrols had failed to stop this Arab Trade as it had practically stopped the European is clear enough from the facts recorded in the preceding chapter. Why this 'policy of restriction' was unsuccessful and how it was finally superseded by a more effective policy will be explained in due course. In this chapter a brief description must be given of the course and character of the Trade by land and sea. There is copious evidence for it. On land the explorers, on sea the naval patrols, saw the Trade in operation at close quarters, and all the former and several of the latter wrote down what they saw.

A supply of slaves, whether for domestic use at Zanzibar and the coast towns or for sale overseas, could only be obtained in the interior, and slave hunting in one form or another was, together with the quest of ivory, the main objective of those Arab caravans which had penetrated so far inland in the course of Said's reign. The composition of a caravan was always much the same—two or three Arab merchants in charge with their half-caste hangers-on, a body of armed slaves, and the long string of porters, slave or free, with the scarlet flag of the Sultan at their head—but its numbers varied from a hundred or so to a thousand and even more. The principal route for slaves in Majid's time ran from Kilwa to Lake Nyasa, the neighbourhood of which was then the chief source of supply; but slave gangs were to be met with often enough on the other 'trunk road' of the day, the route from Bagamoyo to the 'colony' at Tabora and thence to Lake Tanganyika.

At all points on their way inland and back again the traders were anxious to pick up slaves if only in twos or threes. Kidnapping of natives by natives was rife along the main routes, 'for the Arabs buy whoever is brought to them'; and the victims were sometimes caught while walking in the 'bush' quite close to their villages. Occasionally a chief would be tempted to punish crime by selling the culprit to the traders. Livingstone reports a case of an old chief selling 'his young and good-looking wife for unfaithfulness, as he alleged'. But the main sources of supply were the organised slave-raids in the chosen areas, which shifted steadily farther inland as tract after tract became 'worked out'. The Arabs might conduct a raid themselves, but more usually they incited a chief to attack another tribe, lending him their own armed slaves and guns to ensure his victory.[1]

---

[1] Krapf, the C.M.S. Missionary at Rabai, wrote as follows about the Pangani district: 'The Arabs of Zanzibar come here and promise the Segua chiefs a number of muskets and shot for a certain number of slaves; so, when a chief has entered into the contract, he suddenly falls on a hostile village, sets it on fire, and carries off the inhabitants.'

The result, of course, was an increase in intertribal warfare till 'the whole country was in a flame'. A deplorable example was the fate that befell Usambara. Under 'king' Kimweri it constituted a compact little African state in which, as its European visitors testified, a number of kindred tribes had been welded together under a single system of peace and law. But in 1873 Kirk reported its temporary disruption after Kimweri's death.

The tribes commenced fighting with each other. Captives were sold, and slaves brought in thousands into Pangani which suddenly became a great place of export from having imported slaves from Kilwa the year before. This slave war did not last long as the place was depopulated to such an extent that the few remaining villages became afraid; but the same thing still goes on, though to a less extent, here as elsewhere along the coast.

A village having been carried by assault, all the inhabitants who had not escaped or been killed in the fighting were rounded up—except those who were too old and decrepit to be saleable —and the huts were then set on fire. Three villages were once seen burning within two hours. Cattle would be driven off. Standing crops might be cut down or left to rot. There was no one left to cultivate them, unless a handful of fugitives crept back to 'the wreck of their homes'—the half-burned huts, the blackened ground strewn with broken household goods and bits of furniture, the unburied dead, and the silence. This destruction was often widespread. The explorers speak of 'miles of ruined villages'. Nor were the actual slave-raids the only injury done to the countryside. If they occurred in the sowing season, the strife and anarchy they provoked meant insufficient crops and famine. And that in turn increased the Trade; for a starving tribe would sell its own folk for food. 'A chief without food and without the means of buying food will sell off his people very cheaply indeed . . . I have known children of the age of from 8 to 10 years bought for less corn that would go into one of our hats.'

The slaves' worst sufferings were those they endured between their capture and their ultimate consignment to their masters. The march to the coast, to begin with, was a terrible experience. From the Great Lakes it often lasted three months or more. The slaves were usually roped or chained together from neck to neck in gangs, with their hands bound behind their backs, and sometimes they were 'gagged by having a piece of wood like a snaffle tied into their mouths'. If refractory or suspected of trying to escape they were shackled with beams of wood, 'as thick as a man's thigh', it might be, 'and six feet long with a fork at one extremity in which the neck was secured by an iron pin'. Often a longer and lighter piece of wood, forked at each end, was used to yoke two slaves together. If a halt were called for trading or getting more slaves, the gang was herded together in a hastily built stockade. Livingstone once saw eighty-five slaves, mostly boys of about eight, in this kind of pen. But the most striking feature of the coastward march was the Arab's callous disregard of life. It was not only slaves who resisted their captors or tried to break away that were shot down. Often enough the same punishment awaited the slave who from illness or exhaustion could not keep up with the caravan, and in the latter case it was usually a woman. There was plenty of grim evidence to show the explorers that they were on the heels of a slave caravan. 'We passed a woman tied by the neck to a tree and dead.' 'To-day we came upon a man dead from starvation.' 'We passed a slave woman shot or stabbed through the body. . . . An Arab early that morning had done it in anger at losing the price he had given for her because she was unable to walk any longer.' 'One woman, who was unable to carry both her load and young child, had the child taken from her and saw its brains dashed out on a stone.' Sometimes a caravan had to pass through a district in which drought or warfare had caused a famine, and then whole gangs of slaves might be left in the 'bush', sometimes still yoked together, to die of hunger. No wonder that the routes frequented by the slave-traders could be recognised by the skeletons to be seen at intervals beside the track. All in all, the march to the coast was a shocking business—so shocking that those who witnessed and recorded it doubted if their fellow-countrymen at home would quite believe them. Not long before his death Livingstone noted in his journal that in describing the Slave Trade in the interior as he had seen it he had deemed it 'necessary to keep far within the truth in order not to be thought guilty of exaggeration'. 'But', he added, 'in sober seriousness the subject does not admit of exaggeration. To overdraw its evils is a simple impossibility. The sights I have seen, though common incidents of the traffic, are so nauseous that I always strive to drive them from memory.'

Livingstone, Kirk and Waller, the last of whom took part in Bishop Mackenzie's attempt to found a mission station in the Shiré Highlands, all asserted that 'four or five lives were lost for every slave delivered safe at Zanzibar'. That the Arabs should have been so reckless is not easy to explain. Was it just bad temper and brutality? Or was it that the profit on the coast for every slave was so high that it did not seem to matter how many perished on the way? 'It is like sending up to London for a large block of ice in the summer,' said Waller: 'you know that a certain amount will melt away before it reaches you in the country, but that which remains will be quite sufficient for your wants.' Nor was all the mortality due to the rigours and cruelties of the caravans. There was also the bloodshed caused by the raids and the intertribal fighting they provoked. If that were taken into account, Livingstone calculated that the price of every living slave was not five deaths but at least ten. Most of the explorers, indeed, described the areas scoured by the slave-traders as not merely devastated, but depopulated. There is no reason to doubt the information given to Rigby by men who knew the Kilwa slave route.

Natives of India who have resided many years at Kilwa . . . state that districts near Kilwa, extending to ten or twelve days' journey, which a few years ago were thickly populated, are now entirely uninhabited; and an Arab who has lately returned from Lake Nyasa informed me that he travelled for seventeen days through a country covered with ruined towns and villages which a few years ago were inhabited by the Mijana and Mijan tribes and where now no living soul is to be seen.

The explorers told the same story of other parts of the interior. 'The villages were all deserted. . . . The whole country was painfully quiet.' 'The interior is drained of all its working men.' 'Africa is bleeding out her lifeblood at every pore. A rich country, requiring labour only to render it one of the greatest producers in the world, is having its population, already far too scanty for its needs, daily depleted by the Slave Trade and internecine war.' Cameron went so far as to say that, if the

Slave Trade were not stopped, it would 'die a natural death from the total destruction of the population'.[1]

21. Invasions in Central Africa

ROBERT I. ROTBERG *The Transformation of East Africa* (eds. Stanley Diamond and Fred G. Burke) Basic Books, New York 1966; pages 337–9[2]

Sometime during the sixteenth and seventeenth centuries, pastoralists from the north-east and agriculturalists from the north-west entered the upland region that lies between the headwaters of the Zambezi River and the shores of Lake Nyasa. The former, who may have been descended from groups owing loyalties to the interlacustrine Cwezi dynasty, settled for the most part between Lakes Tanganyika and Nyasa. They apparently intermarried with the autochthonous inhabitants, and may gradually have influenced peoples living beyond the zone of their immediate interpenetration. The latter recall intimate connections with the Lunda-Luba empire of Katanga. Perhaps in the seventeenth century, this empire began to disintegrate and, under a number of leaders, segments entered Bulozi, the heartland of Barotseland, and the Kafue basin, while others crossed the Luapula River and then fragmented again to form the Eastern Lunda, Bemba, and Bisa states. Still another emigré section, that of the Malawi under Karonga, continued across the Chambezi and Luangwa Rivers into modern Nyasaland. They gave their name to the lake only

[1] The depopulation of the Shiré Valley as seen by Livingstone was mainly due to the passage of the Fiti (or Mazitu as he called them), a militant Bantu tribe, whose long marauding expeditions were traditional and not due to the Slave Trade. On that account Dr Steere, head of the Universities' Mission at Zanzibar, thought Livingstone wrong in ascribing the depopulation of the interior to the Slave Trade. Captain Colomb also questioned whether it was the Trade rather than wars which the Trade had not provoked that accounted for depopulation. But Steere never went far inland and Colomb never left the coast, whereas Livingstone traversed depopulated areas which had not been exposed to Fiti or Masai raids, and so did Burton, Speke and Cameron.

[2] All footnotes present in the original have been deleted. The paper was written in 1964.

later called Nyasa and, in time, fissiparous pressures brought about further tribal divisions.

On the eve of the nineteenth century, trans-Zambezi contained an amalgam of very different Bantu-speaking Africans, and a few Arab and Indian traders who had already begun to transport copper ingots, wax, salt, and slaves from this region to entrepôts on both coasts. In the far west, in Bulozi along the upper Zambezi, the Luyana governed a number of subject tribes. To the north, the Eastern Lunda dominated a fairly large region between the Lufira and Chambezi Rivers. On their eastern flank, the Bemba raided but, as yet, had failed to usurp the Lunda paramountcy. In the south-east, meanwhile, the Yao raided for slaves and the various Malawi peoples apparently prospered from the products of their lands. Rivalries and wars there were, but ordered government and an atmosphere of calm apparently prevailed until the Nguni irrupted into trans-Zambezia from the south.

In the early nineteenth century, the most important of the Nguni chiefdoms of eastern South Africa began to compete energetically among themselves. Out of this struggle for power the Zulu, led by Shaka, emerged victorious after overwhelming a warrior group loyal to Zwide. A section of this latter group soon followed Zwangedaba, a subordinate of Zwide, out of Zululand. It penetrated the hinterland of what became the colonies of Mozambique and Southern Rhodesia, everywhere gathering adherents, and then, in 1835, crossed the Zambezi near its confluence with the Luangwa River. They settled for a time among the Nsenga and the Cêwa and then moved north, through the western marches of Malawi country. In Ufipa, near Lake Tanganyika, they paused again until Zwangendaba died. Dissident segments then separated from the main Ngoni group. One segment continued north to Unyamwezi, where it later helped chief Mirambo to control the trade routes of Tanganyika. Another faction went east, to attack the inhabitants of Bagamoyo before finally conquering and settling in the Songea district. The majority, however, followed Mpezeni, a chief who seems to have been the legitimate heir of Zwangendaba. He and most of the members of the main section of the Ngoni circled back through the country then dominated by the Bemba and the Bisa.

The wanderings of the segments loyal to Mpezeni finally ended when the Ngoni crossed the Lunagwa River into what became the eastern districts of Northern Rhodesia. Lastly, even before these segments had penetrated into Bembaland, Mwambera, a rival claimant, had led a number of Mpezeni's erstwhile supporters on to the plateau lands west of Lake Nyasa. Another breakaway group followed a similar route down the west side of the lake into the Dowa district. In this process of finding homes for themselves, the various Ngoni segments had thrown the previous inhabitants of trans-Zambezi into turmoil. They had raided the lakeside Tonga, battled with the Tumbuka, and attacked the various Malawi peoples. The Ngoni had pillaged, ravaged, and generally helped to disrupt the pre-existing social equilibrium. By sundering the various tribal loyalties of the peoples of Nyasaland, they may well have smoothed the path for the eventual conquest by Europeans.

To the west, an invading group similarly imposed its rule on the inhabitants of Barotseland. In about 1833/35, the Kololo, a people who had fled Basutoland in the face of Shaka's hostility, plundered their way northward—under the leadership of Sebitwane—through Bechuanaland to the Zambezi, finally settling forcibly among the Tonga or Toka who grazed cattle on the northern shores of that river. Soon the Kololo moved westward, to Bulozi, where the soldiers of Sebitwane defeated a Lozi army. Sebitwane thereafter ruled Barotseland while several of the defeated *Indunas*, or princes, governed independent chiefdoms beyond the northern limits of Kololo power.

Sebitwane evidently ruled harshly and successfully. His son Sikeletu, however, and Mbololu, who soon succeeded Sikeletu, lost the confidence of their supporters as well as their subjects. In 1863/64, conditions therefore proved conducive to revolt. Njakwa, a leading Lozi commander, gathered a large following, obtained the support of Sipopa, a Lozi prince, and freed Barotseland from Kololo domination. Sipopa thereafter enlarged the size and effective power of the Lozi state. During his reign, and the reigns of his successors Mwanawina and Lewanika, peoples living as far from the centre of the kingdom as the Kafue and Chobe Rivers acknowledged the might of the Lozi. Only Europeans proved the undoing of Lewanika.

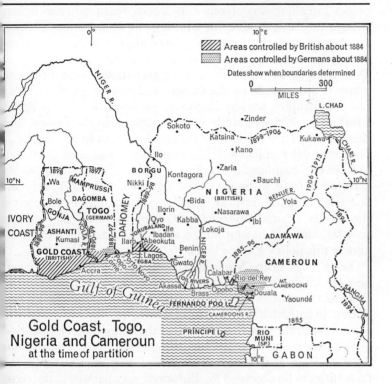

Areas controlled by British about 1884
Areas controlled by Germans about 1884

Dates show when boundaries determined

0   300

MILES

Gold Coast, Togo,
Nigeria and Cameroun
at the time of partition

22. The Berlin Conference

ERIC AXELSON *The Partition of Africa 1875–1891* South African
Broadcasting Corporation, Johannesburg 1964; pages 11–15

The Anglo-Portuguese Treaty of February 1884 would have
given Portugal possession of both mouths of the Congo. It
met with such wide-spread opposition that the Portuguese
government proposed an international conference to resolve the
points at issue. But the British government would not agree,
mainly because it did not wish to be embarrassed at the conference table by France; for France was irate over Britain's
single-handed occupation of Egypt. Then Bismarck suddenly
took the initiative in calling a conference. He suspected Britain
of monopolistic designs in Africa, little realising how anxious

Gladstone was not to extend British authority. Bismarck's main object in calling a conference, however, was further to isolate Britain in his new policy of winning the friendship of France. In August 1884 he formally proposed to the French Prime Minister that they should come to an understanding over West Africa, on the basis of an international commission to guarantee free trade on the Congo, and in other parts of Africa not yet occupied by any European power. The French Prime Minister wanted free trade to be restricted to the Congo, and demanded that the Niger be declared open to free navigation. He remained suspicious of Germany until Bismarck launched in front of his ambassador a diatribe against England, declaring a common front to be necessary against her; he did not want war with England, but she must be given to understand that if the navies of the other nations were to unite they would counterbalance hers; he aimed at an equilibrium of the seas and in this policy France had a great rôle to play.

The French Prime Minister was convinced that Bismarck and he were talking the same language, and invitations went out in their joint name, inviting the states of Europe, and the United States, to attend a conference at Berlin to discuss freedom of commerce in the mouth and basin of the Congo; the application to the Congo and Niger of the principles adopted by the Congress of Vienna for the navigation of the Danube; and the formalities to be observed for European occupations of the coast of Africa to be effective. The British government asked for further information, only to be tartly told that if such questions could be settled by correspondence there would be no point in having a conference. Britain eventually accepted the invitation, but on condition that navigation on the Niger was excluded.

Representatives of fourteen countries met in Berlin in November 1884. Two days before the Conference opened Bismarck asked Malet, the British Plenipotentiary, to meet him. The Chancellor proved to be extraordinarily amiable—he was already finding it difficult to maintain friendship with France. The British ambassador read him his instructions, which revealed a remarkable similarity in the view of the two governments. Bismarck then invited Malet to join him and the French ambassador in deciding certain other matters which had no been included in the published invitation: territorial arrangements were to be settled behind the scenes.

At the opening session Bismarck declared that the primary aim of the Conference was to facilitate access by all commercial nations to the interior of Africa, especially to the Congo basin. Malet added that it would be as well to extend the free trade area to between the Gaboon and the Loge, the French and Portuguese boundaries. The Portuguese delegate calmly announced that his country would guarantee freedom of navigation and commerce as soon as she took over this area.

The Conference appointed a commission to define the free trade area. The hydrographic basin of the Congo was quickly decided on, and also the line of the Loge, but there were sharp clashes of opinion as to where the northern line should run between the Atlantic and the basin, Portugal wishing it to be as far north, France as far south, as possible. A British delegate suggested a compromise line, running inland from the river presumed to enter the sea at Sette Cama, 300 miles north of the Congo. This line was put forward by Stanley, who was officially a member of the American delegation, but in fact an agent of King Leopold. Then Kasson, the chief representative of the United States, declared that American traders were entering the basin also from the east; he demanded that the basin be regarded as extending to within a degree of the Indian Ocean, between 5 degrees north, i.e. on the Somali coast, and the mouth of the Zambezi. Before long he demanded that it be extended all the way to the Indian Ocean coastline. Britain protested that this was a geographical absurdity; and such an extension lay outside the bases of the invitation. But even Portugal accepted this extension, though reserving her sovereign rights, and Malet warned his government that Britain would be isolated, which would be particularly unfortunate if the question of the Niger came up, for Bismarck returned blow for blow. The definition was accepted.

Another commission, meanwhile, was considering how best to secure freedom of trade in this area. Here, to Bismarck's growing indignation, the French representatives revealed whole-hearted opposition to free trade. The French and Portuguese delegates found themselves in the same camp, the British and German in another.

A third commission discussed the setting up of an international body to secure free navigation for the Congo. France demanded that the same free navigation be extended to the Niger. But Goldie Taubman was able to announce at this juncture that he had bought out the last of the rival French companies operating there, and when Britain decided to fall in with Bismarck's territorial programme Bismarck agreed that discussion of the two rivers be separated, and the question of the Niger was quietly dropped.

Then Kasson, the American representative, acting on behalf of Leopold's Association, to safeguard it from attack by any of the powers, proposed that the Congo basin be neutralized. France and Portugal objected, lest their sovereign rights be infringed, and in the end it was decided to leave the powers to declare whether they neutralized their territory or not; all undertook to submit any difference that might arise between them to mediation.

Having settled the first two bases, the Conference could easily have finished the third and risen before Christmas, but for Bismarck's anxiety for a territorial arrangement. This arrangement hinged on general recognition of Leopold's so-called International African Association as a state. It had already been so recognized by the United States Senate thanks to the activities of an American ex-minister to Belgium. The 'New York Tribune' described this as a violation of the Monroe Doctrine, and accused the State Department of having been duped. Leopold now proceeded to dupe the French government. His agents spread rumours that the Association was facing financial ruin. Its President then wrote to the French government that it had no intention of selling out, but if it did it would give France first refusal to acquire its assets—if France would immediately recognize it. France did not at once fall for this trickery, but she supported the Association in case she should come to enjoy its territory.

Next to fall into Leopold's net was Bismarck, who was assured that there would be free trade in the Association's territory, and therefore preferred the Congo to be under its control rather than under Portugal. And Bismarck thought, rightly, that general recognition of the Association would be distasteful to England.

On the eve of the Conference Germany had recognized it, and now Bismarck demanded that Britain do the same. The British government replied that it did not possess the essentials of statehood—it possessed only a few score officials, a few hundred mercenaries, and an inchoate claim to territory. At the beginning of December Bismarck again demanded recognition; without it, there was danger of the area passing into the hands of France; and he hinted at difficulties over the Niger. The Association, meanwhile, was becoming worried lest France and Portugal partition the Congo between them. Leopold sent Stanley on a flying visit to London to warn his influential English friends that if the Association were not given all she demanded she would throw in her lot with France; and he even went so far as to threaten the possibility of war in Europe. Overnight the British Secretary of State for Foreign Affairs was talked into throwing overboard what little remained of the understanding with Portugal, and recognizing the Association. The Foreign Office agreed that the Association have the north bank of the Congo as far as Noqui, the limit of navigation on the estuary, and both banks above Noqui.

Leopold's Association, however, resented having to surrender to France the Niari area, where she alleged she had spent £200,000. This caused a deadlock in the behind-the-doors negotiations, which caused Bismarck to adjourn the Conference, professedly for Christmas. Negotiations between the Association and France continued in Paris. The French Prime Minister refused to pay an indemnity for Niari, but eventually agreed to devote the proceeds of a lottery for this purpose. He refused to bring pressure to bear on Portugal to accept the arrangement, and the negotiations broke down. The British government then told its ancient ally that it did not desire any extension of Portuguese authority, but promised to support her claims south of the Congo if she would abolish differential tariffs in Angola and Moçambique, open the Zambezi to international navigation, and acknowledge the Ruo as the Nyasa frontier Portugal refused.

But by now Bismarck's eyes were being opened to the Association's real nature; he was receiving reports from Nachtigal which revealed that it was just a giant monopolistic, and not very scrupulous, trading concern, Leopold's private property.

Another factor entered into the negotiations. A German concern was planning to establish a colony on the borders of the Transvaal; if Portugal would grant free transit to this colony, Bismarck would assure Portugal of his best offices in the delimitation. In the circumstances Portugal gladly consented to a renewal of the territorial discussions when the Conference resumed in Berlin.

The conference proceeded to the final basis of the invitation. Bismarck accepted a differentiation between annexation and protectorate; but both, to be effective, must be notified to the other powers; and sufficient authority must be set up to guarantee existing rights and freedom of trade.

There was still no territorial agreement. France was persuaded to recognize the Association but still refused to exert pressure on Portugal, nor would Bismarck in view of his secret agreement. The Association conceded Cabinda to be Portuguese; and after identical notes from the three main powers Portugal recognized the Association and signed a treaty defining their common boundaries. The Conference ratified the General Act, and the Association also adhered to it.

The Berlin Conference saw then the birth of the Congo Free State. The wishes of the indigenous peoples were not consulted, of course; its boundaries were completely artificial: heterogeneous tribes were lumped together, while watersheds and meridians cut some tribes asunder. The Conference saw a further breakdown in relations, between Britain and France and Britain and Portugal. It revealed blatant rivalries between the powers. It intensified the scramble for Africa.

23. Annexation of the Congo Independent State

RUTH SLADE *King Leopold's Congo* Oxford University Press for Institute of Race Relations 1962; pages 35–43, 203–8

Leopold II, King of the Belgians
Talented, ambitious and energetic, but strictly limited in scope as the constitutional monarch of a small European state

Leopold II, King of the Belgians, had too little to do, and felt rather too confined in his little kingdom'. He was passionately interested in geography and political science; as Duke of Brabant he had enjoyed travelling in Europe, the Mediterranean and the Far East. Few Belgians of his day were so widely travelled. His passion for geography was no mere romanticism, for he was severely practical, and possessed a good business sense. Long before he reached the throne he became interested in Belgium's economic expansion abroad, and thus in acquiring a colony as an outlet for Belgian manufactured goods. This was the theme of a number of his speeches before the Senate, while a block of marble which he had brought back from Greece for the Prime Minister Frère-Orban, was boldly inscribed 'Belgium must have colonies'.

The young Duke assiduously gathered together a great deal of information on colonial history and administration, and as early as 1865 he made use of it when he produced a 'Note on how useful and important it is for states to possess domains and provinces outside their European frontiers, especially when the extension of the latter is out of the question'. His insistence was almost entirely upon the commercial advantages which the possession of a colony would bring to the Metropolis, but he spared an occasional thought for the colonised:

A successful expedition in China or Japan would make Belgium an important and a very rich kingdom. . . .
Men are not allowed to exploit their fellows, but one who knows the East rests assured that the advent of Europe is a true *deliverance*. Europe would profit from the venture, but at the same time would not impose anything like the burdens which the native Princes put upon their unfortunate subjects. . . .

In short, while Belgium's advantage was the chief consideration, Leopold assumed that her future colonial subjects would benefit from their change of master.

In 1865 the King was thinking of a colony in the Far East; it was not until ten years later that he turned his attention to Africa. In 1866 he wrote: 'It is my dream to found a Belgian company for overseas development with its seat in Brussels, which could gradually do for China what the London East India Company did for the Indian Empire, what the former

Company of the Indies did for Java.' But by 1875 he had failed
to found a colony either in China, the Pacific Islands or North
Borneo, and his attempt to buy the Philippines had recently
come to nothing. So in August he wrote to Baron Lambermont:
'For the present, neither the Spaniards, the Portuguese nor the
Dutch seem prepared to sell. I intend to make discreet inquiries
as to whether there is not something to be done in Africa.'
In December the King showed considerable interest in
Cameron's central African journey, and hearing a false rumour
that the explorer was short of money, wrote to the Royal
Geographical Society offering to pay the expenses of his return
journey to England.

Thus in 1876, when he summoned an international geographical conference to Brussels, Leopold II was clear that he
wanted a colony for Belgium. Its location was relatively unimportant; what mattered was to have an outlet for Belgian trade
and almost any populated part of the globe would suffice.
Since he was late in the field, however, his choice was severely
limited, and the most hopeful possibility was that there was
'something to be done in Africa'. But the limited geographical
choice was not his only difficulty. His speeches in the Senate
urging the need for a colonial policy had not met with an
enthusiastic response. The Belgians had no desire to colonise,
the young nation was glad to be independent at last, was
satisfied with her enforced neutrality, had no ambition
outside her own frontiers and wished to avoid the international
complications attendant upon becoming a colonial power.
If the King of the Belgians was to win a colony for his people, it
would have to be without their co-operation and entirely upon
his own personal initiative and responsibility.

The first expeditions fostered by the African International
Association, which had been set up by the Brussels Geographical
Conference of 1876 and placed under the presidency of Leopold
II, took the east coast route towards the Great Lakes. But in the
autumn of 1877 came the exciting news that Stanley had
successfully descended the Congo river. It was thus clear that
the Congo offered considerable possibilities, and Leopold did
not wish to lose his chance. Two of his envoys appeared at
Marseilles to greet the explorer on his return to Europe, and to
inform him that the King of the Belgians 'would be happy to

hear from him, should he be free and willing to continue and develop his great work'. The King's representatives met with little success, however, for Stanley was still entertaining unfounded hopes that Great Britain would interest herself in opening up the Congo basin. Leopold II did not give up; at the end of 1878 he called together representatives of important financial interests from England, France, Germany, Holland and Belgium, and persuaded them to form a *Comité d'Etudes du Haut-Congo* to study trading prospects in the Congo and the possibility of building a railway to round the cataracts on the lower river and thus link the coast with Stanley Pool. After vainly attempting to rouse British interest in the Congo, Stanley finally consented to lead out the *Comité's* first expedition. Even before he reached Africa, however, the *Comité* was dissolved and the subscriptions returned; this allowed Leopold II to take full control of the Congo enterprise.

His aims were both commercial and political. Earlier, as Duke of Brabant, he had thought of colonial development in terms of a trading company; it was not surprising that his *Comité d'Etudes* was set up to explore the *commercial* possibilities of the Congo basin. But in order to safeguard commercial rights, *political* sovereignty seemed necessary. So when the subscriptions of the members of the *Comité d'Etudes* were returned, and Leopold was left as the sole person to whom Stanley was responsible for the conduct of his expedition, the King was able to give the venture a political twist. It was at this point that a 'republican confederation of free Negroes' with the King at its head, a 'powerful Negro state', was suggested to Stanley. The *Comité* had been dissolved late in 1879, but Leopold continued to use the title as a cloak for his political ambitions in the Congo. In 1882 the title *Association Internationale du Congo* appeared to replace that of the *Comité d'Etudes*; in fact, this association was not international at all, but was entirely an instrument of Leopold II. His aims were well hidden, however; in the early 1880s an impenetrable aura of mystery surrounded the activity of Leopold's Congo enterprise.

For the King was not alone in the field, and he needed to be prudent. It was obvious that each European Power was out for its own national advantage in Africa; the way in which the National Committees of the African International Association had set to work was making this quite clear. So far as the Congo was concerned, Leopold's two rivals were Portugal and France. Portugal was at pains to persuade Great Britain to recognise her long-standing claims to the Congo region. By the Anglo-Portuguese treaty, which was signed early in 1884 but never ratified by England, Great Britain would have recognised Portugal's right to control the Congo mouth, the lower course of the river, and the neighbouring coastline; this would effectively have barred the way to any wide extension of the Association's influence by cutting off access to the sea. While Portugal was active in Europe, France had been active in the field; Count Savorgnan de Brazza, acting ostensibly for the French Committee of the African International Association, but in reality working in the interests of France, had been making treaties at Stanley Pool.

While both Portugal and France were obviously competitors for the Congo region, the aims of the *Association Internationale du Congo* were not so clear. The Association came under fire precisely because of this, and at the end of 1882 Emile Banning put forward the suggestion—never taken up—that Belgium herself should take over, establish her national sovereignty in Africa, and cut short the polemics which surrounded the Association's activities. But Leopold was a master at clever propaganda; he was out to persuade Europe that the *Association Internationale du Congo* was a small, philanthropic, innocuous and non-political organisation which aimed at suppressing the slave-trade and introducing legitimate commerce into the Congo basin, while strongly supporting the principles of free trade. The treaties which Stanley had made with Congolese chiefs secured soverign rights and a commercial monopoly for the Association's stations both in the lower Congo and up the river to Stanley Falls, but little of this was known in Europe not until 1884 did Portuguese and French propagandists obtain examples of the Association's treaties and publish and attack them. Meanwhile, by talking about free trade in the Congo and insisting upon his philanthropic intentions there, Leopold II won to his support against the Anglo-Portuguese treaty both the British trading interests and the English Protestant missionaries in the Congo. Neither wanted to see Portugal or France there; the former objected to the high tariffs imposed by these

Powers, and the latter to Portugal's association with the slave-trade and to the Catholicism of both countries. Great Britain did not wish to take over the Congo herself; her main pre-occupation was to keep the French out. There was opposition to the Anglo-Portuguese treaty both at home and abroad, so it was dropped; as it gradually became evident that the Association had political ambitions in the Congo, it became equally clear that, if strong enough, the Association itself would serve as well as Portugal to keep France out of the Congo. Germany wanted neither Great Britain nor Portugal there; like England, she hoped that the Congo would become a free trade zone, internationally controlled. Thus the King of the Belgians was able to win over both Germany and Great Britain to the support of his 'international' enterprise.

The Berlin West African Conference, 1884–5
When the Berlin Conference opened in November 1884 Leopold's position was therefore a strong one, so long as he played his cards well. As early as April he had secured the United States' recognition of the Association's flag as that of a 'friendly government'. The Americans quite erroneously believed that the free states which the Association intended to establish on the upper Congo would in time be able to govern themselves rather on the model of the recently-established republic of Liberia; there was also in the United States considerable trust in King Leopold's promise of a free trade régime in the Congo basin, and approval for his avowed intention of suppressing the slave-trade.

France had not recognised the soverign rights of the Association before the opening of the Conference, but in exchange for the privilege of buying the Association's assets, should Leopold be forced to sell out by reason of his heavy expenses, she had agreed in April 'to respect the stations and free territories of the Association and to place no further obstacle to the extension of its rights'. In November Germany, like the United States, recognised the Association's flag as that of a 'friendly state'. During the Berlin Conference the Association was gradually to take shape in the delegates' minds as a state with sovereign rights.

The official discussions among the representatives of the

fourteen Powers who took part in the Berlin Conference concerned free trade and free navigation in the Congo and the Niger, the formalities to be observed in the future for valid annexation of African territory, the protection of the native peoples and the suppression of the slave-trade. The Conference had no mandate to deal with territorial questions as such, but behind the scenes claims and counter-claims were fought out, and in practice were regarded as more important than the official business. As to humanitarian questions, little time was devoted to them; the effect of the Conference's deliberations upon the future of the African peoples was less important in the eyes of the delegates than were the spoils to be divided among the European nations.

So far as territorial claims were concerned, it was necessary to prove that the treaties which both the Association and France had concluded with African chiefs were valid (and in the case of the Association, that such treaties could legally be made with a private body). Stanley later stated thus the Association's position at the beginning of the Conference:

The Association were in possession of treaties made with over four hundred and fifty independent African chiefs, whose rights would be conceded by all to have been indisputable, since they held their lands by undisturbed occupation, by long ages of succession, by real divine right. Of their own free will, without coercion, but for substantial considerations, reserving only a few easy conditions, they had transferred their rights of sovereignty and of ownership to the Association. The time had arrived when a sufficient number of these had been made to connect the several miniature sovereignties into one concrete whole, to present itself before the world for general recognition of its right to govern, and hold these in the name of an independent state, lawfully constituted according to the spirit and tenor of international law.

European diplomats at the time of the Berlin Conference were not interested in finding out whether the African chiefs had understood the treaties to which they had affixed their marks, neither were they interested in verifying by what 'substantial considerations' the consent of the chiefs had been bought, nor whether they had the right to make the concessions they did. The latter consideration was only brought up when a certain piece of territory was in dispute between France and

the Association; at one point in the negotiations it was important for the Association to prove that de Brazza had been
mistaken in his estimate of the territorial influence of Makoko,
a chief with whom he had concluded a treaty at Stanley Pool.
It was an unquestioned assumption at Berlin that the European
Powers had the right to annex African territory for their own
advantage, so long as the nominal consent of a certain number
of African chiefs had been obtained.

It was also an unquestioned assumption that the native
peoples would benefit by the change, and indeed that certain
conditions which would ensure that they did so should be laid
upon the annexing Powers. It was the delegates' common wish
not to allow a renewal of 'that policy of extermination of the
natives which had formerly been practised in the two Americas'.
As we have seen, the Africans were theoretically regarded
as having the right of sovereignty and of being capable of
transmitting it to others. Since they had given up this right,
it was recognised that the Powers had a duty to watch over the
preservation of the native tribes and to 'care for the improvement of the conditions of their moral and material well-being'.
This was to be done by the suppression of slavery and the
slave-trade, by protection and favour—without distinction of
creed or nation—of all religious, scientific and charitable
institutions which aimed at the instruction and civilisation of the
native peoples, by giving special protection to missionaries,
scientists and explorers, and by granting freedom of conscience
and religious toleration.

Clearly these were pious hopes rather than a programme
which could be imposed upon the individual Powers; their
fulfilment depended entirely upon the goodwill of the latter.
The Anti-Slavery Society, working through the British delegation at Berlin, had secured a declaration of principle on the
suppression of the slave-trade, but there were no definite proposals for effective joint action on the part of the Powers.
Great Britain also brought up the question of abolition of the
liquor traffic, but vested interests—chiefly German—were too
strong to allow this suggestion to be adopted. The formula
'protection and favour' as applied to religious, scientific and
charitable institutions replaced that of 'favour and aid'. Turkey
had insisted that Moslem missionaries should be placed on an

equal footing with Christian missionaries, but the Powers
regarded Islam as the most serious enemy of European colonisation in Africa; for this reason the meaning of the phrase was
considerably weakened.

Thus, in spite of the lofty sentiments expressed at Berlin,
in practice the extent to which the stipulations of the Conference were applied depended upon the dispositions of the
various colonial authorities. For the Congo itself, it became
clearer as the Conference drew to a close that this dependence
was to be upon the personal will of Leopold II. For one by one
during the Conference the Powers followed the lead of the
United States and Germany in recognising the flag of the
Association as that of a friendly government. Thus in February
1885, on the same day that the Powers of Europe signed the
General Act of Berlin, the Association was able to mark its
own adherence to this Act. During the debates the Association
had hardly been mentioned by name, but the delegates at
Berlin had come to assume that it was to be invested with
authority to carry out the programme which they were laying
down for the Congo basin. Nor were they under any illusion
concerning Leopold's position in the Association, and were not
surprised when he assumed its direction in name, as well as in
fact. Internationalism had served its purpose. De Winton, who
had replaced Stanley as the King's representative in the
Congo, proclaimed the King of the Belgians the 'Sovereign
of the Congo Independent State' at Boma in July 1885; a
month later Leopold II notified the Powers to the same effect.
He was acting in a purely personal capacity; in giving him
permission to assume the sovereignty of the Congo Independent
State the Belgian Parliament had insisted that there was to be
no link whatever between Belgium and the new state save in
the person of their King.

So the inhabitants of some million square miles of African
territory were submitted to the authority not of an elected
European Parliament but of a single European monarch; at
home the King of the Belgians was a constitutional ruler, but in
the Congo he was an absolute sovereign. There could be outside
limitation of his liberty of action only by virtue of international
public opinion and of the enlightened but somewhat vague
prescriptions of the Berlin Act. But in 1885 there seemed no

reason to doubt that the King would use his despotic powers wisely, in pursuit of his avowed objective of bringing legitimate commerce and Western civilisation to the Congo basin. . . .

The Annexation of the Congo Independent State by Belgium

Leopold II had always intended Belgium to benefit by his African possessions; the Congo was to be exploited not for the King's personal profit, but for that of his country. In 1888 he had indicated that he wished to leave the Congo to Belgium at his death. In 1890 the King's financial difficulties were such that he desperately needed the country's assistance if his Congo enterprise was to survive; in July he offered Belgium, in return for a loan of twenty-five million francs, the possibility of annexing his Congo kingdom ten years later. For the moment the idea of a colony was more popular in Belgium than it had been five years earlier; the Financial Commission which examined the King's offer reported that:

For some time public opinion has begun to favour the end of the personal union [between Belgium and the Congo] or at least a direct intervention to help the Independent State. Some impatient elements ask for the immediate annexation of the Congo Independent State by Belgium. Others, more prudent, want Belgium to give financial assistance to the weighty task which has been undertaken by the King.

The Belgian *Parlement* therefore accepted Leopold's offer, and promised the King a loan of five million francs immediately, with two million to be paid annually over a ten-year period.

This amount of money was insufficient, however, to solve the King's financial problems. In 1892 Leopold needed increased resources; in spite of the fact that in 1890 he had bound himself not to contract a loan on behalf of the Congo State without the consent of the Belgian *Parlement*, the King borrowed five million francs from an Antwerp banker, offering forty million acres of land as security, to be forfeited if the loan was not repaid by July 1895. By the autumn of 1894 it was clear that there was no possibility of repaying the loan. It seemed to Leopold that he would be forced to alienate some of his Congo land, but he hoped to do so under conditions more advantageous than those to which he had agreed in 1892. He therefore decided on the creation of a *Société Générale de Cultures*, to which he would sell lands in the Manyema and the Aruwimi basin, around Lake Leopold II and Lake Tumba, but reserving to the State the right to collect the natural products of these lands during a period of fifty years, and to keep two-thirds of the profits from their sale.

Late in 1894 the Belgian Government got wind of the secret agreement which Leopold had concluded with an English syndicate along these lines. The King was forced to make clear to the Cabinet the dire straits he was in for lack of money, which had led him to borrow large sums without the country's permission, and he promised that in future he would not increase the expenses incurred by the Congo administration without consulting the Belgian Government. But in December the Cabinet came to a unanimous decision: that Leopold was to withdraw his decree of November 1894 creating the *Société de Cultures* at once, that it was impossible to modify the convention of 1890 in a way which would allow the King to borrow money without the country's permission, and finally, that Belgium herself would take over the Congo administration immediately. Annexation by Belgium seemed the best way out of a difficult situation, and in January 1895 a treaty ceding the Independent State to Belgium was prepared.

Leopold had been forced to agree to this treaty, and it is very doubtful whether he wanted to give up his power in the Congo during his lifetime. It has been well said that:

In the question of annexation, the position of the Sovereign of the Congo had the merit of a great simplicity; it was directly linked to the financial situation of the State. Leopold II accepted annexation as long as it seemed the only way of delivering the Congo from its financial straits, but rejected it as soon as the Congo had found in the resources of its 'domains' a way to save itself.

In 1895 the Congo State had not yet proved that it was able to save itself in this way, although it was not long before it did so. The King was doubtless greatly relieved, therefore, when public opinion in Belgium refused to support the Government's annexation project, for thus he remained in his position of absolute authority as Sovereign of the Congo Independent State.

The issue of annexation was hotly debated in the country

before the Government laid the treaty of cession before the Belgian *Parlement*. The public became more interested in King Leopold's activities in the Congo than ever it had been previously. The temper had changed since 1890, and the country was sharply divided on the colonial question. On the one hand the Government pushed its colonial propaganda, a *Comité d'action pour l'œuvre nationale africaine* was set up to support annexation, and Belgians with commercial interests in the Congo, notably the Thys group of companies, strongly favoured annexation since they were opposed to the King's policy of creating a State monopoly in Congo commerce. On the other hand, there was violent opposition to annexation on the part of some sections of Belgian opinion.

The Belgian Socialists opposed a colonial policy on principle, and a group of Liberals led by Lorand joined them in anti-colonial propaganda. It was argued that the Congo would ruin Belgium, that it would be too expensive to maintain, and that the Belgian Army would have to defend it. The Socialists believed that millions would be poured into the Congo at the expense of social welfare at home, while a capitalist system had nothing to offer the Congolese themselves. A speaker at one anti-colonial meeting held in Brussels declared that:

The Negro race is handsome and strong. We cannot say the same of all Belgian industrial workers. We are incapable of giving to the Negroes that well-being which we have not yet achieved for ourselves. If one day we manage to shake off the capitalist yoke from which we are suffering and give our European population a true civilisation, then will be the time to think about sharing this prosperous situation with the coloured races. But if all we can bring them is that wage-earning system from which our own workers suffer, in exchange for a condition which is perhaps a happier one under the domination of their Negro chiefs, then we cry: 'Down with the annexation of the Congo! Down with colonisation!'

King Leopold made good use of the opposition to annexation on the part of his critics. He had acquiesced in the decision of the Government in January 1895, but by March the division of opinion in the country was such as to give him hope that annexation could be deferred, and he was openly working for a preservation of the *status quo*. The Government was meeting opposition to annexation within the Catholic party itself, and

feared to lose votes in the next election if it pushed the treaty
between Belgium and the Congo State through *Parlement* in
the face of public opinion. So the treaty of cession was withdrawn; however, to tide the Congo State over its difficulties
Belgium furnished a further loan of six million francs. The
Congo State was to repay its debt in 1901, if annexation did not
take place in that year.

What strikes an observer, looking back, is how little was
known in Belgium about the Congo in 1895:

When we look through the hundreds of polemical articles written in
1895, one striking fact stands out for us today: much was said about
the Congo but scarcely anything at all was known about it. This is
perhaps the outstanding character of the 1895 discussions: they were
concerned with huge, far-away lands about which the greatest
ignorance was displayed.

Arguments for and against a colonial policy were conducted
on the theoretical level; this ignorance of what the Congo was
really like and what King Leopold was trying to do there
continued. Meanwhile the Sovereign, convinced that he knew
better than Belgium how to administer his African territories,
never wavered from a policy hostile to annexation. Thus in
1901, when the question of annexation came up for the second
time and the Government seemed inclined to opt for this, the
personal intervention of the King was decisive in changing its
policy and causing annexation to be deferred once again. This
time Leopold was left freer than before. The repayment of the
Congo State's debt to Belgium was postponed, and the 1890
agreement came to an end, so that the King was free to contract
further debts without the consent of the country, if he so
wished. However, his African kingdom was by this time
enjoying a period of prosperity. In 1891 the Congo State had
produced eighty-two tons of rubber; by 1901 she was producing
6,000 tons a year, and this at a time when the price of rubber
was rising on the international market. Leopold was able to
embark on an impressive programme of public works in
Belgium—including the building of the Colonial Museum at
Tervueren—financed by the returns he received from the
State which at one time had threatened to ruin him.

Finally it was intervention from outside which forced

Belgium to annex the Congo State. The Congo reform campaign showed no signs of slackening in Britain and the United States, and the British and American Governments were forced by public opinion to exert what pressure they could towards a reform of the Congo system. During 1905 the thesis of the 'Belgian solution' appeared in Britain; it was felt that Belgian annexation might be the simplest way out of a difficult situation. The British Government continued to hold that the Congo Independent State was not a sovereign state in the generally accepted sense of the term, and that its Sovereign was answerable to the Powers for the way in which he administered the huge area of African territory which they had committed to his care at the Berlin Conference. But when the other signatory Powers of the Berlin Act had declined the British suggestion of a meeting to consider the Congo question, as the easiest way out the British Government decided to press the Belgian Government to take over the Independent State and put an end to the misrule in the Congo.

In Belgium itself, opinion had been prepared for this step by the books of Cattier and Vermeersch, works based on their study of the Report of King Leopold's Commission of Enquiry and on their awareness of the widespread criticism abroad of the Congo régime. By the end of 1906 the Catholic majority party and the Liberal party were both agreed on the necessity of immediate annexation. Lorand's small anti-colonial group was the one exception among the Liberals, and sided with the Socialists against a colonial policy. The Socialist minority was not unanimous, however; Emile Vandervelde campaigned for immediate annexation as the only possible way out of the situation. On the whole, the majority of opinion in Belgium was in favour of annexation; there was a certain hesitation, however, for it was realised that the end of the Congo Independent State must bring the régime of exploitation to a close. While this was felt to be a good and necessary step, Belgians were rather doubtful as to how much a more humane policy was going to cost the taxpayers.

In any case, pressure from abroad was forcing the Belgian Government to action, in spite of the determined opposition of King Leopold, and in July 1907 negotiations for the annexation of the Congo State were officially begun. The greatest difficulty

came over the *Fondation de la Couronne*. Leopold wished to
continue to exploit this huge territory for the public works he
had begun in Belgium, and at first the Government agreed.
But there was considerable opposition to this on the part of the
Liberals and a large section of the Catholic party; in fact, it
would have been illogical to accept a continuation of the system
whereby Belgium was beautified at the expense of the Congo,
since Belgium was annexing the Congo because of the need to
reform this system. Finally, the King gave in, and in March
1908 agreed to give up all claim to the *Fondation*.

24. Partition of West Africa

J. D. HARGREAVES *Prelude to the Partition of West Africa*
Macmillan 1963; pages 338–48

Survey of the Partition of West Africa, 1885–98

The Berlin Conference caused no sudden change in the basic
attitudes of the European states. After 1885, as before, pressures
for expansion which originated with French or British subjects
on the West African coast were counter-balanced in Paris and
London by diplomatic caution, by the political instinct to avoid
commitment and to economize. The extension of European
control along the coasts meant that the administering powers
were becoming increasingly involved in the affairs of their new
hinterlands; but in practice the inland extension of governmental power was slow and often reluctant.

In June 1885 Great Britain constituted the territories between
Lagos and the Cameroons, together with the banks of the Niger
up to Lokoja and of the Benué up to Ibi, into the Niger Coast
Protectorate; but in principle her governments were willing and
even anxious to leave the administration of the area beyond the
delta to the National African Company, as 'the cheapest and
most effective way' of discharging the obligations to maintain
free navigation which had been accepted at Berlin. (Had Goldie
been able to come to terms with the Liverpool oil traders of the
delta, the government would have been delighted to leave the

entire protectorate to Company rule.) Negotiations about the terms on which this might be done began early in 1886; they did not run smoothly, and Goldie even threatened wildly to transfer his Company's treaty rights to France; but in July 1886 the Charter was finally issued. The Company was empowered to exercise in the name of the Crown all such rights as it might acquire by its treaties in the Niger; it was allowed to levy customs duties for the purpose of covering administrative costs —a provision which afforded an important loophole for oblique discrimination against the imports of competitors, and which permitted the Company to achieve in practice that commercial monopoly which was forbidden by the letter of the Charter. With the fruits of this monopoly the Royal Niger Company (as it now became) created a rudimentary governmental framework which for several years appeared impressive enough to deter France and Germany from any serious challenge on the lower Niger. In practice Company rule had many grave faults and weaknesses; but the British government, as a recent study emphasizes, was still content to leave its major West African interest beneath this light administrative umbrella, while itself devoting slightly increased diplomatic vigour to defending its interests in East Africa.

But it was not only the British government which gave a low priority to West African policy. The fall of Jules Ferry at the end of March 1885, in consequence of a military set-back in Indo-China, meant a pause in the French advance towards the upper Niger. All colonial enterprises were temporarily discredited by the failure of one; the Chambers became even more reluctant to vote funds for military expeditions, just when French troops on the Niger were meeting potentially more formidable opposition. In February 1883 the French occupied Bamako, which at last brought them near the main centre of Tokolor power at Ségou; but, having clashed with Samori's advanced forces near Siguiri, they were forced to recognize the existence of a second formidable African state in the upper Niger. Moreover their own operations (involving requisitioning of foodstuffs and the use of forced labour) had created resistance in the rear. During the middle 1880s substantial French forces had to be diverted into Cayor, where since 1882 Lat-Dior had again been opposing France over the construction of her railway, and into

Galam, where Mamadu Lamina, a well-travelled Muslim
scholar, was organizing resistance from among the Sarakulé.

Fortunately for the French, their enemies failed to combine.
Although Amadu had been re-organizing his dominions with a
view to their eventual defence against France, he seemed equally
determined to resist the challenge to his authority represented
by the rise of rival African empires. Formerly, it is said, he had
held Mamadu Lamina six years in prison; certainly he did not
wish to encourage a militantly Muslim Sarakulé state within
his own sphere of power and influence. He was also on bad
terms with Samori, and seems to have made no serious attempt
to co-operate with him. Prudently enough, Amadu would have
preferred to avoid a battle with the French and their superior
technology; when they appeared willing to co-operate with
him, Amadu responded loyally, signing and observing a new
treaty in 1887. The French were meanwhile more worried
about Samori, who in 1885 turned to the British Governor at
Freetown, offering to accept British protection and seeking an
assured supply of fire-arms. Frightened lest the Niger sources
should come under British control, the French in 1886 and 1887
sent envoys to Samori, and on each occasion claimed to have
obtained his signature to treaties of protection. Whatever
passed on these occasions, Samori certainly did not intend to
alienate his sovereign independence; but the British government accepted the treaties in this sense and did not interfere
when France eventually undertook the task of bringing this
over-mighty protégé to heel.

This temporary shift of French policy was not exclusively due
to the difficulty of obtaining money for military operations.
During the middle 1880s there was some disillusioned reaction,
both in Paris and in St. Louis, against the policies of Faidherbe
and Brière de l'Isle. Galliéni, back in the Sudan as military
commander, but still impetuously following the swing of his
enthusiasms, now proposed the abandonment of the attempt to
reach the Niger by way of the Senegal (and the writing-off of the
ill-fated railway) in favour of developing alternative routes
through Futa Jalon and the *rivières du sud*. From this point of
view, the prevention of any alliance between Samori and the
British was clearly of prior importance. But other African rulers
in the extreme western Sudan might also need to be associated

with French policy. In 1886 Galliéni signed a treaty of protection with Amadu's brother and nominal vassal, Aguibou of Dinguiray, and two years later there were new treaties with the Alimamies of Futa Jalon.

Still other possible approaches to the Niger were also being examined by Frenchmen. Between 1887 and 1889 Captain Binger was carrying out the most important journey of West African exploration since Barth, travelling from the upper Niger to Grand Bassam through Mossi and Dagomba, and so exploding the geographical myth that the 'mountains of Kong' would always prevent commercial expansion from the Ivory Coast in the direction of the Sudan. Verdier's once-despised holdings now began to assume considerable interest. At Porto Novo too there was some talk of redressing the failure on the lower Niger by establishing commercial contact with Boussa by way of Abeokuta; unsuccessful probes in this direction were made by Viard, a former agent of C.F.A.E.

These developments redirected attention to the coastal settlements, suggesting to both sides the need for a settlement of pending Anglo-French boundary disputes. At the same time, the French operations against Lat-Dior and Mamadu Lamina in the Senegal raised difficulties concerning the limits of British jurisdiction in the Gambia valley. For a time the old idea of 'comprehensive dealing' revived. In 1887 a new incident in the Porto Novo lagoon led the Intelligence Branch of the British War Office to prepare a paper on West African problems. General Brackenbury (who had served in Ashanti under Wolseley) argued that such places as Appa and Ketenou were of very minor importance, now that the chance had been lost of uniting Lagos with the Gold Coast; but that Freetown, which the Carnarvon Commission on Imperial Defence (of 1879–82) had designated for re-fortification, demanded prior attention. Samori now seemed militarily capable of capturing Sierra Leone, and reports of his treaties with the French had therefore caused great apprehension. In order to ensure the exclusion of French influence from the near vicinity of Freetown, both inland and on the coast, Brackenbury suggested concessions both at Porto Novo and in the Gambia.

Nothing was done immediately, except to negotiate a *modus vivendi* to prevent further conflicts around Porto Novo; Holland, a former official who was now Colonial Secretary, suggested grouping the various pending boundary disputes into a single comprehensive agreement, but refused to consider ceding the Gambia. But next summer the Gambia question was again brought forward by Hutton, now as eager to promote an exchange as he had once been to block one. His friend Harry Johnston, Vice-Consul in the Cameroons, spent a weekend at Hatfield with Lord Salisbury, and urged the exchange of the Gambia as part of a broadly visionary scheme for the planned partition of the whole African continent. Salisbury, impressed, agreed that Johnston should air his views in *The Times*, in an attempt to influence public opinion; and Holland reluctantly agreed to consider an exchange. But conditions were far less favourable than in 1876. The French felt a less acute need for the Gambia route now their railway plans had been begun, and the general climate of Anglo-French relations was frigid. Even in Britain, the abatement of mercantile opposition would not remove all difficulties; opposition was feared from Irish M.P.s and perhaps from the Queen. So in 1889 it was decided to grasp an opportunity to negotiate a comprehensive frontier settlement which would reduce friction and protect Freetown against encirclement, but without attempting an exchange. A Convention of 10 August 1889 settled boundaries, on the coast and for short distances inland, at the Gambia, Sierra Leone, Assinie, and Porto Novo (where Britain at last withdrew from Ketenou and part of Appa).

During the 1890s the policies of the European powers in West Africa became rather more widely and consistently influenced by new political attitudes, best characterized by that overworked word 'Imperialist'. This is not the place for any serious analysis of these attitudes, nor of the changes in European society which made them so widely acceptable. Their essential features were a new conviction that future economic benefits would follow from the 'possession' of colonial territories, undeveloped and unpromising though these might actually be; and a new readiness to justify the deployment of military force in order to compel recalcitrant Africans to collaborate in the 'civilizing mission' of the Europeans. This 'new imperialism' affected France's African policy earlier than Britain's; its rise is well illustrated by the career of Eugène Étienne, an Algerian-born disciple of Gambetta, who represented Oran in the Chamber after 1881.

Étienne was a friend and former business associate of Rouvier, and served as under-secretary for the Colonies in his government of 1887. He held that office again from 1889 until 1892; it was now re-attached to the Ministry of Commerce, and Étienne himself was given the right to attend Cabinet meetings. Étienne was becoming the leader of a growing colonial pressure-group, which operated inside and outside parliament; he was closely associated with the *Comité de l'Afrique française*, founded in 1890, and in 1892 became chairman of a group of ninety-one colonially minded Deputies, drawn from all parts of the Chamber. Under his direction the advance into *Soudan français* was resumed. Between 1890 and 1893 Amadu's armies were defeated and the Tokolor empire broken; on 16 December 1893 French troops entered Timbuktu. Thereafter they advanced rapidly down the Niger, and into the lands south of the great bend. Meanwhile in Dahomey the insistence of the new King Behanzin upon the independence of his kingdom and its right to Cotonou (which had recently superseded Whydah as the principal port) drew the French into a series of military campaigns, which led to the occupation of Abomey in November 1892 and the dismemberment of the kingdom in 1894.

Now for the first time the French, advancing from two directions, were in a position physically to test that claim to Hausaland which the Niger Company had still not converted into effective control, and to revive their challenge to the Company's monopoly of the Niger navigation below Boussa. It was true that in 1890, in an unguarded moment, the Foreign Ministry had renounced French claims south of a line from Say to Barruwa (and in 1890 had offered the British an even more favourable demarcation line south of Say), but now that circumstances provided the opportunity to pursue more ambitious aims, ingenious men were able to interpret their commitments rather loosely. The famous 'race to Borgu' between Captain Decoeur and Captain Lugard in 1894 opened a new struggle for position on the navigable portion of the lower Niger, a struggle in which really substantial interests seemed to be at stake.

For a time, it seemed that this struggle might become a

triangular one. Although Bismarck showed little interest in his African colonies after they had been marked out, and there was even talk of German withdrawal, both Togoland and Kamerun had nevertheless begun to expand inland, under pressure from local traders or administrators; they began to make their own demands upon German policy. Bismarck's successors, less strongly resolved to maintain the priority of continental over colonial interests, thus found themselves drawn into Anglo-French rivalries in West Africa. In November 1893 the British, by an apparently generous recognition of Germany's claims in Kamerun, tried to use her to block France's expansion from the Congo towards both Nile and Benué; in March 1894 France turned the tables. On the Niger, Frenchmen and Germans rediscovered common interests in opposing the regulations made by the Niger Company; in March 1894 Dr. Kayser, who as Colonial Director in the German Foreign Office was securing a stronger voice for colonial interests in the formulation of national policy, warned the British Ambassador that the Niger navigation might become 'the next great international question'. For a time there was even talk of France and Germany agreeing to give a north-easterly turn to the inland expansion of Togoland and Dahomey, so that both territories might touch the Niger below Boussa; on the other hand Goldie thought of co-operating with Germany in order to seal off French expansion from Dahomey. Nothing important came of these plans for a stronger German role; but they added an extra element of uncertainty to Anglo-French relations during the troubled 1890s.

Until 1895 British governments still tried to limit their commitments in West Africa. Salisbury, who by a decision of 1888 confirmed that British interests in Southern and Eastern Africa should receive higher priority, was successful in imposing 'a selective regulation of the British advance' in the west. He, and his Liberal successors, were under some pressure to be less rigorously selective. During the 1890s merchants and officials on the west coast, supported by Chambers of Commerce in British cities, were increasingly anxious to expand the frontiers of British influence, either by direct action or by supporting Samori in his prolonged resistance to the French advance. But these West African interests represented 'an energetic but not a compulsive lobby in British politics', and could not determine policy. Sierra Leone was finally delimited, within modest boundaries, in January 1895, the Colonial Office complaining that the diplomatists had traded its interests for the sake of gains in 'the Niger-Congo and Nile questions'. To the north of the Gold Coast, some belated efforts were made after 1892 to conclude treaties with the states of the savanna belt; but though most of Gonja, Mamprussi and Dagomba was thus saved for eventual British control, the northern Mossi states could not be kept out of French hands. In Yorubaland the expansion of the Colony of Lagos, though accelerated by Governor Carter after 1892, remained gradual, and subject to restraints imposed from London.

Even on the Niger, where British claims were most valuable and extensive, it was intended to dispose of the revived French challenge by negotiation. But in this as in other aspects of colonial policy there was a notable change of emphasis after Joseph Chamberlain went to the Colonial Office in 1895. This ex-radical businessman saw tropical Africa as an 'undeveloped estate', capable of profitable improvement by energetic and purposeful administration, and by increased public investment. Convinced of the benefits which the discharge of Britain's Imperial mission would bring to all affected by it, Chamberlain insisted on maintaining British territorial claims to the fullest practical extent. In December 1895 he was prepared to protect the lower Niger by a complicated, three-sided, territorial exchange, involving the cession of the Gambia and Dominica to France in return for Dahomey; but when Salisbury preferred a more limited and local negotiation, Chamberlain insisted on some very tough bargaining. As a leader of the Liberal Unionists in a coalition Cabinet, he was powerful enough to veto some of Salisbury's proposed concessions to France, and eventually to initiate a risky policy of replying to French military encroachments in kind. Though increasingly at odds with Goldie over future policy, Chamberlain strongly supported the Niger Company's insistence on keeping the French off the navigable Niger below Boussa, and out of the main part of Hausaland. Salisbury would have preferred to be much more conciliatory over details; however, it seems doubtful whether even he would have conceded anything which he considered essential to the embryonic territory of Nigeria. Despite the growth of anglo-phobe colonial enthusiasm in France, it was doubtful whether that government would deliberately risk war against the British navy for the sake of the Niger; sure enough, on 14 June 1898, they conceded the essential points of the British demands.

This agreement virtually completed the diplomatic partition of West Africa, though both Britain and France still had to undertake military campaigns to make their power effective in Ashanti and in Hausaland, around the middle Niger and on the borders of the desert. One problem which still seemed open concerned the future of Liberia, where there had been frequent rumours during the 1880s and 1890s of impending annexation by either France, Germany, or Britain. Nevertheless this tenacious little Republic, helped by much luck, succeeded in maintaining its national sovereignty. Elsewhere there were frequent proposals for frontier revision, and some succeeded. The most important formed part of the Anglo-French 'Entente' agreement of 1904; but even this included only a frontier rectification in northern Nigeria, a smaller one in the Gambia, and the cession to France of the Isles de Los.

On this occasion the French made another determined effort to obtain all the Gambia; they had discovered that their railway was overtaxing the navigable capacity of the Senegal river, and wanted the Gambia as an auxiliary 'feeder'. They tried again, offering compensation in Asia and the Pacific, and in 1908 Sir Edward Grey apparently agreed that the colony might be ceded without the city of Bathurst, provided the compensation was adequate. In 1911 the French made another overture, sadly mismanaged, asking for huge slices of Nigerian territory at the same time. And even this was not the end of the matter. There is a file in Dakar entitled *Projets d'Échange de la Gambie, 1916–20.* But, apart from the repartition of the German colonies in 1919, the frontiers which had been defined by 1898 were essentially those within which the modern African states have grown to national consciousness and independence. To a very considerable degree, their main configurations had already been foreshadowed by the relations between the European powers and the coastal peoples of Africa before 1885.

25. The background in East Africa

J. FLINT *History of East Africa* (edited by Roland Oliver and Gervase Mathew) Clarendon Press, Oxford 1963; pages 356–7, 358–9, 362–70, 374, 378–85

It would be a profound mistake to imagine that this expansion of European missionary and commercial activity in East Africa was to lead inevitably to the establishment of colonial rule. Politically the British, with their Indian and South African territories, and their powerful navy controlling the Indian Ocean, were in the strongest position. But the British had no desire at all to found new colonies in East Africa. Prevailing economic theories insisted that colonies were a bad investment yielding less in trade returns than they cost in administrative expenditure. The problems of abolishing slavery (illegal in British colonies since 1834), or of persuading Parliament to vote supplies, were enough of themselves to deter any prudent British politician. Even if these objections had been overcome, there would have been no need for the establishment of colonial rule. The British government's task was to create the conditions necessary for legitimate commerce and Christianity to expand and drive out the slave trade. Politically, this meant that the British Foreign Office, acting through its consular officials, sought to strengthen local states which seemed likely to maintain the peace and order necessary for commercial expansion.[1] In East Africa the Sultanate of Zanzibar was an obvious vehicle for such a policy; the only difficulty was that it was a slave-trading state. In 1841 Britain appointed a consul in Zanzibar and began the long process of forcing the sultan to cut down the extent of the slave trade and to seek compensation in expanding his 'legitimate' trade and his political control over the mainland. The principle of Zanzibar independence, enshrined in the Anglo-French Declaration of 1862, was an important part of this policy. After the appointment as consul of John Kirk, who had been with Livingstone on the Zambezi, British pressure on Zanzibar increased to such a pitch that in 1873, under threat of force, Sultan Barghash had to prohibit the sea-borne slave trade

[1] Compare the way in which the British deliberately fostered the growth of strong African states in West Africa, assisting the political ambitions of the city states of the Niger delta, and in Nupe actually negotiating an arrangement whereby British traders were under the Emir's 'protection'.

completely. Zanzibar was now ready, as the British saw it, to go forward as a respectable, enlightened state, and to expand its authority over the East African mainland, maintaining law and order in favour of British explorers, missionaries, and traders. . . .

The first challenge to the idea of using Zanzibar to control East Africa came not from Europe, but from Egypt. This was ironical, for behind the Egyptian challenge lay many of the same attitudes which had prompted the policy in Zanzibar. Since the opening of the Suez Canal in 1869 Egypt had been of particularly vital importance to British interests in India and the East. Yet there was no idea of establishing direct control over Egypt. Though Disraeli was prepared to buy the Khedive Ismail's shares in the Canal Company in 1875, and to acquire Cyprus in 1878, he refused to follow German suggestions that Britain should take Egypt as a colony or protectorate. The right course seemed to be to allow the khedive to modernize his country, and create an efficient army which could secure the Suez Canal from interference. Private capital was poured into Egypt, and European officials were given key posts in the administration. A vital part of Ismail's policy was the need to expand up the Nile to secure complete control of the flow of water upon which Egyptian agriculture was absolutely dependent. Ismail wanted Europeans, and particularly Englishmen, to undertake this task, and to attract them he not only put forward strategic arguments, but fitted his plans into the framework of the legitimate commerce theory, arguing that a trade in Sudanese ivory would drive out the slave trade. In 1869 Sir Samuel Baker, the discoverer of a second source of the Nile in Lake Albert, was appointed governor-general of 'The Equatorial Nile Basin', and by 1872 he had pushed Egyptian authority down to Lado. In 1873 Baker was succeeded by Gordon, and three years later Gordon was in Bunyoro sending messengers to Kabaka Mutesa of Buganda. He had already come to the conclusion that a permanent control of the Nile sources was not possible along the overland route to Cairo. In January 1875 the Khedive Ismail accepted Gordon's plan to seize territory on the east coast and establish a series of military posts linking the coast with Uganda. In November over 500 troops in four warships were landed at Brava commanded by a British officer in the khedive's service. They disarmed the

Zanzibar troops, hauled down the sultan's flag, and left a garrison. They went on to occupy Kismayu and Lamu, and laid claim to the East African coast in the name of Egypt.

Here was a nice problem of judgement for the British Foreign Office: was Zanzibar or Egypt to undertake the opening up of the lakes region and the east coast? Kirk pressed the claims of Zanzibar, Gordon those of Egypt. The humanitarian interests in Britain supported Zanzibar; they were not convinced that the Egyptians had a genuine anti-slavery impulse. The Foreign Office, remembering the humiliation which the sultan had suffered in 1873, and fearing that further humiliation might permanently embitter his attitude to Britain, decided for Zanzibar. Pressure from Britain induced the khedive to order a withdrawal from the coast in January 1876. Already the Egyptian expedition had found that it was too weak to move inland and join Gordon.

Britain had backed the right horse. Ismail still had ambitions in East Africa, and continued to demand a seaport on the east coast; in May 1876 Egypt officially 'annexed' the territories around Lakes Victoria and Albert. But it was all a sham. Ismail's lavish projects were already creating misgivings. Between 1879 and 1882 they would produce a complete breakdown of the experiment of Egyptian independence, with profound results for East Africa. . . .

Meanwhile events in North Africa were forcing Gladstone and his colleagues towards intervention in Egypt. The attempts of the khedives to create an independent Egypt using European personnel and capital had not met with success. Inefficiency and corruption, and usurious interest rates demanded by European financiers, had produced chaos and bankruptcy by the middle of the 1870s. The German Chancellor, Bismarck, had several times urged Britain to take control of Egypt, but British politicians had rightly suspected that his motive was to embroil them in difficulties and weaken Britain's international position. Disraeli, the Conservative Prime Minister in 1878, was convinced that Egypt would be merely 'an expensive encumbrance'. Nevertheless neither Britain nor France, both of whose subjects held large investments in Egypt, could afford to stand aloof, if Egypt's government collapsed. Early in 1879 the Khedive Ismail had been forced to establish a ministry including one French and one British official, so as to give security to investors' interests. When Ismail a few months later tried to rid himself of these ministers, and deal directly with the bond-holders, Britain and France intervened, replaced the khedive by his son Tewfik, and established a joint control over Egypt. This sparked off a nationalist movement among the Egyptian army officers, led by Arabi Pasha, who by the middle of 1882 were in control of Egypt.

Though Gladstone's government was now prepared to inter-vene, it continued to shun any aidea of establishing any permanent or legal form of British control. The object of intervention would be to 'restore the khedive's authority'. Gladstone wanted the intervention to be international, in the name of Turkey, but the French at first insisted that it be limited to Anglo-French forces. By a combination of maladroit diplomacy and political changes in France the outcome was that the British fleet alone bombarded Alexandria on 3 July 1882. Troops were landed, and in September defeated the nationalist forces at Tel-el-Kebir. Britain now controlled Egypt. Yet British politicians, whether Liberal or Conservative, refused to admit that the control was more than temporary. Solemnly and repeatedly Gladstone promised that Britain would with-draw as soon as the khedive's power had been restored, and he was assuming that the work might take months, or a year or two at the most. This was a profound miscalculation. Before Egyptian finances could be made to support a stable régime, and pay interest to the bondholders, the entire structure of the administration, and even the society itself needed to be reorgan-ized. This was a work for decades, as the consul-general, Sir Evelyn Baring, soon realized. In reality the British occupation was as 'permanent' as any other colonial acquisition, and Egypt's interests, including the need to control the waters of the Nile which alone made life in Egypt possible, became British interests. But by persisting in the belief that the occupation was soon to come to an end, the British estranged France and impeded and confused their own attitude to Egyptian problems, sometimes (as with the dispatch of Gordon to the Sudan in 1884) with disastrous results. They also permitted international control of Egypt's finances to continue, which meant that Britain had to curry favour with European powers, especially Germany, in order to secure agreement to financial reforms in Egypt. This often entailed the sacrifice of British interests elsewhere in Africa.

The British occupation of Egypt helped to set off the complicated series of events which led to the entry of Germany as a colonial power in Africa and revolutionized the situation in East Africa. The German Chancellor, Bismarck, wished to exploit Britain's dependence on the German support needed to secure international consent to financial reforms in Egypt. This did not at first mean that Bismarck wished Britain to smile upon the establishment of a German colonial empire at her expense. He was no believer in colonies, which he regarded as useless and expensive liabilities. He poured scorn on the colonial enthusiasts, and refused their demands. 'I want no colonies,' he said in 1871 when it was suggested that Germany should seize colonies from defeated France, 'they are good only for providing offices. For us colonial enterprise would be just like the silks and sables in Polish noble families, who for the rest have no shirts.' In 1872 he rejected a petition for annexation from Fiji; in 1874 he refused a request for German protection from the Sultan of Zanzibar, who was smarting under the British threats which had forced the abolition of the sea-borne slave trade. He welcomed and encouraged proposals by which other powers would set up régimes capable of giving security for German traders, hoping that the United States would establish a Samoan protectorate in 1875, and urging France, Italy, and Britain to carve up North Africa in 1878. In 1880 German merchants were firmly told that they could get no support for their plans for colonization in New Guinea. As late as 1882 the brothers Denhardt could get no support for a request from Simba of Witu for German protection.

After the occupation of Egypt Bismarck hoped that the British government would show its gratitude for German co-operation by facilitating the activities of German merchants overseas. He hoped to be able to stave off the demands of German merchants by persuading Britain to undertake the burden of protection in certain areas. The test came in South West Africa. A German merchant, F. A. E. Lüderitz, had succeeded in obtaining claims to monopolies and land rights at Angra Pequena, and demanded German protection for his settlements. In February 1883 Bismarck asked Britain to declare a protectorate over the region, but received no definite reply. In August the German government told Lüderitz that German protection might be granted, in so far as it did not conflict with British claims. In September the British were again pressed to state what their claims were. Left to themselves, the British government were prepared to admit that there were no British claims to the area, but the intervention of Scanlen, the Prime Minister of Cape Colony, altered the tone of the British reply. On 21 November, pressed once more by the German ambassador, the Foreign Office stated that although they claimed no sovereignty over Lüderitz' concession area, 'any claim to sovereignty by a Foreign Power' between Angola and the Cape frontier 'would infringe their legitimate rights'.

This in itself might have been enough to provoke Bismarck into establishing German protection in South West Africa. When no reply was received to a demand for further elucidation of the British claim made in December 1883, a German protectorate over Angra Pequena was announced in April 1884. But Bismarck had decided to do more than this. He had determined to found colonies elsewhere and to do all in his power to embarrass the British position in Africa. The British government must be shown that German demands could not be ignored. Other considerations, too, played their part in convincing Bismarck that Germany must begin a colonial career, though he still remained unconvinced of the value of colonies. If the colonial programme were directed against Britain, this might soften the implacable anti-German feelings of France, embittered by her defeat in 1870 and the loss of Alsace and Lorraine. Franco-German co-operation on the basis of mutual colonial antagonism to England might even result in greater stability in Europe. Bismarck also calculated that a German colonial policy would enable him to recreate a solid majority in the Reichstag.[1]

[1] Erich Eyck, in *Bismarck and the German Empire*, 1950, pp. 273 sqq., argues that German party politics were the main motive behind Bismarck's decision, and that diplomacy merely provided the opportunity. This view seems to give too little weight to the Angra Pequena affair, which convinced Bismarck that the British were unaware of the diplomatic facts of life. His later refusals to acquire more colonies, and the continuing neglect of existing German colonies, would indicate that the German colonial enthusiasts had little real power in politics.

Britain now faced a most uncomfortable period of German opposition. In July 1884 Germany annexed the Cameroons, forestalling the British consul by a few days. In the previous month French and German pressure had forced Britain to abandon the treaty she had concluded with Portugal by which she had hoped to secure British mercantile interests on the Congo by recognizing Portuguese control. In August the German representative joined with the French in blocking British plans for financial reform put before the London conference on Egyptian affairs. In September the British were forced to recognize German claims to South West Africa from Angola to the Cape frontier. Meanwhile France and Germany had come together to challenge the British position on the Niger and that of her ally Portugal on the Congo. A Conference of the Powers was summoned to Berlin in November to draw up rules for international control of both areas. Britain was only able to preserve her position on the Niger through the breakdown of the shortlived and unstable Franco-German *entente*,[1] but the Congo was placed under King Leopold's Congo Independent State and Portuguese claims were rejected.

The German humiliation of Britain in Africa during 1884 might perhaps have produced the opposite result to that which Bismarck intended. Instead of appreciating how dependent Britain was upon German favour, the Liberal government might have been provoked to take swift action in other areas to forestall possible German moves and to retaliate. Some of the younger and more ardent spirits in the government were so inclined, particularly the radicals Chamberlain and Dilke. There was an opportunity for retaliation in East Africa where Harry Johnston, at that time a young naturalist commissioned by the Royal Geographical Society, had secured treaties with local rulers around Mount Kilimanjaro. In July 1884 Johnston wrote to Lord Edmund Fitzmaurice urging that Kilimanjaro be colonized by English settlers as a British protectorate.

The letter arrived just as Germany seemed about to make a

---

[1] And by the success of the Niger traders, led by George Goldie Taubman, later Sir George Goldie, in purchasing the French Niger firms at the last minute. For details see Flint, *Goldie*, pp. 67–8. For a full account of the diplomacy of the Berlin Conference see S. E. Crowe, *The Berlin West African Conference, 1884–1885*, 1942.

move in East Africa. On 1 October 1884 Gerhard Rohlfs, a noted explorer well known for his advocacy of German colonial expansion, was appointed German consul-general in Zanzibar. In November the German press carried reports that Germany intended to establish a protectorate over Zanzibar. The German government denied these rumours but the British were uneasy. Kirk, acting on instructions, secured a declaration from Sultan Barghash in December that he would cede no sovereign rights without British consent.

Johnston's proposal thus fell upon sympathetic ears, and for the first time the Foreign Office lent its support to a proposal for direct British action in East Africa. But Sir John Kirk was not so enthusiastic; he felt that Africans would resist alienation of their land, and saw in the scheme a dangerous departure from the traditional policy of controlling East Africa through Zanzibar and one which could only alienate the sultan. Yet Kirk agreed that the German threat was real and that something had to be done; there were mysterious German travellers inland, and a German man-of-war on the coast. He therefore urged that the traditional policy be intensified and strengthened; the area should be developed by British persons, but under the sultan's flag.

The forward spirits in the cabinet, including Chamberlain and Sir Charles Dilke, now made what they could of this proposal, canvassing the support of the Foreign Secretary Lord Granville, the Colonial Secretary Lord Derby, and Lord Kimberley at the India Office. On 5 December 1884 Kirk was instructed to urge the sultan to send a military expedition to Kilimanjaro to negotiate treaties with the local chiefs recognizing Zanzibari authority, and to establish posts *en route*. Kirk was to go with the party, and if the chiefs refused to accept Zanzibari authority he was to make treaties on behalf of Great Britain.

All these decisions had been taken without the active participation of the Prime Minister. On 14 December Gladstone attacked the plan at a meeting of the cabinet. Later, writing to Dilke, he described himself as 'puzzled and perplexed at finding a group of the soberest men among us to have concocted a scheme such as that touching the mountain country behind Zanzibar with an unrememberable name'.

Whilst Gladstone irritably restored his authority over his erring colleagues, their fears were becoming realities in East Africa. On 14 November Carl Peters had arrived in Zanzibar with three associates. Peters's group was the most extreme within the German colonial movement. The main body of colonial advocates were organized in the *Kolonialverein*, founded in 1882 with the aim of identifying the colonial demand with German nationalism, to which end they had begun to issue a newspaper, the *Kolonialzeitung*, in 1884. It was a respectable and sober body, attempting to influence the German government through its influential members like Prince Hohenlohe-Langenburg. Peters and the extremists found such methods altogether too slow and uninspiring, and resolved to act independently to force the government's hand. In March 1884, with thirty others, he founded the *Gesellschaft für Deutsche Kolonisation*. This was in fact a commercial company designed to establish a colony; its manifesto stressed the urgent need for direct action before other powers swallowed the whole of Africa. The project was financed by the sale of shares in the *Gesellschaft* which soon raised 175,000 marks. Various projects were submitted to the German Foreign Office for approval, but Peters was merely told not to meddle in overseas policy. He therefore decided to keep secret his scheme for a German East African colony. He and his companions embarked from Europe, in disguise. On arrival at Zanzibar they were told by the German consul that they could expect no official support, and that they would travel on the mainland at their own peril. Nevertheless Peters set off undaunted. By 17 December he was back in Zanzibar with treaties in his pocket which purported to place Usagara, Ungulu, Uzigna, and Ukami under German protection. At about the same time the Denhardt brothers were negotiating in Witu with 'Sultan' Simba.

Returning to Berlin in February 1885 Peters succeeded in maturing his plans with such precision that it is difficult to believe that Bismarck had been unaware of them. On 26 February the Kaiser signed the *Schutzbrief* placing the territories claimed by Peters under German protection, and on 3 March, the day after the delegates to the Berlin Conference on the Niger and Congo had departed, the *Schutzbrief* was published. It was in reality what the British would have called a 'Royal Charter' entrusting the administration of German East Africa to the *Geselleschaft für Deutsche Kolonisation*.

The establishment of the German protectorate brought to an abrupt end the British policy of controlling East Africa through Zanzibar. The Germans had successfully defied the sultan's rights, despite the fact that these were supposedly guaranteed by the Anglo-French agreement of 1862. Moreover it was clear that further German inroads on Zanzibar claims were to come. If the German chartered company wished to pay its way it would have to acquire a part of the sea coast in order to escape Zanzibar customs duties and be able to levy its own. However loudly the Germans might claim that the inland regions had never been a part of the sultan's dominions, they could hardly pretend the same for the coast. There would have to be a frontal attack on the sultan's position.

Britain could have strangled the new German colony at birth by preventing the acquisition of a coastal foothold. But a resolute defence of Zanzibar would probably have needed the rapid declaration of a British protectorate over the whole of the sultan's dominions, the dispatch of numerous treaty-making expeditions to the interior, and the stationing of enough warships in the Indian Ocean to overawe local German naval strength. Such belligerency was not to be expected from Gladstone and his colleagues. The need for German diplomatic support was now more urgent than it had been at the time of the Angra Pequena affair. The Egyptian situation had become a nightmare—the Sudan had risen under the Mahdi and the popular British hero General Gordon had been killed at Khartoum in January 1885. Russia, taking advantage of British preoccupations in Egypt and the Sudan, began to advance into Afghanistan, and Gladstone's government, unable to face public opinion in England with yet another humiliation, tried to stand firm and threaten the Russians with war at a time when England had not a single ally in Europe. When the Russians occupied Pendjeh at the end of March war seemed imminent. . . .[1]

By the autumn of 1886 Bismarck wished to bring the Zanzibar affair to a close. He was still unconvinced of the value of

---

[1] The crisis died down in May when the two powers began negotiation for a settlement by arbitration.

colonies, and wished to limit the expansive designs of Peters and the Denhardt brothers. As usual, the demand for a settlement was accompanied by threats; if Germany did not get her way she would support France on Egyptian questions. In October negotiations were begun in London, and within a fortnight they were concluded.

Coolly disregarding any views which Sultan Barghash might have on the matter, the two powers proceeded bilaterally to define that unfortunate monarch's possessions. The islands of Zanzibar, Pemba, Mafia, and Lamu, the coast from Tungi Bay to Kipini to a depth of ten miles, the towns of Kismayu, Brava, Merka, and Mogadishu with a radius of ten miles around each, and Warsheikh with a radius of five miles, were all declared to be the Sultan's. Britain agreed to use her influence with Barghash to obtain for the German East Africa Company a lease of customs dues at Dar es Salaam and Pangani, to promote a friendly settlement of rival claims in Kilimanjaro, and to persuade the sultan to adhere to the Berlin Act. The coastline of Witu was defined as German. Germany promised to adhere to the Anglo-French Declaration of 1862 (i.e. to maintain the integrity of the sultan's dominions!). Another clause revealed that Britain and Germany had mapped out the lines of future partition of the mainland. The territory between the Ruvuma and Tana rivers was divided along a line from the Umba river to Lake Victoria and the northern portion declared to be a British, the southern a German, 'sphere of influence'. Each agreed not to interfere in the other's sphere, and within its own sphere 'not to make any acquisitions except protectorates'. France was later persuaded to adhere to these arrangements in return for Anglo-German recognition of a French protectorate over the Comoro Islands, where the Sultan of Zanzibar may have possessed some rights. . . .

In May 1887 Mackinnon's newly formed British East Africa Association obtained a concession from Sultan Barghash granting full judicial and political authority, including the right to levy customs duties, over his mainland possessions from Kipini to the Umba river, for fifty years. In return the association was to pay the sultan not less than the present amount which he received in customs duties from the region. By the end of the year the association was claiming sovereign rights to a depth of

200 miles from the coast by treaties made with the inland peoples. At the same time Mackinnon was trying, through Stanley, to enlist Emin Pasha as the association's governor of the Lakes region. The association was already in dispute with the German Witu Company formed in 1887, and early in 1888 began a long dispute with Italy over the sultan's northern ports, Kismayu, Merca, Mogadishu, and Warsheikh. The association was thus laying claim to be the government of the British sphere of influence in East Africa by virtue of the sovereign rights conceded to it by the sultan and the African rulers.

In April 1888 the members of the association made an agreement to form a company which might obtain 'a Charter or Charters incorporating the Company as a British corporate body and under British protection or otherwise'. The company would act as both a trading and development agency, and as an administration. £250,000 was subscribed; Mackinnon was the largest shareholder with £25,000 and other members of his family together subscribed the same amount. Philanthropic interest was very pronounced; Sir Thomas Fowell Buxton of the Anti-Slavery Society subscribed £10,000; Burdett-Coutts, whose wife, of the great banking family, was famous for charitable works, subscribed £10,000; and Alexander L. Bruce, who was connected by marriage with David Livingstone's family and had a strong interest in Nyasaland, subscribed £5,000. Past and present members of the British consular staff in Zanzibar were well represented. Sir John Kirk, now no longer consul-general, Francis de Winton the acting consul, and Frederick Holmwood who had done so much to promote the scheme, each subscribed a modest £1,000. The Sultan of Zanzibar was not entirely forgotten; the agreement laid down that he was to receive, without subscribing capital, one founder's share entitling him to 2 per cent of all profits after 8 per cent dividend had been paid on the ordinary capital, and his share was to be worth one-hundredth of the proceeds of any voluntary sale of the company.

Clearly the promoters of the new company had great hopes that a royal charter would be granted, and their expectations were soon justified, for on 3 September 1888 the British government, almost without discussion, granted the charter

Lord Salisbury now agreed to what in March 1887 he had declared impossible.

The reason for this abrupt change of front lay in developments in the Egyptian situation. When Mackinnon had asked for a charter in March 1887 Salisbury had at that time determined to make a serious attempt to withdraw from Egypt. He sent Sir Henry Wolff to Constantinople to negotiate a British withdrawal within five years, with guarantees for re-entry in case of invasion or anarchy. Wolff's mission came within sight of success; an agreement was actually signed, but not ratified. The conditions that Britain should be given re-entry rights raised such opposition from France and Russia that it came to nothing. The failure of this attempt convinced Salisbury that withdrawal with safeguards was impossible. He would therefore have to make the best of the occupation. The Tripartite Agreement of December 1887, between Britain, Italy, and Austria, brought Britain closer to the German system of alliances, and Salisbury could therefore hope for less German obstruction in Egypt. By the spring of 1888 Egyptian finances were in balance, and the need for international agreement on reform therefore less important. Salisbury now accepted the fact that the British occupation would be a long one.

Once this had sunk home Egypt's interests became British interests. It now became a fixed purpose of Salisbury, and of later Liberal imperialists like Lord Rosebery, to prevent any power with the technical skill to interfere with the flow of water from obtaining a foothold on the Nile. The reconquest of the Sudan would one day have to be undertaken, preferably when Egypt could pay for it. European powers would have to be prevented from controlling the sources of the Nile in Uganda; preferably this must be done without help from the Exchequer and without too many awkward questions in Parliament.

Mackinnon's plans fitted in perfectly with this new strategic thinking. His company promised, at no cost to the taxpayer, to control a part of the East African coast from which the source of the Nile could be most easily reached. Mackinnon's interest in Emin Pasha showed his genuine desire to obtain control of the Lakes region, and it was known that he had plans for a railway from the coast to Uganda. The Vice-President, Sir Thomas Brassey, was one of the greatest of British railway

SNA

builders overseas. The grant of the royal charter incorporating
the Imperial British East Africa Company was an announcement to the powers of Europe that the company was henceforth
not merely the agent of the Sultan of Zanzibar, but an arm of
British Imperial policy.

Once the charter had been granted to the British company a
period of intense rivalry set in, despite the fact that the British
and German governments had agreed in June 1887 to discourage annexations in the Lakes region. But nothing had been
said about protectorates. Both the British and the German
companies felt threatened by the possibility of encirclement by
the other; the British feared a pincer movement linking the
German Witu and East Africa companies in Uganda; and the
Germans feared that Mackinnon's company might join with
that of Cecil Rhodes in establishing an all-British route 'from
the Cape to Cairo' by controlling the area between Lakes
Tanganyika and Victoria.

Thus, though Salisbury was interested only in keeping the
Germans away from Uganda and the sources of the Nile, and
though Bismarck had little sympathy for the German companies' expansionist plans, the fact that the local administrations
were in private hands generated intense Anglo-German
friction. On the coast Mackinnon attempted to squeeze out
the German Witu Company, countered their attempts to seize
Lamu island, and even carried on negotiations with Italy over
the sultan's northern ports to prevent the Germans obtaining
them, despite rebukes from the British Foreign Office. His
efforts met with some success; in August 1889, by arbitration,
Lamu was awarded to the Sultan of Zanzibar, who promptly
ceded it to the British company. The same concession gave the
northern ports to the company, which agreed to transfer them
to Italy in November. In December 1889, after the breakdown
of negotiations by which Mackinnon would have purchased
the German Witu Company, Manda and Pate islands were
occupied by his agents.

Rivalry in the interior was even more serious. Initially the
focus for this rivalry was the presence of Emin Pasha in Equatoria. The Germans were not content to leave the 'rescue' of
their compatriot to Stanley and the British. In the autumn of
1888 they had formed a German Emin Pasha Relief Committee,

and money was subscribed to send Carl Peters to Equatoria. Despite the fact that the German coastal area was in open revolt, and that the German company's powers had been superseded by the appointment of Wissmann as Imperial Commissioner in the spring of 1889, Peters persisted with his plans. Though repudiated by the German government and by Wissmann he set off with 300 men in June 1889. The British company replied by sending an expedition under Frederick Jackson to open a route to Wadelai on the upper Nile and support Stanley.

After both expeditions had left the coast Stanley returned to it in December 1889, having 'rescued' Emin and abandoned Equatoria. Events determined that Buganda should provide a new focus to replace Equatoria; in October 1889 the Muslim faction had deposed Kabaka Mwanga, and the Anglican missionaries appealed to the British company to establish its rule in the kingdom. But Peters arrived first, and in February 1890 he persuaded Mwanga, who had in the meantime regained control, to sign a treaty establishing 'friendly relations with the German Emperor'. When Jackson arrived in April Peters had gone, but faced by opposition from the Catholic party the Englishman could not persuade Mwanga to sign a treaty.

Little news of what was happening in Uganda reached Europe until the summer of 1890. In the meantime the diplomats were moving towards a settlement over the heads of the treaty-makers. In the autumn of 1889 the German government suggested negotiations on outstanding disputes, and since the end of the year Salisbury had been working for a settlement by arbitration. Negotiations began in earnest after the fall of Bismarck from power in March 1890. The ambitions of the British government and those of the British company were by no means identical; Mackinnon was by now determined to make a territorial link with Cecil Rhodes's newly chartered company in the south, and in May he signed a 'treaty' with King Leopold. In return for recognition of his right to certain territories around Lake Albert, Leopold promised to hand over, when convenient to Mackinnon, a strip of territory five miles wide which would link Lake Albert Edward with Lake Tanganyika. Lord Salisbury was much more concerned with the alarming news coming from Uganda, than with the 'all-red route'. In March 1890 it had been rumoured that the Imperial Commissioner, Wissmann, was about to leave for Uganda, and on the last day of that month the Germans announced that Emin was to lead a large caravan to Buganda. The Foreign Office pressed the British company to make some counter-move,[1] and in April it was announced that Frederick Lugard would lead an armed expedition to establish the company's authority in Buganda. In the first week of May news was received of Peters's treaty with the Kabaka. Salisbury was so alarmed that he was not only to abandon the idea of the strip to Lake Tanganyika, but to make a sensational and hitherto unprecedented offer to cede territory in Europe to keep the Germans from Uganda.

On 13 May, meeting the German negotiator Count Hatzfeldt, Salisbury played this trump card. He began with a list of formidable demands; Germany must recognize Uganda as within the British sphere, she must abandon Witu, she must accept a British protectorate over Zanzibar and Pemba islands. In return Britain would drop the claim to a strip of territory to Lake Tanganyika, use her influence to persuade the sultan to sell the German coastal leases outright, and Britain would cede the island of Heligoland to Germany.

An African reader might find it strange, even ludicrous, that the German government should have seized eagerly the chance of acquiring a small, sandy, and almost barren little island in the North Sea in exchange for thousands of square miles of East African territory. But there were special reasons to tempt the Germans in Heligoland. In 1887 construction work had begun on the Kiel Canal, linking the Baltic and North Seas, nationalists were pressing for a programme of naval expansion, and the new Kaiser supported them. The strategists had long argued that the possession of Heligoland was essential if the German navy was to be able to exploit the usefulness of the Kiel Canal in time of war. Thus the Germans were soon biting at Salisbury's bait. Beside Heligoland, Count Hatzfeldt was

---

[1] This has long been a matter of some dispute. The company, when pressing the British government for compensation for the loss of its charter, argued that it had occupied Uganda in response to appeals from the government. As the costs of the Uganda occupation largely caused its bankruptcy, the company claimed that the government was morally liable.

told 'our East African interests merely come forward as matters for concession'. Salisbury had some difficulty with his cabinet, and with the Queen, who was uneasy that British subjects in Heligoland should be thus 'bartered away', but these scruples were overcome, and the agreement was signed on 1 July. By its provisions the British company obtained a solid block of territory, the thorn in its side at Witu was removed, and above all Uganda and the Nile sources had been secured. If the Cape to Cairo scheme was ever to come to fruition there still remained Mackinnon's 'treaty' with Leopold.[1]

A further British attempt to prevent Italy from reaching the Nile from the east coast also affected the frontiers of the British East African sphere. Though the British company and the Italian government had agreed to establish a joint administration of Kismayu, and the company had ceded the four other northern ports to Italy in November 1889, the inland frontier remained undefined. Mackinnon would have liked to arrange a boundary line, but Lord Salisbury was more concerned with the implications of Italian activity farther north. In 1889 the Italians had concluded the Treaty of Ucciali with Emperor Menelik of Ethiopia, which, so the Italians claimed, gave Italy a protectorate over Ethiopia. If this claim could be substantiated it would have given the Italians control of the sources of the Blue Nile. Another Italian claim to incorporate Kassala within the Italian colony of Eritrea would have given Italy control of the River Atbara, a tributary of the Nile. In the autumn of 1890 Baring, the consul-general in Egypt, visited Italy to negotiate directly with Signor Crispi, the Italian Prime Minister. Salisbury told Baring to 'insist on the command of all the affluents of the Nile, so far as Egypt formerly possessed them', but Crispi argued that these rights had been abandoned by Egypt to the Mahdists.

In February 1891 Crispi's government fell, largely as a result of his expensive colonial adventures. His successor, the Marchese

---

[1] In May 1894 the British government made an agreement with Leopold, which would have regularized the Mackinnon-Leopold 'treaty', and allowed Britain to construct a telegraph and a railway between Lakes Tanganyika and Albert Edward, through a lease, 25 kilometres wide. Intense opposition from Germany forced the two parties to withdraw this provision from their agreement.

di Rudini, was willing to come to terms. Agreements were signed in March and April in which Britain recognized the extravagent claim of Italy to a protectorate over Ethiopia, but the boundaries of the supposed protectorate were so drawn that Italy was kept away from the main Nile. Kassala was declared to be Egyptian (though Italy could occupy it temporarily for military purposes), and Italy bound herself not to build any works on the Atbara which might alter the Nile water-level. By thus defining Italy's claims the agreement established a frontier between the British company's sphere and the Italian possessions to the north. British East Africa thereafter was undefined only in the north-west, where its territories touched those of the Mahdist State,[1] which it was assumed would one day revert to British-controlled Egypt. The 'scramble' for East African territory was virtually over. The struggle for the Nile continued, but henceforth the British had to guard only the western approaches to the Nile Basin.

26. Nationalism and imperialism: an interpretation

RONALD ROBINSON and JOHN GALLAGHER *Africa and the Victorians* Macmillan 1961; pages 462–72

Did new, sustained or compelling impulses towards African empire arise in British politics or business during the 1880s? The evidence seems unconvincing. The late-Victorians seem to have been no keener to rule and develop Africa than their fathers. The business man saw no greater future there, except in the south; the politician was as reluctant to expand and administer a tropical African empire as the mid-Victorians had

---

[1] Though in fact the frontier with Ethiopia was undefined, for the Italians failed to subdue that state, which regained its independent stature after the defeat of Italy at Adowa in March 1896. Thereafter it could not be expected that the Ethiopian government should recognize a frontier drawn up by two alien powers. In December 1906 Britain and Ethiopia signed an agreement demarcating the border.

been; and plainly Parliament was no more eager to pay for it. British opinion restrained rather than prompted ministers to act in Africa. Hence they had to rely on private companies or colonial governments to act for them. It is true that African lobbies and a minority of imperialists did what they could to persuade government to advance. Yet they were usually too weak to be decisive. Measured by the yardstick of official thinking, there was no strong political or commercial movement in Britain in favour of African acquisitions.

The priorities of policy in tropical Africa confirm this impression. West Africa seemed to offer better prospects of markets and raw materials than east Africa and the Upper Nile; yet it was upon these poorer countries that the British government concentrated its efforts. These regions of Africa which interested the British investor and merchant least, concerned ministers the most. No expansion of commerce prompted the territorial claims to Uganda, the east coast and the Nile Valley. As Mackinnon's failure showed, private enterprise was not moving in to develop them; and they were no more useful or necessary to the British industrial economy between 1880 and 1900 than they had been earlier in the century. Territorial claims here reached out far in advance of the expanding economy. Notions of pegging out colonial estates for posterity hardly entered into British calculations until the late 1890s, when it was almost too late to affect the outcome. Nor were ministers gulled by the romantic glories of ruling desert and bush. Imperialism in the wide sense of empire for empire's sake was not their motive. Their territorial claims were not made for the sake of African empire or commerce as such. They were little more than by-products of an enforced search for better security in the Mediterranean and the East. It was not the pomps or profits of governing Africa which moved the ruling *élite*, but the cold rules for national safety handed on from Pitt, Palmerston and Disraeli.

According to the grammar of the policy-makers, their advances in Africa were prompted by different interests and circumstances in different regions. Egypt was occupied because of the collapse of the Khedivial *régime*. The occupation went on because the internal crisis remained unsolved and because of French hostility which the occupation itself provoked. Britain's

insistent claims in east Africa and the Nile Valley and her yielding so much in west Africa were largely contingent upon the
Egyptian occupation and the way it affected European
relations. In southern Africa, imperial intervention against the
Transvaal was designed above all to uphold and restore the
imperial influence which economic growth, Afrikaner nationalism and the Jameson fiasco had overthrown. Imperial claims in
the Rhodesias, and to a lesser extent in Nyasaland were contingent in turn upon Cape colonial expansion and imperial
attempts to offset the rise of the Transvaal. The times and circumstances in which almost all these claims and occupations
were made suggest strongly that they were called forth by
crises in Egypt and south Africa, rather than by positive
impulses to African empire arising in Europe.

To be sure, a variety of different interests in London—some
religious and humanitarian, others strictly commercial or
financial, and yet others imperialist—pressed for territorial
advances and were sometimes used as their agents. In west
Africa, the traders called for government protection; in Uganda
and Nyasaland, the missionaries and the anti-slavery groups
called for annexation; in Egypt, the bondholders asked government to rescue their investments; in south Africa, philanthrop-
isst and imperialists called for more government from Whitehall,
while British traders and investors were divided about the best
way of looking after their interests. Ministers usually listened to
their pleas only when it suited their purpose; but commercial
and philanthropic agitation seldom decided which territories
should be claimed or occupied or when this should be done,
although their slogans were frequently used by government in its
public justifications.

It is the private calculations and actions of ministers far more
than their speeches which reveal the primary motives behind
their advances. For all the different situations in which territory
was claimed, and all the different reasons which were given to
justify it, one consideration, and one alone, entered into all the
major decisions. In all regions north of Rhodesia, the broad
imperative which decided which territory to reserve and which
to renounce, was the safety of the routes to the East. It did not,
of course, prompt the claiming of Nyasaland or the lower
Niger. Here a reluctant government acted to protect existing

fields of trading and missionary enterprise from foreign annexations. In southern Africa the extension of empire seems to have
been dictated by a somewhat different imperative. Here the
London government felt bound as a rule to satisfy the demands
for more territory which their self-governing colonials pressed
on them. Ministers did this in the hope of conserving imperial
influence. Nevertheless, the safety of the routes to India also
figured prominently in the decision to uphold British supremacy in south Africa. It was the same imperative which after
impelling the occupation of Egypt, prolonged it, and forced
Britain to go into east Africa and the Upper Nile, while yielding
in most of west Africa. As soon as territory anywhere in Africa
became involved, however indirectly, in this cardinal interest,
ministries passed swiftly from inaction to intervention. If the
papers left by the policy-makers are to be believed, they moved
into Africa, not to build a new African empire, but to protect
the old empire in India. What decided when and where they
would go forward was their traditional conception of world
strategy.

Its principles had been distilled from a century and more of
accumulated experience, from far-reaching and varied experiments in the uses of power to promote trade and in the uses of
trade to promote power. Much of this experience confirmed one
precept: that Britain's strength depended upon the possession
of India and preponderance in the East, almost as much as it did
upon the British Isles. Therefore, her position in the world hung
above all upon safe communications between the two. This was
a supreme interest of Victorian policy; it set the order of
priorities in the Middle East and Asia, no less than in Africa,
and when African situations interlocked with it, they engaged
the serious and urgent attention of the British government. At
the first level of analysis, the decisive motive behind late-
Victorian strategy in Africa was to protect the all-important
stakes in India and the East.

An essentially negative objective, it had been attained
hitherto without large African possessions. Mere influence and
co-operation with other Powers had been enough to safeguard
strategic points in north Africa; while in south Africa control of
coastal regions had sufficed. The ambition of late-Victorian
ministers reached no higher than to uphold these mid-Victorian

systems of security in Egypt and south Africa. They were distinguished from their predecessors only in this: that their security by influence was breaking down. In attempting to restore it by intervention and diplomacy, they incidentally marked out the ground on which a vastly extended African empire was later to arise. Nearly all the interventions appear to have been consequences, direct or indirect, of internal Egyptian or south African crises which endangered British influence and security in the world. Such an interpretation alone seems to fit the actual calculations of policy. Ministers felt frankly that they were making the best of a bad job. They were doing no more than protecting old interests in worsening circumstances. To many, the flare-up of European rivalry in Africa seemed unreasonable and even absurd; yet most of them felt driven to take part because of tantalising circumstances beyond their control. They went forward as a measure of precaution, or as a way back to the saner mid-Victorian systems of informal influence. Gloomily, they were fumbling to adjust their old strategy to a changing Africa. And the necessity arose much more from altered circumstances in Africa than from any revolution in the nature, strength or direction of British expansion.

Hence the question of motive should be formulated afresh. It is no longer the winning of a new empire in Africa which has to be explained. The question is simpler: Why could the late-Victorians after 1880 no longer rely upon influence to protect traditional interests? What forced them in the end into imperial solutions? The answer is to be found first in the nationalist crises in Africa itself, which were the work of intensifying European influences during previous decades; and only secondarily in the interlocking of these crises in Africa with rivalries in Europe. Together the two drove Britain step by step to regain by territorial claims and occupation that security which could no longer be had by influence alone. The compelling conditions for British advances in tropical Africa were first called into being, not by the German victory of 1871, nor by Leopold's interest in the Congo, nor by the petty rivalry of missionaries and merchants, nor by a rising imperialist spirit, nor even by the French occupation of Tunis in 1881—but by the collapse of the Khedivial *régime* in Egypt.

From start to finish the partition of tropical Africa was driven by the persistent crisis in Egypt. When the British entered Egypt on their own, the Scramble began; and as long as they stayed in Cairo, it continued until there was no more of Africa left to divide. Since chance and miscalculation had much to do with the way that Britain went into Egypt, it was to some extent an accident that the partition took place when it did. But once it had begun, Britain's over-riding purpose in Africa was security in Egypt, the Mediterranean and the Orient. The achievement of this security became at the same time vital and more difficult, once the occupation of Egypt had increased the tension between the Powers and had dragged Africa into their rivalry. In this way the crisis in Egypt set off the Scramble, and sustained it until the end of the century.

British advances in tropical Africa have all the appearances of involuntary responses to emergencies arising from the decline of Turkish authority from the Straits to the Nile. These advances were decided by a relatively close official circle. They were largely the work of men striving in more desperate times to keep to the grand conceptions of world policy and the high standards of imperial security inherited from the mid-Victorian preponderance. Their purposes in Africa were usually esoteric; and their actions were usually inspired by notions of the world situation and calculations of its dangers, which were peculiar to the official mind.

So much for the subjective views which swayed the British partitioners. Plainly their preconceptions and purposes were one of the many objective causes of the partition itself. There remain the ultimate questions: how important a cause were these considerations of government? What were the other causes?

The answers are necessarily complicated, because they can be found only in the interplay between government's subjective appreciations and the objective emergencies. The moving causes appear to arise from chains of diverse circumstances in Britain, Europe, the Mediterranean, Asia and Africa itself, which interlocked in a set of unique relationships. These disparate situations, appraised by the official mind as a connected whole, were the products of different historical evolutions, some arising from national growth or decay, others from European expansion stretching as far back as the Mercantilist era. All of them were changing at different levels at different speeds. But although their paths were separate, they were destined to cross. There were structural changes taking place in European industry cutting down Britain's lead in commerce. The European balance of power was altering. Not only the emergence of Germany, but the alignment of France with Russia, the century-old opponent of British expansion, lessened the margins of imperial safety. National and racial feelings in Europe, in Egypt and south Africa were becoming more heated, and liberalism everywhere was on the decline. All these movements played some part in the African drama. But it seems that they were only brought to the point of imperialist action by the idiosyncratic reactions of British statesmen to internal crises in Africa. Along the Mediterranean shores, Muslim states were breaking down under European penetration. In the south, economic growth and colonial expansion were escaping from imperial control. These processes of growth or decay were moving on time-scales different from that of the European expansion which was bringing them about.

By 1882 the Egyptian Khedivate had corroded and cracked after decades of European paramountcy. But economic expansion was certainly not the sufficient cause of the occupation. Hitherto, commerce and investment had gone on without the help of outright political control. The thrusts of the industrial economy into Egypt had come to a stop with Ismail's bankruptcy, and little new enterprise was to accompany British control. Although the expanding economy had helped to make a revolutionary situation in Egypt, it was not the moving interest behind the British invasion. Nor does it seem that Anglo-French rivalry or the state of the European balance precipitated the invasion. It was rather the internal nationalist reaction against a decaying government which split Britain from France and switched European rivalries into Africa.

But the cast of official thinking profoundly influenced the outcome of the emergency. Moving instinctively to protect the Canal, the Liberals intended a Palmerstonian blow to liberate the progressives and chasten the disruptive elements in Egyptian politics. But instead of restoring their influence and then getting out, the need to bottle up anarchy and stave off the French forced them to stay on. This failure to work the mid-Victorian techniques, by coming to terms with the nationalists and finding Egyptian collaborators, meant that Indian solutions had to be applied to Egypt as well. The disenchantment of the 'Guardians' was replacing the liberal faith in voluntary co-operation; and Gladstone's sympathy with oppressed nationalities was hardening into Cromer's distrust of subject races. For similar reasons, official pessimism deepened about the reliability of the Turkish bastion in the Mediterranean; and as the balance tilted against Britain in the inland sea, her rulers realised that they were in Egypt to stay. Weighing the risks of Ottoman decay and the shifts in the European balance, remembering Indian experience and distrusting Egyptian 'fanatics', England's rulers pessimistically extended the search for security up the Nile to Fashoda, and from the Indian Ocean to Uganda and the Bahr-el-Ghazal.

The causes of imperial expansion in southern Africa were altogether different. It was essentially unconnected with the contemporary crisis in Egypt and its consequences in tropical Africa; it moved on a different time-scale, and the impulses behind it were separate. Unlike Egypt and tropical Africa, south Africa was to a great extent insulated from the rivalries of European Powers. Unlike them also, it was being rapidly developed by British commercial interests. The crisis which faced British governments was produced by colonial growth, and not by the decay of a native government. It arose from internal conflicts among the colonists, rather than from rivalries among the Powers. But the south African and Egyptian crises were alike in this: neither was precipitated by drastic changes in the local purposes of British expansion; but in both, the late-Victorians strained to keep up their supreme influence against a nationalist threat, and they were drawn at last into reconquering paramountcy by occupation.

South Africa was a case of colonial society receding beyond imperial control. It was also a case of economic development raising the enemies of the imperial connection to political preponderance over the colonial collaborators. By 1895 the new-found commercial supremacy of the Transvaal was sustaining republicanism and threatening to draw the colonies into a United States of South Africa.

Here also the subjective appraisals of the policy-makers combined with objective situations to produce imperial advances.
British aims in the south were specifically imperial, as they were
not in tropical Africa. For years it had been assumed without
question that south Africa must eventually turn into another
Canada. But it was not only in London that official thinking
was crucial. Their special historiography had taught ministers
that with self-governing colonials it was prudent to follow their
friends and rash to push or thwart them. As a result throughout
the south African crisis, policy had to be warped to the theorems
of the British colonial party.

In 1881 Gladstone had hoped to stultify Afrikaner nationalism by conciliation, as he was to try to do in Ireland. He
switched policy back to the mid-Victorian technique of resting
imperial supremacy upon a responsible ministry at the Cape
and indirect influence over the Boer republics. It was assumed
until 1895 that British immigrants and business would engulf
the republicans and strengthen the natural imperial ties of self-
interest and kinship. Nationalism would be killed by kindness.
So long as London kept in line with colonial opinion and
Britain's collaborators were upheld, south Africa would eventually turn itself into a loyal dominion. In this belief, Colonial
Secretaries from Kimberley to Ripon kept intervention to a
minimum, so as to avert another war between Boer and Briton
and the risk of another Ireland. Hence they went on dismantling
the 'Imperial Factor'. But by 1896 this system of imperial
influence at second hand seemed to have broken under the
strain of internal conflicts. South Africa had outgrown imperial
supremacy in any form; it had passed beyond the power of
British influence to compose the rivalry of its separate states. As
Chamberlain saw it, economic development and political
catastrophe had wrecked the imperial position in south Africa.
It was the Rhodesians' thesis that the Transvaal must be
brought under the control of an English-speaking majority.
Fearing to lose their last allies, Chamberlain and Milner
became their prisoners and followed them over the edge of war.
Drawn on by hopes of re-integrating the empire, hardened by
the recalcitrance of Afrikaner, as of Irish nationalists, and
haunted by the fear of declining national greatness, the Unionists feared that free association would no longer keep south

Africa in the empire. The nostrums of the Durham Report had not worked with the nationalists of the Transvaal, as they had done with those of Quebec. South African pressure drove ministers into action as anomalous as that taken at Fashoda. Admitting that imperial supremacy over white colonies was fast becoming a fiction, they were drawn into trying to restore it in south Africa by compulsion.

There are many evidences that towards the end of the century the wearing out of well-tried devices and the emergence of so many intractable problems shocked ministers out of their self-confidence and turned them to desperate expedients. The beliefs which had inspired earlier expansion were failing. Palmerston's axioms were giving way to Salisbury's re-appraisals. Liberal values could not be exported to all with cases of Birmingham hardware. Self-government would not always travel. Some nationalisms could not be killed by kindness. The growth of communities into harmonious commercial and political partnership with Britain was not after all a law of nature. The technique of collaborating classes had not worked everywhere. And as difficulties and doubts mounted, the men presiding over the destinies of the British Empire found themselves surrounded by the Eumenides.

Why were these catastrophes overtaking them? All the processes of British expansion were reaching their peak. The metropolitan society was putting forth its strongest energies. It was at this climatic point that the social changes in its satellites were quickest and most violent. Hence it was at this time that their relations with the metropolis tended to move into crisis. The colonial communities were breaking off toward full independence; while anti-western nationalism and social upheaval were estranging the non-European partners of British interests. The effects of growth were also coming back to roost at Home. England's rulers were alarmed by the symptoms of disintegration, the demand for collectivism, the decay of the landed interest and the running sore of Ireland. The late-Victorians were confronted with nationalist upsurges in Ireland, Egypt and south Africa, and with their beginnings in India. They were losing the faith of their fathers in the power of trade and anglicisation to turn nationalists into friends and partners. They were no longer so sure as they had been that revolutionary change worked naturally and inevitably to advance British interests. And so they ceased to foster and encourage change and tended to be content to preserve the *status quo*. They became less concerned to liberate social energies abroad and concentrated on preserving authority instead.

Canning and Palmerston had known that the liberals of the world were on their side. But the late-Victorians had to find their allies more and more among Indian princes, Egyptian pashas or African paramount chiefs. Finding themselves less successful in assimilating nationalists to British purposes, their distrust of them grew. And becoming uncertain of the reliability of mere influence, they turned more often from the technique of informal control to the orthodoxies of the Indian *raj* for dealing with political anomalies and for securing their interests. They were ceasing to be a dynamic force and becoming a static power. They were more and more preoccupied throughout the world to guard what they had won; and they became less able to promote progress, as they lapsed into the cares of consolidation.

Fundamentally, the official calculations of policy behind imperial expansion in Africa were inspired by a hardening of arteries and a hardening of hearts. Over and over again, they show an obsession with security, a fixation on safeguarding the routes to the East. What stands out in that policy is its pessimism. It reflects a traumatic reaction from the hopes of mid-century; a resignation to a bleaker present; a defeatist gloss on the old texts of expansion. Perhaps at the deepest level the causes of the British share in the African partition are not found in strategic imperatives, but in the change from Canning's hopes for liberalism to Salisbury's distrust of nationalism, from Gladstone's old-fashioned concern not to turn south Africa into another Ireland, to Chamberlain's new-fangled resolve to re-forge it into another Canada.

The notion that world strategy alone was the sole determinant of British advances is superficial. For strategy is not merely a reflection of the interests which it purports to defend, it is even more the register of the hopes, the memories and neuroses which inform the strategists' picture of the world. This it is which largely decides a government's view about who may be trusted and who must be feared; whether an empire assumes an optimistic or pessimistic posture; and whether the forces of change abroad are to be fostered or opposed. Indeed any theory of imperialism grounded on the notion of a single decisive cause is too simple for the complicated historical reality of the African partition. No purely economic interpretation is wide enough, because it does not allow for the independent importance of subjective factors. Explanations based entirely on the swings of the European balance are bound to remain incomplete without reference to changes outside Europe.

Both the crises of expansion and the official mind which attempted to control them had their origins in an historical process which had begun to unfold long before the partition of Africa began. That movement was not the manifestation of some revolutionary urge to empire. Its deeper causes do not lie in the last two decades of the century. The British advance, at least, was not an isolated African episode. It was the climax of a longer process of growth and decay in Africa. The new African empire was improvised by the official mind, as events made nonsense of its old historiography and hustled government into strange deviations from old lines of policy. In the widest sense, it was an offshoot of the total processes of British expansion throughout the world and throughout the century.

How large then does the new African empire bulk in this setting? There are good reasons for regarding the mid-Victorian period as the golden age of British expansion, and the late-Victorian as an age which saw the beginnings of contraction and decline. The Palmerstonians were no more 'anti-imperialist' than their successors, though they were more often able to achieve their purposes informally; and the late-Victorians were no more 'imperialist' than their predecessors, though they were driven to extend imperial claims more often. To label them thus is to ignore the fact that whatever their method, they were both of set purpose engineering the expansion of Britain. Both preferred to promote trade and security without the expense of empire; but neither shrank from forward policies wherever they seemed necessary.

But their circumstances were very different. During the first three-quarters of the century, Britain enjoyed an almost effortless supremacy in the world outside Europe, thanks to her sea power and her industrial strength, and because she had little foreign rivalry to face. Thus Canning and Palmerston had a very wide freedom of action. On the one hand, they had little need to bring economically valueless regions such as tropical Africa into their formal empire for the sake of strategic security; and on the other, they were free to extend their influence and power to develop those regions best suited to contribute to Britain's strength. Until the 1880s, British political expansion had been positive, in the sense that it went on bringing valuable areas into her orbit. That of the late-Victorians in the so-called 'Age of Imperialism' was by comparison negative, both in purpose and achievement. It was largely concerned with defending the maturing inheritance of the mid-Victorian imperialism of free trade, not with opening fresh fields of substantial importance to the economy. Whereas the earlier Victorians could afford to concentrate on the extension of free trade, their successors were compelled to look above all to the preservation of what they held, since they were coming to suspect that Britain's power was not what it once had been. The early Victorians had been playing from strength. The supremacy they had built in the world had been the work of confidence and faith in the future. The African empire of their successors was the product of fear lest this heritage should be lost in the time of troubles ahead.

Because it went far ahead of commercial expansion and imperial ambition, because its aims were essentially defensive and strategic, the movement into Africa remained superficial. The partition of tropical Africa might seem impressive on the wall maps of the Foreign Office. Yet it was at the time an empty and theoretical expansion. That British governments before 1900 did very little to pacify, administer and develop their spheres of influence and protectorates, shows once again the weakness of any commercial and imperial motives for claiming them. The partition did not accompany, it preceded the invasion of tropical Africa by the trader, the planter and the official. It was the prelude to European occupation; it was not that occupation itself. The sequence illuminates the true nature of the British movement into tropical Africa. So far from commercial expansion requiring the extension of territorial claims, it was the extension of territorial claims which in time required commercial expansion. The arguments of the so-called new

imperialism were *ex post facto* justifications of advances, they
were not the original reasons for making them. Ministers had
publicly justified their improvisations in tropical Africa with
appeals to imperial sentiment and promises of African progress.
After 1900, something had to be done to fulfil these aspirations,
when the spheres allotted on the map had to be made good on
the ground. The same fabulous artificers who had galvanised
America, Australia and Asia, had come to the last continent.

27. Nationalism and imperialism: an alternative view

JEAN STENGERS *Journal of African History* Vol. 3, No. 3, 1962
Cambridge University Press; pages 469–91 (In translation)

As any historian will admit, writing a book with a thesis is both
a great advantage and a great risk. The advantage lies in the
immediate impression that the book gives: the thesis, if sustained with interest, will directly arouse discussion. The risk is
that the book and thesis will not become generally accepted,
not even by specialists, and that if the thesis is strongly criticized, the book may be disregarded as worthless.

This reflection is made after reading the brilliant work of
Robinson and Gallagher, *Africa and the Victorians*. This book,
which presents a thesis 'par excellence', is therefore both
stimulating and exciting. However, we believe its central thesis
to be almost entirely false. The day will come when this thesis
will be rejected; it would be, nevertheless, quite unjust if the
reception of the book itself should suffer. It merits a place of
distinction in the series of works on European politics in Africa.
The authors have made use of widespread documentation, often
new, drawing, for example, to great advantage on the Salisbury
Papers, which shed fresh light on numerous questions. Whether
one is dealing with Egypt, the Sudan, Uganda or South Africa,
one will no longer be able to tackle the issues of British politics
in Africa at the end of the nineteenth century, without taking
into account their analysis. In more than one place, there is

unequal analysis; pages of strong writing and excellent passages alternate with weaker passages where the scholarship at times seems lacking, or where the source of the material seems to have been exploited by the apparent rapidity and inexactness, but where the writing displays an unusual perception. It is necessary, however, to start with the thesis itself. This is called the debate.

Why did there occur the scramble in Africa at the end of the nineteenth century? To this old question, Robinson and Gallagher answer essentially with one word: Egypt. In their opinion, it was the occupation of Egypt by Britain which started it all. 'Without the occupation of Egypt, there is no reason to suppose that any international scrambles for Africa, either west or east, would have begun when they did.' The authors proceed to describe the chain of events by which they feel the Egyptian question provoked the essence of what took place at the end of the nineteenth century.

If, however, there was a series of linked events, was this accelerated by the force of the imperialistic spirit? Not at all, or scarcely so, affirm Robinson and Gallagher. The men who controlled British politics in Africa, the policy-makers, who had conquered an Empire, had the same rules of action as did their predecessors of the previous generations who had not conquered. Only circumstances changed, not the spirit behind the politics.

There was hardly any pressure of public opinion on the leaders. 'Measured by the yardstick of official thinking, there was no strong political or commercial movement in Britain in favour of African acquisitions.' As for the leaders, they never appear to us as true imperialists—as men seeking to build an Empire, whether for political or commercial reasons. Faced with the chain reaction that the Egyptian question provoked, they had to safeguard British interests and the security of Great Britain, and they did this in the same way that Pitt, Palmerston or Disraeli would have done. Their conquests were, for the most part, measures of protection. As Egypt meant the road to India, one can say in the last analysis that the policy-makers considered their African politics in relation to the Orient. 'They moved into Africa, not to build a new African empire, but to protect the old empire of India. . . . The decisive motive behind late-Victorian strategy in Africa was to protect the all-important stakes in India and the East.'

This schematic résumé, although omitting the development of the thesis, allows us to consider its twofold and extreme originality. In part, certainly, Egypt is of first importance. 'The crisis in Egypt set off the Scramble and sustained it until the end of the century'; but from another viewpoint, British colonial imperialism, as it was traditionally conceived, disappears in its mesh. What of the conquest of Africa inspired by a new spirit, a clearly imperialistic spirit that would have arisen at the end of the nineteenth century, and which would have run contrary to the spirit of the preceding age? Nothing of the sort, claim the authors. Everything was done according to political precedents set by the preceding era. The novelty was Egypt, rather than any new conception of the part Great Britain was to play in Africa.

Robinson and Gallagher, in defending this thesis, limit themselves to English politics; but one feels, through various allusions scattered throughout their book, that they almost consider it valid, *grosso modo*, for the other European powers. In this case it would be the very notion of 'the age of imperialism' that would collapse: it would no longer be possible to see the fruits of reason in the division of Africa at the end of the nineteenth century. The particular character which one thought one recognized in imperialism at the time of the scramble would be merely an illusion, a myth.

This was, it must be remembered, the core of a big problem. One might first ask oneself if, in treating this problem, whether for Great Britain alone, or for the European powers in general, the framework chosen by Robinson and Gallagher, i.e. that of Africa, is actually fitting. 'Scramble for Africa' has become an accepted expression. But those contemporaries who were present at the beginnings of the scramble saw it unfolding both in Africa and in Oceania, and it was the 'scramble for Africa and Oceania' of which they often spoke. This was the true scope of the problem, and Oceania certainly takes us far from Egypt.

But since the authors concern themselves solely with Africa, let us confine ourselves to their topic. Are the links which they note between the different phases of the apportionment and the question of Egypt actually realistic? Each case deserves a detailed examination. Newbury does this for Occidental Africa, and the thesis of Robinson and Gallagher does not stand up against his examination. Regarding Uganda, Oliver made what seems to us a fair observation, that in British political dealings with Uganda, concern over protecting Egypt was but a secondary element. 'The strategic importance of Kenya and Uganda was a secondary discovery, made only when it was known that the chartered company was failing.' This was, above all, 'an excuse to hold on'. Occidental Africa and Uganda—two large areas where Robinson and Gallagher's reasoning falls down.

But rather than follow the authors in detail, agreeing with them on one point, criticizing them on another, the problem can be approached from another angle, through an initial question quite different from theirs. Take simply—one might be tempted to say, crudely—the question of priorities. Between 1880 and 1885 the policy of the European powers in Africa took a new turn. As Salisbury said, 'When I left the Foreign Office in 1880, nobody thought about Africa. When I returned in 1885, the nations of Europe were almost quarrelling with each other as to the various portions of Africa which they could obtain.' Between 1880 and 1885, what were, in Africa south of the Sahara, the first moves towards acquiring political control over new lands, what were the first cases of political appropriation in regions which until then had remained free?

Was it Leopold II who began it? One might imagine so, on reading the text of the first treaty signed by the officials of the expedition which he had sent to Africa. In this treaty—which was published in 1884 by the American Senate, to whom the King had sent it—political considerations were in the forefront. The chiefs of Vivee, on the Lower Congo, surrendered to the Comité d'Etudes, an organization acting as a cover for the King, the rights of sovereignty over a part of their territory. That was on 13 June 1880. Had the text been authentic, the political initiative would have been remarkable. Unfortunately, it was not: Leopold II had communicated a forged document to the American Senate. The real treaty of Vivee of 13 June 1880 has now been uncovered; it did not provide for any surrender of sovereignty.

Leopold's undertaking in Africa had not at its outset been

of a political nature. This does not mean that the King, from time to time, had not contemplated political manoeuvres, but they remained at the level of projects without much weight. The motivating idea—the programme, in the correct sense of the word—of Leopold II lay elsewhere; it consisted in organizing the commercial exploitation of central Africa. The chief objectives were to set up trading posts and to establish a great commercial enterprise.

It was only in 1882 that he was forced to change his plans. He had to face a danger, Brazza, who was about to plant the French flag in the regions of the Congo where Leopold II wanted to penetrate, and even in regions where outposts of the Comité d'Etudes had already been established. The only way to stop Brazza, and to prevent his annexations, was to plant another flag before his which would also be the symbol of a political power. Henceforth, Leopold II's aim was to acquire sovereignty.

But all this, beginning in 1882, was only a repercussion of the policy of Brazza, and of the intentions attributed to him. In our search for the first moves, ought we not, in fact, to turn towards France?

It was France, indeed, which initiated what must be considered the two fundamental moves in the scramble. The first was the conclusion of the Brazza-Makoto treaty, and still more its ratification in 1882. The second was the protectorate policy inaugurated in western Africa in January 1883. The first episode is well enough known, although the reasons why France settled in the Congo have never been sufficiently analysed. The second, we believe, has never been highlighted.

In 1882 Brazza returned to France. He brought back what he himself called, and the whole world was soon to call, his 'treaty' with Makoko. There were actually two deeds, judicially rather peculiar, which were obviously not the work of someone skilled in international law, and which dated from September–October 1880. In the first, the explorer declared that he had obtained from King Makoko, the sovereign reigning to the north of Stanley Pool, 'cession of his territory to France', with Makoko making his 'sign' on the proclamation. In the second, he stated that he had occupied in the name of France part of the territory situated on the very edge of Stanley Pool (which was to become Brazzaville). This 'treaty', to use Brazza's term, gave France charge over a very small territory on the threshold of the basin of the navigable Congo, which was of obvious strategic and commercial importance, but which was isolated hundreds of kilometres from both the coast and the existing French possessions.

How many French, British and other officers' treaties of this type—strange and daring—were there in Africa in the nineteenth century, and how proudly did they bring them back to Europe, where the metropolitan authorities, with a smile, acquiesced? Did not Cameron, to cite only one example, draw up in central Africa, in December 1874, an act by which he took possession of the basin of the Congo in the name of the Queen of England? The views of Lt. Cameron are interesting but 'are not destined to be carried out in our generation', an employee of the Foreign Office narrow-mindedly observed, after which a solemn act, without further formality, joined other similar documents in a drawer.

Brazza came close to experiencing the fate common to many officers judged too bold by metropolitan authority. He himself feared that his 'treaty' would not be ratified. In September 1882, while visiting Brussels, he expressed pessimism to Lambermont, secretary to the Minister of the Foreign Office, saying that 'his conviction was that neither the government nor the chambers in Paris would do anything'. Leopold II, who for his part considered Brazza a most dangerous rival, used all his influence to dissuade France from following up this famous treaty. If Brazza's ideas are followed up, he wrote to Ferdinand de Lesseps, 'I'm afraid he will throw his country in the path of annexations and conquests which would infallibly lead other nations to seize other parts of the Congo, monopolizing traffic which is today open to all. It will be the end of all our efforts, the establishment of politics in Africa: the field which we wanted to open will suddenly be closed; instead of having reached the great goal of civilization and humanity to lift the barriers of Africa [the aim that Leopold II himself purports to follow], we will see transplanted there the rivalries and miseries of elsewhere.'

Thus in Paris the Minister concerned—the Minister of the

Navy—was ready to bury the Brazza 'affair'. After having declared in July 1882 that he was avoiding the arrangement made by Brazza, he adopted what was administratively the most effective attitude to ensure that nothing would happen: he kept silent. Yet on 12 October, Lesseps answered Leopold II. He had seen Duclerc, President of the Council and Minister of Foreign Affairs, who, it seems, announced to him his intention to submit the Brazza-Makoko treaty for ratification by Parliament.

What happened? As the French press became aroused the government decided to act. Brazza, with the help of a few friends, had established close relationships with the newspapers and with public opinion. He had communicated with the press at length the account of his explorations, explaining the advantages which his treaty would bring to France, and disclosing the immense economic perspectives that would be opened up in a new colony—the French Congo. As early as the second week in September the newspapers reacted. One after the other, they came out enthusiastically for the exploits of Brazza, his treaty with Makoko and the French Congo. On 30 September the *Temps* noted that 'the press is unanimous in the "affair" of the Congo—for once, all shades of public opinion are in acord'. It was a sort of national plebiscite: 'The whole French press, with a warmth never before kindled by colonial matters, urge the government to ratify the treaty made by de Brazza with the owners of river properties of the Congo.' The Society of Colonial and Maritime Studies, in coming out on 3 October in favour of ratification, could thus write that it was associated with the 'national movement'.

The government must be careful not to give in to the cry of public opinion:

Are we going to refuse a colony that is so rich and so coveted by others? It would be a mistake, for which there would be no excuse. Public attention has been so aroused, national irritation so justly awakened, that a government office which might, through clumsiness or carelessness, lose this exceptionally favourable opportunity to extend our colonial power would have great difficulty in exonerating itself before the Chamber and public opinion.

The government, as we have seen, was to suggest to Parliament the approval of the Brazza-Makoko treaty. It was to be unanimously voted on by the Chamber in November 1882. 'The Chamber,' commented the *Temps*, 'full of spirit and warmth, gave up all opposition: it was truly French.'

The atmosphere of these weeks was one of enthusiastic patriotism. People did not quietly examine the pros and cons; they applauded. To have questioned the words of Brazza, which were the only ones worth heeding to appreciate the advantages of the treaty with Makoko, would have appeared unpatriotic. The lyricism with which the Congo was evoked recalled to mind the leaflets of the colonial societies of the Old Régime.

It would be hard [wrote the *Republique Française*] to present a complete picture of the agricultural and mining wealth of the basin of the Congo—not only does the copper and lead appear in immense quantities in the Valley of Niari, but beds of iron are numerous nearly everywhere from Vivi to Stanley Pool; and gold has been found quite frequently. Ivory and rubber are abundant. The forests are impressive—for their daily cooking the natives burn great chunks of ebony and rose wood. The earth, marvellously fertile, brings forth a great variety of produce. . . .

One cheered, one did not analyse. The correspondent of the *Temps* in Paris noticed this at the end of November:

Never has a Government submitted to parliamentary ratification a treaty of the reality and results of which it knew so little. . . . The Cabinet . . . will have assumed the heaviest responsibility under which a Government can place itself, viz, that of protecting at haphazard, without any precise preliminary information under the mere unreasoning pressure of the public, a foreign adventure of which it has ascertained neither the utility nor the consequences.

In this enthusiasm it is easy to point to the major, even dominant, part played by national pride. Its existence was felt strongly everywhere. Competition in Africa became open between two rivals, Brazza and Stanley. France upheld its champion and wanted him to win. Stanley, upon returning to Europe in 1882, attacked Brazza, declaring that the treaty with Makoko was worthless; another reason for French public opinion to crystallize around the man who bore its colours.

In making Brazza's cause triumph in the Congo, in bringing back this victory for France, revenge was at the same time taken on England. This is where we return to the question of Egypt, but from an angle which Robinson and Gallagher have not perceived. After the blow which the humiliation of the Egyptian occupation had caused, French public opinion instinctively looked for a way to compensate for the British success. It needed a French success. It was at this point that the Congo offered itself. 'It is for us,' wrote a Parisian newspaper, 'the best and surest revenge for the disappointments that we have been subjected to.' Brazza, naturally, did not miss playing on these sentiments.

A speaker who preceded me [he declared at a ceremony at the Sorbonne] said that the English had preceded us everywhere. There is one spot, however, where we had a footing before them, it is the Congo [long applause, notes the recorder]. The French flag floats over this land and Parliament has only to say one word for this land to be ours forever.

The psychological relationship between the Congo and Egypt, seen by various observers, was noted by the shrewd correspondent of the *Kolnische Zeitung*, at the time of the Chamber's vote on the Brazza treaty: 'This matter was considered as a purely patriotic work. Having been supplanted in the Nile by the English, France wants to compensate by supplanting in turn the Belgians and Portuguese in the north of the Congo.' The Egyptian question contributed in a certain and undoubtedly important manner to the installation of France in the Congo.

With the ratification of the Brazza-Makoko treaty in the autumn of 1882, political acquisitiveness came to central Africa. It was the decision taken by France that truly released these acquisitive proceedings. In his letter to Lesseps, of 18 September 1882, Leopold II still evoked the possibility of the Congo being spared the rivalries of politics.

We believe [he wrote] that what is best for commerce, for peace and civilization is to maintain the independence of the native states of the Congo by creating there a few free establishments to serve as guides for them and to direct them by degrees in the path of progress.

The Chamber of Commerce in Manchester, in the first two weeks of November 1882, still proclaimed itself in the same

manner. It asked the British government to reach an understanding with other powers 'in order that the sovereign and
territorial rights of the natives of the Congo and of the adjacent
neutral territories may be respected and maintained'. The
action of Brazza, cheered by the French Parliament, changed
all their perspectives. The entire zone situated between Stanley
Pool, where France had just established itself, and the ocean
appeared to be threatened by the French occupation. To save
the lower Congo and its commercial interest from the perils of
French custom duties, Great Britain preferred the Portuguese
occupation. This preference developed into the Anglo-Portuguese treaty with all its important consequences. For his part
Leopold, whose precautions and political ambitions were still
limited in 1882 to reclaiming the status of autonomy for his
outposts (the 'few free establishments' mentioned in his letter to
Lesseps, and the 'adjacent neutral territories' mentioned by the
friends of the King, in Manchester), began the race, ever more
rapid and more widespread, toward acquiring political sovereignty over these territories. The 'scramble' in this region of
Africa had begun.

In the Congo, French politics had been more chauvinistic
than practical, dictated for the most part by patriotic excitement
rather than by materialistic consideration. In Occidental Africa,
where in January 1883 the second French enterprise took place,
the game was altogether different; with no intervention by
public opinion, it was a game which sought to promote the
interests of national commerce.

Commercial interests and territorial occupation on the Occidental coast have been bound together more than once in the
nineteenth century. This, however, had always taken the form
of limited occupation, primarily concerned with the maintenance of local and regional order. The last of these manoeuvres
for local order to be put into effect 'to maintain the national
commerce' had been the re-establishment in 1882 of the
French protectorate at Porto-Novo.

In January 1883 the apparent purpose became clearer.
From the ministry of the Navy and Colonies in Paris emerged
texts which, when put together, defined a new and what might
be called a great policy. On 19, 25 and 30 January 1883

respectively, three letters signed by the Minister, Admiral Jauréguiberry, struck a new note:

[19 January 1883: Jauréguiberry to Duclerc, President of the Council and Minister of Foreign Affairs:] You know, Monsieur President of the Council and dear colleague, that in acceding to the demands of King Toffa [who asked France to re-establish its protectorate on Porto-Novo], our foremost thought was to protect our very important and prosperous commerce in the region of the Gulf of Benin. Now the French trading posts do not exist merely in Kotonou or at Porto-Novo, but are also established at all the neighbouring points: Gosomey, Abomey, Wydah, Grand Popo, Petit Popo, Porto Segouro and large villages of which some have as many as five to ten thousand inhabitants and do important trading. I feel that it would be wise to maintain national commerce and to avoid the English taxes that threaten it, to extend the French protectorate on all the small territories which extend along a coastline of from 20 to 25 miles from the border west of Dahomey to the English villages of Flohou and Adaffi, the last points east of the Colony of Cape Coast Castle.

The advantages of this policy that I hope you will approve cannot escape you. With the protection of our flag, French commerce, already of great importance, will assume fresh developments. Communications via lagoons with the interior and especially with Dahomey will be facilitated, and we will therefore be in a better position to compete with English commerce.

[25 January 1883: another letter from Jauréguiberry to Duclerc, this time on the subject of the regions of the Niger and the Benoue:] I believe, after having studied the political and commercial situation of these regions, that it is of interest to affirm our politics from this side and that, for the good of our commerce, it is necessary to develop our influence alongside that of the English.

On the right bank of the Lower Niger, noted the Minister, it was useless to attempt anything. The English influence was too strong, the population already 'experienced in the ways of the British Government'. In 'Oriental parts of the delta', on the other hand, there was perhaps a way to deal with the native chiefs; it was to be done with 'the sole preoccupation of assuring the freedom of our commerce', that is, to guarantee 'an independent route avoiding English customs before they spread all the way up to Brass River'.

However, further in the Benoue region, the situation was different. It was possible to 'take a more privileged position'. As the region had been neglected by the English, 'the banks of the Benoue were completely free'. They could therefore have signed

political and commercial agreements with the chiefs of Akoto, Mitschi, and Wukari. . . . A similar policy ably carried out would assure for our traders a route from Lake Tchad and the rich markets of Adamawa and Bornu. . . . The policy which I propose you should adopt would result in the opening of routes to new countries for French trade.

At last, on 30 January, Jauréguiberry was no longer content to recommend a policy—he applied it. Extraordinarily enough, although not without precedent in the history of French colonialism, instead of going through the Diplomatic Corps, which was not informed of his instructions, he issued his order to the Commander of the Naval Division of the Occidental Coast of Africa:

We must [he said] foresee the possible annexation by England of the right bank of the Lower Niger. It is to be feared that the day will come when the English trading posts will extend as far as the mouth of Brass River. I believe it is best to take steps against this contingency in the interests of French commerce now established on the Niger up to Egga, and also on the Benoue where all efforts must be made. It is important that trade should not be affected by English taxes after entering the river.

I urge you to study the measures that could be taken towards this goal. It would be especially interesting to know whether the rivers which join the sea to the East of Brass River, among them the new Calebar and Bonny, are not branches which would be navigable from the delta of the Niger. This point is still doubtful. . . . I would urge you to find out by sending one of your ships to chart the Eastern part of the Niger.

If the new Calebar, the Bonny or some other river has navigable waters which would provide an entrance to the Niger, you should sign political and commercial agreements with the littoral chiefs that would enable us to place these territories under our protectorate.

Furthermore [added Jauréguiberry, still widening his horizons] 'I call your attention to the whole coast, from Niger to the Bay of Banoko.' We are already able to invoke the treaties which we concluded some time ago with the Kings of Banoko.

I think it would be best not to forget these advantages, and if no other nation has preceded us, to sign treaties with the chiefs of the mouth of the river Quaqua, which may become important if it does, as we believe, communicate with the lake of Liba.

These terms of January 1882 thus formulated a policy of political expansion—a protectorate on the coast line from the Gold Coast to Dahomey, political treaties on the Benoue, terms with the chiefs in the Oriental Delta of Niger, the eventual protectorates of Bonny, Old Calabar and that entire region south of the estuary of the Cameroun.

Who were the men who worked it out and under whose influence did they operate? What was the personal role of Jauréguiberry? Did the commercial firms whose interests were involved, notably those in Marseilles, take a direct part in the elaboration of these plans? Many questions remain unanswered, and the secrets of the Naval Office in 1882–1883 await solution.

What is clear is that the Navy did obtain the approval of the Diplomatic Corps for at least a part of their plans. In a letter dated 25 January 1883, relating to the Niger and Benoue, in the handwriting of a responsible officer of the Quai d'Orsay, the following notation was made: 'Write with these views to Mr Mattei.' (Mattei was an agent for the French consulate at Brass River.) On 6 March 1883 instructions were given to Mattei.

Though these plans were grandiose, they were poorly executed and policy defined in January 1883 had, for the most part, produced meagre results. To the west of Dahomey, the plan was much reduced, largely for fear of diplomatic complications. To the east, at the Niger and in the Cameroun, those who sought to execute the new policy with limited means had little success.

The first to appear in these areas was a naval officer, Godin, Commander of the destroyer *Le Voltigeur*, who was in charge of executing the instructions of 30 January. Godin, in March 1883, first went to Bonny, where the chiefs had made a treaty of commerce and friendship with France. Could these terms be transformed into a treaty for a protectorate? Godin immediately decided that 'it was out of the question'.

How and under what claim can one ask for the protectorate of a country where there are eight English commercial firms, two large steamship companies and where trading is such that during eleven days I counted ten steamers entering and nine leaving, all under the English flag, whereas in the forty-two years, since the drawing-up of our treaty, not one French commercial firm had established itself?

The Commander of *Le Voltigeur* therefore limited his aim to renewing the old treaties of commerce. He was unable to accomplish even this, as the chiefs seemed to be afraid of displeasing the British consul.

After this failure Godin, in April, reached the 'Cameroun country'. Again, he found the English influence well established (to the point, he notes, 'that my pilot became very worried at what the English consul would say when he found out that he had been taken into my service'). But on the coast of the river Quaqua, which his instructions had especially emphasized, he found a 'king' who was favourably inclined, the King of Malimba Passall who, without any hesitation, signed a treaty in which he handed over to France half of his territory. Such eagerness seemed strange even to Godin: 'Since I seemed surprised at how easily he had given up his independence, Passall told me: "I have a lot of trouble in governing; when you are here, I will not meddle into anything and will sleep all day." ' Passall, whose English name meant that his power surpassed that of all his neighbours, hardly seems to have deserved this rather glorious designation.

This treaty with Passall, together with the renewal of the old treaties with the Banoko chiefs, constituted the sole success of *Le Voltigeur*'s cruise.

Mattei, later in the year 1883, had even less success. In August, at his consular post at Brass River, he gathered together the local chiefs and submitted to them a treaty, placing 'their country, territories, as well as all their subjects, under French protection and suzerainty'. After a favourable welcome (the chiefs at first wondered if they could not play off France against Goldie, the representative of the English Company whose competition was becoming dangerous), their refusal was clear: England was too powerful. Mattei then arrived at the Niger and Benoue where he was somewhat luckier from a commercial than from a political point of view (he was at the same time the general manager of the French Equatorial African Company of Commerce). Further up the Benoue, at Ibi, he thus managed, before the English traders, to be granted by the Emir of Djebou, 'a spot to be used as a market place'; this was not a political agreement.

The outline drawn up on paper in January 1883 was, however, far removed from its realization on land. The little that the French did was enough to set off the scramble, in much the same way that the approval of the Brazza-Makoko treaty had done in central Africa. There can be no doubt among those who have seen the British documents that it was the French initiatives, as interpreted by the Foreign Office and the Colonial Office, which lay behind the decision taken by the British government to act.

The Brazza-Makoko treaty had already heightened worries for Occidental Africa and the Congo, since a 'coup' like the one Brazza had successfully engineered could be repeated elsewhere, such as on the Niger. 'The tactics . . . of Mr de Brazza may be imitated on the Niger, and that great highway into the interior of Africa be converted into a French river', wrote an influential British businessman to the Foreign Office.

When the news of the re-establishment of the French protectorate in Porto-Novo was received, the alarm was intensified. There followed an announcement that a French warship was in Bonny and that the officers were trying to obtain a treaty with the native chiefs. In these circumstances it became 'a question of the first importance to consider . . . how British interests are to be protected'. By June 1883 Percy Anderson of the Foreign Office had made his point. He brought together the different factors which revealed the nature of the French activities, emphasizing in particular the question of British interests.

The Captain of the *Voltigeur* is trying to induce the natives at the mouth of the Niger to accept his treaties. If he succeeds in this, the final step will have been taken, and British trade will have no chance of existence except at the mercy of French officials.

From this he concludes:

Action seems to be forced on us. . . . Only one course seems possible; that is, to take on ourselves the protectorate of the native states at the mouth of the Oil Rivers, and on the adjoining coast. . . . Protectorates are unwelcome burdens, but in this case it is . . . a question between British protectorates, which would be unwelcome, and French protectorates, which would be fatal.

The subsequent news from the Occidental coast of the treaty with Passall and the activities of Mattei only reinforced this way of thinking, so perfectly formulated by Percy Anderson. And from this reasoning the British government resolved to take action. In a second region of Africa, the scramble had begun.

All this, it might be said, is taking us far away from Robinson and Gallagher's book and from their thesis. But, firstly, in the episodes which we have examined and which are, we believe, the first two acts of the scramble, we can assess the importance of the Egyptian question. This is present in the first of the two episodes—but only because of the bitterness of inflamed public opinion, a connection which does not accord with the argument sketched by Robinson and Gallagher. From the second episode, Egypt is totally absent.

But what appear even more clearly through these episodes are the new characteristics of imperialism, new characteristics which Robinson and Gallagher tend to deny. Analysing the events of 1882–1883, one sees emerging the new face of imperialism, which was to remain until all the territories still free had been divided up. Three trends stand out clearly: the development of colonial chauvinism, the new type of colonial occupation with its aim of economic protection, and the role of public opinion.

National pride, national self-respect and chauvinism influenced colonial affairs with a force which they had never previously known. In this respect Brazza appears as the great initiator. His propaganda of 1882 made use of numerous economic arguments—it drew France's attention to new and fertile lands. But when Brazza was really acclaimed was when he brandished the national flag: it was when he evoked the tricoloured emblem, which he had set up in the heart of Africa, that he gripped public attention and fired the country's enthusiasm. Even the economists who adhered to his views, did so as patriots rather than as economists. Leopold II, a great admirer of Paul Leroy-Beaulieu, said sadly that 'chauvinism seems to possess' the eminent author of the *Colonisation chez les peuples modernes.*

In the settlement of African problems the prestige of each country—and no longer only its interests—was henceforth taken into account. At the end of 1884 negotiations began in Berlin between the ambassador of France and the representatives of the International Association of the Congo, alias Leopold II. There were territorial disputes to be settled. A question of frontiers, but a question also of prestige, as Jules Ferry explained to the ambassador of France:

Even the most suspicious opinion will approve the Berlin arrangements on one condition; this is that a victory over M. de Brazza will not emerge indirectly from it. M. de Brazza is popular, he has a large following, he has been entrusted with a part of our honour, *we need an arrangement which flatters the self-respect of the French public.*

This was the new aspect of colonial policy; it satisfied a need for *grandeur* which, in more than one case, took considerable precedence over considerations of material interest. Yves Guyot, in 1885, shaken in his thinking as a traditional economist, accustomed in all things to calm calculations, wrote concerning the psychological evolution of his fellow-countrymen, and more particularly of their attitude towards the British Colonial Empire: 'We are jealous of this vast domain, and we want to have a similar one to set over against it, at all costs. *We no longer calculate, we listen only to passion.* We want annexations, of which we see only the extent, without worrying about the quality.'

A great country owes to itself, by virtue of the opinion it has of itself, an extension beyond the seas. It thus proves itself and shows others its national vigour. 'We believed', said the German Chancellor in 1890, 'that if we only had colonies and sought an atlas and painted Africa on it in blue, then we would have become a great people.' Not to act, not to extend was to proclaim that one's country was impotent, a prelude to political decadence.

This is what Jules Ferry said in 1885:

Our country must place itself in a position to do what all the others are doing and since the policy of colonial expansion is the general motive which nowadays is worshipped by all the European powers, we, too, must pursue this policy; otherwise there will happen . . . what happened to other nations who played a very considerable role three centuries ago and who today find themselves, however powerful, however great they may have been, reduced to third or fourth class.

It was their rank in the world—this was the new and unprecedented phenomenon which European countries were going
to defend in colonial partitions, especially in the partition of
Africa. There, even more than in Asia or in Oceania, the stake
was clear: it was a continent which was being carved up. The
success of each would be measured visually on the map. 'In
this partition', declared the Comité de l'Afrique Française,
'France has a right to the largest part'. And in seeking to
realize this programme, the majority of those who were to
support the work of the Comité—the many grammar-school
pupils, for example, and officers, who were among its subscribers—would obviously think above all of the greatness of
their native land.

In the race which began, economic preoccupations were
present, to be sure, but often they were different in character
from those of the preceding age. At the period which, when he
was evoking it in retrospect, Jules Ferry justly called the period
of small-scale, piecemeal annexations, of parsimonious bourgeois conquests, the aim had often been to gain economic
advantages, to improve national trade. These were classical,
traditional objectives. French traders on the west coast pressed
for annexations, wishing to procure for themselves a privileged
position.[1] The British consul in the Gulf of Benin, Hewett,
recommended a protectorate policy: he saw this principally as
a means of giving an impetus to national trade, by establishing
direct commercial relations with the hinterland.[2] Calculations
of this kind had a positive character, but very often, from 1882–
1883 onwards, fear of the annexations of others was going to
replace positive calculation. Conquests were made on the
grounds of security, to protect a region from the interventions
of another power, which would make its own commercial
interests prevail there. The colonial revenue of the rival powers

[1] Hutton described to Lister the efforts of powerful firms such as Regis,
Fabre, etc., which want to 'get the government to take possession of places
where they have factories, and their object is to make all other trading
impossible' (memorandum of Lister of 15 October 1883; F.O.84/1807).

[2] One finds the same preoccupation—that of establishing a 'direct
trafficking of the Europeans with the Negroes in the Interior'—in the
memorandum of the Chamber of Commerce of Hamburg of 6 July 1883,
which recommends the occupation by Germany of a part of the African
coast opposite Fernando Po.

thus became the prevailing obsession which took hold of men's minds.

The French Admiralty programme, in January 1883, evoked the possible danger of British trade, against which it was important to take precautions. But the positive aspect in this programme of an offensive at once political and economic was still dominant. The British counter-stroke was to be essentially defensive; they annexed without enthusiasm, because it was absolutely necessary to surpass the French. In the Congo delta, Britain, by pushing forward the Portuguese, did nothing but defend herself against the French menace; French trade would have been the death of British imports in this region.

Is a policy of this type new? Nothing to be sure is ever completely new and one can find precedents for everything. But Gladstone, in 1885, evoked 'the demands now rife . . . for a system of annexations intended to forestall the colonising efforts of other countries'. He explained to Queen Victoria:

Mr Gladstone could not honourably suppress the fact that he himself, for one, is firmly opposed on principle to such a system, and he believes that herein he is only a humble representative of convictions, which were not general only but universal among the statesmen of the first thirty years of his political life.

When one sees on what scale, under the very eyes of Gladstone, the policy which the latter considered contrary to tradition was about to be practised, it is clear that there had indeed been an innovation in the reasons for occupation.

Finally, the third new element: the role of public opinion. In the autumn of 1882, in the affair of Brazza and the Congo, observers were unanimous in stating that the wave of interest in the press and of press comment and public opinion in France was such as a colonial question had never raised before. Thus began, in colonial matters, the series of movements of public opinion of the end of the nineteenth century and the beginning of the twentieth. One must speak in the plural, of movements and not of a movement, for it was never to be a question of one of those passions, such as one found in politics, which literally take possession of people's minds and remain fixed in them. Rather there was a succession of sporadic outbursts of colonial enthusiasm, first in one country then in another. They were to be separated often by periods of virtual indifference, to the dismay of the champions of the colonial cause.

These outbursts, however, which were going to stretch over almost thirty years—until the last was to be produced in Italy shortly before the 1914 war[1]—were to have repeated import-ance in the course of history. The example of 1882, which opened a series, was one of the most characteristic. Carried away by a nationalistic fervour which surpassed and left far behind it all economic considerations, French public opinion, in 1882, practically dictated to the authorities the policy they should follow. The government and the Houses could not, according to the expression of the historian Henri Martin, 'fail in the duty which the unanimous wish of the country imposed on them'. Let us recognize this fact and this date: for the first time in the partition of Africa the imperialistic agitation of metropolitan opinion played the decisive role.

Two years later Germany, in its turn, was to be seized with the colonial fever. It was in almost clinical terms that those who witnessed it, in 1884, described the phenomenon: 'national craving', 'colonial mania', 'colonial fever', 'real fever', 'mania for colonial adventure'. The agitation was to reach such a degree that the president of the *Kolonialverein*, in October 1884, felt himself obliged to guard his fellow-countrymen against the illusions born of an excess of enthusiasm.[2] Bismarck was a man of a different stamp to Duclerc, the President of the French Council of 1882. It is scarcely likely that—as the ambassador of Great Britain to Berlin thought at the time—he let himself be led by public opinion.[3] His stand on

[1] The explosion of chauvinism in Italy, in 1911, is described in remarkable terms by Camille Barrère. The nationalists, he explains, 'demand their share of the spoils': this will be the expedition of Tripolitania (Barrère to de Selves, 20 July 1911; *Documents diplomatiques français, 1871–1914*, 2nd series, vol. XIV (Paris, 1955), pp. 90–3).

[2] *Temps*, 7 October 1884. The Berlin correspondent of the *Globe* noted that, in his opinion, the promoters of colonial policy in Germany, 'were quite unprepared for the amount of rather too zealous enthusiasm their scheme was fated to awake in the public mind' (9 July 1884).

[3] 'It is a remarkable fact that Prince Bismarck, contrary to his convictions and to his will, has been driven by public opinion into the inauguration of a colonial policy he has hitherto denounced as detrimental to the concen-tration of German strength and power.'

colonial matters was a deliberate, wise step, which must be analysed in terms of high political strategy.

But between the policy decided upon by the Chancellor and German opinion there was, nevertheless, a direct relationship: one of the objectives of Bismarck, in placing himself on the colonial scene, was without doubt to find a theme which would help him win the 1884 elections.[1] So once again metropolitan public opinion played a major role albeit in an indirect way.

Africa and the Victorians limits itself to English policy. Does the latter, at the end of the nineteenth century, place us to the same degree in the presence of the new imperialism of which we believe we have brought out the characteristics?

With regard to the economic motives it most certainly does. In 1883–1884, when they took action to forestall France, the British leaders did so, often reluctantly, and sometimes angrily, to halt the terrible French protectionism which they could not allow to spread any further. In 1897, Salisbury said to the ambassador of France: 'If you were not such fierce protectionalists, you would not find us so greedy for territories.' This is close to a permanent argument which had been always—and was still—an important motive. Sir Edward Grey, in a speech in 1898, described the English expansion as having been a means above all of avoiding exclusion:

We had got in the Continent the undeserved reputation of being a jealous, grasping and greedy nation but the truth was we had been forced into the policy of expansion, because if we had not expanded we should have been excluded. I do not entirely accept the doctrine that trade followed the flag, but it had been unfortunately true that where the foreign flag went British trade was certain to be excluded.

Grey was exaggerating, but he was diagnosing one of the major characteristics of a policy which he knew well. Was 'greed' then not a factor in British policy? Had England avoided, in her approach to African problems, the psychosis of national *grandeur*, of getting a place in the sun? The testimonies are numerous which show us that after a certain date—but,

[1] 'The whole colonial history is indeed a swindle but we need it for the elections', he said to one of his secretaries of State.

beyond doubt, later than in either France or Germany[1]—this psychosis did play its part, and that it was as powerful in public opinion as among the men who made the partitions.

Dicey, both a witness and an analyst, spoke in 1890 of the 'popular outcry for extending our empire in Central Africa'. Lugard, both a witness and an historian, was to write later, on the subject of the same period, that 'the popular demand that Britain, as the foremost colonizing power, should not be backward in claiming her share (in the partition of the African continent) was irresistible'. What Lugard and Dicey termed 'popular' related no doubt more to the sphere of the readers of *The Times* and of the *Morning Post*, than to the popular mass; but it was certain that the will to see Great Britain 'take her share' in the partition of Africa emerged like a rising flood, stemming from public opinion toward the leaders. In this motivation, economic preoccupations had a large part, to be sure, but also something else, which was the true imperialism: the will for power.

The Times wrote (in 1889) an admirable leader which summed up the whole matter.

Our large charter companies [it stated] ought to be able to draw into their nets most that is worth having in Central Africa. [It was essential that they should.] Whatever the commercial and economical value of Central Africa may be, there are other reasons why England should keep herself well to the front in its partition. We cannot, with so many eager competitors in the field, afford to neglect any country likely to yield new fields for commercial enterprise; nor can we afford to allow any section even of the Dark Continent to believe that our Imperial prestige is on the wane. . . .

This urgency stemming from public opinion, the implicit protest against the idea that England could be 'left behind in the race for the possession of the equatorial regions of Africa', the pressure which those directing affairs felt from that point on,

---

[1] In 1884 the colonial enthusiasm of German public opinion was as yet only very little communicated to the English public, who observed it with a rather astonished curiosity. 'Englishmen', wrote *The Times*, 'are too little enamoured of Africa to grudge Germans the privilege of seeking their fortunes on its vacant shores' (27 September 1884). The tone as well as the words are significant.

all seem to have been very poorly perceived by Robinson and Gallagher.

Immersed in the events of 1890, they speak, on the contrary, of a 'popular dislike of African entanglement', and write: 'Public opinion in the broadest sense was still indifferent to the issues of tropical Africa.' This they see in the very same year that Salisbury found himself overwhelmed, in his African policy, by a veritable wave of excitement—undoubtedly the greatest to be produced in England by the subject of partition, along with that over Uganda, which was soon to follow—an excitement which a contemporary termed a 'craze'. 'The Stanley craze' (Stanley being the champion of British national-ism who lead the movement) was certainly one of the outbursts which proved that in Britain, as elsewhere, a large portion of public opinion could be aroused in favour of 'African entangle-ments'.

But, one might ask, were the policy-makers also subject to contagion of this truly imperialistic spirit? Robinson and Gallagher portray them to us as apparently reasoning, weighing and calculating with a coldness worthy of their predecessors. Did they not in certain cases let themselves also become caught up in this conquering spirit? One of the scenes which is lacking in *Africa and the Victorians* is that of the visit to Hatfield, in July 1888, by the young vice-consul Johnston, and of his conver-sation with Salisbury, from which emerged an entire plan for the partition of Africa. Was this not an instance in which the imperialist dream merged with political reality—this summer day on which, under the gaze of Hatfield, was evoked a vision of the whole of Africa divided among the big powers?

Furthermore, were the principal authors of the partition, the actual policy-makers, really those London statesmen whose actions and gestures are so closely studied by Robinson and Gallagher? Were not the real leaders those who headed the imperialist movement and left their mark on it, both in London and even more so in Africa itself—men such as Mackinnon, Goldie, Rhodes and Johnston? And was there not evident among these men who, more than any others, produced this imperialism, an element of passion? A French diplomat who met Cecil Rhodes in February 1891 was struck by the 'sacred fire which burned within him'.

Yesterday evening, I had a long private talk with Cecil Rhodes. He is a man of 40 to 45, robust, square-shouldered, with the head and shoulders of a bull. At first glance, he gives the impression of brutal force, but one quickly notices that this force is harnessed to an idea, and that one is facing more than a businessman, more than the instrument of a government or company, but rather an impassioned, violent, daring, tireless agent for British expansion. . . .

Johnston was totally possessed by this 'sacred fire'. It was these men who made the Empire, just as the French military leaders of Occidental Africa forged an Empire, sometimes without the accord of Paris, and just as Leopold II, from his palace in Brussels, created his Empire through unceasingly repeated orders. These are the men who had the passion to conquer vast territories for their countries.

In October 1890 Johnston wrote to Rhodes: 'Farewell till our next encounter. The Empire owes us both at least a tablet in Westminster Abbey, for had we not met and worked together, the British dominions would not have been extended to Tanganyika.' Ten years earlier, no one would have written such a letter on the subject of Africa. It was the new face of British imperialism, a face with new traits, which was revealed.

Finally, let us return to Egypt. Without the occupation of Egypt would things have happened as they did happen in Africa south of the Sahara? Would French public opinion have embraced the cause of Brazza as it did if the Egyptian question had not given it a desire and a need for revenge? Where collective passion is concerned, speculation is almost always vain: in such outbursts of passion there are always too many imponderables which cannot be analysed.

But the scramble also sprang from economic causes. There can be no possible doubt: with or without the Egyptian problem economic factors would, certainly sooner or later, have started the movement.

The fundamental point which must be kept in mind is the following: from the moment that the economic penetration of the Black Continent began, there had been the strongest temptation for each country to keep for itself advantages of one kind or another in the regions which were opened up. The march towards the interior was to be almost necessarily synonymous, in many cases, with acquisition of economic privileges.

Leopold II had been in this respect the great precursor. In 1877, confiding in a Belgian diplomat, he wrote: 'We must be both prudent and ready to act . . . in order to procure for ourselves a piece of this magnificent African cake.'

In this letter of 1877 is then the first written mention of this expression, a 'piece of cake', by a political leader. One must be careful, nevertheless, to remember that what the King envisaged in these first, rather vague, projects, was not the conquest of a part of Africa; what he wanted, above all, was to take his place, his 'piece', in the economic exploitation of the new lands. When, in order to put this plan into operation, he sent Stanley towards the interior of the continent, he ordered him to concentrate first not on political power, but exclusively on economic advantages. The treaties signed by Stanley during the first phase of his expedition—for example, the authentic treaty of Vivee of 1880—are agreements which almost fiercely reserve for the agents of the Comité d'Etudes exclusive economic privileges:

The sole and exclusive right of all foreigners and strangers to cultivate any portion of Vivee district. . . . The sole and exclusive right of all foreigners and strangers to trade in any part of Vivee district. The sole and exclusive right . . . [etc.—this expression recurs like a chorus].

A 'privileged position' was also what the French, as we have seen, wished to acquire on the Benoue: it is what Goldie did, in fact, manage to obtain on the Niger.

Attempts to acquire privileges on the new markets of Central Africa, and the reactions of those opposed to these attempts, made it inevitable that the scramble would be the outcome of such a process.

Remarkably, Leopold II, despite his early entry into this scene, did not unleash this process. In fact, from 1882 on, in a political *volte-face* in which one discerns a touch of genius, he abandoned his vision of a privileged exploitation to become, on the contrary, a champion of free trade in Central Africa; he thus played the card which would lead him to triumph. When certain of the exclusive treaties signed by Stanley and his collaborators in the beginning were disclosed, they evidently embarrassed the King, but he managed to stifle the adverse effect which they produced, with his solemn promises of commercial liberty. The impact was thus greatly reduced.

But whether this was done by Leopold II in the first phase, or by Goldie, or by the French on the Benoue, Africa, or, rather, the interior market of Africa in the 1880s, began to be taken over by commercial competition which would have engendered the scramble in any case, even if Egypt had not existed.

Translated by Dr Ian Lockerbie and Mrs Eugene Praeger

28. Partition: a general view

R. HYAM *Historical Journal* No. 2, 1964 Cambridge University Press; pages 156–61, 164, 165, 167–8

. . . Their [Robinson and Gallagher's] interpretation of the partition as a strategically dominated response to local 'nationalist' challenges has been criticised by reviewers in at least four different ways.

In the first place, some critics think the authors appear to underestimate the importance of prestige as a motive for taking African territory. The authors would admit there is considerable truth in the explanation that the single factor of prestige made the possession of African territory important to France and Germany. But it could be argued that it was also a factor of some weight for Britain too. There were many Englishmen who felt refusal to take formal political responsibility in Africa would be a fatal blow to the advance of the civilizing influences it was Britain's duty to secure. *The Times*, for example, declared Britain could not afford 'to allow any section even of the Dark Continent to believe that our Imperial prestige is on the wane'.[1]

---

[1] *The Times*, 15 October 1889. R. J. Hammond, 'Imperialism: Sidelights on a Stereotype', *Journal of Economic History*, vol. XXI (1961), suggests that except at the end of its career, 'financial gain, as well as decent administration, seem to have been subordinated' in the British East Africa Company 'to the acquisition of territory for its own sake'. Hammond also quotes a Portuguese, Eça de Queiroz, writing in 1903: 'Precisely what preoccupies us, what gratifies us, what consoles us, is to contemplate *just the number* of our possessions; to point here and there on the map with the finger; to intone proudly "we have eight, we have nine; we are a colonial power, we are a nation of seafarers" ' (pp. 583, 589).

In the second place, some readers have felt the authors under-
estimate the strength of the diplomatic or European factors
traditionally considered necessary to explain the partition. The
authors seem to assume those who allege the importance of
diplomatic or European factors are referring simply to 'balance
of power' considerations, but surely what is really important in
this context is the atmosphere created by the events of 1870–71.
The authors repeatedly depreciate the importance of European
factors, but it is doubtful whether they have proved their
assertions to the satisfaction of the unregenerate defenders of the
traditional argument, who might ask why they do not quote
Gambetta's remark, 'In Africa France will make the first falter-
ing steps of the convalescent', or why they do not refer to
Bismarck's contention that his map of Africa lay in Europe. On
the face of it, if jealousy or search for compensation was the
motive driving France forward, the humiliation of France (if that
is what it was) in Egypt in 1882 at the hands of Britain would
hardly seem comparable to the humiliation of military defeat
on her own soil at the hands of Germany in 1871. At any rate,
it is the sort of contention for which one would like corrobor-
ation. It is therefore a little disturbing to find in Brunschwig's
close study of the French records almost no evidence to show
the French thought British action in Egypt humiliating; on the
contrary, in almost every quotation from contemporary
speeches, it is the events of 1870–71 which are referred to again
and again, while those of 1882 are seldom mentioned. It is also
clear from Brunschwig's book that Leopold II of Belgium
caused a great deal more stir in France than Gladstone. The
chief argument for depreciating the importance of the experiences and repercussions of 1870–71 is the apparent time lag
before any definite African result emerged. But why should
there not have been a time lag? As Hargreaves observes, France
had to give priority to European recovery, and common sense
dictated a policy of avoiding colonial quarrels with England.
But on the other hand, the very real amount of French
activity and planning in Africa during the 1870s should not be
forgotten. French interest in Africa was not something which
sprang suddenly to life in 1882. At all events, British statesmen
of the time thought the process of partition closely linked with
the European situation. An interesting illustration of this was

the insistent, and successful, determination of the Viceroy of India, Lord Elgin, in 1896, to transfer responsibility for Somaliland from the Government of India, acting through Aden, to the Foreign Office. Although Elgin admitted Aden was a geographically convenient centre from which to administer the Somali coast, he doubted whether it was possible to adduce any argument

that would, in my opinion, at all counter-balance the great administrative and political inconvenience arising out of the fact that we are not and cannot be fully cognisant of the political considerations which ultimately must decide the action to be taken in this as well as other parts of Africa, because *they are inseparably bound up with European politics.*

In the third place, it has been suggested the authors do not perhaps bring out as clearly as they are unusually well qualified to do the extent to which partition was not merely an African event, but a world-wide phenomenon. Not even so big a subject as Africa can safely be studied in isolation. The idea of a 'partition of the world' was not confined to the imaginations of Rhodes and Chamberlain; it was accepted as a commonplace of actual fact in the most responsible quarters. Rosebery said Britain must not decline to take her share 'in a partition of the world, which we have not forced on, but which has been forced upon us'. Elgin, while Viceroy of India, wrote about 'an era of delimitation, all over the world'; of the 'struggle between civilisation and barbarism which is going on more or less all over the world'. On the European continent the same way of looking at the world situation was also current; witness, for example, the declaration of the Society for German Colonization under Peters in 1884: 'The German nation finds itself without a voice in the partition of the world. . . .' An explanation of the partition of Africa which would be wholly unhelpful in explaining why there was a partition of the Pacific, almost a partition of China, and at a later date a partition of Persia could not really be said to have got to the root of the matter. This is the real weakness of the 'but for Egypt' argument. At this fundamental level of causation, it is doubtful whether historians have improved upon Salisbury's analysis (not quoted in the books under review):

You may roughly divide the nations of the world as the living and the dying. . . . In these [dying] states, disorganization and decay are advancing almost as fast as concentration and increasing power are advancing in the living nations that stand beside them . . . the weak states are becoming weaker and the strong states are becoming stronger. . . . For one reason or another—from *the necessities of politics or under the pretence of philanthropy*—the living nations will gradually encroach on the territory of the dying, and the seeds and causes of conflict among civilized nations will speedily appear.[1]

Salisbury said this in 1898, and by using the future tense he revealed quite clearly the belief that the partition of Africa was only one step in a much wider and continuing process.

In the fourth place, it is thought the authors of *Africa and the Victorians* under-estimate the strength of economic factors. It is one thing to rule out Marxist interpretations; it is quite another to rule out *any* economic explanation from a central position. The authors remind us strategy is not an end in itself (p. 470); safe communication with India was desirable partly for the economic benefits it conferred. But notwithstanding this caveat, they insist economic motives were not uppermost. To establish, however, that Africa did not in fact prove economically interesting to British manufacturers, merchants and investors until the twentieth century had begun, in no way disposes of the possibility that among the original motives of the partitioners was the thought or hope that the possession of African colonies would be economically beneficial, even to the extent of providing areas for colonization. They may have been almost instantly disillusioned, but the expectation would still stand as a necessary part of the explanation of the partition. Salisbury may not have cared much for economic arguments, but there were other important men who cared a great deal. Palmerston is convincingly depicted in this book as the chief architect of Victorian expansion. It is therefore interesting to note that his interest in Africa was economic as well as strategic. As recently as 1862 Palmerston wrote:

I have long been of the opinion that Western Africa will provide a better and a readier source of supply for cotton than India, provided only that the slave trade can be abolished. Western Africa is much nearer than India; labour there is cheaper than in India, and cotton

[1] *The Times*, 5 May 1898. [My italics, R. H.]

grows there in far more abundance than in India, and European goods are much more wanted there than in India.

And to this end, Palmerston wanted the Ras of Abyssinia to reform his internal customs system and provide protection for traders, and the King of Dahomey to use his power and influence to start cotton cultivation; any African ruler asking for Palmerston's support got it only on the condition of economic concessions. Nor did the British need for new sources of cotton supply diminish in the later nineteenth century. Moreover, contemporary commentators, and those men who actually took part in the processes of partitioning in Africa, almost unanimously agreed the motive was economic; and there were in addition others, like Ramsay MacDonald, who while not pronouncing upon the motives for partition, were convinced it was justified on account of economic benefits. Lugard was always categorically clear in his own mind about the importance of economic considerations. In *The Dual Mandate*, the 'immediate cause' of the partition is said to be the rivalry of Britain and Germany in 1884–85, though further back 'one of the more immediate causes which led to the opening up' of Africa was the events of 1870–71, at which time, Lugard adds, the colonization of Africa was believed both desirable and possible. He concludes:

The partition of Africa was, as we all recognise, due primarily to the economic necessity of increasing the supplies of raw materials and food to meet the needs of the industrialised nations of Europe.

Sir George Goldie and Sir Harry Johnston were equally emphatic. The former wrote of Nigeria in 1885:

With old-established markets closing to our manufactures, with India producing cotton fabrics not only for her own use but for export, it would be suicidal to abandon to a rival power the only great remaining undeveloped opening for British goods.

Johnston referred to the situation in British Central Africa in 1889 in discussion with Rhodes in 1893:

The Foreign Office and the Colonial Office then and now entertained very much the same ideas that you and I held about the necessity of extending the British Empire within reasonable limits over countries not yet taken up by European Powers, to provide new markets for our manufactures and afford further scope for British enterprise. But the permanent officials of the Treasury held opinions ... exactly the reverse, and hold them still.[1]

While no-one would say Lugard and those who agreed with him must have been right, and the authors of this book therefore wrong, the consensus of opinion about economic motives is so weighty it is hard to believe it does not contain a measure of truth. It is very likely true economic grounds were not decisive in the minds of those like Salisbury who actually took the decisions. But there are two further points to bear in mind. Economic considerations might have been more important than would appear from government records. As Miss Perham has pointed out, of the five possible reasons for annexing territory— trade, strategy, colonization, philanthropy and prestige—only strategy and prestige necessarily demanded official state initiative. And there is some evidence that even Salisbury sometimes thought in economic terms. Indeed, he is quoted in *Africa and the Victorians* as saying the British object in West Africa was 'not territory but facility for trade' (p. 386). In the last resort, he, like Palmerston and other British statesmen in the past, was prepared to protect trade by taking territory, provided such protection could be proved necessary, and the trade was large enough. Salisbury refused to take more territory in West Africa because the value of trade did not make it worth-while (p. 383), but he was not opposed in principle to taking territory for the protection of trade. In 1893 Salisbury remarked:

We feel that we cannot suffer, more than we can help, that the unoccupied parts of the world, where we must look for new markets for our goods, shall be shut from us by foreign legislation.

[1] Quoted in R. Oliver, *Missionary Factor in East Africa* (1952), p. 124. See also C. W. Orr, *The Making of Northern Nigeria* (1911): the economic motive 'was undoubtedly the primary cause of Great Britain's action in assuming administrative responsibility', for 'economic reasons necessitate the development of the resources of tropical regions'; that European activity in Africa in the later nineteenth century 'was mainly prompted by a desire for fresh markets and a field for commercial enterprise may at once be conceded. But it would be unfair and unjust not to recognise as well that it was prompted also by a real and genuine desire for the welfare of the inhabitants, by substituting an era of law and order for the pitiful condition of insecurity and inter-tribal warfare in which they lived' (pp. 20, 48, 281–2).

Again, because Great Britain chiefly took those portions of Africa where British economic interests were firmly entrenched, where there was a commercial Company to carry the initial administrative burden, it could be said the existence of the British East Africa Company, the Royal Niger Company and the British South Africa Company was crucial in Britain's ability to take formal territorial control of vast new areas. The authors admit (p. 248) Salisbury followed the earlier Victorian canon: he would help those who helped themselves, and so he supported Rhodes' enterprise. They also admit Nigeria and Nyasaland were exceptions to their thesis; what was involved here was the defence of trading or missionary enterprise from foreign annexations (p. 464). But these are highly important exceptions. Furthermore, Chamberlain tends to be represented as an 'exception' to the normal workings of the official mind, as someone who upset the carefully arranged schedule of strategic-ally based priorities. But Chamberlain commanded a great deal of support. Maybe these motives and these attitudes were not so exceptional as they might appear by writing largely from Salisbury's view-point. However desirable annexations may have been on strategic grounds, they would not have been feasible without the existence of these economic interests, and to this extent, at least, economic objectives are an essential part of a complete explanation of the partition of Africa. Strategic imperatives notwithstanding, if the price of taking territory had been an additional large burden on the British taxpayer, the price would have been prohibitive. We are rightly exhorted to look closely at the African scene. When we do so, what stands out is the widespread and intensifying rivalry between localized European economic interests. The most conspicuous and characteristic feature of the 'scramble' on the spot was con-cession-hunting. The Congo was the outstanding case, but also in Swaziland, for example, there were so many Europeans clambering for economic advantages, that King Umbandine conceded in land alone more than the actual total land area of his kingdom. Newbury has drawn attention to the intense commercial rivalry on the West Coast in the 1870s and 1880s; local disputes arising from differential customs zones, sometimes operating in a protective manner (against German or French spirits in British areas, and against English cloth and arms in

French or German areas), created, he believes, a situation only to be remedied by partition: the impulse to extend European rule over the interior came mainly from local traders, supported by commercial and shipping interests in Europe. Departmental minutes do not deny the economic motive. In 1883 Anderson feared British trade would have no chance of existence except at the mercy of French West African officials:

Protectorates are unwelcome burdens, but in this case, it is . . . a question between British protectorates, which would be unwelcome, and French protectorates, which would be fatal. Protectorates, of one sort or another, are the inevitable outcome of the situation . . . they would not be burdensome to the Treasury, for expenses could be managed by manipulating the traders. . . .[1]

In short, it has been hard for critics to avoid concluding the authors of *Africa and the Victorians* may have laid themselves open to the charge of having exaggerated their claim for the more or less exclusive preoccupation with strategic thinking in British ministers. Salisbury was quite able to keep strategic arguments in proper perspective. After all, it was Salisbury who thought 'the constant study of maps is apt to disturb men's reasoning owners', and who said strategists 'would like to annex the moon in order to prevent its being appropriated by the planet Mars'. . . .

But the authors of *Africa and the Victorians* ascribe much more importance to the Egyptian crisis. Might not the opening of the Suez Canal be said to be the decisive event in changing circumstances? The collapse of the authority of the Khedive of Egypt provided the apparently accidental *occasion* for a British occupation, but the chain of events linking the opening of the Suez Canal, Disraeli's purchase of shares in the Company, and the need to substitute Alexandria for Constantinople as the new bastion against Russia, made an occupation likely even without a 'nationalist' rising. Probably only the unfavourable international situation, and the extent to which Egypt had already been drawn within the British system sufficiently to serve objects then in view, restrained the Conservative government from pursuing the idea of occupying Egypt

[1] Newbury, *The Western Slave Coast and its Rulers*, pp. 120–1.

between 1876 and 1878.[1] Nor did the occupation of Egypt in 1882 *necessarily* lead Britain to take more African territory (in fact it increased her reluctance). If she did so, the explanation is not simply that the conditions under which she had hitherto exercised informal control were breaking down as a result of the collapse of political order in Africa (largely the result of earlier European influences), but even more because France and Germany started to take territory for reasons of their own, comprehensible mainly in terms of the international situation in Europe after the upheaval of 1870–71. As Sir Edward Grey remarked in 1902, European countries having decided to embark on the development of the African continent, 'it was impossible for this country to stand aside'. When France, and more especially Germany, between 1883 and 1885, broke the 'gentleman's agreement' that the African coastline should be held only by informal European control, contemporaries thought the partition had begun. The previous British occupation of Egypt did not fundamentally upset the existing situation because neither unilateral action nor permanency had been intended. Leopold's Congo venture probably did not fundamentally affect the situation either. What was decisive was the declaration of protectorates in areas directly threatening existing spheres of informal influence. Hence it is of paramount importance to explain why France, and particularly why

[2] Salisbury wrote in 1877: 'I feel convinced that the old policy—wise enough in its time—of defending English interests by sustaining the Ottoman dynasty has become impracticable, and I think that the time has come for defending English interests in a more direct way by some territorial re-arrangement' (G. Cecil, *Life of Robert, Marquis of Salisbury*, II (1932), p. 130). He felt the geographical situation of Egypt, as well as the responsibility which the English government had in the past incurred for the actual conditions under which it existed as a State, made it impossible to leave it to its fate. Lady Cecil considered that Salisbury 'from his first occupation with the [Egyptian] question, seems to have had no doubt as to what must be its ultimate issue, and at the outset was prepared actively to promote it' (ibid. p. 329). See also W. L. Langer, *European Alliances and Alignments, 1871–1890* (New York, 1950), p. 257. It is interesting to note that Wilfrid Blunt thought the partition 'may be said to have begun' at the Congress of Berlin in 1878, when the joint financial intervention in Egypt was arranged with France, and, as he put it, 'Tunis was given her in return for Cyprus, a scandalous beginning' (W. S. Blunt, *My Diaries*, part II, *1900–1904*, p. 72, entry for 31 August 1903).

Bismarck, acted in the way they did. The interpretation of late nineteenth-century expansion as a series of hardening responses to local nationalisms tells us nothing about the crucial German motivation. Nor can this question be answered by referring to the occupation of Egypt. The fact of British occupation no doubt made it easier for Bismarck to execute his policy of seeming to pick a quarrel with Britain, but he would have had this policy if Britain had never set foot in Egypt. . . . The occupation of Egypt explains to a large extent why Africa was partitioned in the particular way it was: it will help us to explain *how* Africa was partitioned rather than *why* Africa should have been partitioned at all. Egypt was the occasion rather than the efficient cause. Even if it were conceded Egypt 'set off' the partition (and some reviewers have felt hesitation about conceding this), it would still be necessary to explain why Egypt should have been *capable* of 'setting off' the partition (or as reviewers might prefer to say—why it was capable of intensifying or electrifying the existing atmosphere which had already made Africa ripe for partition), and this cannot be done without referring back to the relations between the European powers. Hargreaves once explained the partition in terms of the interaction of international necessities and local colonial pressures; partition was not merely an episode in late nineteenth-century European history, but the culmination of a whole period of Euro-African relations; but it was probably still desirable to give primacy in the exposition to the drives and pressures which ultimately led the European governments to impose their power. This may well be thought slightly nearer the truth than the view taken by the authors of *Africa and the Victorians*, who consider the interlocking of the African crises (to which they give primacy) with rivalries in Europe 'only secondarily' necessary to explain the taking of territory. . . .

The authors of *Africa and the Victorians* tend to portray the partition as a process unfolding with a large element of inevitability from the moment Gladstone entered his 'bondage in Egypt'. This raises a much larger issue: are the authors inclined to overstress the extent to which British statesmen were the prisoners of circumstance, dragged along by situations beyond their control? Attention ought perhaps to be drawn to some possible implications of the authors' view. The very concept of the 'official mind' involves believing ministers were in some ways prisoners of their 'inherited historiography':

Inherited notions of policy in mature bureaucracies sometimes carry ministers along with a logic and momentum of their own. Salisbury and Chamberlain were prisoners of their own conceptions of what had been, what was, and what should be in South Africa. They tended to see the Uitlander crisis not as it was in Johannesburg, but as British ministers had long expected it to be.

Official thinking, the authors say, was in itself a cause of late Victorian imperialism: 'the official mind has to be taken along with the other elements in the problem as a possible cause in its own right'.

This viewpoint seems to stem partly from their belief that there was a large element of the irrational in the partition. But it is perhaps possible to exaggerate this element. Ministers sometimes made remarks suggesting they were bewildered by the suddenness with which new circumstances emerged, but they seldom acted against their sense of reason; in so far as the partition of Africa was a device to maintain peace, it may have been an extravagant exercise, but it was not an irrational one. They did not (and would not have expected to be able to) control the *emergence* of new circumstances, but Salisbury and Bismarck were wholly confident they could control their further development; they were responding to circumstances, but not quite so helplessly as seems to be suggested. The authors' viewpoint almost implies politicians were not really capable of thinking things out intelligently for themselves. When confronted with a personality of outstanding intellectual power, such as Cromer, whose understanding and analysis of the Egyptian situation was, to say the very least, plausible, the authors are inclined to doubt the validity, and indeed the relevance, of his analysis, assuring disconcerted readers he did not *really* understand the situation, or its remedy.

Furthermore, to believe informal methods of expansion were abandoned reluctantly *only* when changed circumstances (usually nationalist crises) made them insufficient, tends to imply two potentially misleading notions, the first being to think it unimportant which party and which persons were in power at any given moment; the second, to deny the existence of any conscious 'imperialists' among British statesmen.

VII. EUROPEAN ENTRENCHMENT

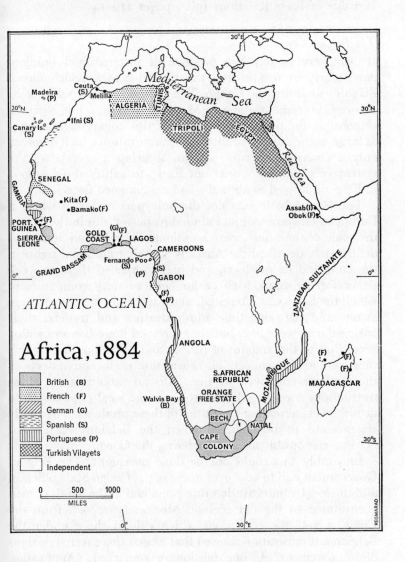

Africa, 1884

British **(B)**
French **(F)**
German **(G)**
Spanish **(S)**
Portuguese **(P)**
Turkish Vilayets
Independent

0   500   1000
MILES

29. Birth of the Belgian Congo

RUTH SLADE *King Leopold's Congo* Oxford University Press for
Institute of Race Relations 1962; pages 210–14

The Belgian Congo

It was very largely the pressure of international opinion,
particularly in Britain and the United States, which forced
Belgium to annex the Congo. The Congo system could not be
allowed to remain unchanged, once Belgium had become
responsible for the administration of this colony eighty times
as large as the mother country. Any annexation which involved
only a change of master without securing a reversal of the
system of government was not likely to satisfy those who—
in Belgium as well as abroad—had campaigned for reform.

The Congo basin was not the only part of Africa where a
European Government had abused its power, but in the Congo
the scale of the abuse was exceptional. The Congo State had
deliberately deprived the Africans of their traditional rights in
the land and its products, and had compelled them to work
either for the State itself or for concessionary companies in
which the State was interested. State and company agents were
at one and the same time administrators and traders; their
basic salaries were low, but they received large bonuses scaled
according to the amount of rubber and other products which
they were able to collect. There was thus no incentive to check
the methods employed by their African subordinates, whose
instructions encouraged them to force the local populations to
furnish ever-increasing quantities of these products. The whole
system had to be changed when the Belgium Parliament
become responsible for administering the Congo.

Inevitably this could not be done overnight. The Belgian
Government had to take over many of the Congo State officials,
and the local administration thus remained in the hands of men
accustomed to the old régime. Missionary reports from the
Congo about the conditions which existed there under the
Belgian administration showed that at first there were few signs
of improvement. As one missionary remarked: 'Annexation
may be proclaimed, but the Natives will not believe it until
forced labour is abolished.' The abolition of forced labour
necessarily involved a heavy financial loss, and thus it was only

gradually that reform could be introduced. The Belgian colonial administration decided to bring the government monopoly in the natural products of the land to an end by easy stages; for one region this was to take place in July 1910, for a second in July 1911, and for the third and last in July 1912.

Leopold II died at the end of 1909, and the change of monarch in Belgium meant a reversal of the royal policy towards the colony. Albert I, who had himself visited the Congo earlier in the year, was determined to use his influence to see that a good proportion of the wealth taken from the Congo was put back into the country for the benefit of the Africans. Although Albert's role, unlike Leopold's up to the end of 1908, was limited to that of constitutional sovereign, the royal encouragement of any plans to advance African interests had a positive effect upon the colonial administration.

By the time the third area came under the reform decrees in July 1912, conditions in the Belgian Congo were very different from those which had existed under the rule of the Congo Independent State. Employees of commercial companies were no longer agents of the administration, the salaries of State officials had been raised, some check on abuse of power had been made more possible by the reorganisation of the judicial system, and the labour tax imposed on Africans had been commuted to a money tax representing a far smaller burden. The United States had already drifted into *de facto* recognition of the Belgian annexation of the Congo, and although in Britain the Congo Reform Association continued to insist that no guarantees that the improvement in conditions would continue had been furnished by the Belgian Government, the official British attitude was affected during 1912 by the general European situation and the threat of war. After a debate in the Commons at the end of May 1913, the British Government finally recognised the Belgian annexation of the Congo in June.

There was no longer any real cause for complaint in terms of current international opinion, for Belgium had proved her willingness to abolish the Leopoldian system of government in the Congo, and to substitute for it one which was more readily approved abroad. It would have been unrealistic to suppose that this could be done in a day. The Congo reform campaign had given Belgians something of a bad conscience in relation to the Congo State, and they were determined to prove that their country was capable of governing an African colony wisely. Leopold's exploitation of the Congo was followed by Belgium's paternalism.

Inevitably, however, the development of the Belgian Congo was affected by the history of Leopold's Independent State. Belgium owed her colony entirely to Leopold II; the King—backed only by a small group of collaborators—had by his own skilful diplomacy secured his recognition as Sovereign of the Congo Independent State in 1885, he had spent his personal fortune on the development of the Congo and when this proved too little he had conceived an economic régime which made the Congo State viable and eventually brought him large returns. Without him, Belgium would never have won her colony. Whereas in the acquisition of other colonies there were usually two factors, the action of a European Government and also that of its nationals on the spot, in the case of the Congo there was only one factor—the iron will of Leopold II. The King successfully urged his fellow-countrymen into a colonial venture on which they would certainly not have embarked without him. It would have been strange indeed had his personal policy in the government of the Congo State not affected Belgian policy in the administration of the Congo.

To begin with, Leopold's Congo was highly centralised; the King kept all the threads of administration in his own hands. This centralisation continued under Belgian rule; all directives came from the *Ministère des Colonies* in Brussels, so that Belgians on the spot, even in areas of European settlement, had little influence on colonial policy.

In the second place, the seeds of a future paradox were there already in the history of the Congo State. On the one hand, Leopold had loudly proclaimed his humanitarian intentions in the Congo, and there is no reason to doubt that he was firmly convinced that his rule would bring great good to the peoples of the Congo by introducing them to Western civilisation. On the other hand, his aims were centred on Belgium itself, for his colonial doctrine was based on the needs of Belgium's economy; the Congo was exploited as a commercial enterprise to increase Belgium's well-being.

The humanitarian aspect was stressed in the Belgian Congo; Christian missions were encouraged, a comparatively wide-spread system of primary education was set up, and strict legislation was introduced to ensure that Africans who worked for Europeans were provided with relatively good living conditions. Progress and civilisation—seen largely in terms of technical advance, native welfare, and the introduction of Christianity—was the ideal put forward by the Belgian Colonial Government. At the same time, Belgium herself drew considerable profit from her colony; the economic reason for Belgium's interest in the Congo was clear enough, although the crude form of exploitation employed by Leopold II had been abolished.

These two aspects were not necessarily incompatible; up to a certain point it can indeed be said that the association between Belgium and the Congo was profitable to both. But in the administration of Leopold's Congo and also in that of Belgium's colony there was a certain blindness which ensured that neither came to a happy conclusion. Leopold II never realised that his methods in the Congo were not compatible with his aims; thus his enterprise ended amid the cries of the Congo reformers and criticism from all sides, leaving the King embittered by what he regarded as an ill-informed and spiteful judgement on his work. Belgium did not realise in time that if an association which had been based on force was going to live on as a freely accepted association which would continue to benefit both partners, it must be carefully prepared by the development of African leadership and of institutions which would provide a means for the formation of opinion, and by a gradual handing over of political responsibility. Thus her ill-prepared transfer of power and the tragic events which followed it brought her nothing but intense criticism from all sides, criticism which Belgians regarded as over-hasty and completely lacking in any appreciation of the positive aspects of Belgian colonial policy.

The element of international intervention has been a constant factor in the history of the Congo. The Congo Independent State was born in 1885 in Berlin at a conference of the Powers of Europe. It was international pressure, with its appeal to the Berlin Act, which brought Leopold's rule in the Congo State to an end; one man's resources alone were clearly insufficient to run an African colony. Belgium's rule in the Congo also ended because of influences from outside; the Congo's isolation from the rest of Africa began to break down after the war, and Congolese opinion—a negligible factor in 1908—increasingly reflected the desire for autonomy which was being manifested all over the continent. But Belgium had lacked the foresight to realise that the end of her colonial régime was so close at hand, and the Congolese had not been sufficiently prepared for the independence which they demanded. Thus the new state was unable to stand on its own feet. The Congo Independent State was born in an international conference; when Belgium granted independence to her colony, the young republic was forced to call the United Nations to its aid. . . .

30. Lugard and Nigeria

MARGERY PERHAM *Life of Lugard* Vol. II Collins 1960; pages 138–50

Indirect Rule: The Idea

No part of history is more difficult to record intelligibly than administration. This is especially true of good administration, for while the bad is generally advertised by the protests of the administered and sometimes defined by the resulting investigation, the good is likely to produce the happiness that has no history. Again, at a later stage, a good system of administration is liable to a peculiar penalty. Created by men, or more likely, by a man, of high ability, it may become sanctified by its own success and be reverently or lethargically prolonged by lesser men until it ceases to meet the changing needs of the time. It can then be displaced only by vigorous action in which condemnation is employed less as a rational process than as an instrument with which to sweep away the obsolete structure. This is to some extent true of Lugard's system which later evoked much criticism. The earliest attack came from the first generation of western-educated Africans, to whom 'Indirect Rule' stood for an alliance made between imperial and tribal authority to restrain their own advance. By the mid 'thirties criticism was being voiced far beyond this group.

But the period with which we are dealing now was one of creation. By the time Lugard left Northern Nigeria, he had constructed both upon paper and in the practice of the men, British and African, who worked under him, what can claim to be the most comprehensive, coherent and renowned system of administration in our colonial history. This was his greatest and most famous work, the achievement of his prime. Not to attempt some analysis of it would be to leave out the main reason why his life deserves to be recorded in full. But there must be a difference in the treatment of such a subject in a biography and that proper to a study of government or of Nigerian history.[1] The full account of Lugard's administrative work, based upon the mass of his official documents, demands a volume to itself. In this chapter and the next, half-way through the narrative of his tenure of office as High Commissioner, we shall do no more than picture him at work at his desk and upon his administrative tours, and consider the nature of his administrative achievement, not omitting to scrutinize it for faults.

His work was shackled by the poverty of his revenue. Today, in Britain and even in Africa, administration is conducted upon comparatively lavish standards, with a parliament which seems willing to vote millions with less reluctance than in Lugard's day it voted thousands. He had to open up a vast region and create a new administration upon a civil revenue made up largely by a small and reluctant grant-in-aid. If he were to administer to his own standards, which, as we shall see, were wholly different from those of the department he served, he had to make up for its inadequacy by the extra energy he forced out of himself and his staff. Shortage of staff, moreover, with shortage of military force, brought closer the possibility that he might at any moment land the imperial government in an expensive and embarrassing disaster.

For the task set him, Lugard was so exactly fitted that his life up to this moment might have been a training especially designed by Providence. He was experienced in every activity that the newly annexed country demanded: in transport and

---

[1] A more general and historical account by the writer will be found in Perham, *Native Administration*.

supply; in survey work; in prospecting for minerals; in dealing with Africans, whether potentates, raw tribesmen or wage labourers. He knew Africa and Africans as did few men of his time. He was a soldier, and a jungle soldier, in a job that was still half military and he had himself created the Regiment he employed. He knew his region, having worked around the middle Niger for six years, helping to win its western frontiers. He had been in contact with Islam and he was an expert upon slavery in a region where it was a major problem. His physique allowed him to do two men's work in a climate and in conditions which halved the capacities of most men. But no list of qualities, however long, would have met the needs of the work if they had not been fused within an ardent temperament and directed by a will of exceptional strength. He entered upon his work with complete confidence. The contrast is arresting between the indeterminate soldier he had been in 1898, when obliged to carry out Chamberlain's directions, and the new administrator with, at least in the earlier years, almost entire freedom of action. Reference has been made to an undated and pencilled paper in his writing which must have been written while he was in England soon after he was appointed or upon the voyage out. In this he laid down the main principles upon which he meant to administer the country.

In the earlier stages of British rule [he jotted down] it is desirable to retain the native authority [an expression which was to achieve a wide-spread technical meaning as a result of his system] and to work through and by the native emirs. At the same time it is feasible by degrees to bring them gradually into approximation with our ideas of justice and humanity. . . . In pursuance of the above general principles the chief civil officers of the Provinces are to be called Residents which implies one who carries on diplomatic relations rather than Commissioners or Administrators.

In the less organized areas, however, their functions would be more administrative and less diplomatic. Legislation would at first be mainly permissive and would be fully enforced only in the most accessible and docile areas and it would allow of great variety in its application. He went on to sketch the legal system through Native Courts and to plan how far he could use his expensive military force as an auxiliary to his inadequate civil service without undermining its discipline and essential character. These and other ideas in his early notes he exactly carried out. The word instinct must not be misused, but at least he had such an aptitude for administration that he hardly seemed to need the processes of reasoning or discussion, either with himself or with others, or even of experiment.

The administrative principles which Lugard developed during the High Commissionership are generally summed up in the words 'Indirect Rule'. Was there, then, an antithesis that could be called direct rule and were there other contrasting methods? To answer this a glance over the earlier phases of British colonial government is needed.

The first stage of British expansion had, in the main, seen British colonists carrying their representative institutions, laws and judicial system with them to the new lands in their ships. When territories inhabited by native populations that lay near to commercial stations or to white settlements were annexed, as along the Guinea Coast or the Straits Settlements, the tendency was still to extend, as far as possible, British institutions without, at first, their representative element. This was introduced gradually and in closely restricted fashion in the form of legislative councils in which officials preponderated over nominated unofficials. Generally speaking, the British authorities, even if they made use of native agents and to some extent recognized native laws and customs, tried to introduce their own institutions and worked in an assimilative spirit. This policy, though the expression somewhat overstates the British form of it, has been called the policy of identity.

This policy seemed desirable when confidence in British civilization was at its maximum—a period which just lasted into Lugard's day—while at the same time both understanding of native society and respect for it were at their minimum. It seemed also a practicable policy, in regions where British rule was developed piecemeal over relatively restricted areas. This was true of the first annexations of tribal South Africa or the first exiguous footholds on the West African coast. But as the nineteenth century wore on, the British, like the Romans before them, found that it was impossible to draw an imperial frontier, and the pace of annexation quickened. Sometimes at a stroke, whether by the use or threat of force or by consent, large tribal or monarchial states were added. No British government of the last century would face the cost or the effort of attempting direct administration of the old kind over such large acquisitions. Lugard's policy of ruling 'indirectly' through the Nigerian emirs cannot therefore, *as a general principle*, be claimed as either inventive or original. Clearly the choice demanded little invention from a governor confronted on the one side with large, semi-civilized but not uncooperative principalities, and on the other by his own absurdly inadequate staff and revenue. Nor, since many other conquerors from the earliest days of history had been faced with much the same position, was the choice very original. Any intelligent conqueror, however self-interested, who had come from a country with a reasonably high standard of order, would hesitate to destroy the structure of a subjected society unless he has some over-riding reason for such action and the means to carry it through. Rome, as Tacitus said, making even kings the instrument of her rule, was of course the most famous empire to adopt this expedient and the story of the three trials and sentence of Jesus Christ is a familiar example of its working. Britain herself, in India, in the Pacific, in South Africa, and even in territories much closer to Lugard's domain, found herself increasingly obliged to recognize princes and tribal chiefs by treaty or by usage and the very term 'protectorate', though it was soon to lose what constitutional meaning it originally had, represented at first a self-imposed restraint by the ruling power.

Lugard as a soldier in India had at least shot tigers in the Indian States. In Nyasaland he had known only backward and broken tribes. But in Uganda, in 1890–92, he had encountered the most advanced kingdom in the whole of East Africa and had been upon intimate terms with its elaborate hierarchial structure. This had led him to publish, in 1893, the principle upon which he believed British administration should be based in that country.

With regard to internal control in Uganda, in my opinion the object to be aimed at in the administration of this country is to rule through its own executive government. The people are singularly intelligent and have a wonderful appreciation of justice and of legal procedure and our aim should be to educate and develop the sense of justice. . . .

An arbitrary and despotic rule, which takes no account of native customs, traditions, and prejudices, is not suited to the successful development of an infant civilization, nor, in my view, is it in accordance with the spirit of British colonial rule. The King has been proved incompetent and useless, but the Resident should rule through and by the chiefs.

We can now see that the application of the indirect principle in Northern Nigeria was original, but not the idea. That great administrator in India, Sir Thomas Munro, had urged it nearly a century before. We have already met in these pages Lord Stanmore who practised this principle in Fiji. Mary Kingsley aired it in her very individual way. Lugard's neighbouring Governor in the Niger Coast Protectorate stated that the paucity of European staff necessitated rule through the chiefs. Coming still nearer to Lugard, Goldie held ideas which appeared to run closely upon these lines and which he defined with characteristic force and clarity. For both the welfare and pacification of the natives, he wrote, 'the general policy of ruling on African principles through native rulers must be followed for the present'. But he added the interesting idea that European methods might be employed in specially suitable districts to serve as models and also as 'cities of refuge' for more advanced individuals. Goldie must often have discussed his ideas with Lugard in the period of their cooperation. But, as we have seen, Lugard inherited very little by way of a working administration from Goldie's Company. In spite of his defeat of Bida and Ilorin in the field Goldie was unable to retain sufficient control over these emirates to establish much more than diplomatic and commercial relations with them. It would not seem, therefore, that Lugard owed much more to Goldie than the confirmation in terms of Nigeria of a principle which he had already defined before he knew either the man or the country. He took over, of course, the same conditions of limited resources in face of strong native states which seemed to impose a tentative 'indirectness' of method.

To emphasize these two conditions in order to disparage Lugard's reputation is to mistake the nature of his achievement. His claim rests not upon his adoption, still less his invention, of the indirect principle, but upon the special methods through which he applied it. It is possible for imperial rulers to use it as a temporary device until they are strong enough to dispense with it as was sometimes the French method, or to express it in terms of mere ultimate sovereignty with the very minimum of intervention in internal affairs, as with Indian states. Or, to take the example of the South African High Commission territories, it was possible, in a spirit of limited liability dictated by economy and the evasion of responsibility, to take over a few superior functions of government and leave the subordinate society to continue to carry out the rest, with little attempt at integration or even at supervision. This last, in varying degrees, was the course already being followed in more than one part of tropical Africa when Lugard took over Northern Nigeria.[1] The distinction of Lugard's system was that he not only preserved native initiative but tried to direct it and, indeed, to incorporate it into his own system. To use his own words, in the first *Political Memoranda* he issued—and of which more presently—he did not ordain

two sets of Rulers—the British and the Native—working either separately or in co-operation, but a single Government in which the Native Chiefs have clearly defined duties and an acknowledged *status*, equally with the British officials.

They were to be an integral part of the machinery of the administration. Such a purpose had nowhere been so consciously attempted: it could not be attained by decree but only by laborious and unceasing efforts in nearly every department of government.

It has been admitted that, principles apart, shortage of political staff was a sufficient reason for a large delegation at first to native authorities. We have seen that in the first two or three years, owing to limitations of finance, Lugard could seldom post more than two political officers to each of the immense provinces he was creating, and often one of these would be sick or on leave. The actual number of men under Lugard was as follows.

---

[1] The policy now being developed in the Union of South Africa is the most extreme form, indeed a perversion, of the indirect principle. Under it Africans who are in large measure economically part of a dominant European-run State are being thrust back politically under artificially revived tribal rule in the attempt to retard and divide them.

	1900–1901	1901–1902	1902–1903	1903–1904	1904–1905	1905–1906	Probable 1906–07
Civil	104	155	163	231*	248	266	288
Military	200	163	157	186†	207	208	187
Total on Estimates	304	318	320	417	455	474	475
Should be in Africa Actually‡	202	212	214	278	310	323	326
Present	—	—	—	—	270	277	—

* Increase due to inclusion of Hausa States (Kano, Sokoto, etc.).
† Increase due to new Mounted Infantry Battalion.
‡ No explanation is given for the omissions under this heading.

It should be noted that the civil staff gradually overtook and passed the military in number. We have already observed that 'civil' staff given here covered all ranks down to foremen of works and masters of the many vessels on the rivers. According to a Colonial Office report upon Lugard's grumblings the number of political officers in the total rose from 9 in 1900 to 40 in 1903, and to 75 in 1905–6.

Lugard did not find it easy to recruit men of the calibre he demanded since he began his administration just as the outbreak of the Boer War called many of the most adventurous spirits to another part of Africa. He was therefore obliged, in face of the paucity of senior civil staff, to make all the use he legitimately could of military officers and he defended this course in words that reveal what he desired from his officers. They were 'an admirable class of men for this work. They are gentlemen: their training teaches them prompt decision'; their knowledge of military law and of survey were assets, they had shown a sympathy and understanding with the people. 'It is, indeed, a characteristic of the British officer that when in civil employ his rule is often marked by less "militarism" than that of the civilian and he is more opposed to punitive operations.' Oxford and Cambridge were, however, now coming forward with offers to train graduates for colonial service and Lugard's men from this source formed a creative nucleus for the new Colonial Service. It is difficult to understand how, with the small

number of political officers he had at any one time in the field,
especially in the first three years, he and they were able to
accomplish so much. The leave system, necessary but costly in
time and money, meant that only two-thirds of his establishment could be at their posts, while there was a large expense of
time in laborious travel, in accompanying military expeditions,
and in sickness.

What were the tasks Lugard asked of his Residents and
Assistant Residents? To say they were to rule through the
chiefs does not take us very far. An immediate question to be
answered was 'What chiefs?' Was it to be the Fulani who had
ousted earlier rulers and imposed themselves over the Hausa
population? The British, coming in, judged them cruel and
oppressive; the test of war showed that their own subjects had
little active loyalty towards them, and at first sight they cannot
have seemed very promising partners for government.

An attempt has been made to picture Hausa society in the
nineteenth century. We must now look more closely at the
Fulani ruling class themselves as Lugard studied them as
candidates for authority under his control. It is easy to recon-
struct the picture these men presented to him, so little in many
outward things had the country changed when the writer first
travelled there, sometimes trekking on horseback, in the early
thirties. They and their large families and many courtiers, com-
fortably settled into the seats of their predecessors, played their
parts as the great men of their world with that dramatic
ostentation which, in industrial civilization, wealth and rank
has largely discarded. In their high turbans, with the characteristic swathe round the chin to keep the blown dust out of their
mouths, their flowing cloaks and brilliantly coloured equestrian
trappings, they would ride out among the earth-stained Hausa
peasantry who would fall prostrate in the fields at their passing.
The rulers had palaces of red mud, with crenellated walls
which extended over acres of ground in the capital cities: these
had high arched halls patterned with arabesques; courtyards;
warrens of rooms for retainers; quarters for slaves and horses
and, shut away in the care of eunuchs, large collections of
women of many tribes. These last, invisible to Lugard or any
other European man, at least until recent days, were shown to
the writer by more than one Fulani emir, who, passing down

the long row of chambers, called each occupant to the doorway and explained how and from where she had been obtained, as a horse-breeder shows off his stud. It was through this luxury and indulgence that many of the emirs, following some greater oriental rulers, had sunk from the physical and religious energy of their conquering forefathers and had drawn negro blood from wives and slave concubines into their Hamitic race, darkening, in many of them, their light colour and thickening their fine-drawn Fulani features and slender limbs. Yet the decline can be over-stated: they still had the habits and the capacities of command and Lugard, obliged to make use of his quick judgment of men, declared them fit to rule.

Had he, indeed, we must ask again, as we approach his situation more closely, any choice? In his *Memoranda* he stated the alternative policy of discovering and reinstating the former Hausa dynasties, and Sir Richmond Palmer informed the writer that a number of Hausa claimants at this time were collected in Gobir hoping to be reinstated. But it is difficult to believe that this restoration could have been possible with his scanty staff and his need for a rapid and tranquillizing settlement. Such a substitution would have ruled out the break-neck speed of his king-making expedition in the spring of 1903. And once a partnership had been made with the interlocked Fulani dynasties, it would have been difficult in honour and in policy to break it.

The indifference, if no worse, of many of the Hausa towards their Fulani ruling caste served, of course, to make these, once the spell of their power was broken, very dependent upon their new masters. The Fulani may have been in some ways able rulers but the evidence of the early European travellers shows how destructive their *Jihad* had been, especially where, as in Katsina, fighting had been prolonged. There is evidence that after nearly a century of assimilation with their subjects they were still regarded as a dominant group, a distinction that was often close to hostility. The Hausa woman, Baba, though she ran into her hut when she saw the first white face, could remark 'We Habe [Hausa] wanted them to come. It was the Fulani who did not like it. When the Europeans came the Habe saw that if you worked for them they paid you for it, they didn't say like the Fulani, "Commoner, give me this! Commoner, bring me that!" Yes, the Habe wanted them; they saw no harm in them.'

The situation might demand the recognition of the Fulani rulers but there was still a wide margin of choice as to their exact status and their powers, and it is at this point that we must begin to distinguish what was peculiar to Lugard's application of the indirect principle. He confessed to the writer many years afterwards that, though he later quoted the example of the Indian States in his *Memoranda* when suddenly confronted with the northern emirs after their rapid collapse, he could only scrape together the vaguest recollections about the position of these states, and was, indeed, amazed at his own ignorance. He had to devise what seemed to fit the immediate situation. It was true that he had thought out the main lines of his settlement long before and had enforced them in Bida but it was now necessary to be more detailed and definite. Lugard's speech in Kano has already been quoted; it shows the main indirect principle; he still had to go a long way in developing it into a system of administration suited to the country.

First, because constitutionally basic, was his determination that there should be no uncertainty whatever upon the question of sovereignty. This, half-consciously perhaps, must have been a main reason for his launching his 1902–3 expedition. The alternative would have been to attempt to secure a treaty, at least with the suzerain state of Sokoto. Or he might have made one of those agreements which elsewhere have tended to confuse both sides by their ambiguous legal status and their tendency to crystallize societies at the very time when annexation was going to bring rapid changes. Lugard's first demand, whether he was looking at authorities above or below him, was always for a free hand. He had not forgotten the hazardous uncertainties of his relationship with Mwanga. So he laid down that the Fulani had lost by defeat the powers—he had then little idea, as he told the writer, what those powers were—that they had won by conquest and recent conquest at that. Now, by grace and not by right, some of these powers would be returned to them by delegation, to be kept according to good behaviour. This settlement, by implication and usage, was made to cover those states which, like Bornu, had acceded by consent and not as a result of conquest. It was upon this constitutional foundation that the Residents were to stand, willing to advise and help, but able with full statutory power, to control and to command. He was quite definite about the contents of this new power. 'This suzerainty involves the ultimate title to all land, the right to appoint Emirs and all officers of state, the right of legislation and of taxation.' He goes on, in this second of his annual reports, to give the underlying reason for his policy.

But in my view the tradition of British rule has ever been to arrest disintegration, to retain and build up again what is best in the social and political organization of the conquered dynasties, and to develop on the lines of its own individuality each separate race of which our Great Empire consists. That has been our policy in India; and Northern Nigeria, though but a third in size, and many centuries behind the great Eastern dependency, still presents to my imagination many strangely parallel conditions. I believe myself that the future of the virile races of this Protectorate lies largely in the regeneration of the Fulani. Their ceremonial, their coloured skins, their mode of life and habits of thought, appeal more to the native populations than the prosaic business-like habits of the Anglo-Saxon can ever do. Nor have we the means at present to administer so vast a country. This, then, is the policy to which, in my view, the administration of Northern Nigeria should give effect, viz., to regenerate this capable race and mould them to ideas of justice and mercy, so that in a future generation, if not in this, they may become worthy instruments of rule.

These passages are important for, in spite of the comparison with India, meaning of course, the Indian States, it is quite clear from the powers he claimed that his system was to be fundamentally different from the almost diplomatic supervision of the British Residents at the courts of Rajahs. The oath of allegiance which each emir had to take was uncompromising.

I swear in the name of Allah, and of Mahomet his Prophet to well and truly serve his Majesty King Edward VII and his Representative the High Commissioner of Northern Nigeria. To obey the laws of the Protectorate, and the lawful commands of the High Commissioner and of the Resident, provided that they are not contrary to my religion. And if they are so contrary, I will at once inform the Resident, for the information of the High Commissioner. I will cherish in my heart no treachery or disloyalty, and I will rule my people with justice and without partiality. And as I carry out this oath, so may Allah judge me.

(Even in an official declaration the emirs are made to follow Lugard's habit of splitting his infinitives!)

Undisputed sovereignty was one of Lugard's principles. The integration of British and native power was another; the two were not to lie together in impermeable strata.

The effect is to still further recognize the Native Administration as an integral part of the machinery of the Government of the country, and to amplify and regularize the position already accorded to it in Proclamations Nos. 1 and 2 of 1906 (Native Revenue and Native Courts). These three important statutes practically contain the whole policy of Government regarding the position, authority, and emoluments of the Native part of the Administration of the Protectorate.

The prestige and influence of the Chiefs can be best upheld by letting the peasantry see that Government itself treats them as an integral part of the machinery of the Administration. . . . They should be complementary to each other, and the Chief himself must understand that he has no right to his place and power, unless he renders his proper services to the State.

The words are clear and firm but their implementation was not easy. Indeed, as we shall see when discussing the judicial system, there were contexts in which Lugard wished to emphasize dualism rather than integration. He made no attempt to deceive himself or his staff about their difficulties. He discussed them frankly and summarized these discussions in his *Political Memoranda*, especially in the one entitled 'Fulani Rule'. In this, it must be admitted, he tended to run together three related but separate issues—firstly, whether the Fulani should rule or be replaced by the old Habe dynasties; secondly, how far Muslim rule should be restored or extended over pagans; thirdly, the question in what measure the power of the emirs should be retained or increased. Immediate decisions answered the first two questions but the last remained, and continued to remain until the eve of independence, open to varying political practice. Not surprisingly, there were differences of opinion among Lugard's first Residents. There was at first a feeling against the emirs who had been in the field as 'the enemy' and in favour of the underdog, the peasantry. This was followed by an early realization that it was impossible, as Lugard pointed out, to take over, or even, indeed, to supervise very closely, the large administrative work of the Fulani rulers. And as many of these quickly showed their intelligence by a co-operative acceptance of their new status most Residents entered into some degree of partnership with them. . . .

31. Indirect rule: French and British methods

MICHAEL CROWDER *Africa* Vol. 34, July 1964 Oxford University Press for International African Institute; pages 197–205

. . . There were such fundamental differences between the French and British systems that, even if both did make use of 'chiefs', it is not possible to place the French system of native administration in the same category as British indirect rule. It is true that both powers had little alternative to the use of existing political authorities as a means of governing their vast African empires, and in most cases these authorities were headed by chiefs. What *is* important is the very different way in which these authorities were used. The nature of the position and power of the chief in the two systems was totally different and, as a corollary, so were the relations between the chief and the political officer, who was inspired in each case by very different ideals.

The British in Northern Nigeria, which became the model for indirect rule, believed that it was their task to conserve what was good in indigenous institutions and assist them to develop on their own lines. The relation between the British political officer and the chief was in general that of an adviser who only in extreme circumstances interfered with the chief and the native authority under him. However, where chiefs governed small political units, and in particular where their traditional executive authority was questionable, the political officer found himself interfering in native authority affairs more frequently than ideally he should. This was true in many parts of East Africa and in parts of Yorubaland, where the borderline between 'advisory' and 'supervisory' in the activities of the political officer was not always clear. Though indirect rule reposed primarily on a chief as executive, its aim was not to preserve the institution of chieftaincy as such, but to encourage local self-government through indigenous political institutions, whether these were headed by a single executive authority, or by a council of elders.[1] In Northern Nigeria a policy of minimal interference with the chiefs and their traditional forms of government was pursued. But Lugard himself had insisted on a reform of the indigenous taxation system and of the administration of native justice when he was Governor of Northern Nigeria and believed that, while the colonial government should repose on the chiefs, their administration should be progressively modernized. And, though his successors left them largely to themselves, Sir Donald Cameron, Governor of Nigeria from 1931 to 1935, who had introduced indirect rule to Tanganyika and held similar beliefs to those of Lugard, was shocked by the situation in Northern Nigeria, where he felt the emirates were fast developing into Indian-style native states.

Indeed, in the earliest inter-war period many emirs and chiefs ruled as 'sole native authorities', a position which gave them for practical purposes more power than they had in pre-colonial days, where they were either subject to control by a council or liable to deposition if they became too unpopular.[2] They were permitted to administer traditional justice, which, in the case of certain emirs, included trying cases of murder for which the death sentence, subject to confirmation by the Governor, could be passed. They administered political units that corresponded to those they would have administered before the arrival of the colonial power. They were elected to office by traditional methods of selection, and only in the case of the election of a patently unsuitable candidate to office would the colonial power

[1] See Sir Philip Mitchell's article on 'Indirect Rule', when Governor of Uganda, in the *Uganda Journal*, iv, no. 1, July 1936, where he says that indirect rule is founded on the assumption that 'every group of people must possess some form of . . . natural authority, normally, of course, symbolized in the person of some individual or individuals'. 'The administrative system called "Indirect Rule" endeavours in each place where it is to be applied to ascertain what are the persons or institutions which the people concerned look upon as the natural authority.'

[2] See P. C. Lloyd's article 'Kings, Chief and Local Government', *West Africa*, 31 January 1953, where he remarks that the Yoruba kings became much more powerful under the British. 'They could only be deposed by the British administration which often tended to protect them against their own people.'

refuse recognition. There was thus a minimal undermining of the traditional sources of authority. The main change for the Fulani Emirs of Northern Nigeria, for instance, was that they now owed allegiance to the British Government rather than to the Sultan of Sokoto, and collected taxes on its behalf, though they retained, in most cases, 70 per cent of the amount collected for the administration of their native authority.

This system of indirect rule was, with modifications, practised wherever possible in Britain's colonies in West Africa and in most of her other African territories. There were notable exceptions, especially in Eastern Nigeria, where the absence of identifiable executive authority in most communities made indirect rule as practised in Northern Nigeria almost impossible to apply. In such societies, British assiduity in trying to discover chiefs, or invent them, might lend colour to M. Deschamps's argument; but, in practice, the goal of ruling through tradit-ional political units on whom local self-government could be devolved was maintained, and after much trial and error a system of democratically elected councils was formulated as most closely corresponding to the traditional methods of deleg-ating authority.

If, taking into account such variations, we use indirect rule in Northern Nigeria as a model we shall see just how greatly the French system of administration in Black Africa differed from that of the British.

The British system depended on the advisory relationship between the political officer and the native authority, usually a chief, heading a local government unit that corresponded to a pre-colonial political unit. The French system placed the chief in an entirely subordinate role to the political officer. M. Deschamps alludes only briefly to the role of the French political officer towards the end of his article, where he hints at the nature of his status as a *roi paternel* or *roi absolu*. But it is important to stress that the chief in relation to the French political officer was a mere agent of the central colonial government with clearly defined duties and powers. He did not head a local government unit, nor did the area which he administered on behalf of the government necessarily correspond to a pre-colonial political unit. In the interests of conformity the French divided the country up administratively into cantons which frequently cut across pre-colonial political boundaries. Chiefs did not remain chiefs of their old political units but of the new cantons, though sometimes the two coincided. In certain cases the French deliberately broke up the old political units, as in the case of the Futa Jallon where their policy was 'the progressive suppression of the chiefs and the parcelling out of their authority'. Most important of all, chiefs were not necessarily those who would have been selected according to customary procedures; more often than not they were those who had shown loyalty to the French or had obtained some education. While the British were scrupulous in their respect for traditional methods of selection of chiefs, the French, conceiving of them as agents of the administration, were more concerned with their potential efficiency than their legitimacy. We need not wonder then that as a young French administrator, after serving in Senegal and Dahomey, M. Robert Delavignette should have been astonished, on his way to duty in Niger, to find that the British political officer in Kano actually called on the Emir when he had business with him and paid him the compliment of learning Hausa so that he could speak to him direct. 'Pour le jeune administrateur français, une telle manière d'administrer avait la charme d'un conte des *Mille et Une Nuits.*' Contrast the position of the Emir of Kano with that of the Alaketu of Ketu in Dahomey. By tradition he was one of the seven most important rulers in Yorubaland, on an equal footing with the Oni of Ife and the Alafin of Oyo. A friend who visited him while Dahomey was still under French rule found him waiting outside the French Chef de Subdivisions' office. He mentioned the fact that the King was waiting to the French administrator, who replied, 'Qu'est ce qu'il va se faire engueuler?', and kept him waiting a little longer.

It is clear then that the French explicitly changed the very nature of the powers of the chief and that 'his functions were reduced to that of a mouthpiece for orders emanating from outside'.[1] This is brought out clearly, for example, in the *Arrêté of*

---

[1] L. P. Mair, *Native Policies in Africa*, London, 1936, p. 210. R. L. Buell in his *The Native Problem in Africa* cites Joost Van Vollenhoven, Governor-General of French West Africa, 1912–17, as describing the chiefs as having 'no power of their own of any kind. There are not two authorities in the *cercle*, the French authority and the native authority; there is only one'.

28th December 1936 on the organisation and regulation of the local indigenous administration in French Equatorial Africa in the section dealing with *Chefs de Canton* (or *de Terre* or *de Tribu*).[1]

The Chefs de Canton (etc.) are recruited:

(i) for preference from among the descendants of old families traditionally or customarily destined to command,

(ii) from among notable natives, literate if possible, who have rendered services to the French cause and who are fitted to fill these functions by their authority or influence in the country,

(iii) from among the *Chefs de Canton* (etc.) who have satisfactorily carried out their functions for at least four years,

(iv) from among old soldiers who have completed more than the normal terms of service and who qualify for special treatment,

(v) from among local civil servants (clerks, interpreters, etc.) who have worked satisfactorily for at least four years in the public service.

The following are the disciplinary measures applicable to *Chefs de Canton* (etc.):

(i) Reprimand by the *Chef de Department*.

(ii) Temporary withholding of salary.

(iii) Temporary interdiction.

(iv) Reduction of salary.

(v) Dismissal.

Since the chiefs did not, except in rare cases, represent traditional authority and, since they were the agents of the colonial power for carrying out its more unpopular measures, such as collecting taxes and recruiting for labour, they were resented in most parts of French West Africa. While they retained no traditional judicial authority such as that of their counterparts in British West Africa in their Native Courts, they were agents of the law, in this case the unpopular system of summary administrative justice known as the *indigénat*.[2] In

---

[1] Translated by T. G. Brierly.

[2] Concessions were made to customary law prior to 1946, when native penal law was abolished and all inhabitants of French Tropical Africa became subject to the French code. Before that time only those Africans who were French citizens could claim justice under the Code. The vast majority

many areas in the post-war period they became identified with pro-French administrative parties, particularly in Soudan (Mali). Hence it was not surprising that when, in 1957, just before the independence of Guinea, Sekou Touré (then Vice-Président du Conseil) decided to do away with chiefs, the operation was effected with remarkably little protest from either the indigenous population or from the French administration that had made use of them. Of the twenty-two Commandants de Cercle, still mostly French, called to Conakry to discuss the proposed removal of the chiefs (from 25 to 27 July) only four felt that the 'chefs de canton' had a useful role to fulfil in the territory, and nearly all confirmed that the chiefs no longer possessed political traditional authority and had become mere agents of the administration. As far as the Commandant de Cercle for Labé was concerned: 'Pour moi, qu'ils soient là ou pas, c'est la même chose.' This is a far cry from Nigeria of the day, where in the North the opposition party (N.E.P.U.) were trying unsuccessfully to rouse the people against the chiefs and where the Government of Eastern Nigeria, an area in which traditionally most societies did not have chiefs, commissioned a former expatriate administrative officer to 'investigate the position, status and influence of Chiefs and Natural Rulers in the Eastern Region, and make recommendations as to the necessity or otherwise of legislation regulating their appointment, recognition and deposition'. In African countries where the British had imposed chiefs, as in Eastern Nigeria and parts of Uganda, their prestige had in fact gone up, but this has certainly not been true in the former French territories.

In formulating these general models it is once again essential to recognize exceptions to the general rule. For example, the kings of the Mossi in Upper Volta, the Fulani Emirs of the northern provinces of Cameroun, and a number of chiefs in Niger retained some power. But in general the French system of administration deliberately sapped the traditional powers of the chiefs in the interests of uniformity of administrative system, not

of *sujets* were subject to the *indigénat* already referred to and to customary law. Customary law, however, was not administered by the chief but by the French administrator, who was assisted by two notables of the area who were versed in tradition. These courts could try both penal and civil cases. Now customary law survives in questions of inheritance, marriage, and land.

only within individual territories but throughout the two great federations of West and Equatorial Africa. Thus it seems somewhat of an understatement to describe the French attitude, as Gouverneur Deschamps does, as 'notre pratique nonchalante à l'égard des chefferies'. Robert Delavignette in *Freedom and Authority in West Africa* (London, 1950) bears this out in his chapter on the Commandant. 'The man who really personified the *Cercle* was the Commandant. . . . He was the Chief of a clearly defined country called Damaragam (Zinder in Niger), and chief in everything that concerned that country'. Yet this was the Damaragam once ruled over by the powerful Sultans of Zinder, who are now reduced to little more than exotic showpieces of traditional Africa. So too does Geoffrey Gorer in *Africa Dances* (London, 1935), when he writes of the 'chefs de canton':

In theory these local chiefs rule under the guidance of the local administrator: in practice they are the scapegoats who are made responsible for the collection of money and men. While they enjoy the administrator's favour they have certain privileges, usually good houses and land and in a few cases subsidies; but unless they are completely subservient they risk dismissal, prison and exile.

Gorer draws attention to a phenomenon that bears out just how much the French had changed the nature of chiefs in West Africa. In Ivory Coast, if a 'chef de canton' with no traditional rights to 'rule' were imposed by the administration, the people often elected in secret a 'real' chief. Delavignette also notes this in *Freedom and Authority in French West Africa*.[1]

---

[1] A somewhat extreme point of view with regard to the French attitude to chiefs, which is the exact opposite of that of M. Deschamps, is held by J. Suret-Canale in 'Guinea under the Colonial System', *Présence Africaine*, no. 29, p. 53 (English edition): 'Between 1890 and 1914 the system of "direct administration" was progressively established. The former sovereigns (including those who had rendered the best service to French penetration) were utterly eliminated and the former political leaders utterly overthrown; ethnic limits, the traditional limits of the former "dwie" in the Futa Jallon, all those were carved up and rearranged at the whim of administrative needs or fancies. The political reality was henceforward the Circle, and where appropriate, the Subdivision, commanded by a European administrator, and below them, the canton and the village commanded by African chiefs described as "traditional" or "customary". In reality, these chiefs in their role and in the powers devolved upon them had absolutely nothing traditional or customary; designed to ensure the cheapest execution (under their

Why this great difference in approach by the two powers to the question of native administration, given that both for reasons of economy had to administer their vast African possessions with the aid of 'chiefs'? The difference has much to do with difference in national character and political traditions. While few would disagree that the British were inspired by the concept of separate development for their African territories, there is still much to debate as to how far the French were inspired by the concept of assimilation even after its formal abandonment as official policy in favour of a *politique d'association*. Only by an examination of the extent of the survival of assimilationist goals in French colonial policy can we understand the reasons for the difference in the two approaches to native administration. This survival showed itself at two levels: as a dominant feature of the *politique d'association* and in the personal ethos of the French political officer.

One of the problems here is to define assimilation. M. D. Lewis has drawn attention to the many definitions of assimilation in use: (1) assimilation as the dominant colonial policy of France, i.e. its dominant and continuing characteristics; (2) assimilation as the policy abandoned in favour of association; (3) assimilation as opposed to autonomy, i.e. integration versus devolution; (4) assimilation as a legalistic definition, i.e. representation in the mother of parliaments; (5) assimilation as civilization; (6) assimilation as representing racial equality as against British tendency to the colour bar; (7) assimilation as a highly centralized form of direct rule of colonies. It is of course difficult to choose any one definition as the satisfactory one. Assimilation as practised in the four communes of Senegal, the only instance of its full-scale application in French Tropical Africa, had the following distinctive features: political assimilation to the metropolitan country through the representation of Senegal in the Chambre des Députés; administrative assimilation by creating a Conseil-Général for Senegal modelled on the Conseils du Départment of France, and by the establishment of municipal councils on the French model; the personal assimilation of Senegalese in the communes by according them the

own responsibility) of the multiple tasks of administration, taxation, forced labour, recruitment etc., they were the exact counterpart of the caids of Algeria, subordinate administrators.'

status of French citizens, though they were allowed to retain their *statut personnel*; the extension of French educational facilities as part of the French *mission civilisatrice*. This policy was abandoned not so much because men like Lyautey and Jules Harmand advocated Lugardian ideas about the relationship between the colonial power and African peoples, but because, to use Lewis's phrase, the French were 'not prepared to undertake the massive work of social transformation which alone could make it a reality'. But the *politique d'association* that succeeded it was certainly not that advocated by Jules Harmand, whereby the colonial power would respect the manners, customs, and religion of the natives and follow a policy of mutual assistance rather than exploitation. Rather it was one in which, while recognition was given to the impracticability of applying a full-scale policy of assimilation to African societies, a number of assimilationist characteristics were retained. First, the goal of creating French citizens out of Africans was not abandoned; it was just made more distant and much more difficult of achievement. Second, there was a high degree of administrative centralization on the mother country, which was not compatible with a true *politique d'association*. We have already seen that the French made little concession to indigenous political units in dividing up their African territories for administrative purposes. Third, the French civilizing mission was not abandoned, and though education might be sparse, it was modelled on the French system. Children spoke French from the day they entered school. No concession was made to teaching in the vernacular as in the British territories. Fourth, individual territories were not considered as having special characters, so that the same administrative organization was imposed on them all. Political officers would be posted from one territory to the other sometimes every other year, which gave them little time to learn the local language or ethnography. On the other hand the British political officer remained in the same territory for a long period of time, and in the case of Nigeria, in the same region; and promotion depended in part on the ability of the political officers to learn indigenous languages. Thus under the French system the one constant for the political officer could only be French culture, while for the British officer every encouragement was given to him to understand the local

culture. As a corollary the French did give some encouragement to the formation of a native *élite*, which was absorbed into
the territorial and federal administrative services, albeit not on
a very large scale. The British, on the other hand, in the
twenties and thirties actively discouraged the formation of a
class of Europeanized Africans, particularly at the level of the
central colonial administration. Miss Perham in the late thirties
was advocating that no African should be appointed to the
administrative service, which she regarded as an alien super-
structure. Rather they should be encouraged to work with the
native administration. Nigeria was, in the words of Sir Hugh
Clifford, Governor from 1919 to 1925, a 'collection of self-
contained and mutually independent Native States' which the
educated Nigerian had no more business co-ordinating than the
British administration. Thus Nigerians were by and large
excluded from the senior service of government, while a number
of French colonials reached high posts in the administration.
Professor Lucy Mair, writing in 1936 about the status of the
educated African in the French colonies, remarked that:

The assumption which governs the whole attitude of France towards
native development is that French civilisation is necessarily the best
and need only be presented to the intelligent African for him to
adopt it. Once he has done so, no avenue is to be closed to him. If he
proves himself capable of assimilating French education, he may
enter any profession, may rise to the dignity of Under-Secretary for
the Colonies, and will be received as an equal by French society.
This attitude towards the educated native arouses the bitter envy of
his counterpart in neighbouring British colonies.

Jean Daniel Meyer in *Desert Doctor* (London, 1960) writes of his
experiences in French Soudan in the Army Colonial Medical
Service before the Second World War: 'My colleague was a
full-blooded Senegalese. He had studied medicine in France,
attending the Bordeaux Naval School, and had the rank of
lieutenant.' Fifth, the African colonies were considered economic extensions of the metropolitan country, and as Albert
Sarraut insisted in his *La Mise en valeur de nos colonies* (Paris,
1923) the colonies should provide assistance to France in the
form of raw materials for her industry, and, in addition to this,
troops in time of war, in return for which the African would

benefit from French civilization. Colonial policy in the inter-war period was to be 'a doctrine of colonisation starting from a conception of power or profit for the metropolis, but instinctively impregnated with altruism'.

Finally it was at the level of the political officer himself that the tendency to assimilation so often manifested itself. Whatever official colonial policy may have been concerning the status of chiefs and the necessity to respect indigenous institutions, it is clear that the majority of French political officers believed sincerely in the French civilizing mission and that it was their role to bring 'enlightenment' to the African. They certainly did not believe that indigenous culture or institutions had anything of value to offer except as a stop-gap. L. Gray Cowan writing in 1958 observed: 'The young *chef de subdivision* in bush is still a proponent of assimilation through the very fact of his education as a Frenchman although it is no longer a part of official policy.' The administrator from republican France, particularly in the inter-war period, had little time for the notion of chiefs holding power other than that derived from the administration itself. This provides a marked contrast with the average British administrator, who believed sincerely that for Africans their own traditional methods of government were the most suitable, provided they were shorn of certain features that did not correspond to his sense of justice. Coming from a country which still maintained a monarchy that had done little to democratize itself on the lines of the Scandinavian monarchies, he had a basic respect for the institution of kingship and the panoply of ritual that surrounded it. The British officer respected his chief as separate but equal, though certainly not somebody with whom he could establish personal social relations. It was the educated African before whom he felt uneasy. Indeed many political officers openly expressed their contempt for the 'savvy boy' or 'trousered African'. In Nigeria, even as late as 1954, one could hear such epithets used by Northern political officers about Southern politicians. The African's place was in the Emir's court, not at Lincoln's Inn or Oxford.

The French political officer, on the other hand, was able to establish relationships with the educated African. M. Delavignette has published in *L'Afrique noire et son destin* (1962) a revealing letter which he received from Ouezzin-Coulibaly, late

Prime Minister of Upper Volta, in 1939, concerning his application for French citizenship. Ouezzin-Coulibaly, then a young teacher in Upper Volta, had been friendly with Delavignette at that time for some ten years and expresses his devotion to France and her cause in the war in the warmest terms:

J'ai été à Sindou et c'est là que la nouvelle de la mobilisation m'est parvenue le 29 Août 1939. J'ai pu admirer dans ce coin de brousse l'affection que les indigènes portent à la France. Le mouvement s'est opéré en silence et avec une rapidité qui suppose une certaine compréhension de devoir. J'en ai été émerveillé et cela c'est votre œuvre, c'est l'œuvre de tous ceux qui ont passé par là et qui ont inculqué au paysan indigène, qu'on fruste à tort, l'idée de la France et de la Patrie.

It would be difficult to find such an intimate relationship between a British political officer and a Nigerian teacher at that period. Even as late as 1954, such contact would have been rare. It would be interesting to make a comparison of the philosophy of the colonial service training courses of France, which were much longer established, with that of the British Devonshire courses.

In conclusion, the differences between the French and British systems of administration in Africa were not only differences in degree but in kind. Both may have used chiefs, but the position of the chief in each system was radically different. The basis for these differences may be sought in the fact that though assimilation as an official policy was abandoned after the early experiment in Senegal, it continued to be a most important inspiration both for the *politique d'association* and for the political officer charged with carrying it out. An understanding of the nature of these differences is not only essential to an understanding of colonial history in Africa, but also to an appreciation of the differences between the two main language blocks in independent Africa today.

32. Early exploitation in the south

G. V. DOXEY *The Industrial Colour Bar in South Africa* Oxford University Press, Cape Town 1961; pages 6–11

Historical Background Prior to 1870

The coming of the European to South Africa was not so much design as the result of the opportunities of geography. It had been the aim of all adventurer explorers from the Middle Ages onwards to discover a sea route to the East and open up a new and safer means of conducting the lucrative Eastern trade in spices and rare silks than by the long, arduous and dangerous land route of the Middle East. The discovery of the West Indies, and for that matter of the Americas as a whole, had been a by-product of this quest, and the Cape of Good Hope was no exception. Africa was the unknown continent and was to remain so until the second half of the nineteenth century. Vast deserts separated the Mediterranean coast-line from the unknown south and on the whole the coast of Africa was forbidding and uninviting. Although legend held that the Phoenicians had sailed their frail craft down the coast of Africa and round its southern shores, few believed that in this direction lay the answer to the quest for an easy route to the East.

It was the Portuguese, at the height of their maritime and commercial supremacy, who eventually turned legend into fact by sailing past what they named the Cape of Storms and reaching India by way of the Indian Ocean. Later, the Dutch and the English followed suit, but few ventured beyond a momentary stay at the Cape itself. However, in 1652, the Dutch East India Company first made use of the possibilities of the Cape of Storms, by then known as the Cape of Good Hope, as a provisioning point and strategic base, and from then onwards the southern part of the African continent was brought within the orbit of European life.

The Dutch were not interested in founding a colony, and the officials who were sent to establish the base were instructed to avoid giving the impression to any indigenous inhabitants they encountered that they had come with the object of colonizing. Nevertheless, from the beginning, the force of circumstances militated against the achievement of these aims and the avoidance of contact between whites and the indigenous Bushmen and Hottentots proved impossible in practice. Thus from the very earliest days, the race problem in South Africa revealed a divergence between what was considered desirable and what was to prove possible.

In spite of the efforts of the Company, and later of the Dutch authorities, to contain the area of white settlement within the effective jurisdiction of the Cape Peninsula, its range was consistently extended and contact with the indigenous inhabitants became greater with the widening of the moving frontier.

By the time the British finally took over the Cape in 1806, South African society had begun to assume many of its contemporary forms. Among most whites there had already developed the illusion of a 'white' country and a refusal to admit to the reality of multi-racialism. Henceforth South African history was to be characterized by the schisms of race. Even the whites were no longer a homogeneous group, for while the French Huguenot settlers of 1688 were to be completely absorbed by Boer culture and language, the British settlers retained their identity and it was the Boer who felt the need to preserve language and heritage against the new-comers. As far as the non-whites were concerned, they found they were unwanted in the new society except for the labour they could provide and when physical frontiers between white and non-white disappeared, the artificial barriers of the colour bar were gradually erected to take their place.

The primitive Bushmen, who with the Hottentots had roamed around what is now the western Cape, proved unable to resist the advance of white settlement and by 1870 they had virtually disappeared. The Hottentots as nomadic pastoralists had not taken kindly to white settlement which threatened their coastal grazing-lands and denied them safety from the marauding Bushmen. Yet by 1800 the frontier had spread to the Fish River, with the Hottentots reduced in numbers and effectiveness through smallpox and white man's liquor. By this stage, however, in the eastern Cape contact had been firmly made with the Bantu tribes, who for several centuries had been making their way through Africa in a south-easterly direction.

The whites had begun to evolve distinct characteristics moulded by the nature of the country and the new society. In the settled areas in and around Cape Town the institution of slavery enabled them to enjoy an existence free from the burden of manual work. Even though slavery at the Cape manifested few of the excesses which characterized it elsewhere, it played a significant part in moulding the attitudes of white South Africans to manual labour and in fostering colour prejudice. The uncivilized heathen non-whites were looked upon as inferior and it was natural that slavery should have reinforced this attitude.

The first slaves had been introduced soon after the arrival of van Riebeeck and his party in 1652. The founder of the settlement had lost no time in asking for slaves to be sent to the Cape —his first request was sent to the Company within six weeks of his arrival—and it is interesting to note that he also advocated the importation of Chinese labourers.

Within a hundred years of van Riebeeck's arrival, the institution of slavery had made an important impact on the whole way of life at the Cape, where the majority of the slaves were concentrated. Further east, existence on the frontier was vastly different: the leisurely, settled plantation existence gave way to a simple, rough way of life which was to mould a race of men, self-reliant, hardy, and resentful of attempts to govern them. It was largely from this type of pioneer that the trekkers of 1836 were drawn.

The nature of the Bantu tribes encountered by the frontiersmen reinforced ideas of racial superiority, and the bitter conflicts with the black people in the eastern Cape served to intensify dislike of British policy which aimed at the gradual assimilation of the races into a common society. From this resentment sprang the idea of the trek, and the famous Retief manifesto which became the guiding light of the Boer people. The bloody wars between Boer and Bantu in the Orange Free State and Natal which followed the trek provided the legends on which young Afrikanerdom was reared. It is common practice today for exponents of apartheid to compare the 'struggle for western civilization' with the exploits of the Voortrekkers against the Bantu. The interior of southern Africa was thus opened up by people firmly convinced of colour inferiority. There was little scope for the ideas of J. J. Rousseau, or for those of the later missionaries who taught brotherly love and equality before God. Nevertheless, where servants were concerned, the attitude of the Boers was strict and paternal rather than harshly domineering.

After 1806 the British were content to remain in the coastal areas: the settlers of 1820 were placed on the eastern frontier and after the annexation of Natal to the Crown in 1843, that territory gradually became anglicized. With the spread of the white frontier, the various Bantu tribes constituting the African population were progressively contained in those parts of the country which came to be known as the Native Reserves. The so-called 'Native Reserves' are today grouped as follows: (1) the Ciskei; (2) the Transkei; (3) the British Bechuanaland Reserves; (4) the Natal Reserves; (5) Zululand; (6) the Transvaal Reserves; (7) the Orange Free State Reserves.

The Coloured People

Slavery was abolished in 1834 and the Hottentots gradually merged with the former slaves to form the Coloured population. The majority of the slaves had come from the East (the Moslem religion has been retained to this day by the Cape Malays who in many respects form a distinct sub-group in the Coloured community). Miscegenation between whites and slaves added to the Coloured population which later was further increased by racial mingling with the Bantu. The majority of the Coloured people worked on the farms or as domestic servants, but many were skilled craftsmen—a tradition which has been maintained through the years.

The Indian Population

The coming of the Indian to South Africa is closely linked with the development of sugar-cane cultivation in Natal in the first half of the nineteenth century. The Zulu proved unwilling to leave the Reserves to work on the plantations and, in spite of attempts to force him to do so, white planters continued to experience a shortage of labourers. Indentured labour had proved a satisfactory substitute for slavery for sugar-planters in Mauritius and elsewhere, and it was only a matter of time before Natal followed suit.

Negotiations began in 1856 for the importation of Indian coolies but it was not until 1859 that the Indian Government finally agreed to an experimental importation. The Indians were brought to Natal at the expense of the authorities and indentured for three years. Employers paid wages of 10s. a month, plus food and lodging, increasing to 12s. in the third year. They had, in addition, to repay the expenses of transporting the Indians.

The first Indians arrived towards the end of 1860 and by 1865 there were well over 6,000 at work. The indentured Indians were mainly low-caste Hindus, but these were soon augmented by the arrival of wealthier and more cultured traders, largely Moslem. As a group, the Indians were to play a significant role in the economic development of Natal, not only in the sugar industry but in coal-mining, agriculture and trade generally. The importation of indentured workers was stopped in 1911, while Act No. 22 of 1913 (the Immigration Legislation Act) gave the Minister of the Interior wide powers to prohibit the entry into the country of persons deemed undesirable and to restrict their internal movement. As will be seen, the restrictions placed on Indians have widened considerably since that date.

The Pre-Industrial Society

By 1870, political boundaries were being finally drawn; the Republics of the Transvaal and the Orange Free State were in being, while the Cape was to be granted responsible government under the British Crown in 1872. Natal was moving in the same direction, and was granted the same status in 1893.

In the economic sphere, agriculture was the mainstay of the whole country: in the Cape, wool had superseded wine as the chief export, and in Natal the sugar industry was becoming predominant. The diamond discoveries of 1869 were to have immediate consequences. They came at a time when agriculture was in the throes of a recession and when the Cape stood to lose much as a result of the opening of the Suez Canal. Yet these immediate, windfall advantages were to be far surpassed by the long-term benefits. With the discovery of diamonds came South Africa's first industrial society and, with it, the problem of the industrial colour bar.

33. Central Africa: the dart of the tongue

PHILIP MASON *The Birth of a Dilemma* Oxford University Press 1958; pages 135–45

Lobengula had in the eyes of his people repudiated the Concession in September of 1889; the Charter, which proceeded from the Concession, was signed in October as the result of a set of forces and personalities operating in London with little knowledge of what was happening in Bulawayo. On the general situation, Moffat, anxious and divided, again provides the commentary; he had written a year earlier:

The Matabele . . . have the notion that they are the people and that they can fight the Boers or even the English. The Chief knows better but he is hampered by the ignorance of his people. It is a problem which occupies my thoughts night and day, how we are to avoid the impending collision. . . . To me the only solution of the difficulty is the breaking up of this tribe, but I should be sorry to be the intermediary, for sooner or later I should have to be the herald of war and not of peace. . . . There is some talk of the whole tribe migrating to the north side of the Zambezi; I hope not, for that simply means carrying thither the same murderous system which they have carried out here—the ruthless harrying of tribe after tribe till there is nothing left but a succession of vast solitudes, which the Matabele neither occupy themselves nor allow others to occupy.

That is the essence of the situation from the Matabele angle. To it may be added on the other side a letter written in March of 1890 by the Secretary of the British South Africa Company to the Imperial Secretary, that is, to the High Commissioner at Cape Town.

Mr. Rhodes [he wrote on 18 March] has for some time felt that to assure the position of the Chartered Company it is necessary to obtain effective possession of Mashonaland in the coming winter [that is, April–September 1890]. He is very strongly of the opinion that this object could not be considered to be obtained merely by sending in one or two prospecting parties and that it is of the utmost importance to form, at as early a date as possible, a substantial nucleus of white population in the country. For this purpose, he does not consider 150 at all an excessive number.

This is the background to all that followed.

The news of the Charter did not reach Matabeleland till the end of January; meanwhile, into the mounting anger and fear of Bulawayo came Dr Jameson. He was a man whose gaiety and ready tongue gave him a charm that can be felt across the years; quick in decision, gallant in action, his personality must have cured his patients as often as his technical skill; even in the posed daguerreotypes of the times, his face is at once sensitive and impulsive, yet his actions show him free from doubts, resolute in the course he was committed to. Lack of patience and over-confidence were later his undoing, but at this stage he was patient in negotiation. Jameson was in Bulawayo by 17 October, before the Charter was actually signed, bringing back with him Thompson and also Sam Edwards, for whom Lobengula had a particular regard. He put the original concession into Lobengula's hands and once again explained it to him clause by clause. The chief now took the line that he had not meant to give a general concession, but only 'one hole to dig in'; the only general part of the agreement was that no one else should have a hole to dig in at all, while Rhodes must ask for each hole, one at a time. During the weeks that followed, it seems to have been Jameson's policy to maintain the Concession but not to insist on it; he would resist any attempt to substitute a less sweeping agreement, but in practice would rather slur over its general provisions and concentrate for the moment on getting permission to 'dig in one hole', and thus to implement it in the eyes of English lawyers.

Into this pool, already turbulent enough, fell one more stone, the news that the Portuguese were trying to extend their influence along the Zambezi by building forts and giving flags to chiefs in Mashonaland. Lobengula dictated a protest: 'I send three messengers with this letter to ask you by what authority you are doing this in a country which belongs to me.' Then, remembering the Moffat Treaty, he sent on 22 December a quite inconsistent message to Cape Town: 'Lo Bengula is not in direct communication with the Portuguese Government; he therefore requests Your Excellency to move Her Majesty's Government and bring to an end these infringements of the territory of a friendly chief.' This incursion increased the general atmosphere of suspicion that was directed against all Europeans, but must on the whole have helped Jameson to persuade

Lobengula that he had to make a choice between evils and that the Company was the least of these. At any rate, he obtained permission to start prospecting to the south of Bulawayo. And a few days later Renny-Tailyour and others who asked for permission to dig were referred to Jameson; the rifles which were part of the payment were put into a store on Lobengula's account; he did not protest and Cooper-Chadwick was appointed to look after them. The Concession was thus, by implication and somewhat half-heartedly, reinstated during December.

By the end of January, the news that the Charter had been signed reached Matabeleland, together with Lord Knutsford's letter of 15 November containing the Queen's advice to Lobengula to deal with the Chartered Company only. The letter was brought by a Captain and a Surgeon-Major of the Royal Horse Guards, with the Corporal-Major of the Regiment and a trooper. The stature, uniform, and accoutrements of this escort were perhaps intended to distract attention from the contents of the letter and in this to some extent they succeeded. Lobengula was interested and impressed; 'he took off and handled one of the cuirasses, asked them to go through the sword exercise, and, in inviting them to attend the "Great Dance" . . . made a point of their appearing in full panoply'. The atmosphere created was favourable; Jameson asked for another indaba a few days later, told Lobengula that the hole he had dug in the south showed no payable gold and said he did not want to extend his digging towards Bulawayo for fear of disturbing Matabele villages. 'Then you had better go somewhere else,' said the chief. Jameson asked if he might go east. The chief agreed; he was shown a map on which had been drawn a route planned by Selous, skirting Matabeleland and leading into the Mazoe country in Central Mashonaland. Might Selous have some of Lobengula's men to cut a road for the wagons? Yes, he might. But, went on Lobengula, making a last dart from the shadow of the landing-net like an exhausted fish, 'go and find out where you want to make your road and then come to me and I will give you the men to make it'.

This was enough. Jameson left on 14 February and by 20 February Sir Henry Loch (who had succeeded Sir Hercules at Cape Town) passed on to Lord Knutsford a telegram that he had received from Rhodes: 'Lo Bengula has sanctioned our occupation of Mashonaland. . . .' This was, quite simply, not true; he had sanctioned the Company's digging in Mashonaland for gold. Sir Henry, however, naturally took the telegram at its face value; he referred to a rumour of an incursion from the South African Republic into Mashonaland; he had already been instructed to warn President Kruger that this would be regarded as an infringement of the Queen's Protectorate. He continued to Lord Knutsford: 'I consider it will be impossible to prevent a rush to Mashonaland goldfield unless British South Africa Company are allowed to anticipate such a move-ment. . . . I earnestly trust that the time and responsibility for giving sanction may be left to me.' Lord Knutsford consulted Lord Salisbury at the Foreign Office. The Foreign Office replied on 7 March 1890: 'His Lordship considers that it would be dangerous to withhold much longer from the High Com-missioner authority to sanction the advance of the Company's armed police force into Mashonaland.' And on 10 March, Lord Knutsford gave the High Commissioner the authority he sought.

Thus a concession which gave Rudd and his colleagues per-mission to mine had been used to obtain a Charter which authorized them to exercise any sovereign rights which might be conceded to them. None had been conceded except at Tati; Moffat's right to try British subjects had so far been assumed without discussion. Permission to dig in Mashonaland had been reported as permission to occupy, and on that report the Secretary of State had empowered the High Commissioner to slip the leash when he judged the moment had come.

Sir Henry Loch, the High Commissioner, was not however immediately satisfied. Preparations for the march of the Pioneers and the occupation of Mashonaland had begun as far back as October of 1889, but Sir Henry understood the legal situation very clearly and had written to the Company:

it will of course be very important, before introducing such a force into Matabeleland . . . to ascertain clearly that its presence there will be acceptable to Lo Bengula. . . . The Company no doubt under-stands that the Concession above referred to does not confer such powers of government or administration as are mentioned in clauses

3 and 4 of the Charter. Those powers will have to be obtained whenever a proper and favourable time for approaching Lo Bengula on the subject arrives.

That time had come and in February 1890 it had been reported that the chief had sanctioned the occupation of Mashonaland, but both the High Commissioner and the Company were aware that it had been a somewhat grudging sanction. This was the more dangerous because the High Commissioner had been misled as to what had been sanctioned. 'It was feared', writes Mr Hole, 'that he [Lobengula] might upset the contemplated expedition by sending objections to the High Commissioner.' So Jameson went back to Bulawayo in April.

He now explained the scope of the expedition. There would be 100 wagonloads of provisions and mining-tools; there would be a detachment of police—to Lobengula indistinguishable from soldiers—to protect the Pioneers. There can be no doubt that Lobengula saw what this meant; he raised every objection he could think of, but to all Jameson found an answer. 'Against whom,' Lobengula asked, 'are these workers to be protected?' 'Against the Boers,' was the doctor's reply, 'against the Portuguese, against anyone else who might molest them.' A much less intelligent man than Lobengula could guess who that 'anyone else' was expected to be; nor could he believe the precaution unreasonable. At last Jameson felt he had no hope of getting further; he announced that he was going and on the last morning, his horses saddled, went to say good-bye to the King.

There was a respect, indeed a guarded liking, between these two men. Lobengula had responded to Jameson's doctoring of his gout and to the gaiety and frankness; he showed again and again that he distinguished between such a man as this and those thinking only of their pockets. On Jameson's side, there lay, beneath the bantering good-humoured firmness that it was proper to display towards a native potentate, a genuine understanding of the King's dilemma; he had, too, a share of the feeling, wide-spread among Europeans, that it was a pity Rhodes could not get his way without causing so much embarrassment to Lobengula, 'who wouldn't be so bad an old buffer if it weren't for the Matjaha'. There was no doubt of his embarrassment today:

The door of the Chief's hut was in two portions, an upper and a lower, and leaning over the lower half he had his last and final interview. The old King was stark naked, somewhat agitated—an unwieldy mass of dark copper-coloured flesh moving restlessly up and down within the dim, uncertain light of the hut.

'Well, King,' said Jameson, 'as you will not confirm your promise and grant me the road, I shall bring my white *impi* and if necessary we shall fight.'

Lobengula replied: 'I never refused the road to you and to your *impi*.'

'Very well,' said Jameson, 'then you acknowledge that you have promised to grant me the road and unless you refuse now, your promise holds good.' Then as the King remained diplomatically silent, Jameson said: 'Good-bye, Chief, you have given your promise about the road and on the strength of that promise I shall bring in my *impi* to Mashonaland'—and he left.

So it was done; an unwilling half-consent from a King who knew that his people were against him, but who realized better than they the consequences of refusal, who believed Jameson's clear statement that his *impi* would come with or without consent and fight if need be.

I know very well [Moffat had written just a year before] that nothing is further from the thoughts of either Chiefs or people than the introduction into any part of their country of a colonizing population. However desirable such a result might appear to us, to the natives it means only one thing, which they have seen . . . over and over . . . further south; it means that the white man having once got one foot planted firmly on their land will soon have both feet on it . . . till he becomes the owner of all the land and the native has become a squatter on sufferance in his own country.

That this was indeed Lobengula's view is clear from what followed when the Pioneer column began to collect on the Macloutsie River. He wrote to Loch a letter for the Queen:

When we joined together, why do you send your *impi*? Rhodes . . . paid me money for which I gave him a piece of ground. . . . If you have heard that I have given my whole country to Rhodes, it is not my words. I have not done so. Rhodes wants to take my country by strength. . . . Your words were, I was to send to you when I was troubled by white men. I am now in trouble. . . .

Loch replied on 4 August:

The Queen assures Lo Bengula that the men assembled by the British South Africa Company were not assembled for the purpose of attacking him, but on the contrary were assembled for a peaceful object, namely searching for gold. . . . They were ordered to travel at a distance from the Matabele kraals and always to recollect that Lo Bengula is the friend of the Queen and that the Queen wishes to maintain peace and friendship with Lo Bengula.

The march of the Pioneers is a story for another chapter. Here it is necessary to complete this account of the chameleon's step-by-step advance with emphasis on the legal aspect: the realities beneath the formal moves are another matter. On 6 June 1890, the Imperial Secretary wrote to the Secretary of the British South Africa Company:

Having carefully considered the political position the Governor and High Commissioner considers the time has arrived to give his consent to the entry of the Company's forces into Mashonaland by the route already agreed upon—that is to say, by a route that will skirt Matabeleland proper and leave all Matabele kraals to the north and west of the expeditionary force. . . . The object to be attained is the peaceful occupation of Mashonaland, and it is desirable that all officers should be instructed to be most careful and prudent in the treatment of the natives . . . and to respect their prejudices and susceptibilities. . . .

On 27 June, the Pioneers crossed the Macloutsie River and on the 30th were met by a party of Matabele with a letter from Lobengula: 'Has the King killed any white men that an *impi* is collecting on his border? Or have the white men lost anything they are looking for?'

To this Jameson replied that this was a working-party, protected by soldiers, who were 'going to Mashonaland along the road already arranged with the King'. The column waited some days for stores, then forded the Shashi on 11 July and the advance proper began. On 6 August another protest was received from Lobengula—alleging that Jameson had agreed to dig only in specified places, that the only place authorized had been near Tati, and that Jameson had misunderstood him when he said good-bye in April. To this the inept reply—sent not by Jameson but by Pennefather, commanding the police—was that the column must march on in accordance with the Queen's orders.

Colenbrander, who brought this letter, was Lobengula's agent, but he felt more at home with the Pioneer column than with the indunas who had been his companions; he talked freely to the Pioneers and gave them his opinion that Lobengula had sent his letter as a move in internal politics, to gain time with the warriors, and did not expect it to have any effect on the movements of the column. The answer, however, abandoned the legal fiction of Lobengula's willing consent and brought in the Crown directly. The Pioneers, it will be seen, had no use for legal fictions. On 12 September, at Fort Salisbury, the Union Jack was hoisted, a salute fired, and 'possession taken of Mashonaland in the name of the Queen'.

The Pioneers had come to occupy Mashonaland. They had each been promised fifteen gold claims and a 3,000-acre farm; the notion that the expedition was intended only to 'dig in one hole' had been reserved for correspondence with Lobengula. But the Pioneers' act in 'taking possession' of Mashonaland was not recognized by the Crown; indeed, it was felt in Cape Town and Whitehall that the next step was to get Lobengula's formal consent to the Company's exercising jurisdiction over Europeans in his territory—a right blandly assumed in the Queen's letter of 15 November 1889. Just a year later, in November 1890, Moffat presented the King with a document that would give the Company this authority and at this Lobengula 'entered at length into the whole question of the concession', protesting that he had never meant to give such a concession and that if he had, it was Lotje's fault, that he had clearly repudiated the concession and given Jameson leave only to 'dig in one hole', that the column should have come to Bulawayo before going to Mashonaland, and—a final grievance—that the High Commissioner and Rhodes had come to the borders of his country without coming to see him. On 1 January 1891, he wrote to the Governor:

Mr. Moffat has asked me to give Mr. Rhodes power to punish those who do wrong in Mashonaland. They ask for this now but they went into my country without doing so. Why do they come now and ask? When did we speak on this matter? Did not the Queen say that I should not give all my herd of cattle to one man? Have I given all my land to the people now in Mashonaland? Who has got the herd to kill today?

ZNA

On 13 April 1891, the High Commissioner proclaimed that 'The country North and West of the South African Republic, West of the Portuguese dominions, and East of the German sphere of influence falls within the British sphere of influence', and that anyone entering this territory with a view to the occupation of land must observe the rules and regulations established by the Company. Ten days later, on 23 April, the Colonial Office told the Foreign Office that Sir Henry Loch had communicated to Lobengula 'his intention to govern and punish the whites in his [Lobengula's] country' and that there was therefore 'ground for assuming the existence of "sufferance" ' on the part of Lobengula, this giving Her Majesty jurisdiction in his country within the meaning of the Foreign Jurisdiction Act of 1890. Next came the Order in Council of 9 May 1891. 'Whereas', it began, the territories of the Charter are 'under the protection of Her Majesty', and 'whereas . . . Her Majesty has power and jurisdiction in the said territories', the High Commissioner may 'from time to time, by Proclamation, provide for the administration of justice, the raising of revenue, and generally for the peace, order and good government of all persons within the limits of this Order. . . .' There followed the High Commissioner's proclamation of 10 June 1891, by which he empowered himself to appoint Resident Commissioners, Inspectors of Police, and Magistrates. It was under this proclamation that Dr Jameson was gazetted Chief Magistrate of Mashonaland on 18 September 1891.

But the Queen's jurisdiction was based on Lobengula's supposed 'sufferance', and he was in fact protesting as vigorously as words would permit. 'There is no probability,' Sir Henry Loch had told Lord Knutsford on 20 November 1890, 'of Lo Bengula granting any concession of jurisdiction.' His sufferance perhaps lay in his holding back his young men from fighting, perhaps in his own knowledge that words would do no good.

When Duke William of Normandy landed in England, he professed to be claiming what was his own, and there was talk of an oath Harold had sworn renouncing his Kingdom. But William has always been known as the Conqueror; his true claim to England was established at Hastings by the sword—and a very good thing for England it turned out to be. Mzilikazi took Matabeleland by the sharp blades of his assegais, and held it by the same title-deeds. In the events that have just been related, an elaborate structure of legality was erected, mainly for the satisfaction of English public opinion. It rested on the fiction of Lobengula's consent. But though Lobengula delegated certain sovereign powers at Tati, nowhere else did he cede or even delegate any authority that had to do with sovereignty. 'Leave to dig' was all he gave; even that was only wrested from him by Jameson's clear threat of force. In the whole series of transactions, only Rhodes and Lobengula are consistent, Rhodes in a conviction that he was 'under an obligation to develop and open up to civilization that part of the country dominated over, not inhabited by the Matabele', Lobengula in a determination to cede no sovereignty but to avoid war, to give up the least that would enable him to keep what remained.

Lobengula could not adopt the policy of Khama, who had unreservedly allied himself to England; his people would not have let him and in any case the whole nature of his state forbade it; there was no room in the *pax Britannica* for a people who lived by raiding their neighbours. He was accused by Europeans of being vacillating and unreliable, but in truth he was like a hooked salmon trying to take out as much line as he could whenever the chance came. The charge of inconsistency might as truthfully be preferred against the salmon, which strives to avoid the gaff and comes towards it only when compelled. And Lobengula proved himself a noble salmon who put up a good fight.

VIII. ETHIOPIA IN THE NINETEENTH CENTURY

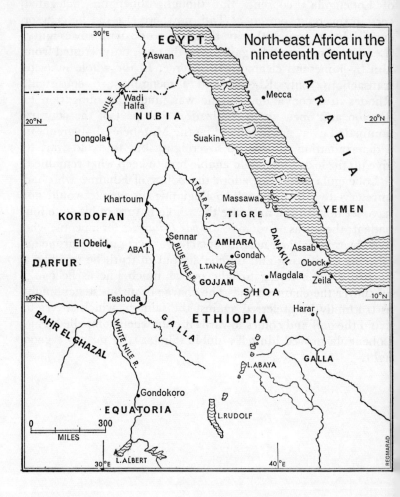

North-east Africa in the nineteenth century

34. Aspects of the survival of Ethiopian independence 1840-1896[1]

SVEN RUBENSON *University College Review*, Addis Ababa 1961;
pages 253, 254-5, 256-9, 261-4

There is one question that seems sooner or later to present itself
to every historian or politically interested person who has to
deal with Ethiopia and its place in Africa today. How did it
happen that Ethiopia as the only old state in Africa preserved
its independence throughout the era of European colonization?
Why did Ethiopia alone survive the 'Scramble for Africa' as a
free nation?

The fact that Ethiopia managed to preserve its independence
through the decades of the 'Scramble' and only suffered five
years of military occupation as an opening chapter to the
Second World War when the tide in Africa was already turning
has naturally influenced the character and outlook of the
Ethiopian people. Ethiopia has something of a unique position
in Africa. It is as true in the historical as in the geographical
sphere that Ethiopia lies neither north nor south of the Sahara.
But the uniqueness of Ethiopia's position in Africa today has
probably more to do with the history of the last century than
with geographical and ethnic considerations. Ethiopians have
barely tasted experiences which have been the daily bread of
other Africans for many decades. In the re-awaking, the
reorganization of Africa today, there is therefore a sense in
which Ethiopia stands alone.

What this actually means, why it is so, depends on the reply
to the question above about the survival of Ethiopian independence.

This question has hardly received a complete or satisfactory
answer yet. The replies most readily found are somewhat
general. They refer to the fact that Ethiopia is an old Christian
country with an ancient culture and common traditions and
history which have made its people conscious of themselves
and their common cause. I do not deny that there may be truth

[1] This article consists of extracts from a paper originally contributed
to *Historians in Tropical Africa. Proceedings of the Leverhulme Inter-Collegiate
History Conference*, held at the University College of Rhodesia and Nyasaland,
Salisbury (published 1962).

in these general explanations, but they often have a tendency to obscure more than they reveal. Only by a careful study of the events of the period do we come close to the solutions.

The factors which played an important role in Ethiopia's successful struggle to maintain its independence can, I believe, be divided into three categories: firstly, diplomatic, political, and military conditions on the European side; secondly, the actual political and military conditions in Ethiopia; thirdly, the serious and repeated miscalculations of Ethiopia's strength by its 'protectors' and invaders. . . .

In Ethiopia two centuries of almost complete isolation were slowly coming to an end during the first half of the nineteenth century. Explorers in numbers unknown before travelled through the country, and Catholic as well as Protestant missions were established there. In the 1840s France and England opened competing consulates at Massawa. France concentrated mainly on bringing the rulers of the province of Tigre under her influence. England sent diplomatic missions farther inland to King Sahle Sillase of Shewa and Ras Ali of Gonder, with whom commercial treaties were negotiated in 1841 and 1849 respectively. European penetration and Egyptian expansion under Mohammed Ali and his successors began to be a menace to the independence of the old, but weak and disunited empire. There was hardly any reason to expect that Ethiopia would avoid the fate awaiting Africa as a whole.

In the person of Tewodros II, Ethiopia, however, in 1855 received a powerful and gifted ruler. He seemed to come from nowhere. But in a couple of years he had swept away all the old feudal princes and himself replaced the last puppet emperor of the Solomonian line at Gonder. His unification programme included reforms to limit the power of local chiefs and centralize the administration and the control over the army. His large army, intended in the first place to pacify the country and later for a campaign against the 'Turks', i.e. the Egyptians, necessitated a larger state income, and Tewodros was not prepared to leave even the old privileges of the land-owning church untouched.

With regard to foreign relations, Tewodros responded favourably to European approaches. But there was in his mind no thought of accepting any kind of foreign protection. It is significant that he saw the importance of making all consular representations reciprocal. This and an attempt to awaken the interests of European powers in his planned campaign against Egypt were his aims in sending Consul Cameron and M. Bardel to London and Paris respectively in November 1862. In its reply the French Government avoided the issue and instead indirectly upbraided Tewodros for having expelled Catholic missionaries from Ethiopia. From the British Government came no reply at all, a fact which greatly contributed to the rise of the Ethio-British conflict, which in its turn ultimately led to the British expedition of 1868. Thus, Tewodros' attempt to give his people a respected place among the nations of the world ended with the catastrophe at Meqdela. . . .

From the viewpoint of Ethiopian history Meqdela as such is but an incident. Probably the respect for European arms and military organization was increased, but then Tewodros himself was fully aware throughout his reign of the importance of modern arms and discipline, so it was certainly nothing new. Instead, the significance of Meqdela seems to lie on the other side. The ease with which the victory was gained was remembered, but the conditions in Ethiopia which made it possible were unknown or gradually forgotten. Consequently, the outcome contributed to a wrong opinion about Ethiopia in political circles in Europe. Why else were all later expeditions into Ethiopia so incredibly insufficient? But this certainly does not mean that Tewodros' reign is insignificant. In spite of his failure to carry out his intentions, some elements in the creation of modern Ethiopia are due to him. First of all he revived the idea of a united empire under one strong, supreme ruler. The Gonderine 'era of the princes' was gone, not to return. The task of unification had begun. Secondly, Tewodros had started the struggle to make Ethiopia diplomatically recognized abroad. His hand was not accepted, and so European consuls and a special ambassador from the Court of St. James ended up in chains. But all his successors immediately approached the British Government asking for recognition as independent rulers and for normal diplomatic relations. Minilik managed to get a consulate at Aden, Yohannis one in London. It may not have meant much to the British Government but it certainly did to Yohannis.

It was during the reign of Yohannis IV (1871–1889) that Ethiopia was to feel for the first time the full pressure of colonial politics and foreign aggression. It is true that Sir Robert Napier withdrew without attempting to secure any British influence in the country. The British Government was very reluctant to have anything to do with Ethiopian affairs for some time. But France remained with its consulate at Massawa, headed by the active and ambitious Swiss Werner Munzinger, explorer, businessman and at times both British and French vice-consul. Farther down the coast, France had purchased the small port of Obock from some local sultan, and Italian interests entered into the area in 1869, when the Società di Navigazione Rubbatino bought the port of Aseb. These ports were, however, too far from Kasa's province to have any direct significance for him, and Minilik's main trade routes to the coast ended farther south at Tajurrah and Zeila.

The main centre of activity was Massawa, which Khedive Ismail had bought from his suzerain in 1865, and the key person in the arising conflicts was Consul Munzinger. Already as French vice-consul he had made several attempts to gain control over parts of Eritrea, particularly the province of Bogos, where he was a great land-owner. He induced Ras Welde Mikael, later so famous, to write to Napoleon III and introduce himself as a prospective ruler of Northern Ethiopia.[1]

When Kasa turned against the Roman Catholic missionaries, Munzinger begged his government to protect them and their followers. But the outcome of the Franco-Prussian war made it necessary for Munzinger to seek other backing if he was to carry out his scheme in the Red Sea area. He had carefully watched the Egyptian policy at Mazzawa and in Eastern Sudan, where Egypt was developing a border in common with Ethiopia and where border incidents were becoming frequent. Now he decided to enter Egyptian service, a decision which is actually the first determining factor in the creation of Eritrea. Instead of protecting European interests against Kasa and at times Kasa's against Egypt, he became the tool of Egyptian expansion. Already after one month as Egyptian governor at Massawa he was ready with his first proposal to Cairo to annex

[1] Archives du Ministère des Affaires Etrangères, Paris (A.E.), *Correspondence politique*, *Massouah*, vol. III.

Bogos, Halhal, and Mareal. Especially if Kasa became engaged with his would-be sovereign Wagshum Gobaze, who had proclaimed himself Emperor at Gonder as Tekle Giyorgis, Bogos should at once be occupied. But then Kasa's victory over Tekle Giyorgis in July 1871 came so suddenly that Munzinger was caught unawares. Only one year later did the plans materialize in an occupation of Bogos and surrounding provinces. Kasa, now Emperor Yohannis, was away in the south, and on his return he contented himself with marching up on the new frontier and sending a special mission to London, Paris, Berlin, and Vienna to protest against the aggression.

He asked for no military protection, but ascertained the rights of Ethiopia to the disputed territory and asked for the 'interference and moral support' of the European powers.[1] War was staved off for three years, during which the Egyptians, however, occupied whatever ports remained along the whole coast of the Red Sea and the Gulf of Aden, thereby profiting from all Ethiopian trade and hindering the import of arms and ammunition. In the summer of 1875 the plans were ready and in October and November four expeditionary forces moved in on Ethiopia from the north and east. The two eastern expeditions, of which one led to the occupation of Harer, were, however, only indirectly a threat against Ethiopia. It was the two northern forces under Munzinger Pasha and a Dane Colonel Ahrendrup that immediately concerned Yohannis. Munzinger was ambushed and killed near Lake Awsa. At the most, one third of his small force managed to reach the coast again. Ahrendrup pushed on with his small army of some 3,000 towards Yohannis' capital Adwa, but met with a crushing defeat at Gundet. About 1,800 lay dead in the valley and the remainder fled, but only a handful reached Massawa. Khedive Ismail understood that he had underestimated his enemy and sent a new force of about 15,000 men under Rhatib Pasha, the commander-in-chief of Egypt's military forces, with an American officer as second in command. His orders were to march on Adwa and force upon Yohannis a battle by which the lost prestige of the Egyptian army could be regained.

The Emperor met the Egyptians at Gura, where a three days'

---

[1] Public Record Office, London, *General Correspondence*, F.O. 1/27B.

battle was fought. Of 5,200 Egyptians involved the first day only 400 returned to their fortified positions intact. The following days were less disastrous, but Rhatib Pasha was happy when he was permitted to evacuate the highlands again.

After years of negotiations, in which General Gordon also was involved, Egyptian-Ethiopian relations were finally normalized by the treaty of Adwa, 3 June 1884, the so-called Hewett treaty. Egypt had to take Great Britain's advice to give up her outlying eastern possessions. The Bogos country was restored to Yohannis for Ethiopia's assistance in saving the Egyptian garrisons there from falling into the hands of the Dervishes. There had been much discussion about giving Yohannis either Massawa or some other port, but the Egyptian Government had refused to negotiate on this condition, and Yohannis was satisfied with 'free transit through Massawa to and from Abyssinia for all goods, including arms and ammunition under British protection'.[1] Whether Massawa remained under Egyptian administration or reverted to the Porte was of little significance to Yohannis, once Egypt's many garrisons on the Ethiopian frontiers were gone and Great Britain had guaranteed Ethiopia access to the outside world through Massawa. It still remained for Yohannis to find out that his friends the British would bring upon his country a worse enemy than Egypt.

By 1882 the Italian Government had taken over Aseb and begun to show interest in its hinterland, particularly Shewa. In the autumn of 1884 it started negotiations with the British Government about taking over the small port of Beilul just north of Aseb, if and when the Egyptian garrison would leave it, or in case some other power, i.e. France, showed interest in it. The Italian Government stressed that it wanted 'a perfect understanding with the cabinet of London'. The British Government took care to safeguard themselves from the accusation of giving 'away that which did not belong to them' and asked Italy to approach the Porte, which had actually received British requests to take over its old ports again. When this had not been done by 22 December, the British Government assured Italy 'that Her Majesty's Government, for

---

[1] Public Record Office, London, *General Correspondence*, 1/30–31 and 93/2.

their part, had no objection to raise against the Italian occupation of some point of the coast between and including Beilul
and Massawa', which under the circumstances amounted to an
invitation.[1]

Thus Massawa was actually offered to the Italians by the
British Government half a year after the Hewett treaty. The
Italians were asked to observe the provisions of the treaty, but
no guarantees for this were required nor was Yohannis informed
of the transfer beforehand. In view of his repeated claims for a
port and the fact that Massawa had been refused to him on the
basis that it was really Turkish and not Egyptian, Yohannis
had good reason for his protests.

Moreover, he was most likely aware that Italy, like Egypt,
would tend to become a more troublesome neighbour than the
Porte had been for centuries. Very soon Italy also blocked the
whole coast and started to advance inland, an advance which
was temporarily stopped by the massacre of a small Italian
force at Dogali in January 1887. The British Government felt
obliged to try to mediate and sent Portal to Yohannis' court. It
now became evident that the British were supporting Italian
claims to all the territories contested between Ethiopia and
Egypt, including Bogos, which the Italians had not yet entered.
This is probably not surprising except from the point of view
that it reveals how little they knew about Yohannis in spite of
all the negotiations in which they had been involved because of
the Ethio-Egyptian conflict. They still thought of him as someone to whom they could offer their good offices and their
protection. But Yohannis would have no more of it:

I can do nothing of all this. By the Treaty made by Admiral
Hewett all the country evacuated by the Egyptians on my frontier
was ceded to me at the instigation of England, and now you come
to ask me to give it up again. . . . As for the complaints they [i.e.,
the Italians] made that they had been badly treated, the fault was
on their side, and they began the quarrel by stopping the Abyssinian
merchants, and by occupying Sahati and Wia. . . . But now on
both sides the horses are bridled and the swords are drawn; my
soldiers, in numbers like the sand, are ready with their spears.[2]

[1] *British and Foreign State Papers*, 1885, Vol. LXXXIX, Egypt No. 14,
p. 58 ff.
[2] F. O. 95/746, G. H. Portal, *My Mission to Abyssinia*, p. 158, 173f.

But Yohannis had other trouble as well. At Adwa he had actually traded one weak enemy, Egypt, for two strong ones, Italy and the Mahdists. He was determined to give in to none, but marched against the Mahdists first, and fell in an otherwise successful battle at Metemma in March 1889. . . .

When the Italians replaced the Egyptians, they also followed the policy of detaching Minilik and Shewa fron Yohannis. They were in a better position than the Egyptians. In the resistance against the latter, the difference in religion was an important factor in raising the population against the invader. Italy offered civilization, trade, and firearms, which Minilik needed for his large conquests of Galla and Sidamo territory. Moreover, no European country had shown open interest in acquiring territory inland before 1885, and the Italian negotiator Antonelli was a capable diplomat. But Minilik was by no means indifferent to what was happening on the coast either. When Yohannis informed him of the Italian occupation of Massawa, Minilik protested to the Italians and asked how they could take such an action without first having agreed with Yohannis.[1] In the following years Antonelli worked arduously with accusations against Yohannis, with promises and gifts to detach Minilik from the Emperor.

In October 1887 this work resulted in a convention of friendship and mutual support. The agreement with Minilik evidently reassured the Italians with regard to their plans of avenging the massacre at Dogali. On the other hand, Minilik was in article 3 assured that the Italians would annex no territory.[2]

There is also no indication that Minilik hoped to benefit from the embarrassment of his sovereign. On the contrary, Minilik made several sincere attempts to mediate between Italy and Yohannis, but failed. In view of the relative independence of the King of Shewa and his never forgotten claims to the imperial throne, Minilik was rather more loyal than one would have expected, in any case far more loyal than the enemies of Ethiopia had hoped.

The common view that Yohannis' reign was a period of

---

[1] *Atti parlamentari. Legislatura XVI. Documenti Diplomatici XV* (*Libro Verde, Etiopia*), p. 191 ff; Cf. *Ministero degli Affari Esteri, L'Italia in Africa. Etiopia–Mar Rosso*, Vol. 1, p. 409 ff.

[2] *Libro Verde*, p. 279 f.

growing disunity in Ethiopia is hardly justified. Within the feudal structure of the empire there seems on the contrary to have been a growing sense of interdependence between the provinces in the struggle against foreign invaders. It was definitely there as a positive force in repelling the attacks of Egyptians and Mahdists. Its final test was the Italian war that ended at Adwa.

Because of Yohannis' death at Metemma it remains an open question whether the friendship between Minilik and Italy could have survived a serious attack on Yohannis or not. Soon after Minilik's proclamation as Emperor the friendship materialized in the treaty of Wichale, 2 May 1889.[1] But the events between that date and the battle of Adwa show that no friendship was possible once Minilik had become aware of Italy's motives in Ethiopia. Antonelli had definitely overreached himself when he attempted to make Ethiopia an Italian protectorate by the mistranslation of an article in a treaty.

Minilik was no man to accept any limitations of his sovereignty. But before he had even discovered the Italian aims in article 17, the friendship was threatened by the Italian frontier policy. At Wichale Minilik had allowed the Italians Massawa and the lowlands occupied in Yohannis' reign as well as a few places on the edge of the highlands. In an additional convention signed at Naples in October it was stated that 'a rectification of the two territories shall be made, taking as a basis the actual state of possession', which meant adjustments in Italian favour, since Italian troops were moving forward all the time.[2] When the convention reached Minilik for ratification, the Italians had reached the Mereb-Bellesa-Muna line, and Antonelli claimed that this was the frontier agreed upon. Minilik refused, and Italy started the old game again but now against Minilik. There was particularly the jealousy between Yohannis' successor in Tigre, Ras Mengesha with his faithful general Alula, and Minilik with his Shewan chiefs, to utilize.

---

[1] *Libro Verde*, p. 434 ff. *Archivio Storico del Ministero degli Affari Esteri*, Roma (A.S.M.A.E.). Trattati, *Etiopia No. 3* with both the Amharic and Italian versions.

[2] A.S.M.A.E., Trattati, *Etiopia No. 4*, English translation in *British and Foreign State Papers*, 1888–1889, Vol. LXXXI, p. 736, f.

The Italian governors in Eritrea negotiated with the northern chiefs, while Antonelli kept on dealing with Minilik at their expense. But evidently the Italians underestimated the ambitions and shrewdness of their counterparts. All they could offer Minilik was more arms and help to subdue Mengesha, which he could do unaided.

Mengesha, being the weaker of the two, was in a sense their natural ally, but then it was actually his and Alula's territory that the Italians were gradually occupying. The most important reason for the Italian failure, however, was certainly the fact that no Ethiopian chief could expect the Italians to grant him what they did not allow Minilik, i.e. the full sovereignty of Ethiopia. It is even doubtful that any Ethiopian prince by 1895 would have been able to command the loyalty of the other great chiefs, if he had himself accepted foreign supremacy.

In spite of this the Italians were still hoping to stop Minilik's advance in 1895 by allying themselves with Ethiopian chiefs. The warnings of Dr Nerrazini, the Italian resident at Harer, that an Italian occupation of Tigre would mean the certainty of war against a united Ethiopia and that 'a war against Ethiopia is a big war', passed unheeded.[1] Both Baratieri and Crispi's government placed their hopes in Ethiopian disunity. Negotiations were kept up or at least attempted with King Teklehaymanot of Gojam, Ras Mikael of Wello, Ras Mekwennin of Harer and, of course, Ras Mengesha, who had been defeated in a premature outbreak of hostilities around New Year 1895. Although Baratieri admitted that 'there was growing up throughout the length and breadth of Ethiopia a kind of negative patriotism', he still hoped to block Minilik's way by a system of alliances from Gojam in the west to Danakil in the east.[2] Even after the first Ethiopian victories at Amba Alagi and Meqele, Baratieri seems to have entertained the idea that Ras Mekwennin or some other great prince would accept a separate peace. It is quite probable that Minilik was kept informed of the Italian approaches to his vassals and generals although the scarcity of known Ethiopian documents makes it impossible to be categorical about this matter. The essential fact is that all the great chiefs participated in the campaign

[1] G. F. H. Berkeley, *The Campaign of Adwa and the Rise of Menelik*, p. 86 f.
[2] Ibid., p. 61.

against the Italians. At Adwa Minilik lined up all of them:
Teklehaymanot, Mikael and Mekwennin, Mengesha and Alula.

It would certainly be a mistake to believe that Minilik by
1896 had completely overcome the internal strife, the jealousies,
and rivalries of the different provincial chiefs. But the growing
menace of foreign interference and aggression had helped
Minilik to carry on the work of establishing his country as a
political and military unit of considerable strength.

Alongside the process of unification went the territorial
expansion in the south and east under the leadership of Minilik,
first as King of Shewa, then as Emperor. As already mentioned,
the original motive for these conquests seems to have been
strategical. Although the new provinces also meant a considerable increase in revenues, the aim of keeping out the European
powers probably remained the major consideration. In a
circular letter in April 1891 Minilik notified the European
powers of his frontiers and added, 'I have no intention of being
an indifferent spectator if far-distant Powers make their appearance with the idea of dividing Africa. . . . As the Almighty has
protected Ethiopia to this day, I am confident that He will
protect and increase her in the future.'[1] The increase was
considerable. By 1896 Ethiopian territory had more than
doubled compared with 1872.

With regard to actual military strength a tremendous
development had taken place. The numbers of soldiers and their
followers had been rather high ever since Tewodros' days.
Figures vary from 50,000 to 100,000 (even more at Gura)
during his and Yohannis' reign with the exception of course
of the army of Meqdela. Minilik's vast conquests necessitated
large armies and also made it possible for him to provide for
them. While Minilik was still King of Shewa and a presumptive
Italian ally, Antonelli in a careful estimation arrived at the
figure of 196,000 for his total forces.[2] But when it came to
meeting him in war, the opinion was that he could in any case
not march more than 30,000 to Tigre. Minilik actually commanded some 80,000 to 120,000 at Adwa. What counted was,
however, the firearms force. Tewodros had probably commanded 10,000 firearms at the most. At Meqdela he had only
2,000 to 3,000 left and they were very inferior compared with

[1] Berkeley, op. cit., p. 35 f.   [2] *Libro Verde*, p. 281 ff.

those of the British troops. He was very proud of his cannon, most of them manufactured in the country, but he had no one to serve them. When the British rewarded Dejach Kasa with 850 rifles and eight cannon in 1868, these were sufficient to turn the scales in his favour in the battle of Asem, where he was out-numbered five to one in man-power by Tekle Giyorgis. Yohannis was landlocked by Egypt and Italy throughout his reign, but he increased his supply by the mostly excellent arms captured at Gundet, 2,200 rifles and 16 cannon; and at Gura, some 8,000 rifles and at least 15 cannon more. Minilik was, in the meantime, in the enviable position of receiving arms for nothing.

Both Egypt and Italy were furnishing him with consignments of arms in the mere hope that they would be used against Yohannis. For his promise of friendship in 1887, for example, Minilik received 5,000 Remingtons. After Minilik had become Emperor the import of firearms increased enormously. Exact numbers are not easy to obtain, but one early Italian account arrives at a total of 189,000 firearms from 1885 to 1895.[1] So sure were the Italians of their new 'protectorate' that they themselves furnished Minilik with arms as gifts as well as with a loan of four million lire, with which Minilik placed orders for arms all over Europe. Arms and ammunition were pouring into Ethiopia particularly through the French port of Obock. By the time the Italians finally grasped the truth that Ethiopia was not their protectorate, Minilik was armed as no Ethiopian ruler before him. He could not only put some 100,000 soldiers in the field, but furnish them all with rifles.

The outcome of the battle of Adwa is well-known. The extent of the Italian disaster is best illustrated by the figures: 17,000 to 18,000 engaged, more than 6,000 dead, 1,500 wounded, about 4,000 prisoners of war. How many Ethiopians were engaged in the battle it is impossible to know, but their losses have been estimated at anything from 4,000 to 10,000 dead and about the same number of wounded.[2] But there were no prisoners of war. The battle-field and the land remained Ethiopian. The

[1] Bourelly, *La Battaglia di Abba Garima*, Appendix D, p. 668 ff. Cf. *Ethiopia—Mar Rosso*, Vol. 1, p. 273 ff. about the earlier consignments.

[2] Berkeley, op. cit., p. 345 f.; Conti Rossini, C., *Italia ed Ethiopia Dal Trattato D'Uccialli alla Battaglia di Adua*, p. 447 ff.

scramble for markets, railways, and influence in Ethiopia continued, but the approach completely changed. Almost overnight the European powers accepted the fact that Minilik was the ruler of a sovereign state and had to be dealt with as such in all affairs concerning his country. This is why Adwa is so important in Ethiopian history; this is why it belongs as much to the twentieth as to the nineteenth century.

The unique position of Ethiopia in Africa does not mean that it was deliberately spared by the European powers. On the contrary, Ethiopia was not treated differently from other African territories. There was no lack of determination in the plans of Egypt and Italy. Egypt finally obtained a free hand and many European and American officers and advisers participated on her side. Italy entered the scene with the full blessing of the British Government. Although she could expect no military support, she did have the moral support of most European countries, and no one would have stopped her had Minilik failed to do so. Britain, France, Italy—all thought in terms of 'spheres of influence' in the colonial sense. The concept of an independent African state was simply becoming obsolete. How far it had gone in Ethiopia's case is evident from the fact that Ethiopia had disappeared as a country from both British and French maps in the years before the battle of Adwa. The first and second editions of Hertslet's 'Map of Africa by Treaty' show it as Italian; 'Carte generale des possessions françaises en Afrique au premier Janvier 1895' shows it as French. There is a sense, therefore, in which the old saying that the defeat of the Italians at Adwa put Ethiopia on the map of the world is true.

But the Ethiopian victory should not have been so unexpected. Ancient Ethiopia had for forty years been involved in a process of placing herself on the map of modern Africa. Under the determined leadership of the emperors Tewodros, Yohannis, and Minilik, and under the constant pressure of foreign interference and aggression, Ethiopia as a modern state was born.

In this process foreign powers unintentionally helped her. Because of the misunderstanding or misinterpretation of Meqdela, Ethiopia was not taken very seriously for thirty years. This underestimation of the political and military strength of Ethiopia gave her the favour of always entering into negotiations and military conflict stronger than her opponents supposed her to be, and each victory in some way or other helped the unification onwards. But this is not the main reason. The survival of Ethiopian independence is in the first place due to the actual growth of political stability in the country and the qualities of its rulers and soldiers, often simply armed but brave peasants. In the same way as internal conditions and not British military power caused the fall of Tewodros, so also internal conditions and not Egyptian or Italian weakness led to the victories of Yohannis and Minilik. Ethiopia was certainly not a mere pawn in the 'scramble for Africa' but a national force which shaped her own fate.

35. Menelik and the European powers

GEORGE N. SANDERSON *Historians in Tropical Africa* University College, Salisbury, Rhodesia 1962; pages 247–52

Sometime in the spring of 1895, when open hostilities with Italy could hardly be postponed much longer, Menelik sent to Omdurman an Abyssinian Muslim called Muhammad al-Tayyib with verbal proposals for better relations. In July or August the Khalifa returned a curt reply requesting a statement in writing. Menelik did not respond until after his victory at Adowa on 1 March 1896; on 25 April he wrote reporting his success and assuring the Khalifa of his continued desire for peace with all Powers, whether his immediate neighbours or not. No specific proposals were made; after the defeat of the Italians Menelik evidently felt for the time being no special need of the Khalifa. This confident mood did not last; Menelik soon realised that the battle of Adowa had not in itself solved the 'European problem', and Kitchener's early victories on the Nile seem to have made him uneasy. In July 1896 he wrote to Omdurman through his official confidant Ras Bitwatid Mangasha offering an alliance against all whites and co-operation against 'the red English'; the letter begins, significantly enough, with a Muslim salutation, and it confirmed a verbal message despatched on 11 June. The Khalifa was prepared in principle to accept an alliance, and despatched to Addis Ababa his trusted envoy Muhammad 'Uthmān; but he attempted to make the impossible condition that Menelik should sever all relations, including commercial relations, with Europeans. As Muhammad 'Uthmān remarked, it was the Negus who took the initiative throughout, while 'Abdallāhi's response remained cold and grudging. Menelik replied that his relations with Europeans were in fact restricted to trade which was essential to his country, offered to supply the Khalifa with arms and ammunition, and, doubtless to convince the Khalifa that the Ethiopian policy of peace enjoyed general support, introduced Muhammad 'Uthmān to his principal Rases, including Takla Haymanot of Gojjam and Mangasha of Tigre, son of Yohannes.

No formal alliance seems ever to have been concluded; but by February 1897 Menelik was causing his important Rases to write almost fulsome letters congratulating the Khalifa on the establishment of cordial relations. The Negus supplied Omdurman with information on the movements of the English; the Khalifa permitted Menelik to subdue the Sheikh of the Banī Shanqūl, who had hitherto pursued a career of successful turbulence while Addis Ababa and Omdurman had disputed his allegiance. In a letter of December 1897 Menelik addressed 'Abdallāhi as 'our superior, venerable, dear friend'; and in the spring of 1898 'Abdallāhi greeted an Ethiopian delegation with an official firework display, arranged for their meat to be slaughtered by Christians, and even provided date wine for their refreshment. Under the pressure of Kitchener's advance, indiscriminate hostility to the enemies of God was yielding to more mundane calculations of political prudence.

The Negus was at pains to protect this hard-won entente against disruption by misunderstandings or frontier incidents. The expedition against the Banī Shanqūl was notified both to the Khalifa and to the local Dervish commander. When in December 1897 Menelik launched a reconnaissance towards the White Nile under *Dejazmach* Tassama, he carefully explained that this expedition was directed against the Europeans who 'intended to enter between my country and yours and to separate and divide us', and explicitly begged the Khalifa not to misunderstand his intentions. He warned 'Abdallāhi impartially against both the French and the British, and exhorted him to 'be strong, lest if the Europeans enter our midst a great disaster befall us'. For Menelik, the main importance of the entente was that it permitted both 'Abdallāhi and himself to concentrate on the 'European problem'. A Mahdist victory over Kitchener would go far to solve that problem, not only for the Sudan, but also for Ethiopia; but if the Khalifa were to be distracted by loss of confidence in the Negus the chances of such a success would be hopelessly compromised. Menelik confined his own struggle to the diplomatic arena, where he successfully played off France against Britain. In the course of that struggle he made promises to both Powers which were flatly contrary to his entente with 'Abdallāhi; but he was determined that these promises should remain unfulfilled.

In the Anglo-Abyssinian Treaty of 14 May 1897, Menelik had undertaken not to supply the Mahdists with arms and to treat them as 'enemies of his Empire'; the British negotiators knew that there had been contacts between Addis Ababa and Omdurman, but were induced to believe that the Negus had coldly rejected 'Abdallāhi's overtures. They were however impressed by the extent to which Menelik seemed to have subordinated his policy to that of France, and for this reason refrained from soliciting active Ethiopian assistance against the Mahdists. Rodd and Wingate were also given the impression that Menelik had with French assistance effectively occupied the Sobat valley; lest he should be stimulated to extend and consolidate this occupation they decided not to press him on territorial questions and even accepted without protest a Note declaring that the Negus would make 'no cession to any Government, whoever it may be'.

Menelik had fobbed off the British with empty words, and had used the French as a shield against embarrassing demands; but he paid for French support not by deeds, but by flattering gestures and unfulfilled promises. The French Resident Lagarde was created 'Duke of Entoto', and Frenchmen were appointed to high-sounding but purely ornamental posts in the Ethiopian administration. The Anglo-Abyssinian Treaty was shown to Lagarde; above all, on 20 March 1897 Menelik concluded with Lagarde a 'Convention pour le Nil Blanc' partitioning the Upper

Nile Basin, between 2° and 14°N., along the line of the Bahr al-Jabal and the White Nile. In order to establish contact with their expeditions from the Bahr al-Ghazāl, the French urged Menelik to hasten the occupation of his share, and the Negus appeared to concur in the organisation of Franco-Abyssinian expeditions with this objective. In fact, he spared no effort to wreck these expeditions. Menelik's guides deliberately misled the French; and his letters of introduction to local Rases seemed curiously ambiguous. But the Rases knew what was required of them; they immobilised the expeditions by impounding their animals, fomenting strikes among their porters, and, on one occasion at least, opposing their advance by armed force. The mythical occupation which had fooled the British must not become a reality, lest it shatter the entente with the Khalifa. Menelik's efforts were not wasted; a depleted remnant of the De Bonchamps expedition did indeed get as far as the Baro-Pibor confluence, but found any further advance was impossible (December 1897). Two of De Bonchamps' survivors later joined, more or less as guests, *Dejazmach* Tassama's expedition; they persuaded Tassama to send them with an escort to the Nile-Sobat confluence, where they planted and immediately abandoned a French and an Abyssinian flag (June 1898). In view of Menelik's anxiety that this expedition should not arouse the Khalifa's suspicions, it seems very unlikely that he can have authorised this action, at once provocative and futile. When Menelik really wished to assert his sovereignty, he normally went about it in a much more business-like manner, and there is rarely any doubt about his intentions.

On his return to France De Bonchamps reported to the Colonial Ministry that 'les Abyssins n'ont pas aidé la Mission; ils ont fait tout leur possible pour empêcher son départ vers le Nil'; and the *Direction d'Afrique* ruefully noted 'combien il parait aléatoire de compter sur l'appui de Ménélik'. Nevertheless, it is Lagarde rather than the Negus whom the received account has cast as the scapegoat for the French failure. Lagarde's failure to co-operate with De Bonchamps did indeed amount at times almost to outright sabotage; and his behaviour was all too frequently, and all too clearly, influenced by personal hostility and professional jealousy. Yet even when the Mission had been placed under his own control, and had ceased thereby to be 'entachée du peché originel', his support remained very lukewarm. Lagarde was however in a position to know something of Menelik's relations with the Khalifa, and it would not be hard for him to draw the conclusion that Menelik was unlikely in this situation seriously to support expeditions to the Nile. But instead of reporting to Paris a development which had emptied of all meaning his own diplomatic masterpiece, the 'Convention pour le Nil Blanc', he attempted on his own initiative to use the understanding between Addis Ababa and Omdurman as a means of offering French protection to the Khalifa.

Lagarde evidently believed that the entente was directed exclusively against the British; and Menelik did not discourage this belief. Early in 1898, in the presence of Lagarde, Menelik handed to his envoy Muhammad al-Tayyib 'a small flag of three colours'. 'Menelik said . . . "Take this flag . . . and give it to the Khalifa, and tell him that if the English advance against him he is to fly it at the head of his army. When they see it they will do him no harm, and this will be the same if the French advance against him." ' But Muhammad al-Tayyib was also told, more privately, to impress upon the Khalifa 'that it was not desirable that either French or English should come into the Sudan'. He was also the bearer of an unsigned message warning 'Abdallāhi to be on his guard against Europeans of all nationalities, and a formal sealed note accrediting him as the bearer of an important confidential message. No pains were spared to prevent the Khalifa from being misled by Menelik's successful deception of the French.

For public consumption, 'Abdallāhi rejected the flag with correct Mahdist intransigence, declaring that 'if Heaven and Earth together should advance against him he would not accept the protection of a European Power', and with this reply Muhammad al-Tayyib was sent back to Addis Ababa. According to the account of Muhammad 'Uthmān al-Hājj Khālid the flag was also returned. But Yūsuf Mikhā'īl states that the Khalifa secretly conveyed the flag to his own house; and he reports, very circumstantially, the proceedings of a discussion in which 'Abdallāhi and his son 'Uthmān Shaikh al-Dīn strongly urged that the flag should be used, and were only deterred from this course by the outspoken opposition of the group led by the Khalifa's brother Ya'qūb.

It seems a paradox indeed that in the spring of 1898 'Abdallāhi should have been inclined to accept the protection of the French flag in spite of Menelik's urgent warnings not to do so. Yet, so far as Menelik is concerned, the paradox is certainly more apparent than real. The promises and gestures of co-operation which he made to the French were as empty as the repeated declarations of irreconcilable enmity to the Dervishes with which he had regaled the British in May 1897, a few weeks after the entente with Omdurman had been consummated. The expeditions which the Negus despatched to the western frontiers of his realm in 1897 and 1898 have sometimes been cited as evidence of French influence; in fact Menelik saw to it that these operations should promote exclusively Ethiopian interests, which he was quite shrewd enough to safeguard without any European prompting. The received tradition that the Negus had committed himself more or less completely to the support of French policy on the Upper Nile evidently requires drastic revision; and the material for this revision seems to be contained in the meagre handful of papers at Khartoum rather than in the copious records of the Quai d'Orsay or the Foreign Office. . . .

36. The Mahdist idea

P. M. HOLT *The Mahdist State in the Sudan* Clarendon Press, Oxford 1958; pages 20–3

. . . The Mahdi himself was originally a member of the Sammānīya order. The founder of this, Muḥammad b. 'Abd al-Karīm al-Sammānī (1718–75), was a member of the Khalwatīya order and a disciple of Muṣṭafā Kamāl al-Dīn al-Bakrī, under whom the Khalwatīya entered into a phase of revival and expansion in the eighteenth century. Al-Sammānī established himself at Medina. The Sammānīya order was introduced into the Sudan about 1800 by Aḥmad al-Ṭayyib al-Bashīr, who had become an adherent while on pilgrimage in the Ḥijāz. Shaykh-al-Ṭayyib, as he is usually called, had much success in proselytyzing for this order in the Gezira. His grandson, Muḥammad Sharīf Nūr al-Dā'im, was Muḥammad Aḥmad's first Ṣūfī shaykh.

Although these new orders which developed in the eighteenth and nineteenth centuries were founded as reformist movements, the traditional pattern of devotion rapidly reasserted itself. The founders and their descendants were regarded as saints. In the Sudan the Khatmīya became assimilated into indigenous Islam. The same phenomenon appears elsewhere, for example among the Sanūsīya in Libya and the Darqawīya in the Maghrib. The Mahdia was intended by its founder to supersede and abolish the orders, but the neo-Mahdism of the present times conforms very closely in practice and outlook to that of the *tarīqas*, with which it has established a *modus vivendi*.

The policy of the Egyptian administration towards Sudanese Islam had two aspects. In the first place the conquest brought the Sudanese more closely into touch with orthodox Islam and its institutions. The Sharī'a, the Holy Law of Islam, had previously had little part in Sudanese life, although nominally the people adhered to the Mālikī *madhhab*.[1] Tribal and local

---

[1] *Madhhab*, often translated 'rite', is the term applied to the four 'schools' or bodies of legal opinion in Sunnī Islam. That the Sudanese belonged to the

custom was in most respects the effective law. The Egyptians introduced a regular system of religious courts administering the Sharī'a according to the Ḥanafī *madhhab*. Mosques were built and trained '*ālims* brought in, while Sudanese students made their way to Cairo to study at al-Azhar, where they had their own hostel, the Riwāq al-Sinnārīya. Some of these Azharite Sudanese played a part in the Mahdia. The rise of a class of trained '*ālims* threatened in the long run the prestige of the older *fakī* class, but the feeble appeal of orthodox teaching compared with the emotional power of the orders was to be demonstrated by the success of the Mahdia itself.

The second aspect of Egyptian policy was to use the leading religious shaykhs, like the tribal chiefs, as instruments of the administration. The Mīrghanī family were especially favoured and the Khatmīya was closely associated with Egyptian rule in the Sudan. But this recognition was to prove double-edged when the personal prestige of the religious leaders became involved in the fortunes of the Egyptian administration. The Mahdist revolution was to overthrow in turn the rule of Egypt, the authority of the tribal notables and the influence of the heads of the orders; yet, as we shall see, the Mahdist state had characteristics inherited from all three of these systems of authority, some aspects of which show great vitality until the present day.

The Mahdist Idea

The idea of a *mahdī* has assumed two main forms in the Muslim world. Among the Shī'a the *mahdī* is equated with the Hidden Imām, whose infallibility and whose return are articles of faith. This view need not detain us since there is no evidence of a direct connexion between Sudanese Islam and Shī'ism, nor of any attempt by Muhammad Ahmad to represent himself as the Hidden Imām returned to rule the Muslim community. Among the Sunnīs, Mahdism is a popular belief, particularly in times of crisis, but it has never been fully integrated into the orthodox faith. It would perhaps be more correct to call

Mālikī school indicates their connexion with North Africa, where this *madhhab* predominates, rather than with Lower Egypt, which is Shāfiī. The Ḥanafī *madhhab*, introduced by the Egyptian conquest, was official throughout the Ottoman Empire.

Mahdism a deposit of ideas and hopes rather than an organized and coherent system of beliefs. To attempt to analyse Mahdism with any degree of rigour does violence to its nature as an essentially popular synthesis of elements, varying in their content and emphasis at different times and in different places.

With this in mind, however, we may note three of the dominant themes of Sunnī Mahdism. The term *al-mahdī* means 'the guided one', a person who has a particular measure of divine guidance and is the repository of esoteric secrets. Furthermore the *mahdī* is *al-imām*, the head of the Islamic community. His function is to restore right governance or, in a traditional phrase, 'to fill the earth with equity and justice, even as it has been filled with tyranny and oppression'. The appearance of the *mahdī* is associated with the approaching end of the world. This is combined in Muslim eschatology with the second coming of Jesus. Sudanese Mahdism has placed the second coming after the manifestation of the *mahdī*. As we shall see, the period after Muḥammad Aḥmad's death saw the appearance of more than one individual who assumed the style of *al-Nabī* *'Īsā*, the Prophet Jesus.

Sunnī Mahdism has thriven in North Africa, where historical circumstances have made further additions to the Mahdist idea. The career of the Mahdi Muḥammad b. Tūmart, the founder of the Almohad movement who assumed the mahdiship in the Maghrib in A.D. 1212, is particularly significant. Like Muḥammad Aḥmad in the Sudan, he was primarily a reformer, preaching in a lax Muslim society against departures from primitive Islam. There are other points of resemblance between the two movements. Both developed on the African fringe of Islam, at the meeting-place of Arab and indigenous cultures. Both directed their energies primarily against an Islamic state and both founders seem to have assumed the title of *mahdī* as a means of acquiring greater authority against the existing government. In both cases, behind the Muslim government immediately threatened by the movements lay the menace of a Christian advance against Islam; the Reconquista was proceeding in thirteenth-century Spain, while during the nineteenth century European pressure was increasingly felt both in Egypt and in the Ottoman Empire as a whole. It is therefore not surprising that the Sunnī *mahdī* is seen as a champion of Islam against the infidel. During Bonaparte's occupation of Egypt a *mahdī* had a brief career in Lower Egypt. In the Sudan Muḥammad Aḥmad became involved in hostilities with forces which were officered by or composed of Europeans and Christians—the Hicks expedition, Gordon, the Relief Force. Nevertheless, it seems that to the Mahdi the infidels (*al-kafara*) were primarily the 'Turks' and that it was against these backsliding Muslims that he directed his *jihād*.

The assumption of the title of *mahdī* by Muḥammad Aḥmad should not conceal from us the fundamental similarity between his mission and the reformist activity described in the preceding section. Long before 1881 he had acquired a popular reputation for sanctity and asceticism, which in different circumstances might have led him merely to found a new order as an offshoot of the Sammānīya. Even the militancy of his propaganda and actions had precedents in the previous century. The combination of zeal to purify the Faith and the recourse to arms against opponents characterized the Wahhābīs. A still closer parallel, since it also developed on the fringe of Islam in the geographical Sudan, is the movement which arose among the Fulani under 'Uthmān dan Fodio (1754–1817). Like Muḥammad Aḥmad later, 'Uthmān began as a reformer and reviver of the Faith. Like him, he was compelled to an Emigration (*hijra*) to escape his enemies and rally his followers. Like him, too, 'Uthmān waged a *jihād* and built up an Islamic state in trans-Saharan Africa. . . .

37. The end of the Khalifa

WINSTON S. CHURCHILL *The River War* Eyre and Spottiswoode 1933 and Odhams Books; pages 433–40

. . . It was at first universally believed that the Khalifa's intention was to retire to an almost inaccessible distance—to El Obeid or Southern Darfur—and the officers of the Egyptian army passed an unhappy fortnight reading the Ladysmith telegrams and accusing their evil fortune which kept them so far from the scene of action. But soon strange rumours began to run about the bazaars of Omdurman of buried weapons and whispers of revolt. For a few days a vague feeling of unrest pervaded the native city, and then suddenly on the 12th of November came precise and surprising news. The Khalifa was not retreating to the south or to the west, but advancing northward with Omdurman, not El Obeid, as his object. Emboldened by the spectacle of two successive expeditions retreating abortive, and by who shall say what wild exaggerated tales of disasters to the Turks far beyond the limits of the Soudan, Abdullah had resolved to stake all that yet remained to him in one last desperate attempt to recapture his former capital; and so, upon the 12th of November, his advanced guard, under the Emir Ahmed Fedil, struck the Nile opposite Abba Island, and audaciously fired volleys of musketry at the gunboat *Sultan* which was patrolling the river.

The name of Abba Island may perhaps carry the reader back to the very beginning of this story. Here, eighteen years before, the Mahdi had lived and prayed after his quarrel with the haughty Sheikh; here Abdullah had joined him; here the flag of the revolt had been set up, and the first defeat had been inflicted upon the Egyptian troops; and here, too, still dwelt— dwells, indeed, to this day—one of those same brothers who had pursued through all the vicissitudes and convulsions which had shaken the Soudan his humble industry of building wooden boats. It is surely a curious instance of the occasional symmetry of history that final destruction should have befallen the last remains of the Mahdist movement so close to the scene of its origin!

The news which had reached Khartoum set all wheels in motion. The IXth and XIIIth Soudanese Battalions were mobilised on the 13th of November and despatched at once to Abba Island under Colonel Lewis. Kitchener hurried south from Cairo, and arrived in Khartoum on the 18th. A field force of some 2,300 troops—one troop of cavalry, the 2nd Field Battery, the 1st Maxim Battery, the Camel Corps, IXth Soudanese, XIIIth Soudanese, and one company 2nd Egyptians—was immediately formed, and the command entrusted to Sir Reginald Wingate. There were besides some 900 Arab riflemen and a few irregular mounted scouts. On the 20th these troops were concentrated at Fashi Shoya, whence

Colonel Lewis had obliged Ahmed Fedil to withdraw, and at 3.30 on the afternoon of the 21st the expedition started in a south-westerly direction upon the track of the enemy.

The troops bivouacked some ten miles south-west of Fashi Shoya, and then marched in bright moonlight to Nefisa, encountering only a Dervish patrol of about ten men. At Nefisa was found the evacuated camp of Ahmed Fedil, containing a quantity of grain which he had collected from the riverain district, and, what was of more value, a sick but intelligent Dervish who stated that the Emir had just moved to Abu Aadel, five miles further on. This information was soon confirmed by Mahmud Hussein, an Egyptian officer, who with an irregular patrol advanced boldly in reconnaissance. The infantry needed a short rest to eat a little food, and Sir Reginald Wingate ordered Colonel Mahon to press on immediately with the whole of the mounted troops and engage the enemy, so as to prevent him retreating before an action could be forced.

Accordingly cavalry, Camel Corps, Maxims, and irregulars —whose fleetness of foot enabled them, though not mounted, to keep pace with the rest—set off at their best pace: and after them at 9.15 hurried the infantry, refreshed by a drink at the water tanks and a hasty meal. As they advanced the scrub became denser, and all were in broken and obstructed ground when, at about ten o'clock, the sound of Maxim firing and the patter of musketry proclaimed that Mahon had come into contact. The firing soon became more rapid, and as the infantry approached it was evident that the mounted troops were briskly engaged. The position which they occupied was a low ridge which rose a little above the level of the plain and was comparatively bare of scrub; from this it was possible at a distance of 800 yards to overlook the Dervish encampment huddled around the water pools. It was immediately evident that the infantry and the battery were arriving none too soon. The Dervishes, who had hitherto contented themselves with maintaining a ragged and desultory fire from the scrub, now sallied forth into the open and delivered a most bold and determined charge upon the guns. The intervening space was little more than 200 yards, and for a moment the attack looked as if it might succeed. But upon the instant the IXth and XIIIth Soudanese, who had been doubled steadily for upwards of two miles, came into line, filling the gap between Mahon's guns and dismounted Camel Corps and the irregular riflemen; and so the converging fire of the whole force was brought to bear upon the enemy—now completely beaten and demoralised. Two Dervishes, brothers, bound together hand and foot, perished in valiant comradeship ninety-five paces from the line of guns. Many were slain, and the remainder fled. The whole Egyptian line now advanced upon the encampment hard upon the tracks of the retreating enemy, who were seen emerging from the scrub on to a grassy plain more than a mile away, across which and further for a distance of five miles they were pursued by the cavalry and the Camel Corps. Three hundred and twenty corpses were counted, and at least an equal number must have been wounded. Ahmed Fedil and one or two of his principal Emirs escaped to the southward and to the Khalifa. The Egyptian loss amounted to five men wounded. The troops bivouacked in square formation, at about four o'clock, near the scene of action.

A question of considerable difficulty and some anxiety now arose. It was learned from the prisoners that the Khalifa, with about 5,000 fighting men, was moving northwards towards the wells of Gedid, of which we have already heard in the Shirkela reconnaissance, and which were some twenty-five miles from the scene of the fight. The troops were already fatigued by their severe exertions. The water pool was so foul that even the thirsty camels refused to drink of it, and moreover scarcely any water remained in the tanks. It was therefore of vital importance to reach the wells of Gedid. But supposing exhausted troops famishing for water reached them only to be confronted by a powerful Dervish force already in possession! Sir Reginald Wingate decided, however, to face the risk, and at a few minutes before midnight the column set out again on its road. The ground was broken; the night was sultry: and as the hours passed by the sufferings of the infantry began to be most acute. Many piteous appeals were made for water. All had perforce to be refused by the commander, who dared not diminish by a mouthful his slender store until he knew the true situation at Gedid. In these circumstances the infantry, in spite of their admirable patience, became very restive. Many men fell exhausted to the ground; and it was with a feeling of immense relief that at nine o'clock on the morning of the 24th news was received from the cavalry that the wells had been occupied by them without opposition. All the water in the tanks was at once distributed, and thus refreshed the infantry struggled on and settled down at midday around a fine pool of comparatively pure water.

At Gedid, as at Nefisa, a single Dervish, and this time a sullen fellow, was captured, and from him it was learned that the Khalifa's army was encamped seven miles to the south-east. It was now clear that his position was strategically most unfavourable. His route to the north was barred; his retreat to the south lay through waterless and densely wooded districts; and as the seizure of the grain supplies which had resulted from Fedil's foraging excursions rendered his advance or retirement a matter of difficulty, it seemed probable he would stand. Wingate, therefore, decided to attack him at dawn.

Leaving the transport under guard by the water with instructions to follow at four o'clock, the troops moved off at midnight screened in front at a distance of half a mile by the cavalry and their flanks protected by the Camel Corps. The road was in places so thickly wooded that a path had to be cut by the infantry pioneers and the artillery. At three o'clock, when about three miles from the enemy's position, the force was deployed into fighting formation. The irregular riflemen covered the front; behind them the XIIIth and IXth Soudanese; and behind these, again, the Maxims and the artillery were disposed. Cautiously and silently the advance was resumed, and now in the distance the beating of war drums and the long booming note of the Khalifa's horn broke on the stillness, proclaiming that the enemy were not unprepared. At a few minutes before four o'clock another low ridge, also comparatively bare of scrub, was reached and occupied as a position. The cavalry were now withdrawn from the front, a few infantry picquets were thrown out, and the rest of the force lay down in the long grass of the little ridge and waited for daylight.

After about an hour the sky to the eastward began to grow paler with the promise of the morning, and in the indistinct light the picquets could be seen creeping gradually in; while behind them along the line of the trees faint white figures, barely distinguishable, began to accumulate. Sir Reginald Wingate, fearing lest a sudden rush should be made upon him, now ordered the whole force to stand up and open fire; and forthwith, in sudden contrast to the silence and obscurity, a loud crackling fusillade began. It was immediately answered. The enemy's fire flickered along a wide half-circle and developed continually with greater vigour opposite the Egyptian left, which was consequently reinforced. As the light improved, large bodies of shouting Dervishes were seen advancing; but the fire was too hot, and their Emirs were unable to lead them far beyond the edge of the wood. So soon as this was perceived Wingate ordered a general advance; and the whole force, moving at a rapid pace down the gentle slope, drove the enemy through the trees into the camp about a mile and a half away. Here, huddled together under their straw shelters, 6,000 women and children were collected, all of whom, with many unwounded combatants, made signals of surrender and appeals for mercy. The 'cease fire' was sounded at half-past six. Then, and not till then, was it discovered how severe the loss of the Dervishes had been. It seemed to the officers that, short as was the range, the effect of rifle fire under such unsatisfactory conditions of light could not have been very great. But the bodies thickly scattered in the scrub were convincing evidences. In one space not much more than a score of yards square lay all the most famous Emirs of the once far-reaching Dervish domination. The Khalifa Abdullah, pierced by several balls, was stretched dead on his sheepskin; on his right lay Ali-Wad-Helu, on his left Ahmed Fedil. Before them was a line of lifeless bodyguards; behind them a score of less important chiefs; and behind these, again, a litter of killed and wounded horses. Such was the grim spectacle which in the first light in the morning met the eyes of the British officers, to some of whom it meant the conclusion of a perilous task prolonged over many years. And while they looked in astonishment not unmingled with awe, there scrambled unhurt from under a heap of bodies the little Emir Yunes, of Dongola, who added the few links necessary to complete the chain.

At Omdurman Abdullah had remained mounted behind the hill of Surgham, but in this his last fight he had set himself in the forefront of the battle. Almost at the first discharge, his son Osman, the Sheikh-ed-Din, was wounded, and as he was carried away he urged the Khalifa to save himself by flight; but the latter, with a dramatic dignity sometimes denied to more civilised warriors, refused. Dismounting from his horse, and ordering his Emirs to imitate him, he seated himself on his sheepskin and there determined to await the worst of fortune. And so it came to pass that in this last scene in the struggle with Madhism the stage was cleared of all its striking characters, and Osman Digna alone purchased by flight a brief ignoble liberty, soon to be followed by a long ignoble servitude.

Twenty-nine Emirs, 3,000 fighting men, 6,000 women and children surrendered themselves prisoners. The Egyptian losses were three killed and twenty-three wounded. . . .

38. The Khalifa in retrospect

P. M. HOLT *Modern History of the Sudan* Weidenfeld & Nicolson and Praeger 1961; pages 105–6

. . . The significance of the Khalifa's reign has not always been appreciated either by his countrymen or by foreign observers. A legend, fostered by war-propaganda, grew up around his name, depicting him as a bloodthirsty and barbarous despot, from whose tyranny the Sudanese were released by the Anglo-Egyptian invasion. The reality is rather different. When he came to power, the initial drive of the Mahdia was at an end. The objects of the revolutionary war had largely been attained. The greater part or the Muslim north was under Mahdist rule. His primary problem was to restore order and make administration effective over a vast area in which four years of warfare against the established government had broken down the habits of obedience. His task was complicated by the uncertain loyalty of the *Awlad al-balad*, from whom the Mahdi had drawn the bulk of his ruling *élite*, and by the insubordination and backwardness of the Baqqara, on whom he himself chiefly relied.

He sought to establish his authority by developing an increasingly elaborate and centralized administration. Although the forms of the Madhist theocracy were retained, the spirit had, by the middle years of his reign, departed from them. The other two khalifas were in no real sense his colleagues; his closest associate in government was his brother, Ya'qub. The great military commands were held almost exclusively by Baqqara. The simple fiscal system of the Mahdi was abandoned. The revenue was augmented by a whole range of new taxes, dues and confiscations, closely resembling the Turco-Egyptian taxes, which the Mahdi had come to destroy. The development of specialized treasuries, notably the Khalifa's own privy treasury, siphoned off from the original *Bayt al-mal* the cream of its revenue. The judiciary similary acquired an increasingly complex organization, although no greater independence of the ruler in the performance of its functions.

The reign of the Khalifa, then, is characterized by the passing of the Mahdist theocracy and the creation of a personal rule exercised through a bureaucracy, largely composed of Sudanese civil servants inherited from the Turco-Egyptian regime. 'Abdallahi prevented the northern Sudan from relapsing into anarchy after the Madhi's death. His success in establishing his control so firmly that it was broken ultimately only by a foreign invader with superior military resources, is a measure of his inherent strength of personality and his administrative talent. Yet the price was high. 'Abdallahi, permanently resident in Omdurman, was never fully in control of his provincial officials, although his system of constant communication with them destroyed their initiative in emergencies. His reliance on the Baqqara opened a rift between himself and the *Awlad al-balad* which weakened the foundations of the state. Finally, the sustained military character of the regime, derived from the revolutionary period, and continued at first in accordance with the policy of the Holy War, and later because of the growing threat from outside, prevented a genuine resettlement of the country. 'Abdallahi was much less a malevolent despot and much more the prisoner of his circumstances than contemporary European writers were willing to perceive. . . .

X. SOCIAL PROBLEMS

39. Economic changes in African urban life

I. SCHAPERA *Africa* Vol. I, 1928 Oxford University Press for International African Institute; pages 179–86, 187–8

... The first effect of contact on the economic life of the Native was thus the substitution of European goods for native products. The white man brought with him new articles of various kinds, many of which appealed to the Native. At first personal ornaments, such as beads, copper-wire, and brass buttons, were most in demand, but gradually the skin clothing of the Native was replaced by blankets, the implements made by the smith were superseded by imported metal goods, the wooden utensils and clay pots by the tin mugs and iron pots of the trader. In this way began a process by which the native products have disappeared to have their place taken by European wares, brought in and sold by trade. The productive work of the native household has been completely changed. The Natives no longer devote themselves to the same tasks as before. The home industries, the only industries there were, are dying out more and more, even in the least affected parts of the native areas; all the kraal handicrafts have suffered, and some have completely disappeared. Moreover new tastes have been created in the Native. The beads and buttons of the early traders have long been superseded by cloth, blankets, iron pots, axes, picks, and knives. Many articles, such as European clothing, groceries, crockery, and in many cases furniture, saddlery, and so on, which were quite recently luxuries, he is now beginning to regard as necessaries; and with the spread of educational influences the demand for them has grown. In progressive districts even the huts are being abandoned, and stone buildings on the European model erected, with corresponding innovations in the form of beds, tables and chairs, table-linen, and crockery. The range of individual possessions is increasing, and in material objects at least the Native is adopting more and more from European culture.

Even more far-reaching in its effect upon the economic life of the Native was the fact that he had to enter into a system of exchange with the traders. In order to obtain European goods he had to exchange something for them. He had to learn how to buy and sell, to familiarize himself with the use of money. In the early days ivory, hides, and gum formed the main articles of exchange, but as the supply of these fell away, and as the wants of the Native increased, he was forced to find some other means of satisfying them. His land he could not part with, as it was vested in the chief, so the three main things he had to offer were his cattle, crops, and labour.

At first cattle were an important article of trade, but it was not long before their importance declined. There were several reasons for this. Under the tribal system the Natives had been in the habit of procuring cattle which they could not acquire in any other way by making plundering forays into their neighbours' territory; and in the earlier years of contact native thefts of European cattle formed an everlasting source of conflict. The herds of the European farmers lay at the mercy of the Native, and if there was any trade in cattle more often than not it was cattle stolen from the Europeans which was traded back to them, or if the Native did part with his own herds, it was only in order to steal them back at the first opportunity. But with the strengthening of the European population on the eastern frontier, and with the establishment of law and order in the native territories, this method of obtaining food and the means with which to pay *lobola* for their wives disappeared. Very shortly, therefore, after the Europeans had asserted their rule, the increase in the native population and the contraction of the sources from which they had derived a livelihood began to show their effects. Then came the famous 'cattle-killing delusion' of 1857, when it is estimated that the Natives slaughtered over 150,000 of their cattle; and the trade in cattle completely fell away. This was followed in later years by the spread of rinderpest to the native territories, which decimated the native herds, and, shortly after Union, East Coast fever and drought still further reduced the native stock. Today the Native is in need of cattle. To him they still are of the greatest value, both as a source of food and especially as the means of obtaining a wife; he will not readily part with his stock, and it may even be said that the desire for cattle has become one of the most powerful motives driving the Native to enter more and more into the economic system of the Europeans.

It is only within recent years that native crops have become of any importance as an article of trade. At the same time the character and scope of native agriculture have improved considerably. Under the tribal system, as we have seen, all the cultivation was done by the women. The crops raised were few in number, and the methods employed wasteful and unproductive. The most important change here was brought about by the introduction of the plough. This was directly due in the first place to missionary effort early in the nineteenth century, but it was afterwards actively and deliberately supported by the administration. The use of the plough has now spread very widely, carrying with it improved agricultural methods, and, what is far more significant, a reconstruction of society. The use of the plough involved the harnessing of cattle; and as the native social and religious system prohibited women from having anything to do with cattle, the men now had to do the ploughing. The change in the native division of labour was profound, even although the other agricultural work, such as hoeing and reaping, still remains to a large extent in the hands of the women.

Accompanying this revolution in the character of native agriculture, there has been a considerable extension in the range of agricultural activity. As a result partly of missionary influence, partly of imitation of European neighbours, landlords, or masters, but due mainly to a policy deliberately carried out by the administration, native methods of agriculture have improved immensely. The Native has begun to grow in quantity for exchange as well as for subsistence; new crops have been introduced with some measure of success, such as wheat, barley and oats, fruit and vegetables, and tobacco; while associations are rapidly springing up among the Natives for the encouragement and training of their agricultural production. Irrigation, agricultural education and individual land tenure, combined with the relative shortage of cattle, are tending to make the Native pre-eminently an agriculturist. The trade in native crops is still proportionately slight, but there seems no doubt that in the course of time it will increase considerably.

The most important factor of change, however, has been the selling of his labour by the Native. From the outset there was the demand by the Europeans for native labour, for cheap unskilled labour, and the Natives have not been slow in responding. This was the case especially after the 'cattle-killing delusion' of 1857, when under the impulse of religious enthusiasm all their existing cattle and crops were destroyed by the Natives at the instigation of the notorious 'prophet' Umhlakaza. As a result nearly 100,000 Natives wandered forth to find some means of living. Relief works were multiplied in the Colony to meet the crisis, and more than 40,000 Natives were taken into service in various parts of the country. From this time on there has been an increasing flow of Natives to the labour market. Domestic service, farm labour, and industrial tasks all called for native employment, and the opening of the great mining industries greatly stimulated the demand. The primary motive which urged the Natives to sell their labour in this way was their need of the money with which to purchase their new requirements. As they became more civilized their wants increased, and in order to satisfy these wants they had to go out to seek remunerative employment. Then also the imposition of the hut-tax by the European government formed an additional stimulus, for the Native had to earn the money with which to pay his tax.

Although in many respects the kraal life of the Natives often remains but slightly altered, the demand for labour has already led to significant changes in their habits and customs. They are still primarily agriculturists or herdsmen working on their own account, but a very large proportion of them have now also become temporary wage-earners. It is a common practice for able-bodied men to leave their homes from time to time to enter the service of white employers, and for this purpose they often travel great distances. As a rule they do not remain employed for more than about six months. In this time they can often, without much difficulty, save a fair amount out of their earnings, and with this money they generally return to their kraals and resume their normal occupations. While this practice takes them into many other employments, it has greatly strengthened their position as agriculturists. With the savings which they bring home they are able to make good the ravages of rinderpest among their cattle and to buy the implements which they need for the cultivation of their fields. In many districts large numbers of European ploughs have in this way been purchased by the Natives. Today this going out to labour has become a regular feature in native life, the principal method by which they can obtain the means to satisfy their new needs and tastes.

The chief result of this demand for labour has been to turn the native population into a class of unskilled labourers, moving about from place to place in search of work. The aim of the Native for the most part still remains to work for a short period only, and then to return home when he has saved some money. But there is now a growing tendency for the Natives to stay at work in the towns for longer periods. They are also beginning to acquire some degree of skill in certain classes of employment, and with this may be associated the fact that a growing proportion of the native population are drifting away from their own districts and living in or near the towns in which they work. These Natives are beginning to look for permanent rather than temporary labour, and are becoming urban dwellers who do not return to their kraals at all. They are becoming detribalized, in other words, and many of them have ceased to be agriculturists and herdsmen, and are now primarily industrial labourers.

It is not difficult to appreciate the effect this has upon the life of the people. The many thousands of Natives constantly employed on farms, railways, and public works, and in mines and workshops, are inevitably being brought into more intimate contact with European civilization and all that it means to them. In the towns they acquire new tastes, new habits, and new vices; they return to their kraals profoundly altered, and with an increasing detachment from the old tribal system. They cannot come into contact with the relative freedom of civilized life, enter into individual contracts, and secure earnings formerly undreamt of, and yet retain their old communal ideas and submit to the caprice and exactions of their tribal superiors. In the kraals also these economic changes are slowly but surely undermining the tribal system. The regular absence at work of the younger men is beginning to leave its mark upon the social life. As long as the period of work away from the kraal was short, the effect was not so serious; but when the intervals began to lengthen the old routine of life had perforce to suffer. Social ties are being weakened, and the families broken up by the long absence of the bread-winners.

The breakdown of the tribal system has been further stimulated by other factors. Of these not the least significant was the decay of the chief's economic functions. This is partly the result of a policy deliberately carried out by the administration since the middle of last century. The chiefs were still recognized by the Europeans as a means of government, but their jurisdiction, more particularly in criminal matters, was gradually transferred to European magistrates and commissioners. They were induced to accept fixed salaries from the government, in return for which they had to surrender their right to fines imposed on their people. They were also deprived of the power of making war against rival tribes, and were thus discredited in the eyes of their people, who looked to war as one of their principal means of acquiring cattle. In this way the chiefs were deprived both of their most important functions in native life and of the chief source by which they derived revenue from their people.

At the same time the ordinary Native, by his contact with the European economic system, learned the meaning of thrift and of personal property; new wants were created, and so were the means of satisfying them; and as the range of personal possessions increased the Natives began to grow reluctant to part with individual gains. Instead of working for their chief they now worked for themselves: the accumulation of wealth became a motive in the life of every Native. Travel and the absence for longer or shorter periods from their home environment widened the breach between the chief and his subjects. The economic reciprocity which entered so strongly into the relations between chief and subjects, and which formed one of the vital features of the native economic system, has broken down almost completely. The chief no longer plays the part of tribal banker: his function as the holder and distributor of all the surplus wealth has been obliterated by the new economic forces.

Another highly important factor in the breakdown of native economic life was the restriction upon territorial expansion. Under the tribal system there was no effective check upon tribal or individual movements, and it was always a basic assumption in native life that there was an abundant supply of land. A tribe which desired new territory would either oust its neighbours or simply move on and take up vacant territory; while similarly any Native whose fields were no longer productive could always find new lands. The enforcing of the Fish River boundary by the colonial government was the first real suggestion of territorial enclosure to reach the Native. Then after a time followed the expansion of the Colony towards the east, and more and more of the Kafir territory came to be absorbed by the Europeans. Moreover under European administration all unoccupied land was made Crown land, and thus a further check was put upon native extension. The main immediate effect of annexation upon the native land system was the transfer of the administration of the land from the chief to the government. This was a direct blow to the power of the chief, who, by losing his right of allotting land to tribesmen except under the direction of the new paramount power, was deprived of one of his important functions in native life. At the same time white farmers occupied large tracts of country in parts of which the Natives had previously been settled, and the native population was confined more and more to lands specially reserved for them. As the European population increased, the movement for the enclosure of the farms was commenced, and the Native began to find himself more and more cramped for space, hemmed in on all sides by fences, and confined to a limited area.

Following upon this restriction of territorial expansion, there has been a profound change in the nature of land tenure. The colonial administration began by adopting the communal system of occupation observed by the Natives in their independent state, and by gradually adapting it to the changing conditions of life attendant upon the march of civilization, prepared the way for the recognition by the people of the advantages of an individual system tending towards the assimilation of European methods. From about 1830 onwards, various attempts were made in the Ciskei to induce Natives to take up land in this way. At first the attempts did not meet with much success, partly because the Native was too attached to the tribal system, partly because of the complexities presented to the native mind by the European laws of transfer. But the spread of education and the increasing disadvantages of the communal system led to a certain amount of land being taken up on individual tenure. The whole movement was accelerated by the Glen Grey Act of 1894, in which provision was made for the settlement of the Natives of Glen Grey district upon the land, allotments being made to individual applicants. The success of this scheme led to its extension by proclamation to the Transkei territories, the measure being made permissive and applicable only to such districts as voluntarily desired to have it. The movement thus initiated proceeded very slowly at first, but is now making steady progress. The way is being prepared for the extension of the system, and in time, no doubt, the whole of the territories will be included under it. . . .

Brief and inadequate as this survey has necessarily been, it has perhaps made clear the main lines along which the modification of the native economic system has taken place as the result of its contact with European civilization. The introduction of the Native to the economic system of the Europeans, the restrictions upon territorial expansion, and the spread of education have combined to weaken the old tribal system and to destroy the vital economic functions of the chieftainship. There has been a considerable change in the habits of many of the Natives. Their methods of agriculture have markedly improved, and their ideas about stock and stock-raising are slowly being influenced for the better. On the other hand some of their kraal handicrafts have been destroyed, and others injured. Moreover the Natives have been introduced to an economic system which was entirely alien to them. They have learned something of the white man's economic motives, and these have modified their habits and outlook.

Most important, and perhaps as the result of all these changes, the Natives have been differentiated into a number of classes. There is in the first place the relatively small class of Natives who still live under the same conditions as prior to the advent of the Europeans, and do not go out to work at all. They do not come into the economic system of the white man, except in so far as they pay taxes and buy goods and perhaps sell a few of their crops. Then there are those kraal Natives who form the great mass of the unskilled labourers of the country, who leave their kraals to work for short periods, and then return home again. This class is still by the far the largest in the native population, and includes the great majority of the able-bodied males and more recently also a number of women. Both these classes still live under the communal system of land tenure. Then there are a small number of independent native farmers who own farms of their own. This is a new class which has come into existence fairly recently, under the system of individual land tenure. Another class consists of those Natives who have no land of their own, but live permanently on European-owned farms, either as tenants, labourers, or squatters. They do not come into the general labour market, but render service for a certain period of each year in lieu of rent to the owners of the farm on which they reside. There is also the growing class of Natives who have become detached from their land, and who now live permanently in urban areas. This class has increased during the last decade, very largely indeed owing to the influence of the Native Lands Act of 1913. Finally there is the class of Natives who are neither agriculturists nor unskilled industrial labourers, but are permanently engaged in various trades or professional occupations.

It will be seen, therefore, that the Natives are now differentiated to such an extent that it is impossible to generalize about their habits and characteristics as a whole. Some are living very much as they did under the old tribal system, others have changed very materially indeed, and approximate to the Europeans both in mode of life, economic occupations, outlook on life generally, and individualism. Between these two extremes there are the great majority who are now in a transitional stage. Any attempt to deal with all these different classes as a single unity is doomed to failure. We must recognize their differences, and approach the particular problems they each present with no illusion about the uniformity of the native question. . . .

40. The slave trade in British Central Africa

L. H. GANN *Rhodes-Livingstone Institute Journal* Vol. 1, No. 6, 1954; pages 39–45, 47–9

The Significance of the Slave Trade

A few areas in Central Africa managed to remain free from the scourge of the traffic in human beings. The great majority, however, did not. It did not matter where the raiders came from, the results of their attacks were always the same. Everywhere there was the same story of burnt villages, of slaughter and the devastation of crops. The loss of life caused by these raids must have been enormous, though it is of course impossible to give any exact figures. Burton, a British explorer, estimated that in order to capture fifty-five women, the merchandise of one of the caravans he observed, at least ten villages had been destroyed, each having a population of between one and two hundred souls. The greater part of these were exterminated or died of starvation. In addition to these losses, there was the loss of life incurred on the road to captivity. This again horrified all observers. The trade must have constituted a severe drain on the manpower resources of Central Africa. It revolted all the moral feelings of Europe. The trade in slaves also constituted a barrier to any political penetration which a European power might undertake.

The slave traders themselves maintained a rival system of political power. Either they established dominions of their own, or else they distributed guns to the indigenous population, so much so that Portuguese-imported guns were even said to be finding their way into Southern Rhodesia. As a British police officer put it, these guns in native hands led to 'an attitude of intolerable independence'. It is probable that had the traffic been continued over long periods, it might have seriously affected the balance of power as between Europeans and Africans in certain regions.

Also, in Livingstone's words, the slave trade would prove 'an insurmountable barrier to all moral and commercial progress' in Central Africa. Commerce could not flourish, as long as potential customers of manufactured goods from Europe were murdered or abducted by men without manufactured goods of their own to sell and thus less interested in building up an internal market. Nor as long as the traffic continued could the African continent become a producer of tropical products.

Again, no European settlement could take place for the direct exploitation of the resources of the country. The Yao slave raiders, for instance, interfered with the labourers on the European coffee estates on Mount Mlanje. In North-Western Rhodesia George Grey, the representative of a great British mining and concession company, complained bitterly to his London office that as long as the Mambari were allowed to carry on their traffic, his work at Kansanshi mine would remain very difficult. His company was not slow to communicate these views to the governing British South Africa Company, to which it was financially allied. The slave trade was thus not only immoral and cruel. As the Commandant of the British South Africa Company's police in North-Western Rhodesia put it succinctly, it also constituted 'iniquitous abduction of valuable labour'.

A system of slave labour could not exist side by side with a system of wage labour. The European mining managers and railway engineers needed African labour. However, they did not want to 'own' Africans and keep them till their dying days. They did not want women. They wanted adult African labourers for limited periods, working for wages and bound to them by contract. They did not want to mobilize their labour through forcible abduction. They were willing and able to recruit labour and to return it to the villages. They were prepared to pay wages. Wages, combined with the indirect inducement of taxation, the lure of new trade goods and the facilities of efficient recruiting organizations, would produce the required hands. The Arab plantation owners or petty chiefs did not have those means at their disposal. Even had they wanted to, they could not have organized a continuous system of wage-labour migration. So they resorted to the man-hunt and employed slaves.

The slave trade also stood for a different attitude towards the Africans in a wider sense. The black slave suffered terribly on the march from the kraal to the coast. Once he had arrived at his destination, however, he usually led a fairly easy life. The Arab or half-caste plantation owner did not stand over him with his watch in his hands, checking results. The Muslim had no watch. He had no production schedule. The European was different. H. Johnston, the first British Commissioner for Central Africa, a very acute observer, was even convinced that it was preferable for the slave to remain with his old owner rather than be liberated and be put in charge of a Christian mission. The Arab's 'tolerable form of servitude' was more agreeable than 'the tutelage of a Christian mission, with its regular hours of work, its plain diet, severe chastity and absence of exhilarating orgies', as far as the slave was concerned.

Again the two civilizations differed in their attitude towards assimilating the African. In most cases the European believed in the segregation of the African labourer. The Arab, on the other hand, believed in assimilation. He took Negro wives. He practised polygamy like the African. Besides, Muslim slavery was not a rigidly fixed status, but one allowing for an infinite number of gradations from misery to wealth. As one observer put it, 'That gaily dressed man with riches of cloth for exchange is a slave, and that poor woman who has brought her basket of meal into the market to sell looks upon him in awe and envy with her companion who carries her ware and who is her slave.' The slave trade stood indeed for 'a rival kind of civilization to that of the white man which it is of a much easier notion for the Negro mind to accept'. One of the two had to go, for between the two 'peaceful co-existence' was impossible.

The Suppression of the Slave Trade

The leading European protagonist in the struggle was Great Britain. She had already taken an active part in suppressing the slave trade on the west coast of Africa in the first half of the nineteenth century. Later Livingstone's denunciations of the slave trade in Central Africa, his discoveries, and his heroic death in Northern Rhodesia roused missionary enthusiasm for the liberation of Central Africa. Side by side with the religious, there were economic motives. Britain had become the world's leading commercial and industrial power. With the growth of her industries, more and more of her people became capable of buying tropical products. One of these was palm oil which Britain imported from the west coast of Africa; and which replaced the slave trade there. Another was cotton. During the American Civil War both American cotton production and exports suffered a very serious drop, and bitter distress resulted in Lancashire. This produced a demand for new sources of cotton, and Livingstone, amongst many others, was greatly interested in the possibilities of Africa for cotton. In addition, Africa might become a market for cotton cloth and other cheap manufactured goods which British factories were now turning out in great quantities. With the opening of the Suez Canal in 1869 and the development of steam ships capable of using it, East Africa became very easily accessible and in 1866 already Great Britain was the foremost White trading power in Zanzibar. There could, however, be no further expansion of trade if the slave trade with its ravages was to go on, and British policy was always bitterly hostile to the traffic.

Missionary, commercial free-trading, and humanitarian considerations thus all combined into a single, consistent and intelligent policy. There could be no evangelization without security of life and property. This security depended on the destruction of the slave trade. This in turn could, however, only be achieved if the traffic in slaves was replaced by some other form of trade in tropical produce. These would supply British factories with their raw materials. They would also create a market for their goods. Improved trade, provided it was not hampered by vexatious tariffs, would help the poor in Lancashire. It would also civilize the African tribesman, giving him new wants and new aspirations. These could be met by hard work and sober living, all of which in their turn would produce an attitude of mind favourable for the reception of the Gospel.

At first Britain used her strong position to check the trade by indirect means. British diplomatic representations to France and to Portugal helped to end the export of slaves from Portuguese territory across the Atlantic and to Mauritius. Diplomacy, backed by sea-power, also induced the Sultan of Zanzibar to forbid the trans-oceanic slave trade in 1873. In return, Britain supported Zanzibar in other ways. Zanzibar, though a Muslim state, was almost a free-trading country and British commercial interests could only benefit from such a policy. Neither warships nor diplomacy could stop the caravans on the mainland, however. Neither could the Sultan do so, for his authority in the interior was of a most shadowy kind. A direct attempt was then undertaken by the 'African Lakes Company', a commercial body formed with missionary support, to oust the Arab slave traders from their foothold on the north end of Lake Nyasa. Open war broke out as the Company attempted to give protection to African tribesmen against the Arabs, and as it attempted to break into the Arab ivory monopoly in the region. There was serious fighting, but the Company was too weak to achieve its aims. H. Johnston therefore negotiated peace between the Arabs and the Company in 1888, which left the Arabs where they were. The missionaries who had settled along the shores of Lake Nyasa from the 1860s onwards were similarly unable to restrain the Yao raiders from their depredations. Effective suppression only became possible once the Foreign Office assumed direct control. This was made possible by a combination of various circumstances. There was the pressure from missionary opinion. There was the failure of 'indirect rule' at Zanzibar, when Germany entered the field of colonial expansion in East Africa. There was Portuguese rivalry as Portugal attempted to make her claims to Nyasaland effective. Besides, Rhodes, one of the greatest captains of industry in South Africa and a firm believer in British colonial expansion, offered financial support to the Imperial Government in return for important concessions. In 1891 the whole of Nyasaland became an Imperial Protectorate and the older policy of non-intervention in the interior had been abandoned.

Johnston, the new Commissioner, did not at once start a general crusade. He possessed neither the military nor the financial resources to do so and at first confined himself to dealing with a minor Yao trouble-maker who interfered with British planters on Mount Mlanje and robbed European travellers. Later he extended his operations to the southern shore of the lake, where he forced most of the slavers to submit. The powerful chief Makanjira, however, resisted vigorously and inflicted a serious reverse on the British. But after a series of minor campaigns, decisive action was taken. A well-appointed seaborne expedition, supported by gunboats, over-whelmed Makanjira's town, which was strongly fortified and defended by cannon, and the east coast of Nyasa was cleared.

In the following year a concerted attack by the chiefs belonging to the Machinga group of Yao in the south was broken up and the stronghold of Mount Chikala was captured. The Mlanje district was finally pacified and by 1896 all the most dangerous chiefs had fled into Portuguese territory.

After the defeat of the Yao in Southern Nyasaland, Johnston at last was in a position to turn on the north end Arabs. Originally he had hoped that it might be possible to collaborate with the Arabs. By 1892, however, Johnston had come to the conclusion that they were the backbone of the slave trade and that in most cases it was impossible to turn them into agricultural producers. In 1896 he launched a strong seaborne force with artillery against Mlozi, the principal Arab chief, and after heavy fighting Mlozi's powerful fortress was stormed, his slaves liberated, and he himself hanged. Thus the most powerful Arab chieftaincy in the region was defeated, and the most important overland caravan route to the coast was closed. Before the destruction of Mlozi's dominion, little serious action had been taken against the Arabs in Northern Rhodesia, as it had first been found necessary to secure the communications in Nyasaland. After the establishment of British rule in that territory, the task could be undertaken effectively. It amounted to little more than a number of police actions. These were based on a series of stations, Fife, Abercorn, Kalungwisi, which had been established from Lake Nyasa to Lake Tanganyika and Lake Mweru, originally as observation posts. In 1895 Dr. Watson, one of the officers of the British South Africa Company, took over the administration of Kilwa island on Lake Mweru, which had become the home of an Arab slave-trading chief. From 1869 the police of the Company fought a series of small engagements against the Arabs, and by the end of 1899 Commissioner Sharpe reported to the Foreign Office that the influence of the Arabs in North-Eastern Rhodesia had disappeared.

The African associates in the trade similarly surrendered after small resistance. . . .

On the British side the key to victory lay in two things: Sikhs and sea-power. Sikhs, who were able to stand the climate better than European troops and who were far cheaper to maintain, formed the backbone of Johnston's force. They supplied that

CINA

element of discipline which local levies lacked and gave the necessary stiffening to the whole force. Sea-power, in the shape of a little squadron of Imperial gunboats, on the other hand, made it possible to control the route across the lake. It made up for any lack of numbers and the difficulties in the way of communications by enabling Johnston suddenly to throw large concentrations of forces against such an enemy as Makanjira or Mlozi, and it also supplied a floating artillery against an enemy ashore that could not be touched by return enemy fire. Johnston, a most able and resourceful amateur soldier, who (like Cromwell) had never had a formal military training, grasped the importance of these two factors from the very beginning, and he carried through the main campaigns to their successful conclusion, despite all military and political obstacles in his way. The shape which the operations thus assumed established an important difference between early Nyasaland on the one hand and Southern Rhodesia on the other. It had been a mounted burgher force that had conquered Southern Rhodesia. The settlers themselves had won the Matabele War, with relatively small help from the Imperial Government. They had vanquished an enemy who relied on the open tactics of the spear crescent, who was helpless against rifle and machine-gun fire and who possessed few firearms, having never seriously tried to trade captives for guns, but either murdered or assimilated them. In Nyasaland events had taken a different course. The settler element, in the shape of the African Lakes Company, had been incapable of dislodging the Arabs, with their breech-loaders. They were neither numerous enough nor sufficiently well armed to take the country on their own. In two subsequent operations the settlers again only played a very minor part. The same was true in Northern Rhodesia during the Ngoni War when the settler element, the few employees of the North Charterland Concession Company, never took any serious part in the fighting. The fact that the region north of the Zambezi was not conquered by settler forces seriously affected the strength of the settler as against the Imperial element in the far north.

In North-Western Rhodesia the slave trade continued somewhat longer. In 1894, after lengthy negotiations, the Foreign Office handed over Northern Rhodesia to the direct administration of the Company. The Company then took over the few administrative stations, such as Fife and Abercorn, which Johnston had established as Imperial Commissioner along the eastern fringe of the Chartered Territory. He administered this territory on the Company's behalf from 1891 onwards. However, the British South Africa Company did not attempt to make its power effective over the vast expanse of bush that covered most of North-Western Rhodesia. It had too many other obligations. Unlike the older 'African Lakes Company', it was not interested in trade, and it had, therefore, no incentive to push on into the interior in search of ivory and rubber. Neither was it associated with missionary interests. Its object was to guide British capital into mining and other capital investments in Rhodesia. The Company had been formed in 1889 at a time when Britain no longer lent to Continental countries to the same extent as formerly, but when British investors had realized—from the 'seventies onwards—the possibilities of investments in colonial and overseas territories. But the Company's investments in the first place lay south of the Zambezi. The copper resources to the north were hardly known. The gold of the Transvaal and of Southern Rhodesia could be worked immediately. It was thus in the south that the Company made its first major efforts, fighting the Matabele War in 1893, later becoming engaged in the Jameson Raid, and finally being forced to suppress a major African revolt in Southern Rhodesia in 1896. In consequence it had at first neither the time nor the money to devote much attention to its distant and speculative possessions in the 'far north'. In North-Eastern Rhodesia it confined itself at first to maintaining the few posts that Johnston had set up. In the north-west it did not even maintain a Resident with King Lewanika in Barotseland.

It was only in 1897 that the Company's first permanent representative took up residence in Barotseland, seven years after the first treaty had been concluded with Lewanika. A year later the first detachment of police set out from the south across the Zambezi into North-Western Rhodesia. A year later Tanganyika Concessions Ltd, a company financially linked to the British South Africa Company, started prospecting seriously for copper along the northern border of the territory and in the

Congo Free State. For the first time European interests had thus become directed to that part of Central Africa.

Despite the late start, the task of pacifying the west was in some ways simpler than it was in the east. For one thing, the Administration could rely on the support of a well-organized and comparatively powerful native state in the suppression of the slave trade, a state which moreover disliked Portuguese encroachments along its western border. Secondly the 'Mambari', with their lack of political ambitions, did not possess the fighting mettle of the Arabs and coast-men from the east. Their suppression was merely a matter of establishing police stations from which patrols would issue forth. The first of these, Kasempa, was established in 1901 and police action was quickly expanded. In 1905 the King of Italy settled by arbitration a long-standing dispute between Great Britain and Portugal over the exact extent of the western boundary of Northern Rhodesia. Once this question was settled, patrols could enter into previously doubtful territory without provoking diplomatic complications. At the same time the slave trade was coming to an end in Portuguese territory itself. In 1902 the Portuguese launched an expedition against the Bailundu, and began to assert their authority effectively in the interior of Angola. Nine years later a terrible famine also struck the slave-trading Ovimbundu. Besides rubber fell in price, as the great plantations of the East Indies started competing with native rubber. All this disorganized trade. The slave trade was further undermined by the building of the Benguella railway from the west coast to the Congo from 1902 onwards. This did away with the need for slave porters. Finally Portugal became a republic in 1910 and the tempo of reform quickened. Slaves were freed and repatriated from the cocoa islands, and the old abuses came to an end. By 1912 the last caravans disappeared. Ten years later the Administration felt itself strong enough to control strictly the possession of firearms by Africans throughout the whole of Northern Rhodesia. This measure had already been taken in the north-east in 1901, and its universal application marked the final pacification of the country. . . .

XI. THE COMPETITION FOR LAND IN SOUTH AFRICA

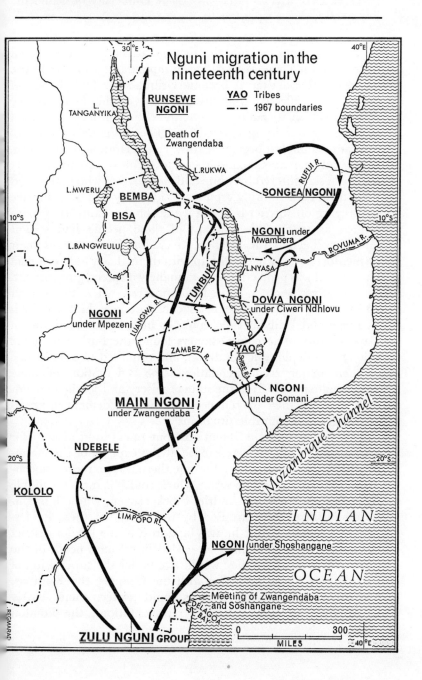

Nguni migration in the nineteenth century

YAO Tribes
– ·– · 1967 boundaries

RUNSEWE NGONI

Death of Zwangendaba

L.TANGANYIKA

L.RUKWA

L.MWERU

BEMBA

BISA

SONGEA NGONI

RUFIJI R.

NGONI under Mwambera

ROVUMA R.

L.BANGWEULU

L.NYASA

TUMBUKA

LUANGWA R.

DOWA NGONI under Ciweri Ndhlovu

NGONI under Mpezeni

ZAMBEZI R.

YAO

SHIRE R.

NGONI under Gomani

MAIN NGONI under Zwangendaba

NDEBELE

Mozambique Channel

KOLOLO

LIMPOPO R.

NGONI under Shoshangane

INDIAN

OCEAN

Meeting of Zwangendaba and Soshangane

DELAGOA BAY

0   300
MILES

ZULU NGUNI GROUP

REGMARAJ

41. Beyond the Orange River

JOHN S. GALBRAITH *Reluctant Empire* University of California Press 1963; pages 54–7, 59–61

. . . The territory across the Orange River from the settled districts of the colony was called Bushmanland until the 1830s. Thereafter for a time it became Griqualand. The change of designation reflected that displacement of the weak by the stronger which to many nineteenth-century observers seemed to have the fatality of natural law. The Bushmen's powers of resistance could not prevail against whites, Hottentots, or Bantu. Some had been absorbed by their Hottentot conquerors; many had been slaughtered by white and African foes who had ousted them from their hunting grounds. When they sought to survive by preying on the herds of the whites or the Bantu they were treated as vermin. A remnant of these people had sought sanctuary beyond the Orange River, but by the 1820s their tormentors had again caught up with them. Their only prospect for survival was protection by a humanely disposed government. In the 1820s such a hope had appeared when the British government, in response to evangelical pressure, had sent John T. Bigge and William Colebrooke to investigate conditions in Cape Colony. The commissioners found the Bushmen in the colony in a deplorable condition, and promised to offer as one of their major recommendations 'the redemption of these unfortunate people from the state of misery and servile dependence to which they are reduced, and their settlement in kraals or villages in favourable situations'.

These were humane intentions, but reservation of land for Bushmen was not expected to be at the expense of the claims of settlers, and south of the Orange there was no more unoccupied land with adequate water which could be made available for a Bushman colony. Andries Stockenstrom, whose humanitarian instincts were aroused by the misery of these hapless people, proposed while he was landdrost of the border district of Graaff Reinet that they be settled in colonies north of the Orange River, where they would live under the supervision of missionaries whose influence with the Griquas, the Koranas, and other trans-Orange peoples could protect them. Partly in response to Stockenstrom's representations, the London

Missionary Society in 1823 established a missionary station north of the Orange River, which was called Philippolis in honour of the society's South African superintendent, Dr. John Philip. But within three years this haven of refuge for Bushmen had become a residence for a section of the Griqua people, and the Bushmen again were forced to withdraw. Concerning the background of this displacement there is general agreement, but also an important area of controversy.

The Griquas were among the peoples who had withdrawn before the advance of European settlement. Their name seems to have been derived from a clan of the Hottentots variously called the Chariguriqua or the Grigriqua. In the latter part of the eighteenth century many of these people, a mixed breed of white and Hottentot, established themselves beyond the Orange River under the leadership of Adam Kok. Associated with the Griquas and eventually amalgamated with them[1] were the Bastaards, also descendants of white men and Hottentot women. Having fled from the colony to escape the oppression that was the lot of the colonial Hottentots, they were understandably suspicious of any gestures by the government at Cape Town to reimpose control over them, but they could not entirely escape the environment from which they had fled. Dr. John Philip later declared that when the missionary John Anderson had first arrived among them in 1800 they were 'a herd of wandering and naked savages, subsisting by plunder and the chase. Their bodies were daubed with red paint, their heads loaded with grease and shining powder, with no covering but the filthy kaross over their shoulders'—a characterization applicable at most to only some of these people. When Stockenstrom observed them twenty years later, the majority were expert horsemen and marksmen with the musket and 'as well mounted and armed as the generality of colonists'. Many wore European clothes. Their borrowing from colonial society undoubtedly was not entirely the result of missionary influence.

The missionaries soon gained an ascendancy over the main body of the Griqua tribes, with the power to make and unmake chiefs. They induced them to accept a relatively settled life in the present Griqualand West. Klaarwater, later renamed

---

[1] The differentiation, however, was not obliterated by the mid-nineteenth century.

Griquatown, became the capital city. The name of Bastaard, offensive to the ears of the devout, ceased to be employed in polite usage. When the leadership of Adam Kok II became unsatisfactory to the missionaries, they prevailed upon him in 1819 to abdicate his 'captaincy' and procured the election of their protégé, Andries Waterboer, a recent arrival from the colony, in his stead. Waterboer thereafter vindicated the confidence of his benefactors by accepting not only their spiritual but their political guidance. He became the model of the Christian chief, a bulwark of order, the defender of the weak. This client kingdom of the missionaries became the instrument of John Philip's policy of interposing 'belts of civilized natives between the colonists and their less civilized neighbours' as a means of stabilizing the border.

A number of the Griquas refused to accept the new order of a missionary-dominated state and left the realm of Andries Waterboer. Some of them swelled the numbers of the banditti who infested the islands and the banks of the Orange River. Others followed Kok into exile. For three years Kok lived with his brother Cornelis at the village of Campbell (named for a missionary); later he lived near Backhouse (named for another missionary) on the Vaal River. But Philip, on his tour of the interior in 1825, found Kok's band, calling themselves 'Bergenaars', wandering in the Modder Valley. Kok asked permission to settle at the Bushman station, and Philip consented. Kok migrated to Philippolis in 1826. By 1829 the Bushmen had been removed from their erstwhile home to another station on the Caledon River, and Bushmanland became Griqualand.

Philip contended that the relationship between Bushmen and Griquas was friendly and that the Griquas were in fact protectors, but one Griqua later testified that 'we exterminated the Bushmen and Dr Philip gave us the country'. Both versions are exaggerations; certainly the Griquas did not exterminate the Bushmen of Philippolis, but neither did they become their benefactors.

Andries Stockenstrom averred that Philip, in establishing a second Griqua community at Philippolis, had, without a shadow of right to alienate the land, ceded possession of the soil from the Bushmen to the new owners, and that he had seen a paper to that effect in the possession of the agent at Griqua-town. Philip retorted that Stockenstrom had twisted the facts. He stated that because there had been some differences of opinion between the Bushman mission and the Griquas, the former had decided to leave and that Kok and his followers were left in possession of the site of the mission and the buildings on it. The transaction to which Kok alluded referred only to the buildings and improvements, for which the Griquas were required to pay, and had no reference to the land at all; but Kok and his advisers had mistakenly assumed that they had purchased the country as well.

Whichever version was correct the consequences were the same; the Bushmen were displaced by the Griquas. . . .

Eastward of Kok's Philippolis lived the Basuto of Moshesh, a people destined to become one of the most powerful adversaries of the land-hungry white settlers, but as yet largely insulated from conflict with the trekking farmers. It was a tribe born of disaster, transformed into a unified people by a masterly leader from the shattered remnants of tribes broken by the *Mfecane*. Moshesh's feat of organizing the resistance of this unpromising human material, first against tribal adversaries, and then against the Europeans, was one of the outstanding accomplish-ments of South African history. So impressive was his achieve-ment that European observers found it difficult to believe that any mere native could have been responsible. Moshesh had grown to manhood as a minor tribal chief in the mountains of the northern part of present-day Basutoland; he and his followers, when attacked by the Mantatees and other tribes set in motion by the war of Chaka, had retreated to the flat-topped mountain of Thaba Bosiu, where he had resisted all efforts to dislodge him and had steadily grown in power as other refugees had accepted him as their leader.

Moshesh was no mere war chief; he was a most astute diplo-mat. He knew how to temporize to advantage, to play off potential adversaries against one another, to utilize every opening to protect the interests of the people, preferably without the necessity of war. The mind of Moshesh, Europeans were forced to admit, was the equal of their own. They noted that his features were regular, his profile was aquiline, and his forehead was well developed, as befitted a man of great intellectual powers. In fact, except for his dark skin, he had the 'look of a European'.

Hordes of Zulus, Fingoes, Griquas, and other attackers had beset Moshesh's strongholds and had been beaten back or had retired in frustration at being unable to come to grips with the defenders. When the raiders withdrew they left the open lands to the west of the mountains scoured of inhabitants. Over these territories Moshesh now asserted his claim, on the justification that the remnants of tribes that had resided there now lived under his chieftainship. The Basuto left their mountain sanctuaries to return to the corn lands of the Caledon River Valley, favoured with rain from the mountains to the east which made possible agriculture without irrigation. By 1834 Basuto families had already resettled forty to fifty miles west of the Caledon.

Moshesh's claims did not go uncontested. An old enemy, the Batlokua chief, Sikonyela, son of that fierce queen who had given her name to the terrible Mantatees, resided with his followers in the upper Caledon. A recent arrival in the lands claimed by Moshesh, the Barolong of Moroko, had settled around Thaba Nchu with the Basuto chief's consent; but dispute over the nature of the Barolong's relationship to Moshesh was soon to produce conflict. Scattered throughout the Caledon also were villages of Korana Hottentots and Newlanders, the latter a half-caste people. Even before the arrival of the Europeans, therefore, the possession of the valley of the Caledon and the plateau to the west was already in dispute among a number of claimants. Further complicating the relationship of these peoples was a collision of the vested interests of two missionary societies. The Paris Evangelical Missionary Society, closely allied to the London Missionary Society, had begun work in 1833 among the Basuto, and its representatives were soon to become not only spiritual counsellors of the Basuto but political advisers of Moshesh. Representatives of the Wesleyan Missionary Society had established themselves in a similar capacity among Moshesh's enemies.

In 1834, with the arrival of Sir Benjamin D'Urban, the Cape received a new constitution providing for the establishment of an executive council consisting of the governor and four officials, and a legislative council including these same officials, the attorney general, and from five to seven appointed citizens of the Cape. The consent of the legislative council was required for legislation, which could be nullified only by the action of the King in Council. But in the primary problems with which the governor had to deal, he remained as his predecessors had been, the virtual dictator of the colony. He was, however, a dictator with little power, for the British government had decreed that he must maintain order at the Cape with a handful of officials and a few hundred troops, and without recourse to the armed citizenry whose slaughter of the natives had provoked the indignation of British society. Further, D'Urban was required in 1834 to supervise the transition of Cape Colony from a system of slavery to a new 'free society'; in fact, he was to preside over a social revolution which had begun with the passage in 1828 of the celebrated Fiftieth Ordinance, freeing the Hottentots from legal disabilities. To carry out this immense undertaking, the governor had at his disposal a few paid magistrates, whose districts averaged between 7,000 and 8,000 square miles.

The prospects for a governor under such circumstances were not promising, and even a salary of £6,000 per year and perquisites offered small compensation. If he was fortunate a governor could hope to leave the colony in no worse state than he found it, but he ran a grave risk that his career would be ruined. In either event he could expect his policies to be attacked by a Cape population which he despised, 'composed of all that is Vulgar, and worthless, and consisting of no conversation but the Gossip and slander of everyone's neighbour or friend, all alike, friend or foe.' He was sent by an economy-minded government to battle against cosmic forces; the result was predetermined. . . .

42. The Great Trek

ERIC WALKER *A History of Southern Africa* Longmans 1959; pages 196–9, 200–5, 206–10

From one point of view the Great Trek was merely an acceleration of a process which had been going on as long as men could remember: the steady drift of Europeans and half-castes out beyond the proclaimed frontiers of the Colony. The trek spirit was inborn in the Boer frontiersmen of the 'thirties. From the end of the seventeenth century the cattle-farmers had followed their migratory farms eastward till in 1775 they had been checked by the Kaffirs along the Fish. There, a generation of young Boers had grown up all looking forward to farms of their own and fretting against Government restrictions which forbade them to go to the Koonap or, 'if it could be, unto the Kat'. The great effort of 1812 which had cleared the Zuurveld had been followed by a revolution in land tenure, for henceforward new farms were to be obtained only at variable quit-rents. Then, as the second generation grew to manhood, the 1820 Settlers had come crowding into the Zuurveld. The Ceded Territory had offered some relief, but the main tide of migration had already turned north-eastward, when woolled sheep followed the Settlers in and Government threatened to auction Crown lands. With a third generation of lads soon to be pro-vided for and drought following drought in grim succession, what could cattle-farmers do but look around for a way of escape from changing conditions which promised to make the old style of life, the *lekker leven*, impossible? Farmers began to drift across the Orange and a big trek was talked of; but it was only organised after the return of the *kommissie* treks, which told the Boers that there were fine and almost vacant lands where today are the Free State and Transvaal cattle and mealie farms and the fertile valleys of Natal. A large and steady emigration would, humanly speaking, have taken place had emancipation, the Xosas and Stockenstrom never afflicted the frontiersmen, for, as Retief told Dingaan, the Colony was too small and the Boers were becoming landless. The Kaffir war cut right across the projected trek, and it was not till the fighting was finished that the first two organised parties crossed the Orange. Even so, Trigardt had been living beyond the borders for three years past and had very special reasons for his final departure. The movement remained on a small scale till the latter half of 1836; then, helped on by a severe drought, the abrogation of martial law and the fading of all hope of land in Queen Adelaide, the Great Trek began in good earnest.

The Great Trek was however more than a matter of mere

belly-need. It was unprecedented in South African history by reason of its organisation, its size and its spirit. The pre-Trek Boers and some of the scattered groups which drifted out of the Colony alongside the Trek parties meant to take the Colony with them as their fathers had done before them. Not so the trekkers of the Trek. Many of them were sons or grandsons of the men of Graaff-Reinet in whom republican ideas had stirred in 1795, and all had grievances. They moved off inspired by feelings towards H.M. Government ranging from bitter hatred to a mild but firm determination to have nothing more to do with it. 'We quit this Colony,' wrote Retief, 'under the full assurance that the English Government . . . will allow us to govern ourselves without its interference.'

Apart from the general desire for land, the motives of the Trekkers varied almost from family to family. There was the new system of land tenure administered by a haphazard Lands Department. Complaints were frequent of high and unequal quit-rents, of favouritism in the allocation of farms, of delay in the issue of title-deeds after survey, of the possibility that titles would be withdrawn and fresh fees charged. There was pro-found dissatisfaction with the nature of the Government. Officials representing the central power had never been popular on the Frontier even when checked by local heemraden, and now the heemraden were no more. All the evils, wrote the Natal Volksraad in 1842, arose from the lack of representative government. Perhaps that was an afterthought; nevertheless, as soon as the Trekkers could organise their own states, the first thing they did was to revive the courts of the landrosts and heemraden and restore the field cornets to all their old powers and more also. Nor was there enough even of this purely official government near the Frontiers. Not only were many of the field cornets incompetent to perform such duties as remained to them, but the magistrates were too few to permit of the farmers complying with the law. Again, Government set limits to the powder trade and forbade reprisals; but it did not protect. Uys is said to have trekked because the mountains near his home were full of Kaffirs armed with muskets, though his enthusiasm for Natal and his indignation that his wife should have been haled to court, there to answer a charge brought against her by a Hottentot, also explain his action. What though Mrs. Uys was acquitted, there was the delay and expense of the journey to the far-distant magistracy, a difficulty which gave a farmer the choice between marching errant servants to court for punishment with all the risk attendant on leaving the homestead unguarded, or of taking the law into his own hands at the risk of incurring the penalty of the law. On all sides the cry went up that there was no security on the Frontier.

There were also financial grievances. Government held that it had done its duty when it had paid and paid heavily for defence and supplies; but two years after the close of the Kaffir war requisition notes were still unhonoured and changing hands cheaply. Moreover the colonists, both Afrikaner and British, had expected that, since there were to be no land grants, Government, which had made them buy at auction their own recaptured cattle during the war, would make good their war losses. This Glenelg declined to do, in spite of the plea of D'Urban and Napier that it would be worth while checking the Trek at the cost of a bad precedent. Some Trekkers, like Uys, complained that they ought to have been let off the payment of taxes for a year or two; one, Jacobus Boshof, mentions the redemption of the paper money as a grievance. . . .

Had there been no land available outside the Colony there might have been a rebellion even against a government which, as the fate of the Slachter's Nek rebels witnessed, took rebellion seriously. As it was, the Boers trekked. Once the movement had begun, it gathered speed by its own momentum. The knowledge that there was no legal bar, once martial law had been abrogated, decided many; others went because the leading man in their district went or because their neighbours trekked and they feared isolation. Some moved off to help their comrades after the early disasters in Natal; others when victories like Blood River showed them that they could safely do so; others again when Napier, D'Urban's successor, showed that he meant to uphold the treaty system. Nor was 'enthusiasm' wanting. 'We rather withdrew,' wrote Anna Steenkamp, 'in order thus to preserve our doctrines in purity.' 'They fancy they are under a divine impulse,' wrote one observer; 'the women seem more bent on it than the men.' From the start, petticoat influence was strong among the Trekkers.

The parties, drawn almost entirely from the frontier districts, marched as a rule under the leading local official, like Retief, or the family patriarch, like Jacobus Uys.[1] Fairbairn went too far when he said that they abandoned nothing of value. There were, indeed, no Groot Constantias in the East and families rarely occupied the same farm for two generations, but many of the houses were substantial. He was on firmer ground when he said their wants were few and 'even the luxury of bread is not universal amongst them'. Game was plentiful; the creaking, tilted waggon with its straining team of oxen could carry wife and children and 'the family pot', while beside the waggon padded cattle and sheep in herds surprisingly great considering the drought and the wastage of the war.[2] Ammunition presented few difficulties to those who had hard money, and the Boers readily changed the paper proceeds of their farms at the rate of 23s. for each English sovereign. Some farms were simply abandoned, but many were sold at reasonable prices, considering that the absence of title-deeds in many cases diminished their value. Prices naturally fell when numbers of farms were thrown on the market; nevertheless, the proverbial exchange of a farm, which had originally been a free grant, for a waggon and span of oxen was not always a bad bargain at a time when waggons and oxen were in great demand.

Once they had crossed the drifts of the middle Orange into Griqua Philippolis, the Trekkers had before them a huge parallelogram of grasslands: the present Free State, half Bechuanaland and two-thirds of the Transvaal. To the west the grass faded away into the Kalahari Desert; on the east it was bounded by mountains; on the north by mountains again and the deadly tsetse fly of the Limpopo valley. Just beyond the Orange were pre-Trek Boers, who by no means welcomed the new arrivals, and Griquas centring round the L.M.S. stations. Abram Kok reigned at Philippolis itself in the room of Adam II, deceased, and away to the west, beyond the lower Vaal,

---

[1] The leaders and localities of the principal parties were (1835–37): Trigardt and van Rensburg (Albany and extra-Colonial); A. H. Potgieter (Tarka); Cilliers and Liebenberg (Colesberg); Maritz (Graaff-Reinet); Retief (Winterberg); Uys (Uitenhage); Jacobs (Beaufort West).

[2] 113 folk from Tarka took £60,000 worth (Chase, II. 106). 29 small parties or families from Tarka took 6,156 cattle and 96,000 sheep (Cory, III. 404). In 1836, 27 people lost 96 horses, 4,671 cattle and 50,745 sheep to the Matabele (Chase, I. 134).

Andries Waterboer ruled at Griquatown and Cornelis Kok at Campbell. Eastwards on either side of the Caledon river lay Bantu and half-breed clans with their missionaries. The Berliners cared for the Koranas at Bethanie, but on the western bank of the Caledon the Wesleyans held most of the field. They were at Imparani among Sikonyela's Batokua, at Merumetsu with Taaibosch's Koranas, with Baatje's half-breeds at Platberg, and with the Barolong of Moroko and Tawane at Thaba Nchu. The Paris Evangelicals were with Lepui's Batlapin at Bethulie and with the Bataung at Mekuatling; but their main field was among the Basuto to the east of the Caledon at Morija and, after 1837, at Thaba Bosigo, Moshesh's capital. All these Caledon chiefs, big and little, were *amici* of the Colony, 'white men under the white King'.

On the western side of the grasslands the L.M.S. men had long been with the Batlapin at Robert Moffat's Kuruman. More recently American Zulu missionaries had settled at Mosega with the Matabele. Msilikazi's kraals lay north of the Vaal grouped round Kapain and Mosega. Around them lay a waste of Matabele making, and beyond, on the edge of the Kalahari, lurked the remnants of Gasiyitsiwe's Bangwaketse, Secheli's Bakwena and further north at Shoshong, Sekhomi's Bamangwato. In the mountains of the north-eastern and eastern Transvaal lay the Batlou at Makapans Poort, the Maguamba in the Zoutpansberg, the Bapedi, kinsmen of the Basuto, in the Lulu Mountains and the Swazis on the crest of the Lebombo. To the east and south-east of the Drakensberg the land fell away, step by step, till it flattened out into the narrow tropical coast strip of Zululand and Natal. In what is now Portuguese East Africa Manikusa did what he chose, while the Portuguese cautiously reoccupied the posts on the lower Zambesi and the coast which his Shangaans had recently sacked. To the south, from the border of Swaziland to the Umzimvubu river, were lands densely peopled only where Dingaan's Zulus lived between the Mkusi and the Tugela rivers and a few clans huddled in the foothills of the Drakensberg mountains or round the English hunters at Port Natal. Between the Umzimvubu and the colonial frontier were the Pondos and the other coast tribes of Kaffirland.

Had the *Mfecane* not swept so much of the country bare of

inhabitants, the tribesmen might have been able to hold the line of the Orange or, in the last resort, the Vaal as doggedly as the Xosas had long held the line of the Fish river. As it was the only enemies the Trekkers had to fear in the plains immediately north of the Colonial boundary were Griquas, armed indeed with firearms and horses like themselves, but a mere divided scattering of folk, and, far away in the background, the Zulu and Matabele impis which, for all their valour, had no missile weapons other than the light throwing assegai and had never even seen a horse. The Trekkers with their heavy muskets, horses and stout waggons soon found that, unless they were cornered or surprised, the odds were all in their favour, and that the country was admirably adapted to their style of fighting except in the wooded hills and valleys of Natal and Zululand and, presently, the mountains of Basutoland. The enemy could be seen far off on the great plains, and there was usually time to form laager as in Potgieter's fight with the Matabele at Vegkop, waggon locked to waggon by the trek-chains in a great ring and the space between the wheels filled with thorn bush. Or, if the men were out unhampered by waggons and families, there was room to ride up within range, fire, retire to load and then fire again with the heavy roers (elephant guns) which 'kill at a great distance', till the enemy gave way as at the rout of the Matabele in the Marico battle. Sometimes, as at the crowning mercy of Blood River against the Zulus, the two tactics could be combined. A very few decisive battles were enough to make the Trekkers masters of open country which had been cleared of most of its inhabitants either by death or displacement during the *Mfecane*.

The first two trek parties fared ill. Trigardt and Jan van Rensburg journeyed together far into the Transvaal. There they separated, Jan van Rensburg's people to be wiped out by hostile tribes in the lower Limpopo valley, and Trigardt's to find rest in the Zoutpansberg. Presently, sadly reduced by fever, they stumbled on to Delagoa Bay, whence most of the survivors were brought by sea to Natal in 1839. The later parties followed in their tracks. Potgieter, Carel Cilliers and Barend Leidenberg joined hands beyond the Orange, and with them went a boy of ten, Paul Kruger, future President of the South African Republic. Potgieter, most restless of all the

Trekkers, went north, naming many of the Free State rivers and making verbal treaties of friendship with neighbouring chiefs. From his base camp in what is now the northern Orange Free State, he pushed on with a small party to find Trigardt and a road to Delagoa Bay. At the Zoutpansberg he found Trigardt; but he failed to find the road to the sea, and on his return home he learnt that the Matabele, who resented the presence of armed bands in their country in place of the hunters and the men of God who had always asked the King for 'the road', had destroyed the Leidenbergs on the northern bank of the Vaal. He himself was glad to beat the Matabele off at Vegkop at the price of losing his cattle. Moroko, the Barolong chief, and his Wesleyan missionary, the Rev. William Archbell, helped him back to Thaba Nchu, and there he was joined by a new party of Trekkers led by Gerrit Maritz of Graaff-Reinet.

Of the five things needful to the formation of a republic Potgieter had done one: he had surveyed the land. But it still remained for the Trekkers to acquire that land, to frame government machinery, to come to terms with their non-European neighbours and to win recognition of their independence from H.M. Government. They first faced the problem of government. It was not an easy task. Unlike the emigrants drawn from all the strata of old-established societies, who went to North America in the seventeenth century or to Australasia and the eastern Cape Colony in the nineteenth, the Trekkers were, with hardly an exception, men of one class only. They were stock-farmers, of all civilised men the least accustomed to common action and the restraints of the law. They lacked political experience; there were few among them who were competent to carry on public business; they were self-reliant to a fault; their leaders were jealous of one another; they had, as yet, no sure abiding place in the great plains. And they must build their state from bedrock upwards. Their first constitution was of such a rudimentary nature that it has since been disputed whether it can be called a constitution at all. At Thaba Nchu, 'Het Volk' (the People) elected Maritz, a man of some education and legal experience, as landdrost, and six other men to act with him as bench, legislature and council of war administering such laws as might be agreed upon by a general meeting of all the men of the trek party. Potgieter and Maritz then led their fighting men and a few Griquas, Koranas and Barolong against the Matabele. They read them a sharp lesson at Mosega, regained captured waggons and cattle and returned to Thaba Nchu with the American missionaries, who despaired of the Matabele after a year's experience and hoped for better success with the kindred Zulus near Port Natal.

Piet Retief then rode in with four hundred followers. He was the ablest of the Voortrekkers and, helped by the quarrels of Potgieter and Maritz, soon established his ascendancy. At Vet river, the Thaba Nchu constitution was adapted to the new conditions and confirmed by the Nine Articles of association. Maritz remained President of the Volksraad and the landdrost of that body when it should sit, like the House of Lords, in a judicial capacity; but Retief was elected Commandant-General and Governor with an elected Council of Policy to assist him. Retief's Governorship and the Council of Policy, which was probably the Volksraad in another form, were the nearest approach to a civil as distinct from a military executive that the Trekkers were to have for many years. Thus entrenched as head of the state, Retief organised the church. For lack of a fully ordained minister and in spite of the furious opposition of Potgieter, who would have preferred the ministrations of the Wesleyan, 'Aardspiel' of Thaba Nchu, he appointed the ex-mission teacher, Erasmus Smit, to conduct services. He then turned to deal with the pressing matter of native policy. He bade his commandants shed no innocent blood on patrol nor take Bushman children as apprentices without their parents' consent, and made treaties with neighbouring chiefs, notably with Moroko, the good friend of the Trekkers, and with Sikonyela and Moshesh. None of these treaties survive, possibly because they were verbal; but, on the analogy of treaties concluded soon afterwards, they must have provided for peace, amity and leave for the white man to occupy land, probably in return for a consideration.

At this stage, Jacobus Uys and his famous son, Piet, arrived from Uitenhage, closely followed by Jacobs and his neighbours from Beaufort West. Now that some four to five hundred fighting-men were assembled with perhaps a thousand waggons, Retief felt strong enough to deal decisively with the Matabele. Fear of the Griquas and, more certainly, quarrels among the

leaders ruined his plans. Potgieter, who wished to trek north of
the Vaal as far away as possible from British influence and find
a port on the East Coast, finally parted company with Maritz;
Uys with 170 followers formally repudiated Retief's authority
and proposed to found a state in Natal at his leisure on U.S.A.
principles; Retief himself decided to go to the Promised Land
of Natal, the point of contact with the outer world and the
vantage ground from which to bargain for independence and
friendly relations with the British. So Retief rode down to
Port Natal with a few friends to get into touch with Dingaan,
while Potgieter and Uys with 135 men and a few of Tawane's
Barolong defeated the Matabele in a nine days' running fight
along the Marico river without the loss of a man. Msilikazi,
who had been roughly handled a little before by the Zulus,
withdrew northwards beyond the Limpopo into what is now
Matabeleland, and Potgieter claimed all the lands that had
been subject to him from the Vaal to the Zoutpansberg, and
the Kalahari to Rhenoster Poort. The Trekkers were thus
potential masters of all the open grasslands from the Griqua
borders to the edge of the tsetse belt. They hoped soon to be
masters of Natal also. . . .

So far from being solved the native question had been
immensely complicated by the Trek. It was this fact which had
to be faced by the new Governor, Sir George Napier. He was a
Peninsular veteran like D'Urban, but, unlike him, a convinced
negrophilist avowedly prepared to make the best of the treaty
system and to send on Stockenstrom's letters promptly to
Downing Street. Soon after landing he visited the Eastern
Frontier (few Governors were to omit that formality for many
years to come) and found some of the clans stealing extensively,
and the drought, which helped to explain the prevalence of
theft, making the tracing of the spoor and, therefore, recovery
difficult. He condemned the bush of the lower Fish river as a
boundary, demanded the reinforcements which D'Urban had
asked for in vain, tried to move the Fingos back further into the
Colony away from the Xosas who still hankered after the cattle
stolen by their 'dogs' during the late war, threatened Macomo
and the emigrant Tembus with reprisals if they did not behave
themselves and, on the advice of Stockenstrom, made defensive
alliances with the friendly Gunukwebes in the Ceded Territory.

At that very moment he was robbed of Stockenstrom's services. To the unbounded joy of the Easterners, the Lieutenant-Governor lost a libel action which he had brought against one of his critics and sailed for England, leaving Colonel John Hare, an honest man of no great ability, to act in his stead.

Napier, meanwhile, tried to stop the Trek and persuade the Trekkers to return home. He enlisted the help of the border officials and of the Dutch Reformed Church clergy, who disapproved of a movement which was taking so many of their flocks beyond the reach of civilisation and the means of grace, pressed for compensation for war losses and security of land tenure, and even had a hurried and unavailing interview with a Boer deputation on the northern border. All he could do was to issue a warning that no ex-slaves might be taken beyond the frontiers as the day of complete freedom was due in December, and to send a field cornet, Gideon Joubert, to bring back smuggled apprentices into the Colony. Joubert returned with forty, having left over a hundred behind at their own request, two of whom were, however, sent back presently by sea from Natal to receive their freedom.

From the time of Napier's visit to the northern border till the middle of 1842, Transorangia was left to take care of itself and Natal became the storm centre of South African politics. Gardiner had taken up his duties as magistrate at the Port and persuaded Dingaan to cede the southern half of Natal to the Crown, waive his claim to runaway subjects and receive an Anglican missionary, the Reverend Francis Owen, at his kraal of Umgungundhlovu. On the other hand, Gardiner was powerless to check gun-runners, for he had no prison and no police and, now, the majority of the English defied him, repudiated the Royal claim to Natal and declared their independence. They welcomed Retief to the Port and sent one or two of their number with him to interview Dingaan. From him Retief received the promise of land, presumably the whole of Natal, provided he recovered Zulu cattle stolen by Sikonyela and, added the King, 'if possible, the thief as well'. So Retief rode homewards to be met by his own followers and those of Maritz pouring down the passes of the Drakensberg and forming laager among the rolling hills of northern Natal in breach of their promise to stand fast till he should return. However, he recovered the Zulu cattle, took all Sikonyela's horses and guns, and then, in spite of more than one warning and the entreaties of Maritz, rode off to Dingaan's kraal with seventy followers, thirty coloured attendants and an English interpreter from Port Natal.

Retief and his men rode into a death-trap. For some time past Dingaan had been growing uneasy at the news of the doings of these white men mounted on 'hornless cattle' and armed with the guns he coveted. Retief himself had told him how they had routed his deadly enemy, Msilikazi, at no loss to themselves and the King had plagued his missionary to teach him 'what he really wanted to know, the use of firearms'. Now the Boers had come 'like an army from the direction of Msilikazi' to build houses in his country, their leader was actually at his kraal with just such a commando as had harried the Matabele at Mosega, and the rest of them were scattered unsuspecting among their tents. It was a chance not to be missed. After a day or two of negotiation, during which he called up reinforcements, Dingaan signed a deed giving Natal to Retief and his followers and, having thus enticed them all into his kraal unarmed, slew them and the Hottentots without the gate.

At first Dingaan thought of making a clean sweep of the white men in his country, but after some hesitation he let the English and American missionaries get away. On the other hand he at once sent his impis to fall upon the Boer laagers. The slaughter at Weenen followed; but the other laagers stood firm, Potgieter and Uys came down from the High Veld and joint action was arranged with the English. Disaster ensued. Neither of the Boer leaders would serve under the other or under Maritz; Uys was trapped by the Zulus and killed; Potgieter, who had never liked the Natal adventure, rode back to the High Veld; one English expedition effected little, a second was destroyed, and the Zulus, storming down to Port Natal, drove the survivors and the missionaries on shipboard.

The fortunes of the Trekkers were now at their lowest ebb, for the Zulus had thus far killed 361 of their number and about 200 of their Coloured servants besides thirteen Englishmen and many of their Bantu followers. Then the tide began to turn. The Trekkers might hope that Andries Pretorius of Graaff-Reinet, who had visited them before the recent disasters, would

give such a good report of Natal in the Eastern districts that
many of his neighbours would be tempted to join them, and,
then, that the very news of their misfortunes would arouse many
more to come to the rescue. It proved indeed to be so. True,
Maritz died, but the Natalians founded their capital of Pietermaritzburg. Carel Landman, Maritz's successor, gained
possession of the Port with the consent of the few surviving
English, and in due time Pretorius came back with a strong
following, took the lead and began to plan vengeance on Dingaan. On the other hand, the redcoats came close on his heels.
From the first, Napier had wished to send troops to Port Natal
to keep order and check the Trek. As confused rumours of
strife between Boers and Bantu in various parts of the hinterland
drifted in, he had become more insistent and had at last wrung a
grudging consent from Glenelg on condition that there was no
'colonisation'. He promptly sent Major Samuel Charters with
a hundred men to the Port to restore peace and prevent the
importation of warlike stores or the formation of an independent
government; but now that he realised that there was no hope
of inducing the Trekkers to return to the Colony, he urged
Glenelg to set up an administration in Natal subordinate to
that at Capetown. Charters meanwhile occupied the Port; but
in spite of his efforts to stop Pretorius, the latter marched into
Zululand and, on 16 December 1838, overthrew many of
Dingaan's impis at the three-hour battle of Blood River.
Pressing on, Pretorius occupied the smouldering ruins of
Umgungundhlovu and found the deed of cession in Retief's
wallet beside his bones on the Hill of Execution hard by.

Though some three thousand Zulus were slain at the cost of
three Boers slightly wounded, the victory of Blood River by no
means broke the Zulu power. It did, however, clear the way
for the organisation of the most elaborate Trekker republic
yet attempted around the church which the Natalians built at
Pietermaritzburg as a thank-offering for their deliverance.
This Republic was a continuation of that founded at Thaba
Nchu and Vet river, for six of the seven members of the High
Veld Raad had trekked down into Natal, with instructions
drawn up based on existing regulations. These instructions,
with additional rules to meet new circumstances, were now put
into force. A Volksraad of twenty-four members, two from

each field cornetcy elected annually on adult white male suffrage, served as legislature, court of appeal and, in many respects, executive as well.

43. Boer and Zulu

RUPERT FURNEAUX *The Zulu War* Weidenfeld & Nicolson and J. B. Lippincott 1963; pages 13–16

Once again the Boer wagons lumbered over the Drakensbergs. But as long as Dingaan ruled the Zulus, the Boers felt insecure. They learned that his brother, Panda, was planning a revolt; secret messages were exchanged. Panda and Pretorius agreed to act together to rid Zululand and Natal of the treacherous Dingaan. Supported by a Boer commando, Panda defeated Dingaan, who fled and was soon murdered.

The good-natured Panda now ruled in Zululand. The Boers settled in Natal, forming an independent republic like that of their brothers in the Transvaal and Orange Free State. But they had reckoned without the British. Determined to retain their colony of Natal, the Cape government sent troops to Durban. After several clashes, the Boers submitted, and a treaty was made between the Government of Natal and Panda, defining the Zulu frontier on the Tugela River. Peace reigned in Natal, and throughout South Africa. By the Sand River Convention of 1852, the British recognised the right of the Boers of the Orange Free State and of the Transvaal to manage their own affairs and govern themselves without interference, according to their own laws.

In Zululand Panda's sons, Cetewayo and Umbulazi, fought for the succession; in 1856 Cetewayo defeated his brother in a bloody battle and became the heir to the throne. In 1861 Theophilus Shepstone, the Secretary for Native Affairs in Natal, came to Zululand and recognised Cetewayo as Panda's successor. When the old king died in 1873, Shepstone returned to attend Cetewayo's coronation as a mark of respect. He took the opportunity to secure from the new king certain promises,

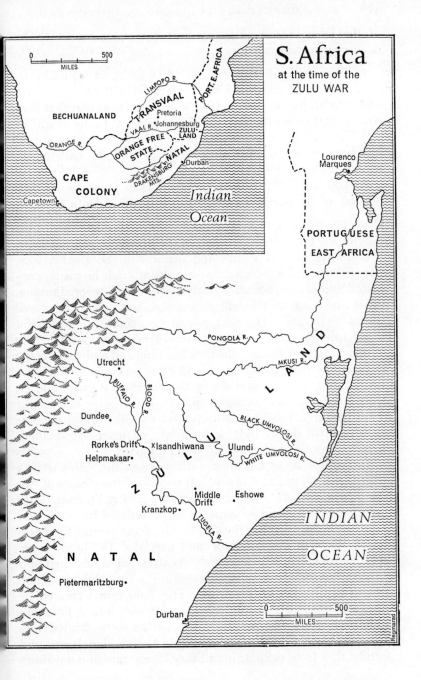

S. Africa
at the time of the
ZULU WAR

0 — 500
MILES

PORT. E. AFRICA

LIMPOPO R.

TRANSVAAL
Pretoria
Johannesburg
VAAL R.
ZULU-
LAND

BECHUANALAND

ORANGE R.

ORANGE FREE
STATE

NATAL
DRAKENSBURG
MTS.
Durban

CAPE
COLONY

Capetown

Indian
Ocean

Lourenco
Marques

PORTUGUESE
EAST AFRICA

PONGOLA R.

Utrecht

MKUSI R.

Z U L U L A N D

BUFFALO R.

BLOOD R.

Dundee

BLACK UMVOLOSI R.

Rorke's Drift
Helpmakaar

x Isandhiwana

Ulundi

WHITE UMVOLOSI R.

Z U L U

Middle
Drift

Eshowe

Kranzkop

TUGELA R.

N A T A L

INDIAN

OCEAN

Pietermaritzburg

0 — 500
MILES

Durban

Regmand

in the form of the following four principles by which his country would be ruled:

1. That the indiscriminate shedding of blood would cease.
2. That no Zulu would be condemned without open trial, and without public examination of all witnesses; and that each convicted man would have the right of appeal to the king.
3. That, once a trial had taken place and the right of appeal had been exercised, no Zulu life would be taken without the knowledge and consent of the king.
4. And that for minor crimes the loss of property, all or a portion of it, would be substituted for the death penalty.

Cetewayo's failure to keep these 'promises' became one of the excuses for the British invasion of Zululand six years later.

Cetewayo, son of Panda and nephew of the great Shaka, was left to rule his people, 250,000 strong, rich in cattle, contented and prosperous after thirty-two years of peace. Prophet, priest and king, an efficient rain maker and driver out of evil spirits, Cetewayo was popular with his people, who, cheerful and happy in their well-ordered existence, grouped together in their scattered kraals—the men building and maintaining the huts and herding the cattle, the women, several wives to each man, tilling the soil and doing the domestic work. Children were loved, but were brought up in strict discipline and taught good manners, sobriety, honesty and morality. Adultery was punished by death, but a form of restricted love-making between youths and maidens was permitted.

In the middle of the nineteenth century, the Zulus were a noble race, refined and brave. But they were the victims of two dangerous national habits: superstition and militarism. They believed in evil spirits who had to be propitiated by magic and could only be exorcised by the death of the person they possessed. Fear of the witch doctors pervaded the land; every man, particularly if he were rich in cattle, might be 'smelt out' as a harbourer of evil spirits, dangerous to his neighbours, and put to death with all his house. The Zulu army, created by Shaka to make his people great, had grown into a Frankenstein's monster. The youth of the nation were drafted into regiments according to age groups. Abandoning home and family, they lived celibate in military kraals, minding the king's cattle and acting as the national police force while drilling for war. No young soldier was allowed to marry without permission of the king, who seldom granted it until the soldier was nearly forty years of age, or until he had killed an enemy in battle, when by national custom he could request the privilege of restrained sexual intercourse with any girl he met. The army was his career, and war afforded the only chance he ever got to gain honour and cattle. Not unnaturally the Zulu army clamoured for war. Cetewayo put them off with excuses, but the pressure increased; for militarism was as much a part of the Zulus' national life as religion was of the Jews'. War and life were inseparable. Sooner or later, the Zulu army, exultant in its manhood but frustrated by inactivity, would prove a stumbling block to peace.

XII. UNIFICATION OF SOUTH AFRICA

44. The Boer War

J. S. MARAIS *The Fall of Kruger's Republic* Clarendon Press, Oxford 1961; pages 323–32

The advent of Joseph Chamberlain as colonial secretary marked the turning-point in Anglo-Boer relations during the last two decades of the nineteenth century. Up to that point the clash between Britain and the South African Republic had been on the outposts. The outcome of this 'battle of the outposts' was the virtual encirclement of the two Boer republics with British territory, and in particular the denial to the Transvaal of access to the sea. There remained the neutral port of Delagoa Bay, but the neutrality of the bay was precarious. When Chamberlain became colonial secretary in 1895 the struggle was transferred to the citadel itself, within which the Trojan horse in the shape of the Uitlander population had been introduced during the preceding decade. Before the end of the year there followed the Jameson raid. To Chamberlain the raid was by no means an unmitigated disaster. 'I even regard it as possible', he wrote after the fiasco, 'that it may bring matters to a head and lead to the settlement of many pending questions.' The question we must try to answer in conclusion is: Which of these 'questions' were soluble without war and which insoluble; or in other words, what was the war about?

There are those who have answered the question in accordance with some doctrine of historical determinism. It has been said, for example, that the war was one between the sixteenth (or seventeenth) and the nineteenth (or twentieth) centuries with the implication that it was inevitable. Sir James Rose Innes in his valuable *Autobiography* does not adopt the war-of-the-centuries view, but considers, nevertheless, that war was inevitable. I do not see how the historian can adopt a determinist standpoint. The 'inevitable outcome' is, actually, descried only after it has come about. When it is descried in advance, it usually fails to take place. Determinist history implies in fact a claim to omniscience.

The responsibility for the war has often been laid at the door
of the mining magnates. More precisely, it is alleged that they
engineered the war for the sake of their dividends. But the
interests of these financiers or 'capitalists' required certain well-
understood reforms in the administration of the republic, not
an attack on her independence. For the purpose of promoting
these interests united action by the capitalists was desirable and
practicable. But it became impracticable when these limits
were transgressed. This was one of the lessons driven home by
the fiasco of the raid. An important section among the capitalists
were altogether opposed to the plan of an armed rebellion, and
even among those who supported it there were misgivings about
the political aims of their leader, Rhodes. This distrust of
Rhodes the statesman contributed its share to the ruin of the
enterprise. Yet it remains true that a powerful group of capitalists played a leading and indispensable role in the plot that
led to the raid. Chamberlain kept in the background, intending
to show his hand only after the capitalists had led Johannesburg
into actual revolt.

In the prolonged crisis that culminated in war the roles were
reversed. In 1895 Rhodes and a number of Rand capitalists
took the lead, but counted on the support of the British government at the critical moment. The mess they made of the enterprise taught the capitalists their lesson. They withdrew into the
shell out of which they had ventured in 1895, and left the political initiative to the British government. As the crisis deepened
they emerged out of their shell once more, this time as instruments of British policy. They acted now as men under orders,
relying on the superior political wisdom of the professional
statesmen.

It was not until late in 1897 that the capitalist front could be
effectively reconstituted with the circumscribed object of taking
united action in the interests of the mining industry. But in their
attitude to the republican government the capitalists continued
to differ among themselves. The most important of them, the
Wernher-Beit firm, remained uncompromisingly hostile. But
certain other big firms did not share this hostility. In January
1899 Milner and Chamberlain took the important step of
arranging joint action between themselves and the chamber of
mines in opposition to the dynamite monopoly. They were

making a bid for the support of the capitalists during the critical months that lay ahead. The bid was sufficiently, if not entirely, successful. The joint action against the dynamite monopoly led directly to the fateful negotiations between the republican government and the capitalists, in which the latter were guided by the advice of the senior partner, the colonial office. But even at this juncture, the capitalists were not unanimous. They could not agree on the demands to be made on Kruger. It was not only 'foreign' firms like those of Goerz and Albu that were unwilling to ask too much, but also a 'British' firm like the Consolidated Goldfields. It was partly due to his awareness of this fact that Fitzpatrick broke up the negotiations and handed over the job to the British government. When the latter took over, the capitalists retired into the background. Those of them who did not agree with the British government's policy were prepared to acquiesce under the combined pressure of the colonial office and Wernher, Beit & Company.

A well-known historian declared recently:

The essential British problem in South Africa was strategical and political, not economic. . . . The British needed a united white South Africa in order to have strategic security at the Cape—the linch-pin of the British Empire. . . . The naval station at the Cape was . . . fundamental to them. . . .

Though British statesmen undoubtedly attached great importance to the naval base at Simonstown, it is not clear why a united South Africa was necessary for the security of the base. The British garrison and naval squadron provided an effective enough guarantee. The game that was played in South Africa in the 1890s was for other stakes than the security of Simonstown. In the eyes of British statesmen a united South Africa——like a united Canada and a united Australia—would be a source of additional strength to the British empire instead of a source of expense. It is true that Lord Salisbury appears not to have agreed with this view; but Salisbury was in a minority in his cabinet.

'No one', writes professor C. W. de Kiewiet, 'who has read . . . the records of British policy since the achievement of Confederation in Canada can miss the picture of a British Government

groping for some means of ending South African disunity.'
So far, so good. But he then goes on to write as if he had adopted
as his major premiss the theory that the political federation of
South Africa was an historical necessity. It is an assumption
that lies at the base of a great deal of South African historiography. Those who write history in this way naturally conclude
that the opponents of federation could not but be swept aside,
since they had placed themselves athwart the destiny of South
Africa. But I have said already that the historian cannot steer
by the light of a determinist philosophy.

It was the Great Trek of the 1830s that was responsible for
South African disunity. The British government was naturally
reluctant to acquiesce in the birth of a second source of 'White'
political power in South Africa. It took that government the
best part of twenty years to make up its mind to recognize the
independence of two Boer states in the interior, and then only
after annexing the coastal republic of Natal and in the confident
anticipation that the inland states would remain of small
account, if indeed they managed to maintain themselves at all
in the face of internal dissensions and Native hostility. But what
if the new states survived and grew in strength? The only step
taken by the British government in the early days to insure itself
against such an eventuality was to veto a union between the
two republics. It was a significant step; but it did not go far
enough since it failed to forestall an inter-republican alliance.
The next step, taken much later, was to propose a South African
federation under the British flag. But two successive attempts
to put the plan into practice encountered armed resistance
and by 1896—after the failure of the second attempt—the
prospects looked particularly unpromising.

Federation was the ideal solution, but it might not be attain-
able. The British authorities felt therefore that they had to
provide some alternative answer to the problem of the duality
of political power (or will) in South Africa. They found the
answer in the concept of paramountcy or supremacy. British
paramountcy proved to be an elastic term, but even in its
mildest interpretation it meant the denial of full republican
independence. The republics, and more particularly the
Orange Free State, got an unmistakable taste of paramountcy
when the British, after intervening in quarrels between the

latter state and independent Native chiefs north of the Orange, annexed both the territory of Basutoland and the diamond fields of Griqualand West (1868–71). The annexation of the South African Republic in 1877 was a vigorous demonstration of paramountcy, undertaken with a view to South African federation. When the republic was restored in 1884, certain limits were set to its independence particularly in regard to treaty-making power. But the claim to paramountcy, while it included and was partly expressed in these legal limitations, was not exhausted by them.

That the British authorities, speaking in the name of a powerful empire, should assert their paramountcy over two republics struggling to find their feet was natural. It was equally natural that the republics should oppose the claim. Having undertaken the responsibilities of independence, they claimed also its rights. It was not really a question of petty African communities claiming to be 'ordinary European states'. It was a question rather of the meaning of political independence. (This is not to deny that it was in fact European jurists and statesmen who were the creators of modern international law—not, however, for Europe only but for the world.) As for paramountcy, the republics did not formally repudiate the claim as an abstract proposition. But they protested whenever its application affected their interests. They did not, however, carry their protests to the length of armed resistance except in the case of the annexation of the South African Republic.

When it had become clear by 1895 that the gold-fields of the Witwatersrand had vast potentialities, the problem of the duality of political power began, in the eyes of British statesmen, to take on a new urgency. Writing to Chamberlain late in 1896 on 'the South African question' Selborne remarked:

In a generation the S.A.R. will by its wealth and population dominate South Africa. South African politics must revolve round the Transvaal, which will be the only possible market for the agricultural produce or the manufactures of Cape Colony and Natal. The commercial attraction of the Transvaal will be so great that a Union of the South African States with it will be absolutely necessary for their prosperous existence. The only question in my opinion is whether that Union will be inside or outside the British Empire.

About two years later Milner expressed the fear 'that the overwhelming preponderance in wealth and opportunity on the side of the Transvaal may turn the scale against us'. As for Chamberlain, he publicly warned the two republican presidents in 1897 against aspiring to an independent federation.

The colonial office had in its files many warnings that Britain might lose the loyalty of the British settlers not only in the Transvaal but throughout South Africa. Rhodes had sent such a warning shortly after the raid. Greene sent another early in April 1897. He was describing a dinner party given by Abe Bailey, one of Johannesburg's mining magnates. Jorissen of the republican bench urged those present 'to foil him in an attempt . . . to frame a new Constitution which would give the Uitlanders all the rights they wanted', including a seven years' retrospective franchise, on condition that they 'renounced allegiance to the land of their birth and agreed to accept the Transvaal as their own country'. Most of Jorissen's hearers thought that he spoke with the knowledge of his government.

The judge's advice to the Uitlanders [continued Greene] to renounce their nationality, and rely on the good faith of the Government of the Republic, could only, I think, be intended as a bait to induce them to abate their confidence in the Imperial Government. At present, in consequence of the recent public utterances of the Secretary of State . . . the Imperial feeling on the Rand is growing in strength; but when we consider that a considerable proportion of the community entertain a certain misgiving as to the thoroughness of Imperial policy . . . a movement such as that advocated by . . . Jorissen might find some . . . support.

At about the same time J. W. Leonard, a leading Johannesburg Uitlander and at one time attorney-general of the Cape Colony, declared in an interview reported to the colonial office:

It is essential that England should re-establish her lost prestige in South Africa. This is the last chance she will have of retaining the loyalty of Englishmen and others . . . in the country. . . . Kruger would welcome the support of such men gladly, provided that they had thrown over England. A little time back he sent me a message offering to make me attorney-general of the Transvaal on that condition.

The determination to forestall an independent United States of South Africa lies at the root of British policy after the proving of the deep levels on the Rand. The longer the South African Republic retained her independence the greater seemed the risk that the British colonies would be attracted away from the empire. For some time after the raid there was not much the British authorities could do to checkmate the republic. Their first opportunity to assert themselves came in April 1897. The April demonstration was followed within six months by the assertion of suzerainty. Suzerainty was intended to underpin or legalize paramountcy, and to issue in complete British control over the republic's foreign relations. If this could be achieved the danger of the republic's taking the lead in the formation of an independent federation would be considerably reduced.

The danger might be reduced; it would not be eliminated. It would persist as long as the republican government was a Boer government. It would in fact persist as long as the republic, whether her government were Boer or Uitlander, remained outside the empire. Indeed, it was the prevailing opinion in the colonial office, until Milner appeared on the scene, that it would not be in the interests of Britain to convert the Boer state into an Uitlander republic owing to the risk that the latter would be a more efficient nucleus of an independent federation. Chamberlain himself shared this opinion.

Milner's importance lies in the fact that he converted the colonial office to his solution of the 'duality' problem. He did not fear a republic which admitted the Uitlanders to citizenship. On the contrary he held that she would become a part of the empire, provided that Britain obtained complete political equality for the new citizens without delay and at the same time mastered the republican will to independence.

But if the republican will to independence was not mastered, what would then be the ultimate outcome? Undoubtedly, declared Milner, an independent Republic of South Africa (though the British naval base at Simonstown would be secure for a long time). We have seen that this was also Selborne's view. Milner, however, was the man on the spot and he undertook to enlighten the colonial office that the independence of the South African Republic was incompatible with the interests of Britain because the republic was the prime cause of the growth of Afrikaner nationalism throughout South Africa. Afrikaner nationalism was the real enemy. What was this Afrikaner nationalism of the late 1890s? Its portrait as painted by Milner looks remarkably like the visage it wears today when it has grown to full stature as the result of the Anglo-Boer war and an effort extending over half a century. A nationalist himself, he recognized the symptoms of a malady to which the patient was not to succumb until many years later.

Milner was not interested in the purely cultural aspect of Afrikaner nationalism. It was the political aspect that worried him. 'The Afrikander Nation idea', if it ever came to fruition, meant political independence.[1] 'To afrikanderize' meant to him to become 'a virtual Republican'. This explains how he could lump together all the Cape opponents of his policy—starting from staunch supporters of the imperial connexion like de Villiers and Schreiner and continuing via Hofmeyr, who had no objection in principle to the British flag, to out-and-out republican members of the Afrikaner bond—as the Afrikaner or Dutch party. It appeared to him that even the 'imperialists' among his opponents, in their solicitude for the interests of South Africa and their fear of the disastrous after-effects of war, were willing to take a chance with regard to the imperial connexion. This he was not prepared to do. (In any case he thought that the after-effects of war would be good.) Whether at the cost of war or not it was his firm resolve to secure South Africa's connexion with the empire for ever. That is the explanation of his desire to see the 'Afrikander Nation idea' doomed. That explains also what he meant when he spoke of 'the great game between ourselves and the Transvaal for the mastery in South Africa'. He meant that unless the republic changed its character, its assertion of independence would be copied sooner or later by the rest of South Africa. But the transformation would have to be quick and radical. That was the

---

[1] Chamberlain, after a long course of instruction from Milner, put the point thus: 'The Dutch [i.e. Afrikaners] in South Africa desire, if it be possible, to get rid altogether of the connection with Great Britain, which to them is not a motherland, and to substitute a United States of South Africa which, they hope, would be mainly under Dutch influence.' Chamberlain's memorandum for the cabinet, 6 September 1899. Chamberlain papers, B.

reason why he insisted that the Uitlanders should be admitted to the republican franchise, not in gradually increasing numbers, but 'wholesale' and on an equal footing with the Boers. If the former course was followed the Uitlanders might 'afrikanderize', i.e. become supporters of republican independence. If they were admitted 'wholesale' by the action of Britain, they would 'burst the existing mould' and the republic would cease to have a will of her own.

The republican government realized too late what it meant to have Chamberlain as a challenger. If it had appreciated its peril, it might sooner have taken appropriate action. As things turned out, the republican record with regard to reform was one of procrastination. The procrastination can be explained. But the fact remains that it was fatal. By the end of 1898 the final crisis had overtaken the republic. Yet as late as the end of April 1899 Smuts still believed that Britain would not go to war unless she had a formally good *casus belli*. As British policy gradually unfolded during the succeeding months, the republican leaders came to the conclusion that Britain was aiming a mortal blow at their independence. Once they had reached that conclusion, they decided to fight. They believed that they stood a chance of winning, especially if they could strike before the British were ready. In spite of a discouraging report from Leyds late in September, they hoped for foreign intervention. Even if they did not win, they may have hoped that Salisbury's government would fall if they held out long enough, and a more sympathetic government take its place. But calculations such as these do not constitute the reason why the republics went to war. After the outbreak of war de Villiers wrote: 'With these people the preservation of their independence is a sacred mission.' Up to the very end he had urged the republicans to give way if they could do so 'without actual dishonour'. Shortly before the Bloemfontein conference his brother Melius wrote to him: 'Men like Mr. Hofmeyr also to some extent forget that the S.A.R. like the Free State has a certain measure of self-respect. . . .' On 16 September the government of the South African Republic sent Hofmeyr its last word: 'We are fully impressed with the very serious position in which we are placed, but with God before our eyes we cannot go further, without endangering, if not totally destroying, our independence. This

Government, Parliament and people are unanimous on this point.' The Free Staters' last word had already been spoken by Fischer: 'We have honestly done our best, and can do no more. If we are to lose our independence,[1] since that is what is demanded, leave us at all events the consolation that we did not sacrifice it dishonourably. . . .'

45. White South Africa united

L. M. THOMPSON *The Unification of South Africa* Clarendon Press, Oxford 1960; pages 480–3

The Union was launched on a wave of optimism. There was a widespread belief, in England and in South Africa, that Boer and Briton would spontaneously fuse into one nation. It was to be a prosperous nation, efficiently exploiting the natural resources of the country. It was to be an expansive nation, peacefully absorbing the High Commission Territories, Southern Rhodesia, and, perhaps, the other British colonies and protectorates in central and even east Africa. Like Canada, Australia, and New Zealand, it was to be an active partner in the British Empire.

How firmly based was this orthodox view? If the arguments that had been used by men like Smuts and Merriman in support of their prediction of an Anglo-Boer fusion are examined, they are found to be sweeping and insubstantial. For example, the fact that most Britons as well as Boers were Protestants did not warrant the deduction that there was no religious obstacle to their fusion, for there were fundamental differences between the social teachings of the Dutch Reformed Churches and those of the other Christian Churches in South Africa (including even the Presbyterian Church). Nor did the fact that both Boer and Briton were mainly of Teutonic descent warrant the deduction that racial sentiment would not hold them apart. Racial sentiment is the product of historical as well as biological factors, and the historical experiences of Boer and Briton had been very dissimilar. The tensions of the period when the British

[1] Fischer was identifying his state with the South African Republic.

imperialism was at its height, culminating in the war of 1899–1902, had left diverse deposits of remembered strivings and sufferings, and although most white South Africans professed the orthodox view in public, there were not very many like Botha, Smuts, and Merriman, to whom it was a reality and not a mask, a permanent way of life and not a stepping-stone towards another goal. From the British South African mind the aspirations which Milner had fostered had not been wholly deleted. Men like Fitzpatrick were still hoping that the tempo of economic development would be increased to such an extent that the British element would sooner or later outnumber the Afrikaners and the Afrikaners would sooner or later be dena-tionalized, so that the South African nation would become essentially British in culture and feeling. In many an Afrikaner mind, on the other hand, an exclusive national ideal and a republican yearning were still present. The belief that the preservation of the Afrikaners as a distinct people was an object of the divine will was deeply engrained and persistently propagated by predikants. Many Afrikaners who had hitherto supported, or at least not actively opposed, the policy of Botha and Smuts had done so in the realization that it was sound tactics—a means of obtaining concessions from Britain. But now that South Africa was united and the imperial factor was virtually eliminated, were not different tactics called for? Would not the conciliation policy, if persisted in, produce the very results which Fitzpatrick desired?

Of these two deviations from the orthodox view, it was the Afrikaner one which was the more formidable. Even under the propitious circumstances of the period immediately after the war, British immigration had not reached a decisive scale. British South Africans had not acted in unison, and Afrikaner national consciousness had not been undermined. In the 1910 election a significant proportion of the English-speaking voters preferred labour or independent candidates to Unionists and there was still no sign of a *British* South African national spirit. Africaner nationalism, on the other hand, had a powerful institutional basis in the Dutch Reformed Churches, a vigorous cultural basis in the language movement, and a potential leader in Hertzog. In these circumstances the short-term prospects of the Union would hinge upon the relations between Botha and

Hertzog. Perhaps regular contact in the Cabinet would allay their mutual suspicions and yield some compromise between the policy of conciliation and the policy of protection for the Afrikaner. Alternatively, their differences might become accentuated to breaking-point, as Jameson had predicted. In that event the stage would be set for the creation of an avowedly nationalist Afrikaner party—and once such an organization existed there could be no knowing what its ultimate character would be, for a party which is nourished by racial fervour generates its own dynamics.

Ultimately, however, the fate of the Union and its prospects of peaceful territorial expansion would depend mainly upon the capacity of white South Africans to establish satisfactory relations with their Coloured, Indian, and African fellow countrymen. So preoccupied had they been with other issues for more than a decade that they had not paid much attention to this question, save when it had been forced upon them by the Natal Native Rebellion and by the need to devise the franchise sections of the Union Constitution. It remained to be seen whether the British hope that white South Africans would become increasingly liberal was justified, or whether, as more non-whites acquired western skills and western aspirations, the whites, outnumbered as they were, would seek to maintain their supremacy at all costs—even at the cost of denying any non-white an effective say in the government of the country. Already there were signs that the liberal tradition of the Cape Colony might be overwhelmed. Negrophobic views had been expressed in the Cape Parliament as well as the other colonial parliaments, and the crude ideas of the Labour Party had attracted many of the Witwatersrand voters. What if such a policy were to be adopted by one of the major parties? Might it not be a perfect prescription for victory at the polls? Moreover, it was being claimed that there was moral justification for racial discrimination. The 'kafir', it was said, was 'naturally' inferior to the white man—'something between a child and an animal'. He was being spoilt by contact with whites and it was therefore in his own interest that the contact should cease. He should be 'separated' from the whites and allowed to develop 'along his natural lines'. Such writers did not explain what they meant by the 'natural lines' of African development; nor did they explain how white South Africans, who had been dependent on non-white labour ever since the time of Van Riebeeck, were to be persuaded to do without it; nor did they define the positions which were to be occupied by the Coloured and Indian peoples of South Africa. Nevertheless, few white South Africans agreed with Schreiner that the orthodox ideal of a white South African nation was incomplete on the ground that the Coloured, the Indian, and the African, as well as the white inhabitants of the Union, should be regarded as parts of the new nation and potential citizens of the new State.

The founders of the Union believed that a Sovereign Parliament would be the best constitutional instrument for the handling of these difficult problems. They had buttressed this belief with many arguments, of which some were dubious interpretations of history, others were false prophecies, and none was conclusive. In following the British example, they had ignored the fact that in so far as the flexible character of the British Constitution met the needs of the British people, that was because they had become a comparatively homogeneous people, and their respect for constitutional conventions, for political compromise, and for personal liberty was strong enough to form an effective barrier against arbitrary action by the government of the day; whereas the essence of the problem confronting South Africa was that her peoples were extremely heterogeneous, and the colour consciousness of most of the whites and the national exclusiveness of most of the Afrikaners were potent enough to override any feelings they may have had for conventions, for compromise, and for the liberties of others. Since a flexible Constitution provides no legal safeguards against arbitrary government, it was the very worst prescription for such a country. So long as Afrikaners remained in a political majority they would have the opportunity, and therefore the temptation, to stand together, to obtain control of Parliament, and to impose their will on the other inhabitants. A division of powers, territorially between the centre and the regions, and within the centre between the Legislature, the Executive, and the Judiciary, would have provided the only sound basis for concord in South Africa. The Constitution of the United States of America would have been a better model than the British Constitution.

Select Bibliography

ALGER, PAUL *La France en Côte d'Ivoire de cinquante ans d'hésitations politiques et commerciales, 1843 à 1893* Dakar 1962

ALLEN, BERNARD MEREDITH *Gordon and the Sudan* London 1931

ANSTEY, ROGER T. *Britain and the Congo in the Nineteenth Century* Oxford 1962

ASCHERSON, NEAL *The King Incorporated: Leopold II in the Age of Trusts* London 1963

ASHFORD, DOUGLAS E. *Political Change in Morocco* Princeton 1961

BAUER, P. *West African Trade* London 1956

BERBAIN, SIMONE *Études sur la Traité des noirs au golfe de Guinée, le comptoir français de Juda au XVIIIe siècle* Paris 1942

BIOBAKU, SABURI O. *The Egba and their Neighbours, 1842–1872* Oxford 1957

BOAHEN, A. ADU *Britain, the Sahara and the Western Sudan, 1788–1861* Oxford 1964

BRUNSCHWIG, HENRI *Mythes et réalités de l'impérialisme colonial français, 1871–1914* Paris 1960

— *L'Avènement de l'Afrique noire du XIXe siècle à nos jours* Paris 1963

BUELL, R. L. *The Native Problem in Africa* New York 1928

BURNS, ALAN M. *History of Nigeria* revised edition, London 1963

CHURCHILL, WINSTON S. *The River War* London 1899

CORNEVIN, ROBERT *Histoire du Dahomey* Paris 1962

— *L'Historie du Togo* Paris 1959

COUPLAND, REGINALD *The British Anti-Slavery Movement* London 1933

— *East Africa and its Invaders From the Earliest Times to the Death of Seyyid Said in 1856* Oxford 1938

— *The Exploitation of East Africa, 1856–1890: The Slave Trade and the Scramble* London 1929

CROWDER, MICHAEL *The Story of Nigeria* London 1962

CURTIN, PHILIP D. *The Image of Africa: British Ideas and Action, 1780–1850* Madison 1964

DELAVIGNETTE, ROBERT LOUIS *Freedom and Authority in French West Africa* London 1950

DODWELL, HENRY H. *The Founder of Modern Egypt: Mohammed Ali* Cambridge 1931

DONNAN, ELIZABETH (ed.) *Documents Illustrative of the History of the Slave Trade to America* Vols. 1 and 2, Washington 1930–1939

FLINT, JOHN E. *Sir George Goldie and the Making of Nigeria* London 1960

FRANKEL, S. H. *Capital Investment in Africa* Oxford 1938

FREEMAN-GRENVILLE, G. S. P. *The East African Coast: Select Documents* Oxford 1962

FURNEAUX, RUPERT *The Zulu War* London 1963

FYFE, CHRISTOPHER H. *The History of Sierra Leone* London 1962

GRAY, JOHN MILNER *A History of the Gambia* Cambridge 1940

HAILEY, LORD *African Survey* London 1938 and 1956

HALLETT, ROBIN 'The European Approach to the Interior of Africa in the Eighteenth Century' *Journal of African History* Vol. IV, 1963, pp. 191–206

HARGREAVES, JOHN D. *Prelude to the Partition of West Africa* London 1963

— 'The Slave Traffic' in A. Natan *Silver Renaissance* London 1961

HILL, RICHARD LESLIE *Egypt in the Sudan, 1820–1881* London 1959

HODGKIN, THOMAS L. 'Islam, History and Politics' *Journal of Modern African Studies* Vol. I, 1963

HOLT, PETER MALCOLM *The Mahdist State in the Sudan, 1881–1898* Oxford 1958

KIEWIET, C. W. DE *The Imperial Factor in South Africa* Cambridge 1937

LLOYD, ALAN *The Drums of Kumasi: The Story of the Ashanti Wars* London 1961

MANNIX, DANIEL P. and COWLEY, MALCOLM *Black Cargoes: A History of the Atlantic Slave Trade, 1518–1865* New York 1962

MARAIS, J. S. *The Fall of Kruger's Republic* London 1961

MARLOWE, JOHN *Anglo-Egyptian Relations, 1800–1953* New York 1954

MÜLLER, FRITZ FERDINAND *Deutschland-Zanzibar-Ostafrika* East Berlin 1959

OLIVER, ROLAND *Sir Harry Johnston and the Scramble for Africa* London 1957

PERHAM, MARGERY *Life of Lugard*, Vols. I and II, London 1960

PERHAM, MARGERY and SIMMONS, J. *African Discovery* London 1942

PORTER, ARTHUR T. *Creoledom: A Study of the Development of Freetown Society* London 1963

RENOUVIN, P. *Les Politiques d'Expansion Imperialiste* Paris 1949

RITTER, E. A. *Shaka Zulu* London 1955

RIVLIN, HELEN A. B. *The Agricultural Policy of Mohammed Ali in Egypt* Harvard 1961

ROBINSON, RONALD and GALLAGHER, JOHN *Africa and the Victorians: The Climax of Imperialism in the Dark Continent* London 1961

SANDERSON, G. N. 'The Foreign Policy of the Negus Menelik, 1896–1898' *Journal of African History* Vol. V, 1964, pp. 87–98

SCHNAPPER, BERNARD *La Politique et le commerce français dans le Golfe de Guinée, 1838–1871* Paris 1961

SLADE, RUTH *King Leopold's Congo* London 1962

SMITH, MICHAEL T. *Government in Zazzau, 1800–1950* London 1960

THOMPSON, LEONARD M. *The Unification of South Africa* London 1960

WARD, WILLIAM E. F. *The History of Ghana* London 1958

WYNDHAM, HUGH ARCHIBALD *The Atlantic and Slavery* London 1935

Chronological Table

The following list of dates is intended only as a guide and is not exhaustive. In order to facilitate an understanding of comparative trans-continental developments the following events have been listed in chronological order rather than by country or region.

1800	Emergence of Dingiswayo, Chief of Mtetwa
1802	Usuman dan Fodio revolts against rulers of Hausaland, starts *jihad*
1804–1830	Holy War of Kanuri against the Fulani
1804	Hijira by Fulani leaders (Shehu Usuman dan Fodio and sons Abdullahi and Muhammed Bello) in Hausa state
1804	Islam rebellion
1804 (23 February)	Flight of Fodio and followers from Degel
1804 (May)	Usuman attacks neighbouring Goberawa towns, raising standard of revolt
1804–1809	Conquest of the Hausa states by Usuman dan Fodio
1805	Usuman dan Fodio captures Birnin Kebbi, Zaria
1805	Muhammed Ali is appointed Wālī, governor of Egypt
1806	Britain captures Cape Town
1806	Ashanti defeat Fantse at battle of Abura
1806	Said-bin-Sultan usurps Muscat sovereignty in East Africa
1807	Usuman dan Fodio enters Katsina
1807	Prohibition of slave trade
1807–1846	Burkomanda II, XVIII
1807–1885	Second period of Euro-West African trade
1808	Abolition of British slave trade in Africa
1808	Usuman dan Fodio captures Daura and Gobir
1808	Fulani of Bornu rise against Sultan
1809	Usuman dan Fodio conquers Kano

1810	Usuman dan Fodio victory complete. Sokoto now capital. Establishment of emirate of Katagum by Ibrahim Zaki
1810	Slave trade treaties initiated by Britain
1811	Ibrahim Zaki leads Fulani *jihad* against Bornu. Bornu under Shehu al-Kanemi conclude peace, found new capital of Kukawa
1812	Fulani conquer most of western province of Bornu
1813	Ahmadu revolts against semi-pagan rulers of Maçina
1814	Town of Kukawa, built by Al-Kanami, to become new capital of Bornu
1815	British-Portuguese treaties on slave trade ending Portuguese slave trade
1815	Death of Shaikh Ahmad al-Fijani
1817	Afonja, kakanfo of Ilorin, rebels against Aole, alafin of Oyo
1817	Juaben becomes greatest military power in Ashanti Empire
1817	Death of Shehu Usuman dan Fodio
1818	Ahmadu bin Hammadi Boubou of Maçina defeats Bambara and Fulani armies
1818	Jihad raised by reformer Ahmadu bin Hammadi
1818	Dingiswayo killed by Zwide, Chief of Ndwande
1820	Muhammed Ali begins policy of gradual amelioration in Egypt
c. 1821–1837	Mzilikazi conquers Shona people
1821	Shaka defeats Zwide
1821	Assassination of Muhammed wad Adlan (1808–1821), regent of Sennar. Turko-Egyptian army of Muhammed Ali occupies Kordofan and Sennar
1822	Britain signs slave trade treaty with Seyyid Said of Zanzibar (Moresby Treaty)

1822	Foundation of Liberia
1823	Baguirmi invades Bornu
1823	Battle of Musfeia; Fulani defeat of Bornu
1824	Party of English traders go ashore at Fort Natal to seek audience with Shaka, King of the Zulus
1824	Shaka cedes Durban to Britain
1824	Egypt: Organization of two councils: (1) *al-Majlis al-Alī*; (2) *Majlis al Jihadiyah*
1826	British defeat Ashanti at Katamansu
1826–1827	Ahmadu conquers Timbuktu
1827	Turkey declares war on Russia
1828	Fiftieth Ordinance in South Africa, freeing Hottentots from legal disabilities
1828	Dingare assassinates Shaka and Uhlangare
1829	Death of Abdullahi, son of Shehu Usuman
1830	Beginning of fourth, or modern, period of North African history. French army landing in Algiers
1830	Shehu al-Kanemi makes peace with the Sarkin Musulmi
c. 1831	Establishment of fourteen Muslim emirates controlling 180,000 square miles, in allegiance to an emir, Al-mu minin, in Sokoto
1831	Asantahene renounces sovereignty over Fantse
1832	Syrian Council of Grand Notables convoked to deliberate on affairs of the peoples
1832	Seyyid Said transfers capital from Muscat to Zanzibar
1832	Kumasi makes war on Juaben
1833	Egyptian Polytechnic School established as training school for college
1833	Said-bin-Sultan concludes commercial treaty with United States
1833–1835	Kololo flee from Basutoland and plunder northwards to Zambezi river

c. 1833–1835	Kololo under Sebitwane migrate northward through Bechuanaland to settle among plateau Tonga
1834	Egyptian Shaikhs directed to nominate members of Superior Council
1834	Abolition of slavery in British colonies
1834	Death of Osei Yaw Akoto. Accession of Kwaku Dua I, asantahene
1834	Sir Benjamin D'Urban arrives in Cape Town. New constitution
1835	Shehu al-Kanemi dies
1835	The Great Trek starts
1835	Treaty between Dingaan and British, recognizing British occupation of Natal
1835	Zulus migrate northwards across Zambezi river
1835	Treaty with Spain illegalizing slave trade ships
1835	Abd al-Jalil of Tunis marries sister of Sultan of Bornu
1836–1837	Fulani finally defeat Yoruba and Oyo
1837	Reformation of Egyptian council, *al Majlis al Ali*, as *al Majlis al Kabir*
1837	France occupies province of Constantine (Western frontier of Tunis)
1837	Death of Muhammed Bello, son of Shehu Usuman
1837–1838	British policy of maintaining status quo with Bey of Tunis
1837	Death of Al Kanemi
1837	Al Hajj 'Uman writes *Suy af al-sa'id*
1838 (6 February)	Dingaan ambushes Retief in Natal
1838 (16 December)	Pretorius marches into Zululand, defeats Dingaan at Blood River
1838	Egyptian Council, *al Majlis al Kabir*, disbanded

1839	Al-Hajj settled in the Futa Jallon with following of Talaba
1839	Said-bin-Sultan concludes commercial treaty with Britain
1839	Treaty to abolish slave trade between Britain and Bonny
1840	Siege of Ostogbo by Fulani
1840	Said shifts seat of government from Muscat to Zanzibar
1840	Commercial agreement between Cameroons and Britain (ratified 1842)
1840–1843	Isles of Nossi-bé and Mayotta acquired by France
1841	Warrington invites Abd-al-Talil of Tunis to meeting
1841	British Consul (Hamerton) appointed in Zanzibar to end slave trade
1841	Treaty between England and Sahela Selassie, *ras* of Shoa (Ethiopia)
1841	Palmerston issues Memorandum on Negotiation with Chiefs of Bonny
1841	New treaty between Britain and Bonny
1841	Britain and Old Calabar sign Treaty of Amity and Commerce
1842	Treaty by Britain with Eyamsa and Eyo for abolition of slave trade, ratified 1843
1842	Tunisian Sheikh Abd al-Jahil murdered
1842	Tunisian slave importation abolished
1843	Britain annexes Natal
1843	British resume administration over settlements in Gold Coast
1843	Free Labour Emigration system introduced by France—'voluntary emigration'
1843	Death of Fulani reformer, Ahmadu bin Hammadi
1843	Introduction of Sanusi order into Cyrenaica

1844	Said-bin-Sultan concludes commercial treaty with France
1844	Death of Ahmadu
1845 (18 March)	Treaty of Lalla Maghnia, between Morocco and France, defining 100 miles of the Algerian and Moroccan border
1845	Kosoko deposes Akitoye as ruler of Lagos
1845–1850	Crisis in Algeria
1845	Treaty between Said and Britain forbidding export of slaves
1846	Sultan of Wadai conquers Bornu, ending Sef dynasty
1846	'Umar defeats Sultan of Wadai
1846	British Proclamation liberating all slaves
1846	War of the Axe between Britain and Xosas in South Africa
1847	Britain annexes territories south of the Orange river to Cape Clay
1848	Military bases established by Al-Hajj at Dinguiray
1848	Slave trade treaty with King Pepple of Bonny
1849	British Consul (John Beecroft) appointed to Niger Coast
1849	Beecroft appointed British Consul for Bights of Benin and Biafra
1849	Treaty between England and King Rao Ali of Gondar
1851	British capture Lagos and restore Akitoye to the throne
1852	Sand River Convention recognizing right of Boers of Orange Free State and Transvaal to self-government
1852	'Umar bin Sa'id defeats Bambara chiefs
1853–1856	Livingstone's explorations in Central Africa
1854	Portugal extends Free Labour Emigration system to Moçambique

1854	Nioro, capital of Kaarta, falls to 'Umar
1854	Louis Léon César Faidherbe becomes governor of Senegal
1855	Accession of Teodros II in Ethiopia
1855–1862	Overthrow of Ahmadu's empire by Al Hajj Umar
1858–1877	Mohamed Abu Sekin XX
1858	Richard Francis Burton becomes first European to see Lake Tanganyika
1860	First Indian slaves arrive in South Africa
1860	Faidherbe and 'Umar agree to separate zones of influence in Western Sudan
1861	'Umar takes Ségou
1862	Foreign invasion destroys dynasty of Al-mu-'minin of Sokoto. Control seized by Al-Hajj 'Umar
1862	Al-Hajj 'Umar bin Sa'id invades Maçina and ends reign of Ahmadu
1862	Anglo-French Declaration of Zanzibar's independence
1862–1863	'Umar destroys Hamdullahi, conquers Maçina, sacks Timbuktu
1863	Africans enter legislature in British Sierra Leone
1863	Ashanti invade British-held territory
1863–1864	Fulani rebellion, 'Umar killed
1863–1873	Porte bestows on Ismail (Egypt) right of primogenitive sovereignty
1863–1864	Mbolulu leads revolt of Lozi against Kololo domination. Sipopa becomes king (litunga)
1863	Protectorate established over Porto Novo
1864	Death of Al-Hajj
1865–1867	French occupation of the Mellacourie
1865	Galla stricken by smallpox epidemic and attacked by Somali
1865	Khedive Ismail buys Massana

1867–1874	Reign of Kofi Karikari of Juaben
1868 (10 April)	Battle of Magdala. Teodros II kills himself. Nafeer returns to coast
1868	British enter Ethiopia under Sir Robert Napier
1869	Italian Società di Navigazione Rubbatino buys post of Assab
1869	Opening of Suez Canal
1869	Malagasy—Queen Ranavalona II baptized
1871	Mokrani's revolt against the French in Algeria
1871 (July)	Kash victory over Tekle Giorgio
1871–1889	Johannis IV of Ethiopia
1872	Cape Province in South Africa granted responsible government under Britain
1872	Ashantis, led by Amankwa Tia, invade Juaben
1872	Dutch withdraw from Gold Coast following attacks by Fantse
1873	Sultan of Zanzibar forbids slave trade
1873	Elmira captured by British
1873	Sultan Barghash prohibits seaborne slave trade
1873	Conflict re-opens between Britain and Ashanti
1873	Samori ibn lafíya Ture over-runs Kankan
1874 (January)	British invade Ashanti kingdom
1874	Abolition of domestic slavery in Ghana
1874	Treaty of Fomena between Britain and Ashanti
1874	Ashanti undertake indemnity
1875	Kumasi invades and defeats Juaben
1875	Disraeli purchases Khedive Ismail's shares in Suez Canal Company
1875	Khedive Ismail accepts Gordon's plea to seize East coast and link with Uganda
1875	Church Missionary Society sends first missionary doctors to East Africa

1875	Financial and economic crisis in Constantinois, Algeria
1875	Conflict between Khedive Ismail and Johannis IV. Ethiopians win battles of Gundet and (later) of Gina
1876–1880	Juabens emigrate to Protectorate, founding new settlements
1876	Egypt annexes territories around Lake Victoria and Lake Albert
1877	Successful descent of Stanley down the Congo
1878	King Leopold creates *Comite d'Études du Haut-Congo* (England, France, Germany, Holland, Belgium). This soon dissolved, leaving Belgium alone with Congo enterprise
1879	Khedive Ismail establishes ministry including one French and one British official for the security of investors
1879	Britain and France intervene after Ismail's death, establishing joint control over Egypt
1879	British victory over Zulus in Anglo-Zulu war
1880	Death of 'Umar
1881 (March)	Battle of Kebemma, Ethiopians defeat Mahdists but Tchaimis killed
1881	Muhammed 'Ahmad ibn 'Abdullah proclaims himself the Mahdi
1881	French occupation of Tunis
1882	Nationalist movement, led by Arabi Pasha, gains control of Egypt
1882	British fleet bombards Alexandria, defeats nationalists
1882	Britain occupies Egypt
1882	Formation of *Association Internationale du Congo* under Leopold
1882	British defeat Ahmad Arabi at al-Tall al-Kabir
1882	Ratification of the Brazza-Makoto Treaty
1883	Mahdists defeat large Turko-Egyptian army

1883–1918	Abd er Rhamane Gaurong II, XXI. Treaty with France
1883	France occupies Bamako, seeking approach to the Niger
1883 (January)	French protectorate policy inaugurated in West Africa
1883 (6 July)	Memorandum of the Chamber of Commerce of Hamburg recommending the occupation of a part of the African coast opposing Fernando Po
1883	Bismarck asks Britain to declare protectorate over South West Africa
1883	German occupation of South West Africa
1884	Berlin Conference—fourteen countries represented
1884 (3 June)	Hewett Treaty between Egypt and Ethiopia
1884	Anglo-Portuguese treaty giving Portugal control of both mouths of Congo (never ratified)
1884	Germany annexes South West Africa
1884	German protectorate over Angra Peguena
1884	German annexation of Cameroons
1884	Carl Peters founds *Gesellschaft für Deutsch Kolonization*—a commercial company designed to establish a colony in Africa
1884	American Presbyterian mission reaches Gabon
c. 1884	Beginning of French invasion of Sokoto
1885	Leopold declares 'Sovereign of the Congo Independent State' at Boma
1885–1898	Partition of West Africa
1885	British declare protectorate over Niger districts
1885	Death of Kumasi
1885	Bismarck signs *Schutzbrief* placing territories occupied by Peters under German protection
1885	Fall of Khartoum. Death of Gordon

1886	Britain annexes Bechuanaland
1886	French defeat Samori at Niagassola
1886–1887	France sends envoy to Samori
1886	Galliéni signs treaty with Amadu's brother, Aguibou of Dinguiray
1886 (January)	Massacre of small Italian force at Dogali by Ethiopians
1887	Amadu signs treaty with France
1887	Eugène Etienne becomes French Under-Secretary of Colonies
1887	French victory over Mahmadou Larmine; Samori signs treaty with French
1888	Accession of Prempah in Ashanti
1888	Abushiri ibn Salim al-Harthi leads Tanganyikan resistance to German forces
1888	Africans enter legislature in Ghana
1888	Rudd Concession in Matabeleland
1889 (2 May)	Treaty of Wuchali (Menelik of Ethiopia and Italy). Massana to Italy
1889 (August)	Lamu awarded by arbitration to Sultan of Zanzibar
1889 (December)	Manda and Pate isles occupied by British East African Association
1889	Treaty of Vecian (Italy and Menelik of Ethiopia)
1889	Abushiri defeated by combined European forces at battles of Bagamoyo; Abushiri hanged by Germans
1889	Convention settles boundaries of the Gambia, Sierra Leone, Assinie and Porto Novo
1889	French repeat victory over Samori at Kenedongon
1889 (October)	Charter granted to British South Africa Company
1890	Pioneer column travels to Mashonaland
1890	Pioneer column enters Matabeleland

1890 (1 July)	Anglo-German agreement (Heligoland exchanged for Uganda)
1890	Foundation of *Comité de l'Afrique française*
1890–1891	Portuguese defeat Ndunduma, chief of Bihe, in Angola
1890–1893	Amadu's armies defeated by France
1890	Cecil Rhodes becomes Prime Minister of Cape Province
1890	American Presbyterian missions reach Libreville
1890	Frontier Police Force founded in Sierra Leone
1891	Rabah occupies Baguirmi and invades Bornu
1891	Anglo-Italian treaty, partitioning Sudan and East Africa from Ethiopia and Somali plateau
1891	Guinea, Ivory Coast, Dahomey constituted as unitary colonies of France
1891 (May)	Britain declares protectorate over Nyasaland districts
1892	Occupation of Abomey by France
1892–1893	Baguirmi falls to Rabah
1892 (29 February)	Casimir Maistre signs Treaty of Protection with Mlsang Dallem, Chief of Galcis of Lai
1893	Matabele war. Death of Lobengula
1893	Sultan of Bornu killed by Rabah
1893	Rabah sacks Kukawa
1893	Nuoro attack defeats Toro
1893	Conquest of Kingdom of Dahomey by France
1893	French troops enter Timbuktu
1893	France captures Djenné, Bandiagara and Maçina
1894	In South Africa, Glen Grey Act, setting up elected district councils
1894	Rabah reduces Bornu and establishes exploitative state
1894	European control of Sokoto. Destruction of emirates

1894	Dismemberment of Tokolor Kingdom
1894	'Race to Borgu' between Captain Decoeur and Lugard
1894	British protectorate declared over certain regions of Sierra Leone
1894 (16 June)	Decree of first federal authority in French West Africa
1895	East African Protectorate (Kenya) established
1895	Malagasy: French defeat Merina at Battle of Tananarive
1895	British conquer Oyo, completing subjugation of Yoruba city-states
1895	Agreement reached on Sierra Leone frontier
1895–1918	Sayid Muhammed ibn 'Abdullah Hassan (Mad Mullah) active against British in Somalia in jihad
1895	Britain proposes protectorate of Ashanti
1895	Portuguese defeat Gungunhana, chief of the Shangaan, at battle of Manjacaze, occupying Gazaland
1896	Jameson Raid, Matabele rising
1896	Sir Francis Scott invades Kumasi
1896 (1 March)	Battle of Adurá. Ethiopia defeats Italy
1897 (20 March)	*Convention pour le Nil Blanc* between Menelik and the French resident Lagarde. Upper Nile Basin (between 2° and 14°) partitioned
1897 (14 May)	Anglo-Abyssinian treaty, in which Menelik agrees not to supply Mahdists with arms
1897 (October)	Emile Gentil signs treaty with Abdessamane, Gaurong II of Baguirmi
1897	Portuguese, under Joaquim Augusto Mousinho de Albiquerque, inflict final defeat on Moçambique tribesmen
1897	British occupy Bida and Ilorin
1897	Frontier between Somalia and Ethiopia traced by Major Nerazzini and King Menelik

1897	French conquer Gao and Zinde
1898	British occupation of Benin
1898	Mende rising in Sierra Leone
1898	Capture of Seunory by Colonel Audéoud
1898	France concedes to British demands in Nigeria
1898	Anglo-French treaty (N. Dahomey to France, N. Nigeria to England)
1898	Britain collects House Tax in Sierra Leone Protectorate
1899–1902	Boer War

Index